# The East Coast
A pilot-guide from the Wash to Ramsgate

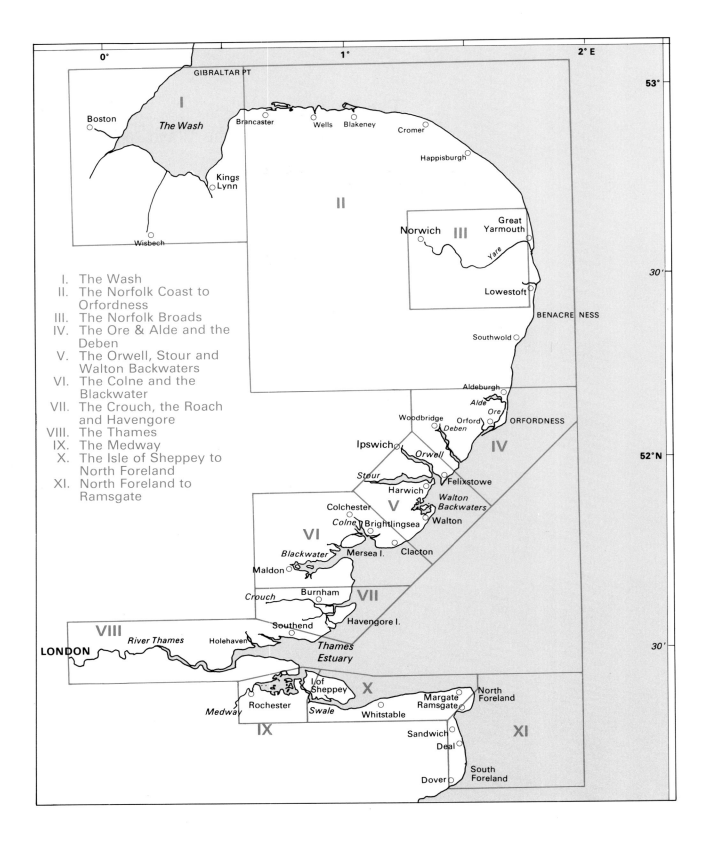

I. The Wash
II. The Norfolk Coast to Orfordness
III. The Norfolk Broads
IV. The Ore & Alde and the Deben
V. The Orwell, Stour and Walton Backwaters
VI. The Colne and the Blackwater
VII. The Crouch, the Roach and Havengore
VIII. The Thames
IX. The Medway
X. The Isle of Sheppey to North Foreland
XI. North Foreland to Ramsgate

# The East Coast

A PILOT-GUIDE FROM THE WASH
TO RAMSGATE

Derek Bowskill

Imray Laurie Norie & Wilson Ltd
St Ives Cambridgeshire England

Published by
**Imray, Laurie, Norie & Wilson Ltd**
Wych House, St Ives, Huntingdon,
Cambridgeshire, PE17 4BT, England.
☎ (0480) 62114 *Fax* (0480) 496109
1992

© Derek Bowskill 1992
1st edition 1984
2nd edition 1987
3rd edition 1992

British Library Cataloguing in Publication Data
A catalogue record for this book is available from the British Library

ISBN 0 85288 158 4

CAUTION
Whilst every care has been taken to ensure accuracy, neither the Publishers nor the Author will hold themselves responsible for errors, omissions or alterations in this publication. They will at all times be grateful to receive information which tends to the improvement of the work.

PLANS
The plans in this guide are not to be used for navigation. They are designed to support the text and should at all times be used with navigational charts.

The last input of technical information was May 1992.

Printed in Great Britain at The Bath Press, Avon.

# Contents

# Foreword

There have not been many months in the past eight years when I have not been cruising the area covered by this pilot-guide. During that time, I have come to enjoy, respect, admire and fear this sometimes lush, sometimes bleak; sometimes remote, sometimes only-too-accessible; sometimes uncivilised, sometimes over-refined; sometimes vulgar, sometimes effete and decadent; sometimes ever-alert, sometimes torpid and somnolent; sometimes green and blue and white, but mainly muddy and grey; and never dramatically rocky but always potentially treacherous East Coast of ours! I hope that my perception of it will be acceptable as a celebration; and, in addition, that this volume will be of actual, practical help. I shall be most grateful to hear personally from any skipper who can offer comment, advice, corrections, amendments or information that will enable me to improve the accuracy and/or increase the usefulness of this work.

So many people have helped me during the years I have been occupied with this guide that to mention them all would be to devalue each. However, some persons have been invaluable in ways they may never know about, and it is by way of paying tribute to their many and varied, if not indeed diverse and even disparate, contributions that I name them.

Sadly, the first two must now be *in memoriam*: Jack Toogood (of the Red Blood, the Blue Eyes, the Open Mind and Golden Heart); Jack Bradley (my Sea Man for all Sea Sons); Ian Rennie and Tim Ascot; both of Ramsgate and elsewhere; Sonny (The Cromer Light) a whelker (and so much more) from Wells-next-the-Sea; Charlie Brinkley and John Lineham, pilots both, from the Deben, the Wash; the master of Shuttlewood's Boatyard on the Roach, a certain Mr Norris; Chris Reynolds-Hole, the residing genius behind Bradwell Marina; the eponymous owner of Titchmarsh Marina, Walton-on-the-Naze; and Captain David Garside, harbourmaster *extraordinaire* of King's Lynn; a Q.Fl navigational aid of few words, much sagacity and wit, completely (but unboringly so) reliable – and a scourge of all water borne idiots.

I have been accompanied on this project (at times in the flesh, but more often wraithly in mind and spirit) by my First, Second and Third Mate. My lifeline in times of great joy or fear or sorrow (for the human condition is such that sooner or later we all need to express or at least try to communicate our significant experiences and feelings) was the telephone link with She who was (usually anyway) Standing By: Anthea.

However, this dedication must over-ride all other factors and acknowledgements, and I now make it with great surges of gratitude and humility, to the men of the RNLI.

Derek Bowskill
Pool-in-Wharfedale 1984

## Foreword to the Second Edition

'Much have I travell'd in the realms of gold
And many goodly states and kingdoms seen;'

So wrote Keats, and I wonder what kind of wild surmise he would have had, 'like some watcher of the skies' if he had been scanning Britain. I am still ambivalent to the East Coast and North Sea. At best, they are what Brid and Skeggyites call ' bracing'; at less than best, they are heavy and grey, and can only too easily become drear and daunting.

Nevertheless, they have about them that which can engage and enthrall. They have engrossed me by their constant state of flux; and although there is not always 'full fathom five' in their cruising rounds, it could well have been said:

'Nothing of them that doth fade,
   But doth suffer a sea-change
Into something rich and strange.'

I am grateful to all who have told me of those special changes that, just like fate, are ready for you the minute you think you have worked it out.

Derek Bowskill
Pool-in-Wharfedale 1987

# Foreword to the third edition

It is many years now since *Valcon* and I first left Ramsgate harbour and turned starboard for the Thames Estuary and the East Coast rivers. Since then, I have cruise-coasted, mainly single-handed and almost non-stop, from the Scottish border to the French Riviera and from Land's End to the Costa del Sol via the inland waterways of England and France.

In all that time, the force and spirit of the East have never left me, and as I look back on my frequently bleak but always challenging years on the coastal waters from Ramsgate to the Wash, they still arouse vivid memories tinged with awe and affection. Little that is 'of the essence' has changed, though there has been marginal mutation, occasional innovation and much refurbishment.

However, this guide has been through something of a radical sea-change; while it has not experienced a reversal in its fortunes it has been turned back to front. And why? Mainly because the cruising folk I have met who have been good enough to speak to me about the book have said, 'Don't you think it goes the wrong way?' or, alternative, 'Don't you know most people want to do it the other way round?'; and, in addition, 'What about the Broads, you don't say half enough!'

So, wanting to please and hoping to sell more copies, this edition has been completely revamped. It now travels southerly and with the consequential rearrangement, contains a special section relating to the Norfolk Broads. I hope the changes are improvements.

Derek Bowskill
Pool-in-Wharfedale 1992

# Acknowledgments

I am grateful to Ian Martin of *Challenger* at Gibraltar Point for keeping me informed and up to date on the ways of Wainfleet and the Wash.

Readers are occasionally good enough to write with good wishes and better info. One such soul is Patricia o'Driscoll who hails from London SE23. She said, 'I have been given a copy of the second edition of your book *The East Coast* and write to offer a little information. Some might be useful for a subsequent edition, and some is just by the way. My knowledge of these waters comes from 11 years commercial barging, 1959–1970.'

# Introduction

This volume is not intended for use as a *pilot* (in the strictly understood Admiralty usage of that word) nor as a set of *sailing instructions* (for those intrepid explorers who are never content until they have piloted themselves through every single puddle on any given patch). It is intended to be a practical *cruising guide/companion*: providing any visiting skipper with all the appropriate (that is, sufficient and necessary) information that is needed to navigate the area safely and efficiently – when used in conjunction with the relevant Admiralty and/or Imray charts.

The *guide* sections of the book offer hard facts in the form of diagrams, sketch maps, chartlets and clearly laid out details of port information and so on; while the *companion* sections set out to describe the areas and venues in a way that is informative but also discursive and entertaining. These comments and commentaries are meant to pass on not only useful thoughts and ideas about actually cruising the area, but also something of the *genius loci* that is to be experienced.

## Buoyage diagrams

These diagrammatic representations of the buoyed channels referred to in the volume are intended for use both in planning a trip and in actually following a course in practice. The aim has been to simplify the representation so that in practical terms 'buoy spotting' and/or 'buoy hopping' have been made easier.

The preferred course is central (along the tinted path) and on the immediate left and right hand lanes are those buoys it is considered important to *confirm* and on the outer lanes are those it is important to *check* (for both positive and negative affirmation since, when crossing the close-in estuary waters of the Thames, for example, it is only too easy to become confused in poor visibility by those buoys that are, and are also hoped to be, on the other side of an unpleasant bank or spit).

No attempt has been made to indicate direction on these buoyage diagrams (as they are meant to be enabling devices to be used in conjunction with the appropriate charts), and while they are not to scale, not even roughly so, in practice it is hoped that they will be of assistance in checking and checking off the buoyage as it comes and goes.

The idea is that the mariner, with the diagram laid out in front of him, will be able to gauge very easily what is to the right and what is to the left without difficulty; thus facilitating navigation and helping to give everyone a fair share of whatever 'views' there may be.

## Chartlets and sketch maps

These have been provided with the intention of giving an overall 'view' of the area, or detailed sketches of particular approaches. It is quite clear when considering the information they offer whether they are suitable for 'navigation/pilotage' or not. In fact, most of them are not, and are only to be used in conjunction with the appropriate Admiralty/Imray charts. Depths where given are in metres and all bearings are true.

The plans in this guide have been based on British Admiralty charts with the permission of the Hydrographer of the Navy.

# Weather

| Beaufort No. | Description of wind | Velocity in knots | Velocity in mph | Velocity in km/h | Sea state code | Sea state term | Sea criterion | Wave height in metres | Land observations |
|---|---|---|---|---|---|---|---|---|---|
| 0 | Calm | <1 | <1 | <1 | 0 | Calm glassy | Like a mirror. | 0 | Calm, smoke rises vertically |
| 1 | Light air | 1–3 | 1–3 | 1–5 | 1 | Calm rippled | Ripples. | 0–0·1 | Direction of wind shown by smoke drift but not by wind vanes. |
| 2 | Light breeze | 4–6 | 4–7 | 6–11 | 2 | Smooth wavelets | Small wavelets. | 0·1–0·5 | Wind felt on face, leaves rustle, ordinary vanes moved by wind. |
| 3 | Gentle breeze | 7–10 | 8–12 | 12–19 | 3 | Slight | Large wavelets. | 0·5–1·25 | Leaves and small twigs in constant motion, wind extends light flag. |
| 4 | Moderate breeze | 11–16 | 13–18 | 20–28 | 4 | Moderate | Small waves, breaking. | 1·25–2·5 | Raises dust and loose paper, small branches are moved. |
| 5 | Fresh breeze | 17–21 | 19–24 | 29–38 | 5 | Rough | Moderate waves, foam. | 2·5–4 | Small trees in leaf begin to sway, crested wavelets form on inland waters. |
| 6 | Strong breeze | 22–27 | 25–31 | 39–49 | | | Large waves, foam and spray. | | Large branches in motion, whistling heard in telegraph wires, umbrellas difficult. |
| 7 | Near gale | 28–33 | 32–38 | 50–61 | 6 | Very rough | Sea heaps up, foam in streaks. | 4–6 | Whole trees in motion, inconvenience felt walking. |
| 8 | Gale | 34–40 | 39–46 | 62–74 | | | Higher longer waves, foam in streaks. | | Breaks twigs off trees, generally impedes progress. |
| 9 | Strong gale | 41–47 | 47–54 | 75–88 | 7 | High | High waves, dense streaks of foam, spray impairs visibility. | 6–9 | Slight structural damage occurs (chimney pots and slates removed). |
| 10 | Storm | 48–55 | 55–63 | 89–102 | 8 | Very high | Very high tumbling waves, surface white with foam, visibility affected. | 9–14 | Seldom experienced inland, trees uprooted, considerable structural damage occurs. |
| 11 | Violent storm | 56–63 | 64–72 | 103–117 | 9 | Phenomenal | Exceptionally high waves, sea covered in foam, visibility affected. | >14 | Very rarely experienced, accompanied by widespread damage. |
| 12 | Hurricane | >63 | >72 | >118 | | | Air filled with spray and foam, visibility very severely affected. | | |

# Glossary of some terms used in shipping forecasts

### Anticyclone

A region characterised in the barometric pressure distribution by a system of closed isobars, with the highest pressure on the inside. It is also known as a *High*. The circulation about the centre is clockwise in the northern hemisphere, anticlockwise in the southern hemisphere.

### Backing

A change in the direction of the wind, in an anticlockwise direction.

### Cold front

The boundary line between advancing cold air and a mass of warm air under which the cold air pushes like a wedge. Its passage is normally accompanied by a sharp shift of wind, a rise in pressure, a fall in temperature and dew-point, and a period of rain, often heavy; sometimes there may be a line squall or thunder. The cold front was originally called the squall line.

### Cyclone

A name given to the tropical revolving storms of the Bay of Bengal and Arabian Sea. Sometimes used as a general term for tropical revolving storms of all oceans, or in the form *Tropical Cyclone*. Depressions of the Temperate Zones were formerly often referred to as cyclones, but *Depression* or *Low* is now used to distinguish them from the tropical storms. The term *cyclonic depression* is still sometimes used for a depression, as also is *extra-tropical cyclone*. (*See* also **Winds**.)

### Depression

A region characterised in the barometric pressure distribution by a system of closed isobars, having lowest pressure at the centre. The circulation about the centre is anticlockwise in the northern hemisphere and clockwise in the southern hemisphere. A depression is described as *deep* when encircled by many isobars close together and is said to be *deepening* when the pressure at the centre is decreasing. The word *shallow* is used to describe a depression which has few isobars. A depression is said to be *filling up* when the central pressure is increasing.

### Fog

A term used when the visual range is less than 1000m.

### Further outlook

A statement in brief and general terms appended to a detailed forecast and giving the conditions likely to be experienced in the 24 hours or more following the period covered by the actual forecast.

### Gale

A mean wind of at least Beaufort force 8 (34–40 knots) and/or gusts reaching 43–51 knots. The term *severe* or *strong gale* implies a mean wind speed of at least Beaufort force 9 (41–47 knots) and/or gusts reaching 52/60 knots.

### Gale warnings

The term *imminent* implies within 6 hours of the time of issue: *soon* implies between 6 and 12 hours: *later* implies more than 12 hours. Gale warnings remain in force unless amended or cancelled. However if the gale persists for more than 24 hours after the time of origin the warning will be reissued.

### Gust

A momentary increase in the strength of the wind, much shorter-lived than a squall and different in nature, being due mainly to mechanical interference with the steady flow of air, especially around large obstructions.

### Land and sea breezes

Local winds caused by the unequal heating and cooling of adjacent land and water surfaces. The sea breeze usually sets in during the forenoon and reaches its maximum strength during the afternoon. The land breeze may set in about midnight or not until early morning.

### Pressure systems

In weather bulletins the terms used to describe the speed of movement of pressure systems is as follows:
Slowly – less than 15 knots
Steadily – 15 to 25 knots
Rather quickly – 25 to 35 knots
Rapidly – 35 to 45 knots
Very rapidly – more than 45 knots

### Ridge

A ridge or wedge of high pressure is the converse of a trough, and is indicated by isobars extending outwards from a high pressure area. It corresponds to a ridge running out from the side of a mountain.

### Squall

A sudden increase of wind speed by at least 16 knots or by at least three stage of the Beaufort Scale, the speed rising to force 6 (22 knots) or more and lasting for at least one minute.

### Storm

A mean wind speed of at least Beaufort force 10 (48–55 knots) and/or gusts reaching 61–68 knots. The term *violent storm* implies a mean wind speed of at least Beaufort force 11 (56–63 knots) and/or gusts reaching 69–77 knots.

## Trough

The word trough is used in a general sense for any 'valley' of low pressure, and is thus the opposite of a 'ridge' of high pressure. A special form of trough was formerly known as a V-shaped depression. Frequently a front lies in a trough.

## Veering

A change in the direction of the wind, in a clockwise direction.

## Visibility

In weather bulletins the words *poor visibility* implies a visual range of between 1000m and 2 nautical miles; *moderate* is equal to a visual range of 2–5 nautical miles; *good* is applicable when visibility is greater than 5 nautical miles.

## Warm front

The boundary line at the earth's surface between advancing warm air and a cold air mass. Precipitation usually occurs within a wide belt (some 200 miles) in advance of the front. Passage of the front is usually marked by a steadying of the barometer, a rise in temperature and a dew-point, and a shift of wind.

## Waves

*Length of swell waves*

| | |
|---|---|
| Short | 0–100 metres |
| Average | 100–200 metres |
| Long | over 200 metres |

*Height of swell waves*

| | |
|---|---|
| Low | 0–2 metres |
| Moderate | 2–4 metres |
| Heavy | over 4 metres |

## Winds becoming cyclonic

A term used to indicate that there will be large changes in wind direction across the track line of a depression within the forecast area. Such changes are considered to be too complicated to be given in detail.

# Buoyage

## IALA SYSTEM A

### Lateral Marks

### Safe Water Marks
(mid-channel and Landfall)

#### Port hand

All red
Topmark (if any): can
Light (if any): Red

#### Starboard hand

All green
Topmark (if any): cone
Light (if any): Green

Red and white vertical stripes
Topmark (if any): Red ball
Light (if any): Iso, Oc, LFl.10s or Mo(A)
(White)

### Cardinal Marks

NW

NE

**N Mark**

Black over yellow
Light (if any): V Q (white)
or Q (white)

**W Mark**

Yellow with black band
Light (if any):
V Q(9)10s (White)
or Q(9)15s (White)

Point
of
Interest

**E Mark**

Black with yellow band
Light (if any): V Q(3)5s (White)
or Q(3)10s (White)

**S Mark**

Yellow over black
Light (if any): V Q(6) + L Fl.10s (White)
or Q(6) + L Fl.15s (White)

SW

SE

### Isolated Danger Marks
(stationed over a danger with navigable water around)

Black with red band
Topmark: 2 black balls
Light (if any): Fl(2) (White)

### Special Mark

Body shape optional, yellow
Topmark (if any): Yellow X
Light (if any): Fl.Y etc..

## Key to symbols used on plans

| | | | | | |
|---|---|---|---|---|---|
| Visitors' mooring | | Public telephone | | Parking for boats/trailers | |
| Visitors' berth | | Post box | | Laundrette | |
| Yacht marina | | Customs | | Caravan site | |
| Public landing | | Chandlery | | Camping site | |
| Slipway for small craft | | Public house or inn | | Nature reserve | |
| Water tap | | Restaurant | | Harbourmaster | |
| Fuel | | Yacht or sailing club | | | |
| Gas | | Toilets | | | |
| Post Office | | Public car park | | | |

# Major lights and radiobeacons

An outline sketch map showing the positions of the major navigational aids of the area. This map is intended merely for general consultation and convenience and is not suitable for navigation.

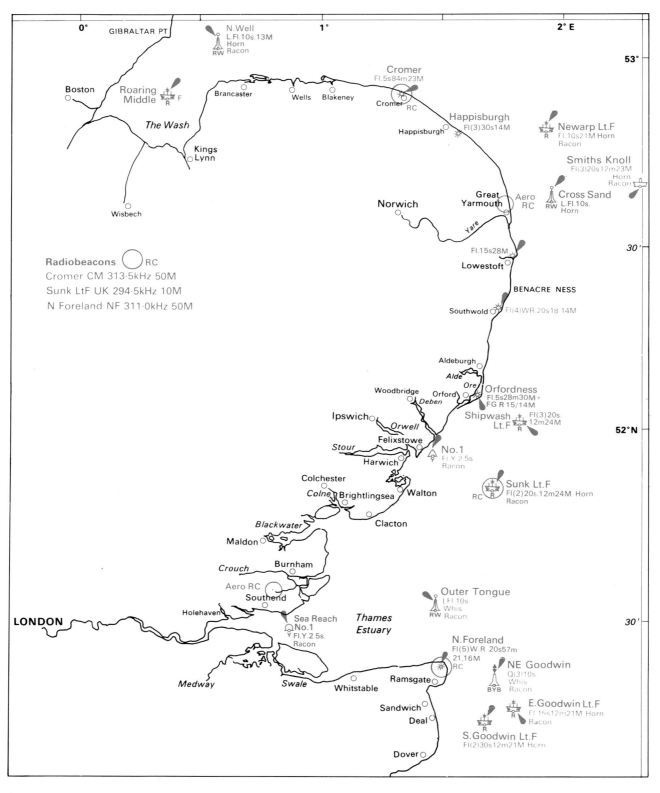

# Coastguard and lifeboats

An outline sketch map showing the positions of the coastguard and RNLI stations of the area.

(LB) Lifeboat    IR Inshore rescue boat only
(CG) Coastguard

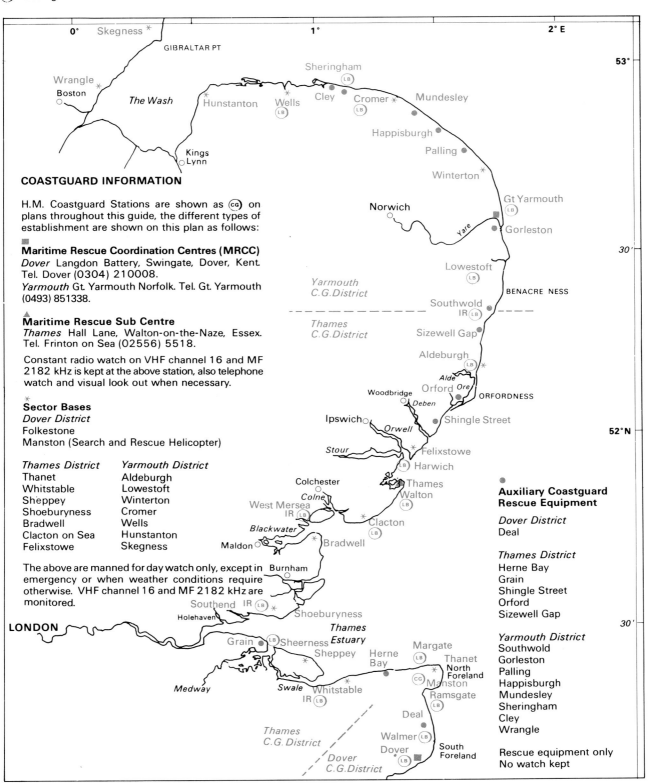

## COASTGUARD INFORMATION

H.M. Coastguard Stations are shown as (CG) on plans throughout this guide, the different types of establishment are shown on this plan as follows:

■ **Maritime Rescue Coordination Centres (MRCC)**
*Dover* Langdon Battery, Swingate, Dover, Kent. Tel. Dover (0304) 210008.
*Yarmouth* Gt. Yarmouth Norfolk. Tel. Gt. Yarmouth (0493) 851338.

▲ **Maritime Rescue Sub Centre**
*Thames* Hall Lane, Walton-on-the-Naze, Essex. Tel. Frinton on Sea (02556) 5518.

Constant radio watch on VHF channel 16 and MF 2182 kHz is kept at the above station, also telephone watch and visual look out when necessary.

✻ **Sector Bases**
*Dover District*
Folkestone
Manston (Search and Rescue Helicopter)

| *Thames District* | *Yarmouth District* |
|---|---|
| Thanet | Aldeburgh |
| Whitstable | Lowestoft |
| Sheppey | Winterton |
| Shoeburyness | Cromer |
| Bradwell | Wells |
| Clacton on Sea | Hunstanton |
| Felixstowe | Skegness |

The above are manned for day watch only, except in emergency or when weather conditions require otherwise. VHF channel 16 and MF 2182 kHz are monitored.

**LONDON**

● **Auxiliary Coastguard Rescue Equipment**

*Dover District*
Deal

*Thames District*
Herne Bay
Grain
Shingle Street
Orford
Sizewell Gap

*Yarmouth District*
Southwold
Gorleston
Palling
Happisburgh
Mundesley
Sheringham
Cley
Wrangle

Rescue equipment only
No watch kept

# Radio stations

An outline sketch map showing the various radio stations in operation within the area.

ⓒ Coast radio station

ⓟ Port radio

ⓜ Marina radio

ⓢ Special radio

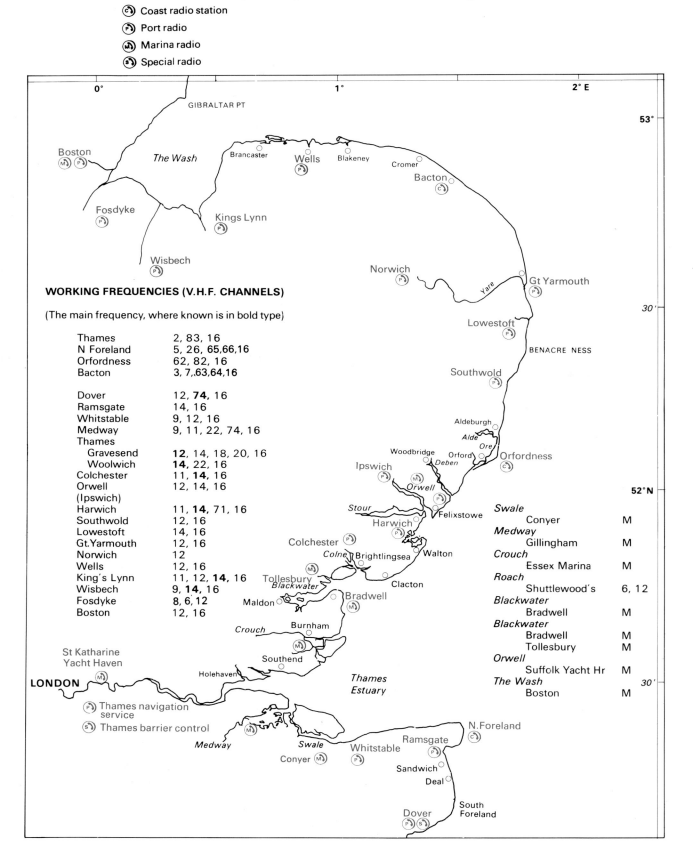

**WORKING FREQUENCIES (V.H.F. CHANNELS)**

(The main frequency, where known is in bold type)

| | |
|---|---|
| Thames | 2, 83, 16 |
| N Foreland | 5, 26, **65,66**,16 |
| Orfordness | 62, 82, 16 |
| Bacton | 3, 7,,63,64,16 |
| | |
| Dover | 12, **74**, 16 |
| Ramsgate | 14, 16 |
| Whitstable | 9, 12, 16 |
| Medway | 9, 11, 22, 74, 16 |
| Thames | |
|   Gravesend | **12**, 14, 18, 20, 16 |
|   Woolwich | **14**, 22, 16 |
| Colchester | 11, **14**, 16 |
| Orwell | 12, 14, 16 |
| (Ipswich) | |
| Harwich | 11, **14**, 71, 16 |
| Southwold | 12, 16 |
| Lowestoft | 14, 16 |
| Gt.Yarmouth | 12, 16 |
| Norwich | 12 |
| Wells | 12, 16 |
| King's Lynn | 11, 12, **14**, 16 |
| Wisbech | 9, **14**, 16 |
| Fosdyke | 8, 6, 12 |
| Boston | 12, 16 |

| | | |
|---|---|---|
| *Swale* | | |
| | Conyer | M |
| *Medway* | | |
| | Gillingham | M |
| *Crouch* | | |
| | Essex Marina | M |
| *Roach* | | |
| | Shuttlewood's | 6, 12 |
| *Blackwater* | | |
| | Bradwell | M |
| *Blackwater* | | |
| | Bradwell | M |
| | Tollesbury | M |
| *Orwell* | | |
| | Suffolk Yacht Hr | M |
| *The Wash* | | 30' |
| | Boston | M |

# Appropriate charts for the East Coast

In the preparation of this volume (and indeed at most other times as well) the author has always used both Imray and Admiralty charts. The range of Imray charts for the East Coast fits very well with the divisions to be found in this volume.

## BRITISH ADMIRALTY CHARTS

### Passage charts

| Chart | Title | Scale |
|---|---|---|
| 1408 | Harwich to Terschelling and Cromer to Rotterdam | 300,000 |
| 2182a | North Sea – southern sheet | 750,000 |

### Approach/harbour charts

| Chart | Title | Scale |
|---|---|---|
| 106 | Cromer to Smith's Knoll | 75,000 |
| 108 | Approaches to the Wash | 75,000 |
| 323 | Dover Strait – eastern part | 75,000 |
| 1183 | Thames Estuary | 100,000 |
| 1185 | River Thames – Sea Reach | 25,000 |
| 1186 | River Thames – Canvey Island to Tilbury | 12,500 |
| 1190 | Flamborough Head to Blakeney Pt | 150,000 |
| 1200 | The Wash Ports | Various |
| 1491 | Harwich and Felixstowe | 10,000 |
| 1503 | Outer Dowsing to Smith's Knoll | 150,000 |
| 1504 | Cromer to Orfordness | 150,000 |
| 1536 | Approaches to Great Yarmouth and Lowestoft | 40,000 |
| | Great Yarmouth haven: Lowestoft harbour | 6,250 |
| | Approaches to Lowestoft | 20,000 |
| 1543 | Winterton Ness to Orfordness | 75,000 |
| | Southwold harbour | 10,000 |
| 1593 | Harwich channel | 10,000 |
| 1594 | River Stour – Erwarton Ness to Manningtree | 10,000 |
| 1605 | Thames Estuary – Edinburgh channels | 15,000 |
| 1607 | Thames Estuary – southern part | 50,000 |
| 1610 | Approaches to the Thames Estuary | 150,000 |
| 1698 | Dover harbour | 6,250 |
| 1827 | Approaches to Ramsgate | 12,500 |
| | Ramsgate harbour | 5,000 |
| 1828 | Dover to North Foreland | 37,500 |
| 1834 | River Medway – Garrison Point to Folly Point | 12,500 |
| 1835 | River Medway – Folly Point to Maidstone | 6,000 |
| | Continuation of the River Medway to Maidstone | 25,000 |
| 2482 | River Medway and the Swale | 25,000 |
| | Ferry Reach | 12,500 |
| | Rochester | 12,500 |

## IMRAY CHARTS

### Passage charts

| Chart | Title | Scale |
|---|---|---|
| C25 | Harwich to the River Humber and Holland | 239,300 |
| C30 | Thames to Holland and Belgium Harwich and North Foreland to Hoek van Holland and Calais | 182,000 |

### Approach/harbour charts

| Chart | Title | Scale |
|---|---|---|
| C1 | Thames Estuary. Tilbury to North Foreland and Orfordness | 122,000 |
| C2 | The River Thames. Teddington to Southend. Teddington to Vauxhall. | 17,000 |
| | Vauxhall to Barking | 14,000 |
| | Barking to Southend | 40,000 |
| C8 | North Foreland to Beachy Head and Boulogne | 115,000 |
| Y6 | Thames Estuary – Northern Part | 112,000 |
| Y7 | Thames Estuary – Southern Part | 116,000 |
| Y9 | The Wash | 87,000 |
| Y14 | The Swale | 26,530 |
| Y15 | Rivers Ore, Alde and Deben | 29,000 |
| Y16 | Walton Backwaters to Ipswich and Woodbridge | 32,000 |
| Y17 | The Rivers Colne to Blackwater and Crouch | 49,000 |
| Y18 | River Medway. Sheerness to Rochester with River Thames, Sea Reach | 21,000 |
| C28 | The East Coast. Harwich to Wells | 126,000 |
| C29 | East Coast of England. Whitby to Harwich | 261,000 |

# Further reading

*North Sea (west) Pilot* (NP 54)
*Dover Strait Pilot* (NP 28)
Both published by the Hydrographer of the Navy

*North Sea Passage Pilot* Brian Navin, published by Imray, Laurie, Norie and Wilson Ltd
*The Tidal Havens of the Wash and Humber* Henry Irving, published by Imray, Laurie, Norie and Wilson Ltd
*East Coast Rivers* Jack Coote, published by Yachting Monthly
*The Pilot's Guide to the Thames Estuary* 1960 Lt Col W. E. Wilson, published by Imray, Laurie, Norie and Wilson Ltd
*Macmillan & Silk Cut Nautical Almanac*
*Reed's Nautical Almanac* published by Thomas Reed Publications Ltd
*Cruising Association Handbook* published by the Cruising Association
*London's Waterway Guide* C. Cove-Smith, published by Imray, Laurie, Norie and Wilson Ltd
*Inland Waterways of Great Britain* L. A. Edwards, published by Imray, Laurie, Norie and Wilson Ltd
*The Shell book of Inland Waterways* Hugh McKnight, published by David and Charles Ltd
*The Coast of South East England* J. Seymour, published by William Collins Ltd
*Northeast Waterways* Derek Bowskill, published by Imray, Laurie, Norie and Wilson Ltd

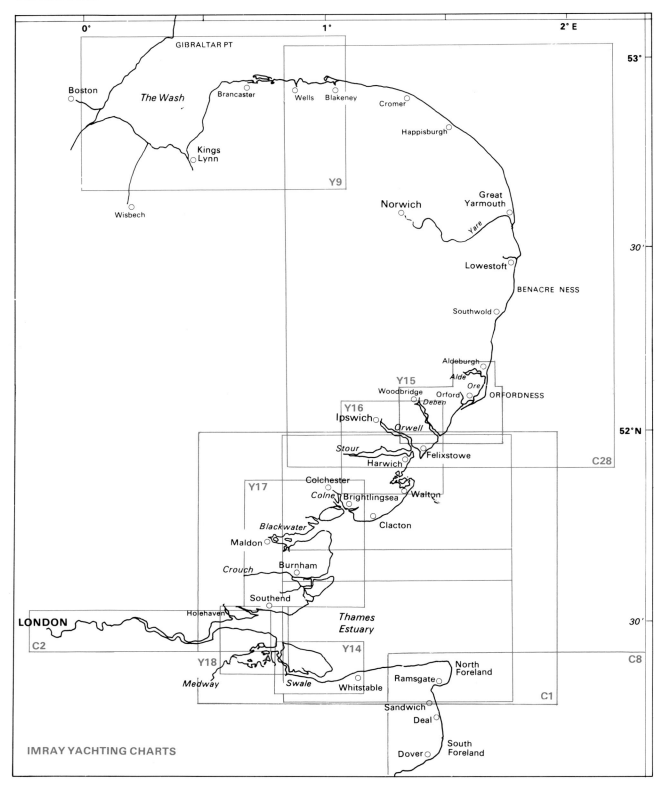

IMRAY YACHTING CHARTS

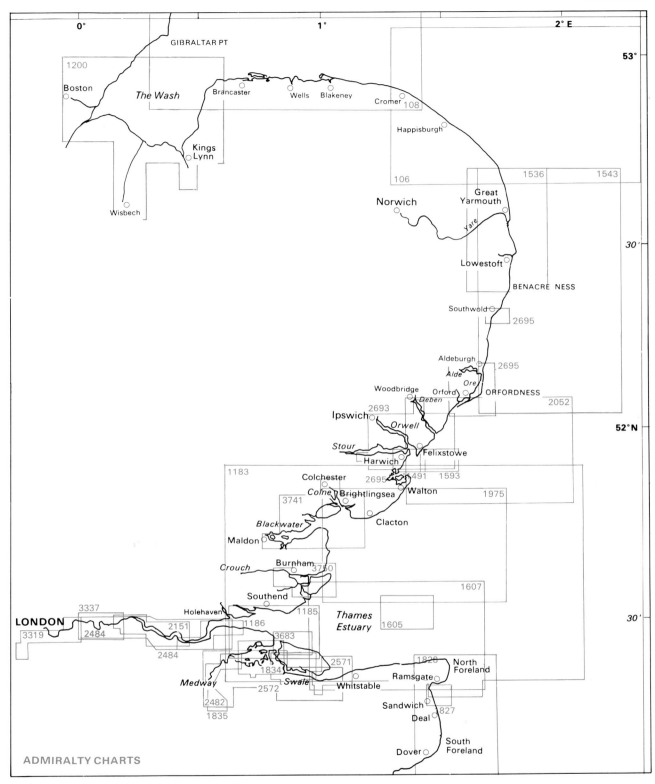

ADMIRALTY CHARTS

# Tidal information

The following average time differences on high water at Dover will give approximate times of high water at each point.

| | |
|---|---|
| Deal | +0015 |
| Richborough | +0015 |
| Ramsgate | +0020 |
| Margate | +0040 |
| Whitstable | +0110 |
| Harty Ferry | +0120 |
| Milton Creek | +0130 |
| Sheerness | +0130 |
| Queenborough | +0130 |
| Rochester Bridge | +0150 |
| St Katharines Dock | +0240 |
| Teddington Lock | +0345 |
| Leigh-on-Sea | +0120 |
| Southend Pier | +0115 |
| Burnham-on-Crouch | +0100 |
| Hullbridge | +0115 |
| Paglesham | +0110 |
| Havengore Bridge | +0100 |
| Sales Point | +0040 |
| Colne Point | +0050 |
| Brightlingsea | +0100 |
| Wivenhoe | +0115 |
| West Mersea | +0100 |
| Bradwell Quay | +0100 |
| Tollesbury | +0100 |
| Heybridge Basin | +0130 |
| Walton-on-Naze | +0030 |
| Hamford Water | +0035 |
| Harwich | +0045 |
| Manningtree | +0110 |
| Pinmill | +0100 |
| Ipswich | +0120 |
| Felixstowe Ferry | +0020 |
| Woodbridge | +0130 |
| Orford Haven | +0000 |
| Orford Quay | +0100 |
| Aldeburgh (R. Alde) | +0145 |
| Snape Bridge | +0345 |
| Southwold | −0055 |
| Lowestoft | −0145 |
| Gt Yarmouth | −0210 |
| Blakeney Point | −0500 |
| Wells Bar | −0500 |
| Burnham Overy | −0420 |
| Brancaster Staithe | −0430 |
| Kings Lynn | −0445 |
| Wisbech | −0455 |
| Boston | −0500 |

The figures against the arrows denote mean rates in tenth of a knot at neaps and springs. Thus 06·11 indicates a mean neap rate of 0·6 knots and a mean spring rate of 1·1 knots.

Based upon British Admiralty information with the permission of the Controller of HM Stationery Office and the Hydrographer of the Navy.

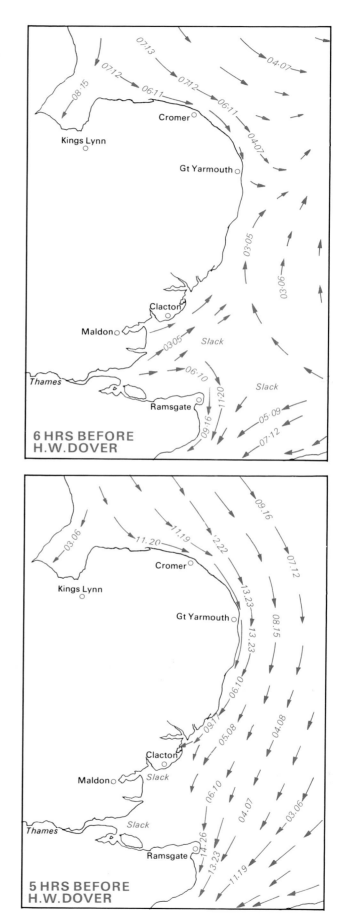

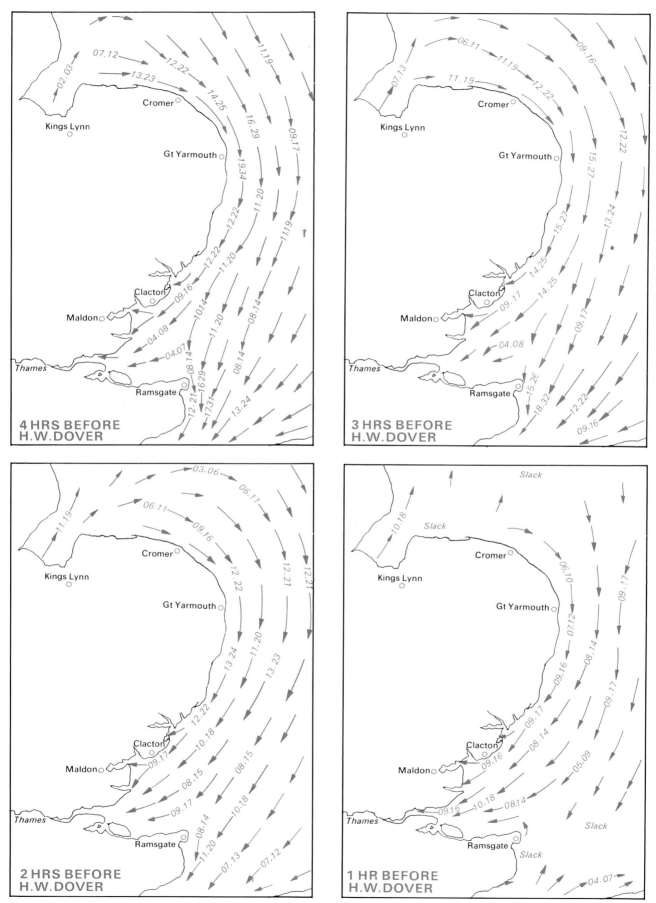

4 HRS BEFORE
H.W. DOVER

3 HRS BEFORE
H.W. DOVER

2 HRS BEFORE
H.W. DOVER

1 HR BEFORE
H.W. DOVER

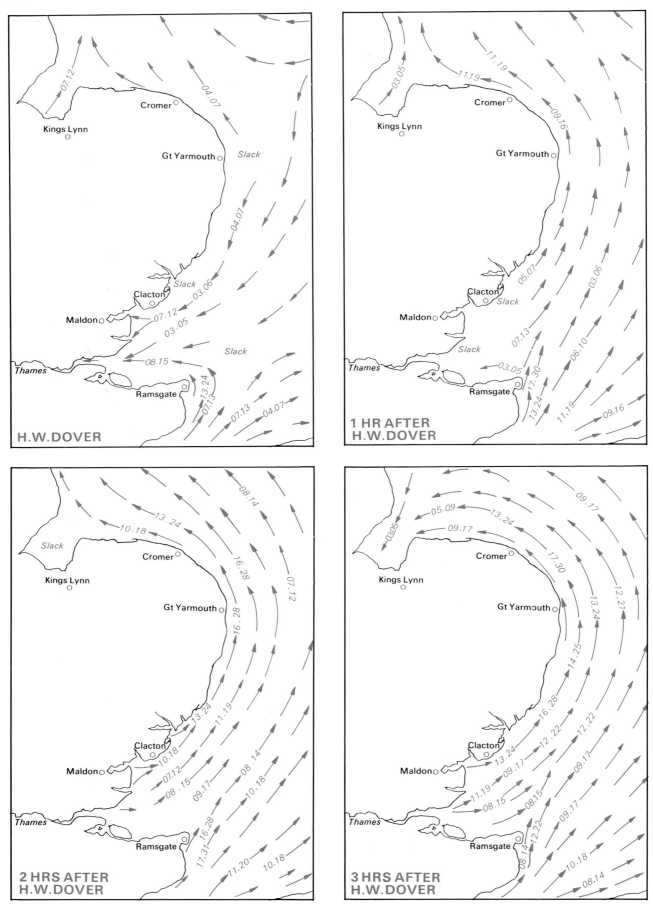

H.W. DOVER

1 HR AFTER
H.W. DOVER

2 HRS AFTER
H.W. DOVER

3 HRS AFTER
H.W. DOVER

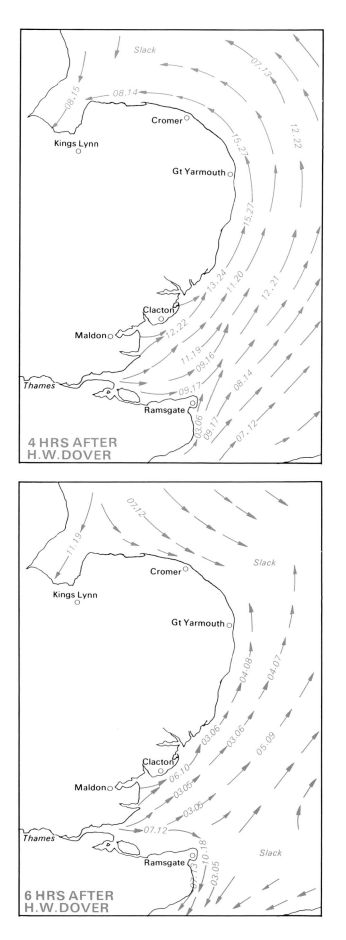

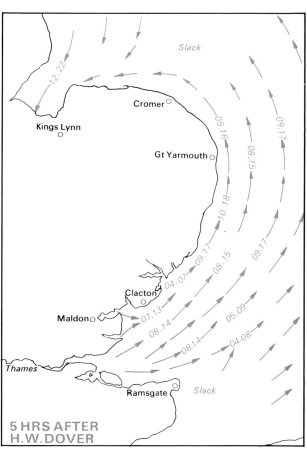

# I. THE WASH

## By way of introducing the Wash

Let me begin by straightway declaring a partiality: I know of no cruising ground; no tideway; no set of tortuous channels, genuine and false; no assortment of bars, banks and braes; nor any array of harbours, communities and settlements that can offer the rich rewards of a month in the country of the Wash. Thus my partisan enthusiasm encourages me to declare, Paul-wise, the Wash capable of being all things to all men.

Great indeed are the rewards of the Wash, but there is a price to be paid if you want to navigate these cruising grounds without fear or favour, and in comfort and relaxation. There is an old French proverb, 'In the country of the blind, the one-eyed man is king.' It could be appropriately adapted, 'In the waters of the Wash, the four-eyed look-out is boss.' That is, if 'waters' is the best word to describe the 250 square miles which are as extraordinary as they are intriguing; for half the Wash dries out at low water, and much of what is left consists of ever-shifting sand and mudbanks. One way of keeping in the credit columns of the good books of the Wash gods, is to acknowledge the price of survival as eternal vigilance: the *genius loci* is only too ready and able to test the heedless, the reckless and the over self-assured. Many there are who have been found wanting.

Some skippers approach cruising the Wash as they would crossing the North Sea; while others make as little of it as they would the New Junction Canal or Nun Monkton Pool. The wise skipper does both by preparing for all contingencies and then setting out to enjoy the experience; to return to base without having lost anyone, bumped into anyone, or broken anything.

The attractions of the Wash range from the amiably prosaic to the unnervingly poetic, with myths and legends in a profusion to rival even seals and sandbanks. Cockling and musselling are popular. At weekends, hordes from the four ports go out for a day's digging and/or scratching. Fishing, although no longer as good as it used to be, is also customary; and if you are to take home a catch that is in any way worthwhile you do need to know a fair amount about the ways of the Wash and its elusive shoals. Fish, that is: the sandy kind will hardly ever elude you for long unless you are extremely limited in what you want to explore.

The Wash can change its character in less than an hour. One minute you can be basking with the seals in glorious sunshine and five minutes later be completely disorientated in one of the fog banks that fall without warning ... and hang around without respite as the tide turns into a fast, undeniable unrelenting force.

Indeed, I remember one occasion when the waters of the Wash were oily calm; the airs were so light, they were incapable of inducing a ripple on the glassy surface. There was no movement nor any sign of life. No bird flew near; no seal swam by; nor was there another vessel in sight. *Valcon* and I had the Wash to ourselves so far as I could see: and that was all of fifty metres. The rest was thick fog, with the Wash merging so effortlessly into its blanketing shroud that I could distinguish nothing. In some of my more extreme hallucinations, I began to take on the mantle of King John.

## Approaches

You can work the tides favourably coming from the south, carrying a sympathetic stream all the way from Great Yarmouth. Cruising at 6–7 knots, you will find yourself turning into the Wash at the same time as the stream does. Thus you make excellent time without needing to force anything.

When entering the world of the Wash, the same buoy, the *N. Well* safe water mark, significant and symbolic, comes first and needs to be identified whether you are coming from the *Dudgeon*, *Dowsing* or *Humber* light vessels. After that, progress is south westerly straight through The Well and into Lynn Deeps; and finally on to the well-known banana-boat light float, the *Roaring Middle*. Craft from Blakeney or Wells-next-the-Sea may use the Stiffkey Overfalls – Bridgirdle – Sledway – Woolpack passage and go straightway on to the Roaring Middle; while those with draught, craft and local knowledge suitable for Brancaster, Overy and Thornham will probably prefer the close inshore route just to the south of Gore Middle and Middle Bank, by the Bays.

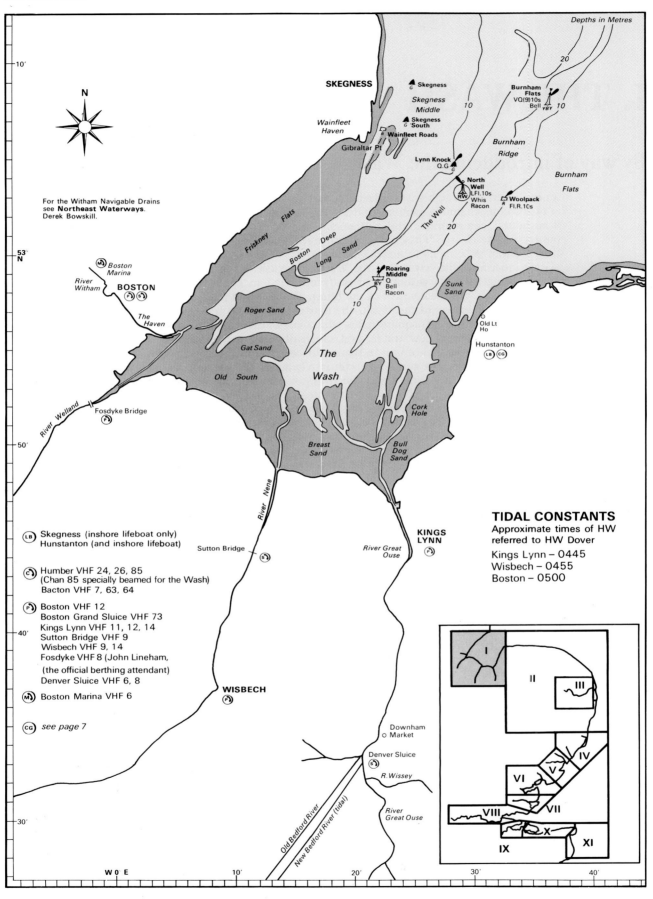

Depths in Metres

SKEGNESS

Skegness

*Skegness*
*Middle*

Burnham
Flats
VQ(9)10s
Bell

*Wainfleet*
*Haven*

Skegness
South

Wainfleet Roads

Gibraltar Pt

*Burnham*
*Ridge*

Lynn Knock
Q.G.

*Burnham*
*Flats*

North
Well
LFl.10s
Whis
Racon

Woolpack
Fl.R.10s

*Friskney*
*Flats*

*Boston Deep*

*Long Sand*

*The Well*

20

Boston Marina

River
Witham

BOSTON

Roaring
Middle
Q
Bell
Racon

*Sunk*
*Sand*

The Haven

Roger Sand

10

Old Lt
Ho

Hunstanton

*The*

*Wash*

Gat Sand

Old South

River Welland

Fosdyke Bridge

Cork
Hole

Breast
Sand

Bull
Dog
Sand

River Nene

KINGS
LYNN

*River Great*
*Ouse*

For the Witham Navigable Drains
see **Northeast Waterways**.
Derek Bowskill.

Sutton Bridge

**TIDAL CONSTANTS**
Approximate times of HW
referred to HW Dover

Kings Lynn – 0445
Wisbech – 0455
Boston – 0500

(LB) Skegness (inshore lifeboat only)
Hunstanton (and inshore lifeboat)

(C) Humber VHF 24, 26, 85
(Chan 85 specially beamed for the Wash)
Bacton VHF 7, 63, 64

(P) Boston VHF 12
Boston Grand Sluice VHF 73
Kings Lynn VHF 11, 12, 14
Sutton Bridge VHF 9
Wisbech VHF 9, 14
Fosdyke VHF 8 (John Lineham,
(the official berthing attendant)
Denver Sluice VHF 6, 8

(M) Boston Marina VHF 6

(CG) *see page 7*

**WISBECH**

Downham
Market

Denver Sluice

R. Wissey

Old Bedford River

New Bedford River (tidal)

River
Great Ouse

I

II

III

IV

VI

V

VII

VIII

X

IX

XI

A similarly close inshore passage for those with local knowledge is to be found when coming from the Humber or the north. It is a tempting short cut if bound for Boston or Fosdyke: past Skegness (*Skegness* green conical; and *Skegness South* green conical) and into Wainfleet Road and Swatchway (*Wainfleet Roads* red can; *Inner Knock* red can; *Swatchway* green conical) and then past *Pompey* (green conical) and *Parlour Channel* (with its westerly entrance marked by *PB* red can) into Boston Deep. It is, of course, necessary to use one of these approaches when proceeding to Gibraltar Point and/or Wainfleet Creek/Haven.

At the northeast corner of the Wash is Hunstanton, with its old but unmistakable lighthouse. It is not always easy to pick out the Hunstanton light or Hunstanton/Gore Points – annoying, since, as the Admiralty *Pilot* says, it is 'a cliff composed of marl, and grey and red chalk; it is remarkable both for the variety of its colouring and as the only cliff in the vicinity.' It also says, 'The rapidity of the tidal streams in this bight, the low elevation of its shores, and the mist which almost constantly prevails, render its navigation difficult, and a more than common degree of care is necessary.'

This is the corner you round when coming up from the south, be it nearby Wells or faraway Ramsgate. Nearby, there are two water towers and an old windmill, but, again as the Admiralty *Pilot* says, 'It is not always easy to identify objects ashore.' A pity, since there are also the remains of St Edmund's Chapel, Hunstand Hall, the Octagon and an Anglo-Saxon burial ground. In fact, the area is littered with remains of one kind or another from the Iron Age, Anglo-Saxons and the Romans; and coins, hoards, cremation and burial grounds abound – after all, it must not be forgotten that the great House of Sandringham (not at all easy to identify from anywhere since close inspection is not invited) is close by … and they must know where all hidden things are.

Strangers tend to stand well offshore, using the main channel into N. Well; but there are inshore channels for those who know or who have the right kind of shoal craft to find out. There is nothing shoresides and little offshore to tempt the visiting mariner close in to Hunstanton (although the pathway for the old once much-used commercial route channel is still quite clear) and most visitors will, in any case, be making straight for Boston Roads and the Freeman Channel or the Sunk and the King's Lynn Channel. All in all, by land or sea, it is an area to be taken slowly but surely; and so it is across the water, coming round the bend from the Skegness direction, where, at the northwest corner, there is a different tale to be told.

# Gibraltar Point and Wainfleet Haven

The south coast of Lincolnshire is like that of the north coast of Norfolk nearby: long, low, flat and featureless, with anything resembling a harbour an immediate boon and blessing. While there is plenty of tourist-resort-life ashore, it is nevertheless very much of a long havenless-haul from the northern delights of Brid, Scarboro' Fair and Spurn down the coast to the northeast corner of the Wash. But there you find the famous resting place and watering hole of the Gibraltar Point, somewhat incongruously named, since nothing could be less like the high reaching 2½ square miles of Spanish peninsula rock at the gate to the Mediterranean. Tucked away behind it is the quiet refuge known variously as Wainfleet Swatchway, the Roads and Wainfleet Haven (Steeping River, if you incline to a riparian point of view). The area is also thrice blessed by the presence of those special features: Wainfleet Harbour; the nature reserve; and the Seacroft golf course.

South of Saltfleet (a now miniature but once thriving harbour of old world charm, virtually inaccessible except to the cognoscenti) and close to archetypally bracing Skegness (even more inaccessible except by beaching, Breeches buoy or traffic jam) Wainfleet is not the kind of haven to recommend itself to the chance visitor who is on the lookout for an easy-in-and-out, lazy mains-powered weekend away from none of it all. In fact, the whole area is a vast nature reserve with a visitors' centre and field station that offers a commanding view over the Wash.

Wainfleet Haven itself lies at the outfall of the Steeping, a river that is tidal up to Wainfleet all Saints almost five miles inland. Once busy with big commercial shipping, it is now silted up, and must be deemed no more than a decently attractive mud creek. It is approached by a channel that is narrow, tortuous and shallow, and in the main is given over to two kinds of wild life: first, flora, fauna and birds of a feather; and second, those eccentric sailors who are attracted by its idiosyncratic charm, the exigencies of time and tide and the frequently changing course of the channel. Nonetheless, it is a most useful reserve destination should you happen to be running late on the tide for Boston. However, it must be added that it is not a suitable harbour of refuge for any stranger or first time visitor caught out by adverse weather conditions.

The Skegness Yacht Club is active in the Haven, as are, still, one or two local professional fishermen. It is also a delight to find that the place possesses real live toilets, an unexpectedly welcome facility in such a remote haven.

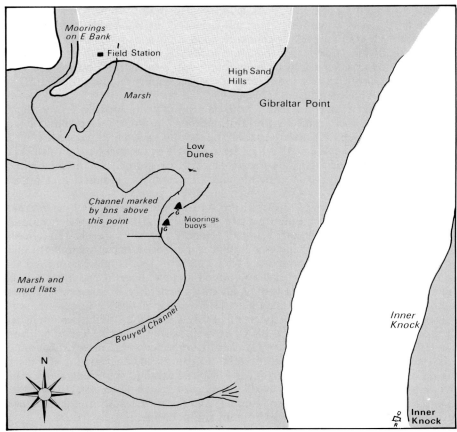

**WAINFLEET HAVEN**

Wainfleet was once a major port; now all that remains is the small
haven by Gibraltar Point.

Access is not dangerous, but neither is it easy, and the best plan is to visit shoresides at low water and make as many local contacts as possible, hoping for help when your proposed trip comes up. It is not a place for nervous skippers or crews who don't keep their eyes skinned.

Coming from the north, to find the River Steeping channel, you make for the green buoy marking Skegness Middle and then leave *Skegness South* to starboard tending southwesterly for Wainfleet Roads, continue thus down to the red *Inner Knock Fairway* buoy by the Wainfleet Swatchway. From the south, via the Well or Boston Deep, you make for the yellow *No.1 DZ* and the nearby green *Swatchway* which will take you more or less northerly to the *Inner Knock*.

You then search out the first *Wainfleet Channel* buoy. While none of these is quite as obscure as the *Pye End* buoy at Harwich, they can occupy more than one pair of fine eyes in the dark misty-grey that so often passes for light in the Wash. The last series of legs of the approach channel is marked by the Skegness Yacht Club with spar buoys along the outer, seaward section and beacons for the final stretch up to the haven proper.

Ian Martin is a worthy local contact, to whom I am indebted. He works his fishing boat *The Challenge* out of the haven and listens on VHF. He described the channel in these terms. 'Where it traverses the beach, there are small spar buoys with light reflectors, red to port, green to starboard. Where it traverses the marsh, there are beacons, red can tops to port, black or green triangular top marks to starboard. At night, there is an 'unofficial' light that can help: the north trap light on the nature reserve field station.'

The club has also managed to establish moorings for about thirty boats up to 10m LOA and 1·5m draught. However, the top range of such vessels cannot navigate the channel on neap tides.

Two or three visitors can usually be accommodated if of shallow draught and with ability to sit up when dried out. If in doubt, and there is no one to assist, tie up alongside the fishing boat or motor boat astern of it. It is vital that you stay on board at subsequent high waters in case they are going to sea. Access is 2 hours either side of HW springs, 1 hour neaps. Offshore banks reduce the swell in onshore winds; and strong S winds reduce the height of HW, especially neaps.

For any one staying more than few days in the Wash, it will be impossible not to become aware that there is an RAF range in the vicinity of Wainfleet. However, the river marks its legal boundary, and anyone navigating the channel into Wainfleet Haven will stand into no danger. Normally, the range operates only during the daylight hours on Mondays, Wednesdays and Thursdays, but its franchise is for weekdays up to midnight. RAF Command HQ listens on VHF channel 16 and can be contacted by land line ☎ (0754) 880325.

Whether on deck taking a strong sundowner; peering from the observation room of the nature reserve; or out on the no-man's-land that is the foreshore of Gibraltar Point's mud-flats, Wainfleet Haven offers an excellent location from which to observe some of the area's bleak attractions; and a splendid opportunity to come face to face, if not to grips or terms, with the Wash.

# The Witham to Boston

## Approaches

Out in the broader expanses of the deeper channels the buoyage is big and unmistakable, and decisions about final destinations can usually be postponed until *Roaring Middle* is in sight. Then it is a case of left, right or centre, depending on whether you want King's Lynn, Wisbech or Boston.

From the *Roaring Middle*, Boston Roads leads to the Freeman Channel. The international buoyage system is owned and maintained by the Port of Boston Authority, and after recent refurbishment (in the Freeman, Boston Deep and Parlour Channel) is excellent to follow. If used without cut corners, it makes the approach a simple and straightforward matter.

A favourite spot to anchor while awaiting a tide to Boston is in the area of Clay Hole, and nearby buoys *11* and *Golf*. Clay Hole is as well a protected spot as you can hope to find in the Wash, but in fact I prefer to go not quite to *Clay Hole* and to use *High Horn* instead; but wherever you are waiting for the tide you will be sure to see the fishermen queueing up just before it is time to go in.

After that, *Tab's Head* and *Dolly Peg* show the way into the New Cut to the Haven and the River Witham. *Tabs Head* is left to port for Boston. It is possible to get closer in by watching your water through the channel almost up to *India*, but this is almost pointless since a rushed start merely means chancing an encounter with the bottom. That is, if you manage to find your way across the bar in the first place. Tide times for entering the river are the same as the others in the Wash: not better than three hours before high water.

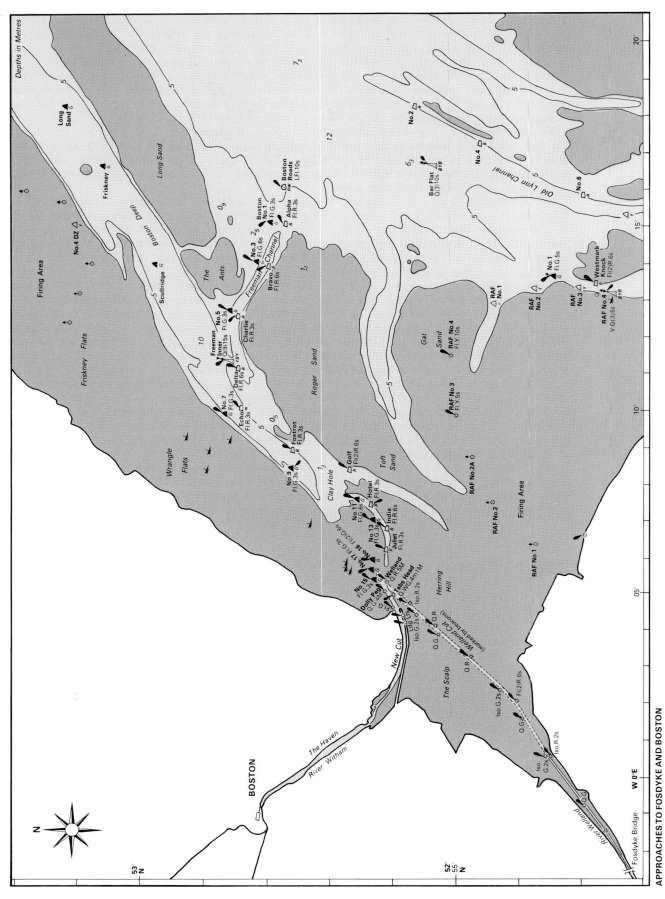

APPROACHES TO FOSDYKE AND BOSTON

# BUOYAGE

## Approaches to Wisbech

| Check | Confirm | Confirm | Check |
|-------|---------|---------|-------|

**River Nene (Wisbech Cut)**

⊙ Tr

Tr. ⊙

☀ F.G.+Q.G.

☀ **West End Bn**
Fl.G.5s.3M

**Big Tom**
Fl(2)R.10s
☀

☀ **Walker**
Fl.G.2s.

☀ **Double Brush**
Q.G.

☀ **Dale**
Fl.G.5s

**Trial Bank**
Fl(2)5s
☀

○ **R.A.F.**
Y **No. 6**

▲ **Fenland**
G Fl(3)G.10s

Y ○ **R.A.F.**
**No. 5**

**R.A.F.**
**No. 4**
VQ(3)5s BYB

○ **Bn**
Y

**Westmark**
**Knock**
Fl(2)R.6s
▧ R

△ **R.A.F.**
Y **No. 3**

▽ **No. 1**
G Fl.G.5s

△ **R.A.F.**
Y **No. 2**

**No. 4**
▧ R

△ **R.A.F.**
Y **No. 1**

▲ **Bar Flat**
G **(Pilot Station)**

**No. 2**
▧ R

**No. 1**
V.Q.Bell
▲
BY

**Boston Roads**
L.Fl.10s
⊡
RW

**Sunk**
Q (9) 15s. YBY

▲ **Roaring Middle**
BY Q
Bell

The Wash

## Approaches to Boston & Fosdyke

| Check | Confirm | Confirm | Check |
|-------|---------|---------|-------|

**New Cut (channel to Boston)**
**Ldg Lts F.W.on Masts**

**Tabs Head**
Q.W.G.
☀

▲ **New Cut**
☀ Fl.G

▲ **Dolly Peg**
☀ Q.G.

**Welland**
Q.R.5M
▧

**Juliet**
Fl.G.3s
▧ G

▲ **Boston No. 17**
G Fl.G.3s

**India**
Fl.R.6s
▧ R

▲ **Boston No. 16**
G Fl(2)G.6s

**Hotel**
Fl.R.3s
▧ R

▲ **Boston No. 13**
G Fl.G.3s

▲ **Boston No. 11**
G Fl.G.6s

**Golf**
Fl(2)R.6s
▧ R

**Foxtrot**
Fl.R.3s
▧ R

▲ **Boston No. 9**
G Fl.G.3s

**Echo**
Fl .R.3s.
▧ R

▲ **Boston No. 7**
G Fl.G.3s

**Freeman**
**Inner**
Q(9)15s
YBY

**Delta**
Fl.R.6s
▧ R

Boston Deep

**Charlie**
Fl.R.3s
▧ R

▲ **Scullridge**
G

▲ **Boston No 5**
G Fl.G.3s

**Bravo**
Fl.R.6s
▧ R

▲ **Boston No. 3**
G Fl.G.5s

**Alpha**
Fl.R.3s
▧ R

▲ **Boston No. 1**
G Fl.G.3s

**Boston**
**Roads**
L.Fl.10s
RW

▲ **Roaring**
BY **Middle**
Q
Bell

The Wash

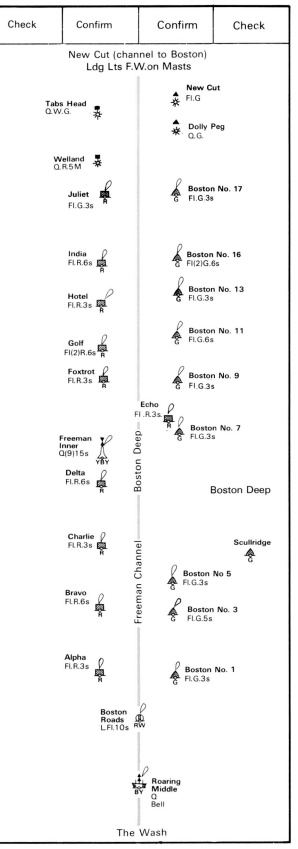

It is also somewhat foolish to arrive at Grand Sluice before the lock has enough water; and, what is of greater significance, before there is enough depth in the upper parts of the river to keep you well above the nasty sundries that decorate the bottom: a choice selection from old car chassis and concrete works on the steeply sloping sides to eel nets and plastic bottles harnessed together in mid-stream (with some in a very prop-threatening formation). An inspection of the river at low water will convince you of the need for caution and accurate pilotage.

To catch the first-level opening of the Grand Sluice, you do need to be off to a good start. With no more than a metre's draught, there will be no problem, but with one and a half you will need all your skill to keep out of keel-scraping trouble.

## The New Cut and the Haven

The channel is more or less central with only the normal hazards of tide-time port and river navigation. The banks are well marked with beacons as an additional aid, but in normal conditions they are not needed for reference, as all is plain sailing until you reach the area of the docks, where life can become a bit hectic. A radio request to the harbourmaster (VHF channel 12) will bring you the state of shipping movements. This is worth having since room to manoeuvre is at a premium and there is little space for Combined Ops with commercial traffic and leisure craft. Co-operation between the two worlds has always been a pleasing aspect at Boston.

The docks are not available to pleasure craft except in an emergency. Mooring is just possible below the first bridge on the port hand where the bottom is soft mud. Under favourable circumstances, craft can stay afloat at all states of the tide. However, laying alongside this short length of wall is a risky affair, only to be considered if you have a robust vessel with sturdy tackle and a stalwart crew who will be staying on board. To go any further means dismasting to negotiate the river bridges and the lock at Grand Sluice.

There are also other possible moorings beyond the (swing) railway bridge to the docks: private jetties and berths, near-berths and so-called berths where, even if you could trace the owner for permission, you would find they are not really suitable for fragile leisure craft. Nevertheless, they are much valued and in great demand, and there have been 'ideas' and somewhat vague 'plans' afoot to improve and reorganise the area and its facilities. As usual, conflicting riparian interests stand in the way. Boats take the (soft mud) bottom.

If you have lowered your gear to get through the Grand Sluice lock, you will also be able to pass under all the bridges up the Boston River. The last stretch of the river before the lock is the one where special care must be taken if you are 'early' on the tide and trying to catch the first pen. The bottom is tricky: although there are not as many eel nets as there used to be, there are still enough to warrant a watchful eye, and the presence of rocks and a generally foul bottom are to be found reaching from the port bank to mid-stream. However, if you keep the railway signal in line with the last lamp standard on shoresides you will clear all the obstructions. The worst area is just after the footbridge, where it is foul on both sides and the stretch is generally shoal.

Finally, there is the immediate approach to the lock itself, Grand Sluice!, which is an ugly-looking, threatening affair, with accompanying gates that can spew out races at a rate of knots to compete with anything that Charybdis could do. True, the rocks roundabout are nothing like Scylla, but care is still called for if sluicing is going on: the process can be so vicious that a small boat skipper can easily find himself in trouble if he is without plenty of power.

On some occasions you will need to manoeuvre/jill around; and the powerful eddies need to be watched. It is a good idea for all skippers to let the lock keeper know of their ETA; he can then try for the engineers' co-operation so that cruising folk are put about as little as possible.

The lock office is equipped with a telephone and answering machine (☎ Boston (0205) 364864) and also on VHF channel 16 and 73, on which dual watch is maintained. As a final resort, Captain Hulland, the Boston harbourmaster, will consider passing on a message from you via the telephone if the necessity should arise. The lock is in fact available at tide times during both night and day for anyone making a genuine seagoing passage or requiring a haven from the Wash. However, since there is only one keeper, he appreciates not having to work nights as well as days.

If you have to wait outside the lock, moor only between the ladders, where if you draw less than 1·5m you will be able to stay afloat at all times. If you draw more, you may touch bottom on springs. The bottom is hard concrete. It is quite flat, but since it is hard, exposed engines or outdrives are at risk. There are standard traffic signals. While the navigation is theoretically open from October to April the river is often run low, so a passage can be well nigh impossible. British Waterways Board who run moorings on the 'fresh' side of the river only, say 'Boaters are requested to book passage through this lock at least one hour before the level of the tide on which they wish to proceed through the lock.'

When going to Boston it must be preferable to go to the trouble of taking down masts (if necessary) and going through the Grand Sluice lock into the fresh water of the river, and Doris

Farmer's marina. This incisive business lady will welcome you with such charm and friendly efficiency that you will be tempted to stay longer than your planned allotted span. In addition to the usual chandlery, they carry Admiralty charts, and there are mains water and electricity at the berths, with diesel nearby. They keep a listening watch whenever they can on channel 6. You can telephone the marina at Boston ☎ (0205) 364420 to let them know you are visiting and they will have a place ready for you if at all possible. It is a very popular spot in season.

You will see none of this until you have passed through the heart of Boston, on the navigation that runs right through the centre of the town. What you can see, however, halfway between the town and the sea, if you have an eye and a mind to seek it out, is the commemorative tablet raised to the Pilgrim Fathers. Not even many of the contemporary Americans who make pilgrimage to Boston (Lincs) from Boston (Mass, USA) manage to get a proper view of the stone. But what they do get is a good view of the tower of the Church of St Botolph, known locally as the Stump. Indeed, dull would he be of eye who could pass by a sight so striking in its dominance: it is not easy to be out of its purview for many a mile. Its higher echelons are now prohibited to the public on account of the growing popularity of suicide attempts from its balconies.

# Boston

No skipper ever finds himself in Boston by chance. It is so far inland from the North Sea as to make a 'chance' call out of the question. Its position at the end of the Witham and Fosdyke Navigation demands that real thought must be given to getting there; and any navigation from salt to fresh, or vice versa, for any yachtsman not based in the area, is one that requires serious thought.

There are so many excellent reasons for making a special trip to Boston, that it is of no consequence that there is little chance trade. The reasons are basically twofold: the welcome you will find on the upstream of the lock, at the BWB and marina moorings and the local clubs on the other side of the river.

Approaching Boston from upstream, on what is known locally as 'the Fresh', on the right hand bank you will come across the first of the clubs. This is the hand-powered coterie who row the stretch in any kind of weather; on the same side and almost immediately after them are the powered boats of the Boston Motor Boat Club: and finally, just before the whirlpools of the Grand Sluice are the moorings of the Witham Sailing Club.

And then there is the town itself: the shopkeepers of Boston all seem to be related to one another, and if they are not, then they are close friends. If they do not have what you want, they rest not until they have determined which of their contacts will come up trumps and have shown you the way and taken you by the arm a goodly distance en route. No doubt there are thieves, rogues and vagabonds in Boston but I have never encountered a single one.

When it comes to boatyards, there is no shortage of people to assist, maintain and/or repair. Pre-eminent, and offering a comprehensive service is the old established family business of R. Keightley & Son. They like all boats and love old ones. They are to be found at their yard: Willoughby Road, Boston. ☎ Boston (0205) 363616.

It so happens that I can personally vouch for the fact that Boston (Mass) can, somewhat improbably, rival Boston (Lincs) when it comes to the preparation and dispensing of fish'n'chips; but when it comes to salted and/or cooked meats, especially chaps, Boston (Lincs) acknowledges no rival.

From Boston you can cruise the waters of the Wash at leisure and you can also start on the long journey of exploration into the inland waterways of the northeast, starting perhaps with the deliciously named Witham Navigable Drains. Boston is one of my favourite ports of call, and is certainly within easy distance of so much of contrast that it is difficult to think of a home port that could offer more.

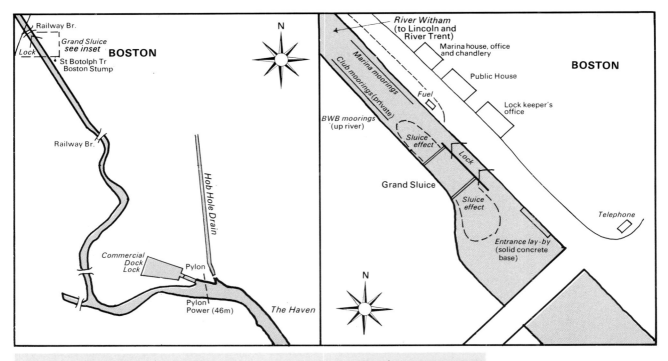

Boston: The Grand Sluice is an area that demands a powerful engine if you are not to be left at the mercy of its currents. The lock gates are to the right

The River Witham: although a busy river and a popular spot, there are few facilities on the salt-side of the Grand Sluice for pleasure craft. As the picture shows the mooring opportunities are not civilised

Boston Stump has for centuries been a sounding board and a
landmark for Wash navigators.

Mooring for pleasure craft in Boston's tidal stretch is not without
its hazards.

# The Welland to Fosdyke

## Approaches

Approach and anchoring are the same as for Boston and the Witham, but if anything, it is prudent to leave a little more time before entering Welland Cut, for there are some parts where the bottom is uneven and 'close'. Additionally, the flood tide can really move up to the bridge, and it is unsafe to have your bows stuck fast with a spring flood up the stern (see Great Ouse below). Access should therefore be best considered as +/−0200 HW from the mouth of the river.

*Tabs Head* and *Welland* beacons show the way into Welland Cut. *Tabs Head* is left to starboard. Fosdyke Bridge must be deemed to be the head of navigation for visitors. If you cannot pass under the bridge, turn well before it so that you have plenty of time to stem the tide, which can get up to 5+ knots. A good idea is to start turning just before you reach the moorings on the starboard (north) hand. Your turn should be made to the north, and it is essential to have plenty of power. Mooring is not without problems, and a prior visit or telephone call should be made.

# The River Welland to Fosdyke Bridge

Welland Cut runs through low-lying marshlands where shortly after entering are to starboard one or two 'last ditches' (they can hardly be called channels) where those with a mind to get well away from it all can navigate at springs, to find truly better 'oles. It is a pleasant, wild-life anchorage in the back of beyond Boston, and provided you are fully self-supporting or enjoy tripping the light fantastic in the dinghy. The only risk is that you will become so lotus eater-like that you will get neaped.

The entry to the River Welland is by *Tabs Head* and the Cut and lies between the sandbanks of Herring and Scalp. Up to *Cut End* and the *Welland* the buoyage is standard and well lit. Welland Cut channel is straight, trained by walls and marked by beacons on its bank. These are lit and most have radar reflectors.

The only hazards are the power of the flood and the few hills and humps that you will undoubtedly find if you try to get in too early on the tide. The most sensible course when tackling the Welland and Fosdyke for the first time is to contact John Lineham. Wherever you find him, you will get a good tale, excellent conversation, first rate assistance and as much advice as you can take.

The quayside at Fosdyke (on the starboard hand going upstream just before the bridge) is a dramatic place to berth. Not only is there the usual amazing rise and fall of the Wash tide with its equally amazing fast flood; but there is also the complication of strong back eddies created by the masonry and support of the bridge; and Fosdyke is a very substantial affair that will see off any attacker. Reserve power is important so you can turn easily and hold your own without stress.

Fosdyke is a small commercial quay with no official or special facilities for yachts, and getting a line to that high jetty can be a fraught job: first there is the power of the flood stream to be negotiated, and that must be accomplished by starting to turn well before the end of the moored boats on the starboard hand. You should turn to the north (starboard) unless you want to risk being carried on the bridge by main force. Finally, if you have gone in early, there will be a good height up to the quay for throwing a line, even if there is someone waiting. It is not a trip to tackle lightly (nor one for a craft a bit short on long strong warps) and there are few services and even less to see; but, it is a 'must' as one of the few remaining 'open' ports left in the UK. In any case, all time and effort expended will be well rewarded once you have been overwhelmed by the looming silhouette of Fosdyke bridge at sundown and have turned to the Ship Inn for sustenance.

From Fosdyke it is not far to either Surfleet or Spalding, nor is it far to Boston, and for once it is actually possible to get there without anchoring outside in the Wash; by just turning the corner at Tabs Head into the River Witham. Even more than with Boston does it obtain that you will not find yourself here by chance. It is an open port, and business has increased so much that there is no guarantee that you will be able to get a berth of any find at the quayside, let alone one that is convenient and comfortable. If you can get under the bridge, or if you have been able to succeed with the telephone manoeuvres needed to get it to open, you will find there are substantial moorings on the starboard hand, and plenty of good yeoman stock to see that you are looked after like a gentleman. (That is, if you can convince them that you are such a person; and take your minder if you are not, for everyone round these parts is a great respecter of persons of good renown.)

There is little in this part of the world that is clichéd or plastic, and for that reason alone it is worth a trip. The shop is well stocked; the beer is good; and the company is even better. In the wise locals you will find friendly advisers who are expert on the ways and wiles of the Wash. If you keep your ears and eyes open while you stay for a while at Fosdyke bridge, you cannot fail to be impressed for there will be much to read, mark, learn and inwardly digest for mind and body alike.

The surrounding area is given over to agriculture, and a hard time some of them have scratching a living from meagre smallholdings. On one of my many weatherbound stopovers at Fosdyke, I found myself disconsolately gazing across a tiny patch of cauliflowers. Within minutes, I was cheered right out of my miserable self by the cauligrower himself who approached with a gift-sack of four prime specimens. He would permit no money to change hands, but I was able to trade drinks with him later. Fosdyke is an unique experience; best appreciated by those with a penchant for the recherché. Its indigens antedate the Romans.

### Fosdyke Bridge local regulations
Sadly, this bridge no longer opens. Its clearances are:
MHW Springs 2·37m MLW Springs 7·67m
MHW Neaps   4·17m MLW Neaps   7·22m
Any enquiry should be directed to the Works Manager, LCC Highways and Planning, ☎ Holbeach (0406) 22181/2, or LCC Bridges ☎ Lincoln (0522) 553020.

# The Nene to Wisbech

## Approaches

Once again approach and anchoring are similar, with no better than half tide access. In fact, access should be best considered as +/−0200 HW from the mouth of the river. For the Nene, the first buoy to pick up after *Roaring Middle* is the *Bar Flat* (green conical, unlit) which is the pilots' station in fair weather. (In bad weather, they stand by at the *RAF No.5*.) After the *Bar Flat*, the Wisbech Channel itself is well marked.

1·5m craft can reach the wreck buoy *RAF No.4*, where there are suitable places to anchor at low water, except for big springs, when it is risky for those without local knowledge. Then it is a case of waiting for at least an hour after the flood has started to run if you want to be sure of getting inland without finding bottom. For some years now there has been a trial bank about two miles to the south of the anchorage, monitoring the wonders and powers of the local elements. A local rule of thumb is that when there is water all round its base wall it is possible for 1·5m craft to gain Wisbech.

The channel then carries one last standard buoy, *Fenland*, after which it is marked with beacons, all of which are starboard hand. Although the chart shows variety if not indeed whimsy with regard to the channel in this area, there is little point in trying to find it, as a directly straight course (just west of south) one hour after the flood will keep you safe. The RAF beacon *No.5* should be kept well to starboard. After the Fenland buoy, there is a smart turn to starboard (much sharper than the charts indicate) to pick up the beacons which are all starboard hand until you come to the last, *Big Tom*.

These beacons are best left about a cable away; but you do need to be close enough to be certain that you are not lining up a member of the fraternity of cranes, posts, perches and derricks that litter the shore. The beacons lead to *Big Tom* and *West End* which mark the start of the training wall. Big Tom is left to port and *West End* to starboard.

Just after the beacons is Crabs' Hole and then Tycho Wing's channel leads to the two (now disused) lighthouses, one of which was home to painter/naturalist Peter Scott. They are still in decent fettle and stand reminders of things past.

## Sutton Bridge

Then it is straight ahead to Sutton Bridge, just like its counterpart in Goole. The bridge master actually keeps a listening radio watch on channel 9 and on channel 16 every hour. But with advance notice he will co-operate on to channel 14 via 16. You can telephone him on Holbeach (0406) 350364. Sutton Bridge represents the last chance to find a mooring before the town itself. There is a staging by the West Old Light and near the swing bridge the remains of an old dock

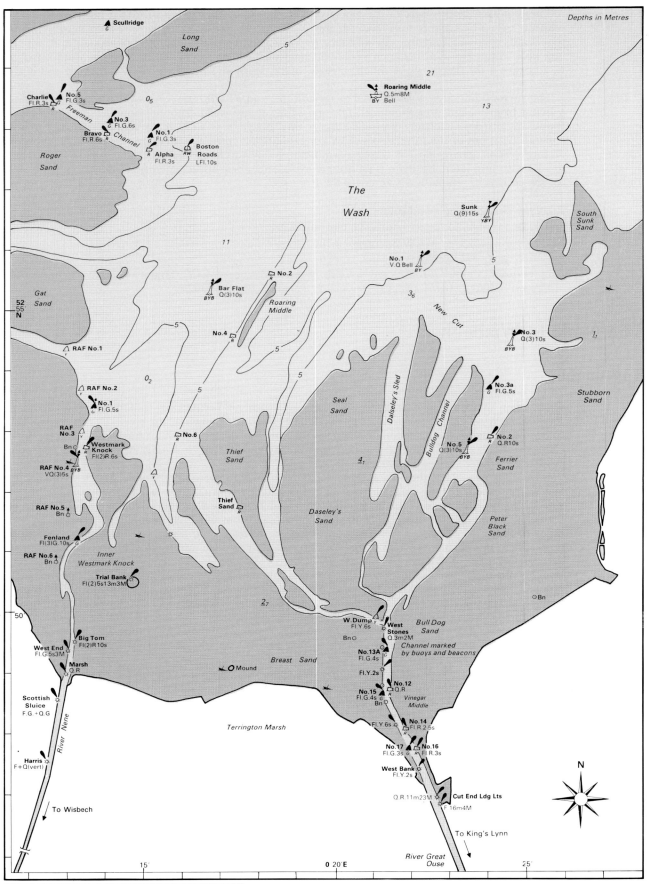

Depths in Metres

**Scullridge**
G

Long
Sand

5

21
**Roaring Middle**
Q.5m8M
BY Bell

13

**Charlie**
Fl.R.3s
**No.5**
Fl.G.3s
G

Freeman

**No.3**
Fl.G.6s
G

**Bravo**
Fl.R.6s
R

Channel

**No.1**
Fl.G.3s
G

**Alpha**
Fl.R.3s
R

**Boston
Roads**
LFl.10s
RW

*The*

*Wash*

**Sunk**
Q(9)15s
YBY

South
Sunk
Sand

Roger
Sand

11

**No.1**
V.Q Bell
BY

52
55'
N

Gat
Sand

5

**Bar Flat**
Q(3)10s
BYB

**No.2**
R

Roaring
Middle

3,6

New Cut

1,1

△ **RAF No.1**
Y

0,2

**No.4**
R

5

5

5

5

**No.3**
Q(3)10s
BYB

Stubborn
Sand

△ **RAF No.2**
Y

**No.1**
Fl.G.5s
G

**No.3a**
Fl.G.5s
G

**RAF
No.3**
Y
Bn

**Westmark
Knock**
Fl(2)R.6s
BYB
R

**No.6**
R

Seal
Sand

Dalseley's Sled

Bulldog Channel

**No.5**
Q(3)10s
BYB

**No.2**
Q.R10s
R

Ferrier
Sand

**RAF No.4**
VQ(3)5s

Thief
Sand

4,

**RAF No.5**
Bn

Y

**Thief
Sand**
R

Daseley's
Sand

Peter
Black
Sand

**Fenland**
Fl(3)G.10s
G

**RAF No.6**
Bn

*Inner
Westmark Knock*

**Trial Bank,**
Fl(2)5s13m3M

2,7

○ Bn

**Big Tom**
Fl(2)R10s

**W.Dump**
Fl.Y.6s

**West
Stones**
Q.3m2M

Bull Dog
Sand

**West End**
Fl.G 5s3M

Bn○

*Channel marked
by buoys and beacons*

**Marsh**
Q.R

**No.13A**
Fl.G.4s
G

**Scottish
Sluice**
F.G.+Q.G

**Breast** Sand

○ **Mound**

Fl.Y.2s

**No.12**
Q.R
R

**No.15**
Fl.G.4s
G

**No.14**
Fl.R.2.5s
R

*Vinegar
Middle*

Bn○

**Harris**
F+Q(vert)

River Nene

Fl.Y.6s

*Terrington Marsh*

**No.17**
Fl.G.3s
G

**No.16**
Fl.R.3s
R

**West Bank**
Fl.Y.2s

Q.R.11m23M
F 16m4M

**Cut End Ldg Lts**

To Wisbech

N

To King's Lynn

15'

0 20'E

25'

*River Great
Ouse*

**APPROACHES TO THE RIVERS GREAT OUSE AND NENE**

The River Nene: there is seldom any need to have to wait for the keeper at Sutton Bridge; especially if you shout him up on VHF at a reasonable time before you expect to pass through

The River Nene: one of the old lighthouse towers; still standing in a decent sate of repair as a reminder of days gone and things past. This was at one time the home of painter/naturalist Peter Scott

and also the summer facility pontoon of the Peterborough Yacht Club. An over-tide stop is possible at all three by negotiation should the need arise; but that would only be for the departing visitor, for no inward-bound skipper would want to delay the experience of the capital of the Fens.

# Wisbech

In Wisbech itself, there is generally a mooring space to be found on either hand just below the bridge; but the only sure way of obtaining a good berth is by 'divining' one or by ingratiating yourself with the local populace. Without thinking or blinking, everyone will deny all knowledge of the port, in particular protesting ignorance about who is the legal and/or regular occupant of each berth – and whether he/she will be using it on that tide ... or indeed on any subsequent tide.

This is a well-known ploy at all moorings, but Wisbechians have elevated it to a fine art. Of course, the moment you have made fast the last line to your chosen spot, there will be someone 'passing by' who will be delighted to inform you that 'Fred' is coming up the river on the last of the flood. When you have finally unmade your lines and cast off, you will just be in time to get out of trouble and deep water by turning with the tide to mosey down the river and into deeper waters still.

However, this can all be circumvented by calling the harbourmaster ahead of time, or tying up smartly near his office and going ashore before you can be accosted. While accommodation for yachts is limited, there is usually 'just one more space, if you don't want to stay for too long.'

For all but shallow draught boats (less than 1·2m), below the bridge at Wisbech is considered to be the head of navigation. If you display the usual courtesies to the working boats in the area, you should have no difficulty in gaining a decent berth for a short stay. Skippers wishing to go further up river should contact the lock-keeper at the weirdly named Dog in a Doublet lock well in advance, since there is often a shortage of water to get you through to Peterborough. The town bridge itself contrasts unfavourably with the cast iron railings and 'heritage' merchants' houses. Close by, port hand on entry, are the diminutive offices of the harbourmaster and a little further upstream below the bridge by the 'traditional' visitors' berths, the much more impressive edifice of the police force.

If Fosdyke represents the recherché experience, then Wisbech must offer the eccentric essence of the Fens. It is a collection of opposites; and while they are not actually warring factions, they create an ambivalent atmosphere in the town. One that is reinforced if you should wander into the police station, to be told, as you well might, that Wisbech had the highest crime rate, pro rata, in the country. While Wisbech is undoubtedly a place of superb interest and character, and well worth a visit for domestics, food and drink, it does not cater much for the boater's specialised needs.

In spite of sinister tales and legends, my experience has been that the folk of Wisbech wish neither to trap nor to ensnare the visitor. They are only too keen on a new face and foreign blood to frighten off a potential 'friend' in any way; and of course the tourist brings with him real money. In this unusual township you will find the old and the new, the stylish and the plebeian, the rich and the poor, the generous and the greedy, and the licentious and the prude, side by side and almost hand in hand; for it is a place of captivating contradictions. Wisbech is not a place to be passed over, underestimated or missed out in any way.

# The Great Ouse to King's Lynn

## Approaches

From *Roaring Middle*, you pick up *Sunk*; note in passing *No.1* and make for *No.3* which marks the last edge of the 5 metre line. The favourite deep water anchorage is around *Cork Hole*; for those wanting to go closer in, there are also safe 'oles near *No.2* and *No.5*; in sight of the tide gauge, which is much used by the pilots. From here on, the channel is well marked by buoys, but between *No.7* and *Lynn Cut* (with the training walls) the buoys are likely to be changed at short notice with more buoys being laid as and when necessary. On my first visit to the Great Ouse (and the Wash as it happened), Captain David Garside, King's Lynn harbourmaster, gave me full details of all the latest buoyage changes on VHF. That kind of co-operation is as unusual as it is welcome.

As far as a time to start is concerned, that depends very much on your draught, speed and destination. There is no point in beating the flood, for that only encounters the bottom; but it is unwise to be late if you are enroute for Denver Sluice lock, for there is the question of headroom under the many bridges on the Great Ouse. This is a matter for some study, and prospective navigators should contact the lock-keeper at Denver and/or a local pilot who will advise and/or assist.

I was originally advised to let the flood run for about an hour before trying to make way inland, and I have found nothing wrong with this counsel. Some local fishermen set off earlier, but they know the shifting ground and not many of them draw two metres as do some of the Boston boats. Unless you personally know who is in front, it is better not to follow. So, access is best considered as +/−0200 HW from the mouth of the river.

I well remember one of my early visits to King's Lynn. I was anchored towards the southeast corner of the Wash near the Sunk Sand waiting for the tide into the Ouse. I reported my position and my intentions to King's Lynn Radio and relaxed. As usual, I pretended to fish. 'Pretended', that is, as in 'pretender: one who makes baseless, false or insupportable claims'; for I am successful in the piscatorial stakes only when mackerel are shoaling like the crazed Gaderene, with their fishy eyes fixed on the tackle for their self-immolation. Even then, my hooks, lines and sinkers are more perilous to me than to the fish. As if to confirm my inefficiency and lack of intimidation to surrounding life, wild or otherwise, I was closely encountered by three seagulls, all of a particularly impertinent bent. For a long time, I thought I could hear them in telecommunication with a band of seals, letting them know how pathetic this human was.

In keeping with this wheeling indifference, I was solicited, or so I thought, by a solo seal; but all he/she did was to sidle close to *Valcon's* stern and wallow off after a massive show of indifference. I was jolted back into the other world of the Wash only by a call from King's Lynn wanting to know why I wasn't on the move and telling me that if I didn't get up there soon I would lose the light.

It was relaxing to be in waters where every buoy was on station with a name that could be easily read and a light that showed at the advertised times and intervals. Up to that moment the Wash had disclosed nothing of its inmost nature and little of its deep-seated disposition. It had been a trouble free inland sea.

Not wanting to overtake the young flood, for I wasn't really late on the tide, I tried to glide slowly and effortlessly along with it, looking to discern something of its special qualities. As I moved slowly through the narrow channel, the still exposed banks of mud unfolded to each side in sad but splendid grandeur. The ribbon of the rising tide showed me the way as clearly as ever did the Yellow Brick Road to its four arcane space travellers. It led me on through an apparent maze of undulating contours where steep mounds and elongated humps lay like the carcasses of prehistoric amphibians. As the setting sun slanted on the banks and the relatively motionless waters, it seemed to sculpt mountains emerging from a slow stream of lava.

Occasionally, the shriek of a seagull or the baying of a seal would filter through the slight mist to add yet another aspect of other-worldliness to my circumstance. It was a vast vista; the whole scene majestic and compelling. I only wish that all my entrances to the Great Ouse could have been so mild and wonderful.

If conditions are a bit rough, not at all unknown in the Wash, a protected anchorage can be found, as suggested above, near Cork Hole, where the surrounding sands afford some shelter. From there onwards, the channel leads to a section that has for years been stabilised by a training wall. It dries to a dramatic height but offers no threat to any skipper navigating properly. However, there are those who take pride in cruising without charts and for whom local advice is immaterial. Some such foolish folk have, in justice, found themselves ensconced literally high and dry on top of one of these walls; a consummation devoutly not to be wished.

# King's Lynn

Now; there are all kinds of Lynns; and King's Lynn itself has not yet made up its mind whether to stay plebeian or to take on the more up-market Lynn Regis as its nomenclature. Since there is a North Lynn and a South, as well as a West Lynn, it is ironic that there is no sign of the best known of all: East Lynne. The major problem is that while Lynn is busy with big commercial shipping traffic, it has virtually no facility for visitors. This is sad, since the old town is a splendid place.

The docks are exclusively for commercial traffic, except for emergencies. Tradition has it that alongside the quays there are 'barges' that stay afloat at all states of the tide; and against which a yacht may moor without fear or favour and free of fee. This is not the case in many ways: the barges do not stay afloat; the bottom in that region is foul in the extreme; leisure craft are not permitted to moor there; and since no berth exists, it can be neither f.o.c. nor paying. Yachts may moor there just as sheep may safely graze in the company of wolves.

Tradition also informs that you may berth free of charge in front of the very Customs House indeed; and finally that you can 'arrange something' with the fishermen who use Fisher Fleet, Purfleet and Mill Fleet. More likely, they will 'arrange' something with you; and to their advantage. As T.S.Eliot says, 'tradition without intelligence is not worth having.' In this case, certainly, intelligence can often be the better part of tradition.

I know some of the brazen souls who have tried for a berth with the fishing brethren in Friars Fleet; and they have regretted it only slightly less than those who have been reckless enough to leave their boats at Boal Quay, unattended, failing to think of local 'trespassers' and completely ignoring or being in ignorance of the rate, rise and fall of the Great Ouse. For example, the flood can run through Lynn at such a rate that many of the buoys, including the one off Friars Fleet, can be dragged right under.

The river deserves its adjectival Great, being long, strong and tortuous, with its deep water at the extreme edges of some of its very tight bights, where unfortunately the bottom can be foul. It floods for between 2 and 3 hours, consequently ebbing for all of nine to ten. The Admiralty *Pilot* quotes the streams at four knots but at times I have been able to make only minimal headway against a spring flood; and *Valcon's* Parson's Pike twin 56hp diesels, will, at full throttle, push her at 7+ knots.

Although King's Lynn is a thriving port and a splendid place to visit shoresides, sadly, there are only minimal facilities for yachts. Recent changes have brought modest improvements and there are some new mooring buoys in the river to starboard just below the first big bridge. Even so, visitors should start to make enquiries about a possible booking well ahead of their expected arrival.

Should you luckily happen to have a mooring within hailing distance of the East/West Lynn ferry, you will find that the ferrymen are more than pleased to help you across. The Ouse may be no Styx, but I am always happy to look upon the Lynns on either side of it as my Elysian Fields while I am in the neighbourhood.

King's Lynn will advise about tide heights and times (and of course help in emergencies); and in any case it is always a good idea to let King's Lynn harbour radio know what you are doing and get a traffic report from them.

Before we move on upstream, let us consider the procedure for leaving Lynn for the Wash. It makes no difference where you are heading for, you will still need to leave King's Lynn with the ebb and anchor in the Wash to await the flood for one of the other three ports. If for any reason you should quit King's Lynn on the flood, don't be surprised to notice that people walking on the banks are likely to overtake you. It is only the river doing its usual stuff.

There are those who will tell you that it is possible to get from one port to another without anchoring off. This is true for a passage between Boston and Fosdyke, but you still need speed and draught in the right combinations. As for the rest, they are routes used over the centuries by

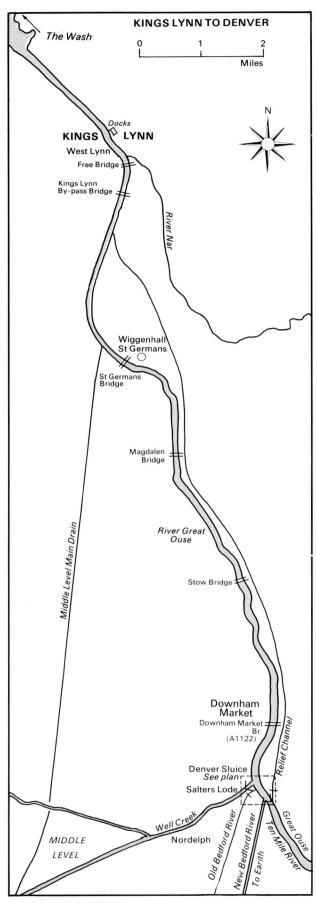

**KINGS LYNN TO DENVER**

0      1      2

Miles

The Wash

*Docks*

**KINGS LYNN**

West Lynn

Free Bridge

Kings Lynn
By-pass Bridge

*River Nar*

Wiggenhall
St Germans

St Germans
Bridge

*Middle Level Main Drain*

Magdalen
Bridge

*River Great
Ouse*

Stow Bridge

**Downham
Market**
Downham Market
Br.
(A1122)

*Relief Channel*

Denver Sluice
*See plan*

Salters Lode

*Well Creek*

Nordelph

*MIDDLE
LEVEL*

*Old Bedford River*

*New Bedford River*

*To Earith*

*Ten Mile River*

*Great Ouse*

## BUOYAGE
### Approaches to Kings Lynn

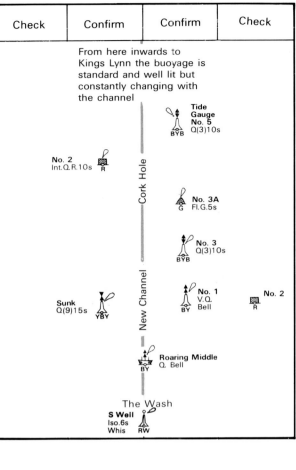

| Check | Confirm | Confirm | Check |
|---|---|---|---|

From here inwards to
Kings Lynn the buoyage is
standard and well lit but
constantly changing with
the channel

Tide
Gauge
No. 5
Q(3)10s
**BYB**

No. 2
Int.Q.R.10s
**R**

*Cork Hole*

No. 3A
Fl.G.5s
**G**

No. 3
Q(3)10s
**BYB**

Sunk
Q(9)15s
**YBY**

*New Channel*

No. 1
V.Q.
Bell
**BY**

No. 2
**R**

Roaring Middle
Q. Bell
**BY**

The Wash

**S Well**
Iso.6s
Whis  **RW**

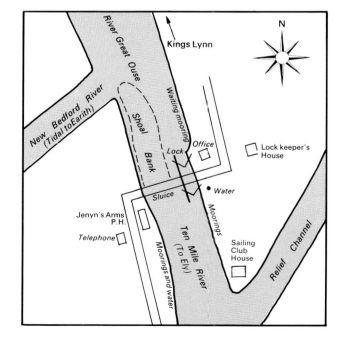

*River Great Ouse*

Kings Lynn

N

*New Bedford River*
*(Tidal to Earith)*

*Shoal Bank*

*Waiting mooring*

*Lock*  Office

Lock keeper's
House

*Sluice*

Water

*Moorings*

Jenyn's Arms
P.H.

Telephone

*Ten Mile River*
*(To Ely)*

*Moorings and water*

Sailing
Club
House

*Relief Channel*

fishermen, pirates and smugglers. The buoys or marks (if there at all) are not easily understood, and many folk have come to grief trying such 'short cuts' over the sands. Indeed, some rash skippers have ended up with their craft actually sitting on one of the training walls. It is worth noting that in some places there is a vertical drop on one side of the wall, and a long, gradual slope on the other; no soft mud berth to plop safely into by mistake.

So, the next stage is out to the *Lynn No.1* north cardinal buoy and from there to your favourite sandbank. The Wash is completely exposed to northeasterly winds and when the wind is against the ebb even the best found boat becomes uncomfortable in the nasty conditions that can arise in as little as a Force 3. Shelter is to be found in the protection of the sandbanks at low tide and these are the places to make for even if you have to sweat it out in lumpy conditions before they top out. Popular for this manoeuvre, because it is central, and also affords the best shelter, is the Freeman Channel and its famous Roger Sand.

# The Great Ouse: King's Lynn to Denver Sluice

In general, cruising folk go to King's Lynn only to leave it behind en route for Denver Sluice. To be able to do that, careful study of tides and bridge heights is called for, and sound advice on those matters can be gained free of charge from Ely Marina or Denver Sluice Lock.

Generally speaking, it is not wise to be leaving King's Lynn until the flood has been under way for about an hour. For all but the most eccentric keeled and air-draughted craft, this should prove the best compromise; achieving a smooth trip, no encounter with bed or bridge, and arriving at the lock when there is plenty of water all round and the flood is beginning to lose its ferocity.

Caution is required, especially at springs, when navigating early on the tide, when the young flood is up your stern. Should you dig into a mud bank or just catch an unexpected hillock in the channel, you can be keeled over with the wheel snatched out of your hands and the boat suffering scouring in minutes. In such cases, fast and expert action is essential if the vessel is not to be lost.

Bridge heights are critical on the Great Ouse between King's Lynn and Denver, for there is nowhere to moor on that stretch of potentially dangerous river. It is not a place to get caught out. The following guide is published by Anglian Water. 'As an indication of the headroom available under bridges, the following table gives the approximate headroom for a spring tide of 7·2m and a neap tide of 6m on the Alexander Dock gauge (King's Lynn).

There are also some overhead pipelines, but they are high enough not to be a problem.

*Bridge headroom*

|  | *Springs* | | *Neaps* | |
| --- | --- | --- | --- | --- |
|  | HW | LW | HW | LW |
| Downham Market | 2·6m | 7·5m | 3·7m | 7·0m |
| Stow | 2·4m | 6·5m | 3·8m | 6·6m |
| Magdalen | 2·3m | 7·3m | 3·7m | 7·1m |
| St Germans | 2·5m | 7·6m | 3·9m | 7·4m |
| Free | 2·8m | 8·8m | 4·2m | 8·0m |

It is a much easier proposition to go from Denver to Kings Lynn than it is to do it the other way round. (If you need a pilot for this river, you need him to bring you up; and Louis Doubleday pilot, mortician and mead purveyor extraordinaire is the man to use. His mordant approach to life is well worth the fee for starters).

The Denver lock keeper will help to sort you in and out and, like many of his vocation (yea verily, for it is an eccentric calling) is often to be found working well beyond the normal demands of duty. 1990 saw Denver Bert retire after 42 years; and all users and Ousers will wish him well. In my experience, most lock keepers seem to be called Bert; but God bless all lockies, Bert or no!

The community at Denver is an interesting one and while there are only the basic facilities of food and drink there is pleasant shopping to be found not far away at Downham Market.

Things have changed at Denver since my first visit; the full refurbishment has been completed, and locking is much smoother. Nevertheless, I am confident that Denver will never succumb to the rat race or be a centre of *la dolce vita*; although there is an hospitable pub with noisy peacocks for company. There are Anglian Water limited stay moorings along the northerly bank, but there is shoaling at the sides. All in all, Denver Sluice guards its secrets too jealously for any chance visitor to find it an appealing proposition.

A point worth noting is that the Great Ouse from Denver to the Wash, although downhill all the way, can also offer its challenges; especially to those who want to get out early for a day in the Wash. Once, I had to negotiate the tricky stretch below Denver in thick fog. On a river with such testing bends and awkward bridges it is best to have more on one's side than near zero visibility. However, since time and tide (and buttered eggs) wait for no man, I had to be away. Happily, I managed to negotiate the tantalising ribbon of fast water without accident, but I had no chance to see anything but the under-arches of the bridges at those quaintly named places, Wiggenhall St Mary Magdalen, Wiggenhall St Mary the Virgin and Wiggenhall St Germans. It was an exhausting process, and not one to be recommended without an alert crew with better than average eyesight.

Over the years, I have been taken to task by some local cruising folk for what they consider to be my over cautious attitude to the problems of pilotage in particular in the Great Ouse and in general in the Wash. (In fact, the most recent of my critics accosted me as far away as Puerto Sotogrande, on the Costa del Sol, next Gibraltar.)

True for those with local knowledge gained over years of experience neither the Ouse nor the Wash possesses attributes that cannot easily be overcome or circumvented if you have the cruising time at your disposal; but for the rest of us, it must make sense to treat the area with the respect it is entitled to, and in my book that means care, caution and concern.

# Denver to Ely and Bedford

Denver is best visited only if you are going on to Ely (Denver to Ely 17M) and beyond, otherwise the difficulties tend to be out of all proportion. In addition, it is worth noting that you can get neaped at Denver!

With 1·8m draught, it is possible to get to Ely, but first there is the long straight stretch of the locked section to enjoy. The junction with the Wissey (navigable to Stoke Ferry with 1·0m draught) is a difficult one: the turn is sharp and the entrance is narrow with a tight bend almost immediately after. After the junction, you will next pass the old Ferry Boat Inn, HQ of the Denver Cruising Club, and then find another junction marked by the Ship Inn: The Little Ouse River which is also known as Brandon Creek (navigable to Brandon with 0·75m draught). Many folk stop at the intriguingly named Prickwillow community for its museum, pottery and herb gardens.

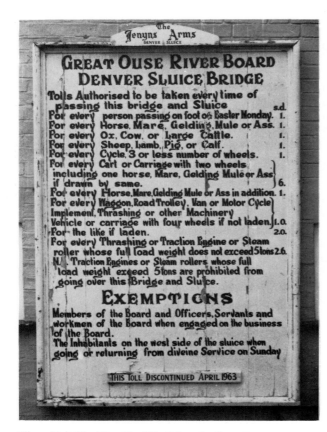

'Fings Ain't Wot They Used To Be' on the Great Ouse

The lock at Denver has never been easy to negotiate, but recent improvements have done much to prevent this kind of conglomeration.

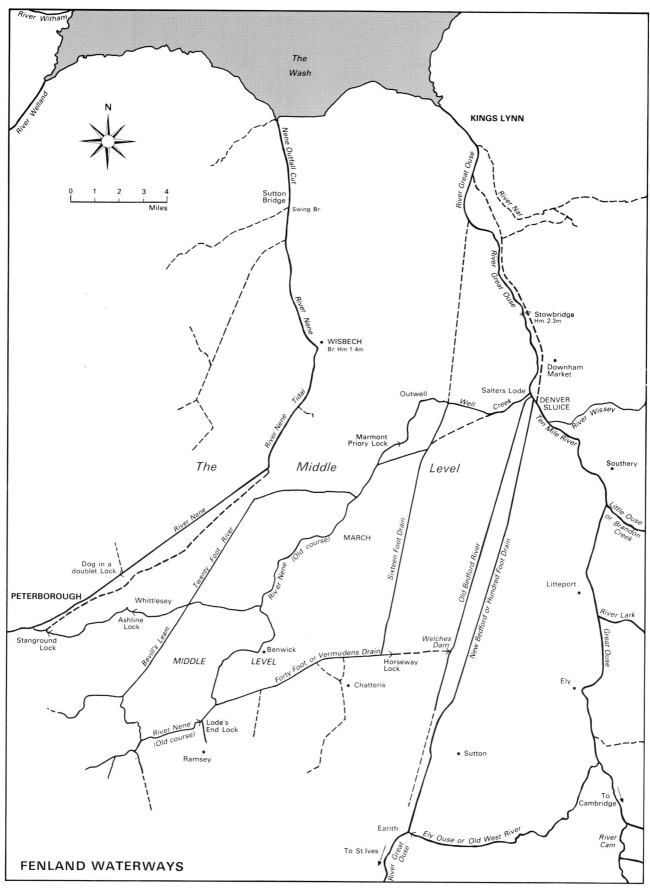

River Witham

The
Wash

River Welland

N

KINGS LYNN

Nene Outfall Cut

River Great Ouse

River Nar

0  1  2  3  4
Miles

Sutton
Bridge

Swing Br.

River Nene

River Great Ouse

Stowbridge
Hm 2·3m

WISBECH
Br Hm 1·4m

Downham
Market

River Nene Tidal

Outwell

Well    Creek

Salters Lode

DENVER
SLUICE

River Wissey

Marmont
Priory Lock

Ten Mile River

The      Middle      Level

Southery

River Nene

Little Ouse
or Brandon
Creek

Dog in a
doublet Lock

Twenty Foot River

River Nene (Old course)

MARCH

Sixteen Foot Drain

Old Bedford River

New Bedford or Hundred Foot Drain

Litteport

PETERBOROUGH

Whittlesey

River Lark

Ashline
Lock

Bevil's Leam

MIDDLE      LEVEL

Benwick

Forty Foot or Vermudens Drain

Welches
Dam

Great Ouse

Stanground
Lock

Horseway
Lock

Chatteris

Ely

River Nene
(Old course)

Lode's
End Lock

Sutton

Ramsey

To
Cambridge

Earith

River Cam

To St.Ives

Ely Ouse or Old West River

River Great Ouse

**FENLAND WATERWAYS**

Before you reach Ely, there is the small community of Littleport on the northerly bank, with the first marina and the well known and even better patronised Black Horse. Next is the junction with the River Lark (navigable to Isleham with 1·2m draught, and to Judes Ferry with less than 0·6m).

Then the capital of the Fens: a settlement encompassing all the sophistication of marina-cum-cathedral life to be enjoyed in a city with a population doing its best to keep at the 10,000 mark. Ely is an eccentric, fascinating and beautiful place. Of its many contrasts, the one I found most appealing was that of the cathedral on the hill, surveying the land for miles around, and the boating centre with the threateningly competitive name of Babylon.

However, let it quickly be said that there is nothing whorishly corrupting about the area; and while there is no actual hanging garden, the trees that are at hand offer a pleasing backdrop for the many cruising boats that tie up there. The mooring berths are amongst the most pleasant I have thrown a bowline at, and their proximity to first rate hostelries and the excellently restored Maltings, an example of picture book architecture, makes a stay there an attractive proposition.

It is something of a long haul up the hill to the cathedral and the market place, but the architectural delights, the comprehensive range of shops and the friendliness of one and all make the climb worthwhile.

In Ely, not everyone will try to rook you as soon as look at you. Indeed, the marina and chandlery in the city centre are both welcoming, efficient and no more expensive than they have a right to be, offering the services they do which are remarkably good. It comes as quite a surprise to find such a first rate chandlery so far from the sea and so thoroughly well equipped for big boats in what is in, after all, no more than a smallish boating centre.

The thing for which Ely is most famed, its cathedral, is into its own version of Thatcherism, and possesses a clear understanding of the phrase, 'Charity begins at home'. The Ely Order was founded in AD673 by St Etheldrida who was born in AD630 and died in AD679. The saintly lady is frequently known as Audrey, a corruption of Etheldrida. At the local annual fair, cheap jewellery and showy lace called St Address's Lace were sold. From these events came the word *tawdry* which has come to mean anything gaudy, in bad taste and of little value. In *A Winter's Tale*, Shakespeare has it thus: 'Come you promised me a tawdry lace and a pair of sweet gloves.' The nearby market offers contemporary bargains of all kinds, but few are tawdry.

Back by the waters of Babylon, there is usually 2m up to this point, with no one even dreaming of tidal rises and falls.

The next leg, to Pope's corner, takes you deep into Fenland. The Fish and Duck Inn stands sentinel at the junction with the Old West River and the Cam. My own reading of the charts told me that I should not be able to get very far, but some experts claiming local knowledge maintained that I should be able to reach Cambridge. It never does to ignore local knowledge completely, so I set off, albeit warily. I had only gone a few miles when *Valcon* began to display tell-tale signs of the proximity of the river bottom. That was at Pope's Corner, where there was supposed to be a pub of legendary hospitality. God's Law meant it would not be open for the likes of me; and, sad to say, God triumphed over the Pope in that area and *Valcon* was forced to retreat.

So, it is here that all 1·75m craft must retreat, in spite of the Authority's claims. The surveying officers must have been optimistic, for there were discrepancies of up to half a metre between the published figures and the actual navigable depth.

The River Cam leads on to the lock at Bottisham, pronounced locally by those who know as Bo'isham, and then into the heart of Cambridge.

The first item of interest on the main river is the Stretham Engine used for drainage. Originally it was steam, but it is now oil fired and is maintained by the Preservation Trust. The Old West River, which leaves the tidal Ouse at Earith, is the old course of the river before the New Bedford was cut. It takes you through increasingly pretty scenery with plenty of distractions in the form of bridges, pubs and the like (for example, Wooden Bridge, Twenty Pence Inn, Smithy Fen Farm and Hermitage Lock). At Earith, there is plenty to entertain and an unexpected short stretch of tidal river, where the rise and fall can reach 0·75m at springs and big freshets.

Then in close succession come Holywell (with its delectable thatched cottages) and St Ives (derived from St Ivo, the Persian bishop). The former has its famous legends of riverside moanings and hauntings at the site of the Ferry Boat Inn; probably special manifestations of the spirit world brought on by overindulgence in the world of the spirituous. The second has a claim to fame for boating folk as the HQ of Imray, Laurie, Norie & Wilson. In addition, it has a fascinating six-eccentric-arch stone bridge.

Then, on up to Huntingdon and Godmanchester, the river is seen at its best and the really productive efforts of the riparian protectors are to be noted and enjoyed by all. You are plunged not only into gorgeous scenery but also into the depths of English and Saxon history, both religious and profane: Abbots abound; Cromwell was born close by; there are links with Beckett and Catherine of Aragon; and round almost every corner there is a modest pub, homely inn or fashionable hotel. All tastes are catered for. The names of the townships say it all: Offords Cluny and Darcy; St Neots; Eaton Socon; and Barfords – Little and Great.

The tale continues with little variation until you reach the outskirts of Bedford. Actually, the River Great Ouse rises 90 miles above Bedford, but that is not navigable, and the present head of navigation is deemed to be Cardington Lock (just outside Bedford) or Bedford Lock in the town itself.

From here to the Wash it is a cruise of some 75 miles with 16 locks. Much of it is flat; much of it is pretty; little of it is overcrowded; and you can count on true Fenland hospitality no matter where you stick your land anchor. Truly a river of variety, multiplicity and continuing charm, challenge and interest.

# The Wash – general cautions

If there is one thing a stranger should not to do in the Wash, it is to try to save time, or even a 'tide' by cutting corners and using one of the 'local knowledge only' mini channels that seem to offer a swift and safe passage.

The other 'one' thing not to do in the Wash is to follow one of the fishing boats that seems to be going your way. It is very likely that (a) the skipper can follow the 'water marks' much better than you can; and (b) that his vessel, although looking deep-draughted, is in fact a very shallow design and you end up with mud on your hull and egg on your face ... both of which are normally distressing to a cruising yachtsman. Nothing is ever lost by waiting in the Wash.

The Ouse, Nene, Welland and Witham all suffer from banks and bars, and all must be deemed inaccessible until at least 3 hours before high water. Craft of 2m and more are advised to wait at least half an hour longer (please see text). Make no mistake: the streams can attack you. The Admiralty *Pilot* quotes them at four knots and says, 'The streams are reported to be strong,' but in both the Great Ouse and the Welland I have had cause to be grateful for *Valcon's* diesels, which will give me just 8 knots, enabling me to progress over the ground at a rate of about 2 knots.

Since the rise and fall can achieve 9m, sound, long, strong warps are essential and so is absolutely reliable ground gear. It is asking for trouble to rely on mooring in any of these rivers except by the towers and Sutton Bridge on the Nene. It is essential to keep to the buoyed channels and to maintain a close look out for the training walls.

Bridge heights are of significance on the Nene and the Welland only if you intend to proceed upstream of Wisbech or Fosdyke. On the Witham, there are four between the railway swing bridge and the Grand Sluice; and if you can get through the lock you will be able to get under the bridges but masts will have to be lowered.

### Distance between ports (Nautical miles)

|  | *Denver* | *Lynn* | *Wisbech* | *Fosdyke* | *Boston* |
|---|---|---|---|---|---|
| Denver | – | 14 | 45 | 46 | 48 |
| Lynn | 14 | – | 31 | 32 | 34 |
| Wisbech | 45 | 31 | – | 30 | 32 |
| Fosdyke | 46 | 32 | 30 | – | 10 |
| Boston | 48 | 34 | 32 | 10 | – |

### Distances to Deep Water (Nautical miles)

| | | | |
|---|---|---|---|
| King's Lynn to Cork Hole: | 8 | to No.1 light buoy: | 12 |
| Wisbech to Bar Flat: | 16 | to Sutton Bridge: | 6 |
| Fosdyke to Clay Hole: | 8 | | |
| Boston to Clay Hole: | 6 | | |

The cruising man who has not tried the Wash is to be envied for all the many contrasting experiences that lie ahead of him. It is not the ideal place for the novice (but anyone having been initiated into boat handling in it will seldom find more challenging grounds) but there is no long haul between landfalls and the main buoyage is well nigh impeccable. Indeed, novice and expert should both find the Wash worthwhile, for it is a place of mystery, magic and continuing challenge: a veritable trap for the unwary; falsely comforting to the unheeding; temptingly seductive to the overconfident; apparently without hazard, horror or even minor obstacle to the foolhardy; yet always rewarding to any realistic skipper who is as he should be respectful, appreciative and cautious.

## BOSTON

**Charts**
Imray Y9
Admiralty 1200

**Tides**
Immingham +0030, Dover −0500

**Authorities**
*Boston Harbour*
VHF Ch 12 (−0300/+0200 HW and office hours)
☎ Boston (0205) 62328
*Boston Grand Sluice Lock*
Dual watch VHF Ch 16 and 73
☎ Boston (0205) 64864 (24 hour answering service)

## WISBECH

**Charts**
Imray Y9, C29
Admiralty 1200

**Tides**
Immingham +0300, Dover −0500

**Authorities**
*Wisbech Harbour*
VHF Ch 9, 14, 16 (from −4 HW when vessels are expected)
☎ Wisbech (0945) 582126
*Sutton Bridge*
VHF Ch 9

## KING'S LYNN

**Charts**
Imray Y9
Admiralty 108, 1200

**Tides**
Immingham +0030, Dover −0445

**Authorities**
*King's Lynn Conservancy Board*
Harbourmaster, Captain David Garside, Harbour Office, Common Staith, King's Lynn, PE30 1LL ☎ King's Lynn (0553) 773411
VHF Ch 11, 12, 14, 16 (office hours and −0400 to +0200HW)
*Denver Sluice*
VHF Ch 6 and/or 8 ☎ Downham Market (0366) 382340

**Pilots**
Louis Doubleday ☎ Wisbech (0945) 773285
J. Memeter ☎ King's Lynn (0553) 761703
J. K. Wilson ☎ Pymoor (035387) 309
John Lineham ☎ Fosdyke (0205) 85618

## KING'S LYNN TO BEDFORD

**Restricting Dimensions**
*Draught* 1·75m to Ely; then decreasing until more than 1·3m is a liability; particularly at the sides, especially for bilge keelers.
*Length* 25·8m
*Beam* 3·1m
*Air Draught* 2·2m

**Denver Sluice**
☎ Downham Market (0366) 382340

**Chandlery**
*Ely Boat Chandlers*, 21, Waterside, Ely. ☎ Ely (0353) 663095

**Marinas and Boatyards**
*Harry Kitchener Marine*, Priory Marina, Barkers Lane, Bedford ☎ Bedford (0234) 51931
*Kelpie Marine*, A1, Roxton, Bedfordshire ☎ Bedford (0234) 870249

The Wash: this light float is perhaps one of the best known (and best loved since it usually means that sanctuary is nigh) navigational marks in The Wash

*River Mill Boats*, School Lane, Eaton Socon, St Neots, Huntingdon, Cambridgeshire ☎ Huntingdon (0480) 73456
*St Neots Marina*, St Neots, Huntingdon, Cambridgeshire ☎ Huntingdon (0480) 72411
*Crosshall Marine*, Crosshall Road, St Neots, Huntingdon, Cambridgeshire ☎ Huntingdon (0480) 72763
*Buckden Marina & Leisure Club Ltd*, Mill Road, Buckden, Huntingdon, Cambridgeshire ☎ Huntingdon (0480) 810355
*Hartford Marina*, Banks End, Wyton, Huntingdon, Cambridgeshire ☎ Huntingdon (0480) 454677
*L. H. Jones & Son*, The Boathaven, Low Road, St Ives, Cambridgeshire ☎ Huntingdon (0480) 494040
*Westview Marina*, High Street, Earith, Huntingdon, Cambridgeshire ☎ Ramsey (0487) 841627
*Hermitage Marina*, Earith, nr. Huntingdon, Cambridgeshire ☎ Ramsey (0487) 840994
*Quiet Waters Boathaven*, High Street, Earith, Huntingdon, Cambridgeshire ☎ Ramsey (0487) 842154
*Twenty Pence Marina*, Twenty Pence Road, Wilburton, Ely, Cambridgeshire ☎ Cottenham (0954) 51118
*Bridge Boatyard Ely Ltd*, Bridge Road, Ely, Cambridgeshire ☎ Ely (0353) 663726
*Ely Marina*, Waterside, Ely, Cambridgeshire ☎ Ely (0353) 664622
*Annesdale Marine*, Riverside Boat Yard, Annesdale Dock, Ely, Cambridgeshire ☎ Ely (0353) 665420
*Littleport Boat Haven Ltd*, Littleport, Ely, Cambridgeshire ☎ Ely (0353) 861969

The approaches to the rivers in The Wash are littered with all kinds of beacons, markers, gauges and so on. This is one sited on one of the Ouse training walls

# II. THE NORFOLK COAST TO ORFORDNESS

## Passage

'Small craft are cautioned that there are no accessible harbours along the North Norfolk coast under conditions of strong onshore winds, i.e. N of E or W. In these conditions the outer entrances of the small harbour along the coast become a mass of broken water and marks are difficult to see. Conditions rapidly worsen when the ebb stream begins to run or if there is swell as a result of a previous onshore gale'.

Thus, the Zarathustra of the Admiralty *Pilots*. Not only is it worth committing to memory; it should be burned into the brain, especially that of skippers who are planning a first time visit to this stretch of coast where the people are so warm and welcoming and nature can be so cold, menacing and implacable.

There is more to the story than that quote from the Admiralty *Pilot* indicates. Further handicaps come with the low-lying coastline which is noted for its haze, mist and fogs which, combined with the shortage of conspicuous landmarks between Cromer and Hunstanton lighthouses, can make for a difficult time in spotting marks and entrances. In addition, even once 'safely' across the bars, the channels inside can be just as difficult a) to observe and b) to distinguish one from another, for many there are that will lead you into ways of unrighteousness. In this low coast of creeks, streams and near ditches, many can be seen but few should be chosen, and only one followed. Spotting and following that right one can sometimes involve real detective work. All very pleasant on a sunny Sunday afternoon with a high water neap, but much less reassuring of an autumn evening with an onshore breeze and an ebb tide.

The North Norfolk coast, from the northeast corner of the Wash to Cromer on the bend, is an exposed stretch of coastline. So severe can be the conditions that every solitary haven, no matter how modest, is worth a ransom to mariners. In particular, they are blessed refuges from the dangers of those strong winds that infest the area almost as much as the legendary mist and fog. Quite clearly, with a spiteful wind from the north, the cautious mariner will be inside waiting, and not outside wanting.

However, these are not new phenomena. They, and their accompanying dangers, consequent especially to strangers, have been known to every fisher and lifeboatman, every coastguard and harbourmaster from Thornham to Cromer to Winterton Ness over the years and centuries. They take for granted their obligation to be not only on hand whenever the need should arise, but to be ready, almost waiting, for the stranger's call for help. This is undoubtedly the most reassuring feature of an otherwise quite inhospitable 50 miles of coastline.

It is also worth noting that if conditions get really bad, it can be worse in the Wash than further out in the North Sea; and it is a long haul from Great Yarmouth to Grimsby.

So, settled conditions, with a good forecast and decent visibility, I consider to be mandatory for a first visit to the North Norfolk coast. It may mean waiting for longer than you would wish, but the people and the places in the nearby Wash will more than amply repay the small price of that insurance. Boston, Wisbech and Wainfleet Haven are all good berths; and from the south there is the choice of Lowestoft and Southwold. Great Yarmouth can just be considered a possible candidate, but it is at best a long haul down the Yare from the Haven Bridge; and the happier alternative of opting for the improved hospitality and services in the Broads, or at least above Haven Bridge, add the further complications of longer distances and the opening times of the bridges.

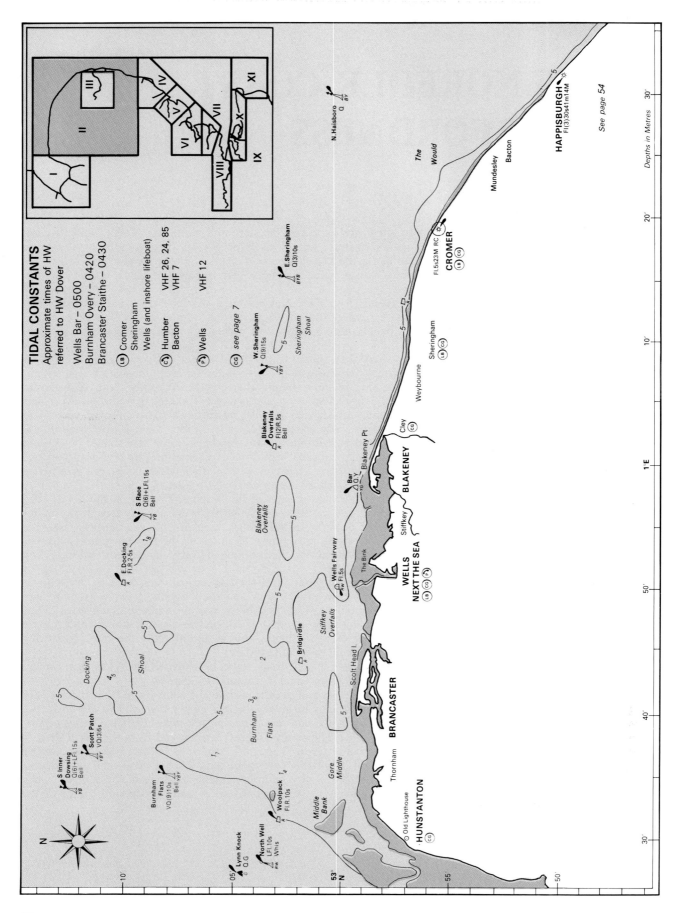

## TIDAL CONSTANTS
Approximate times of HW
referred to HW Dover

Wells Bar – 0500
Burnham Overy – 0420
Brancaster Staithe – 0430

(LB) Cromer
Sheringham
Wells (and inshore lifeboat)

(C₁) Humber    VHF 26, 24, 85
Bacton    VHF 7

(P) Wells    VHF 12

(CG) *see page 7*

*Depths in Metres*

*See page 54*

HAPPISBURGH Fl(3)30s41m14M

Mundesley
Bacton
The Would

N.Haisboro Q BY

CROMER
Fl.5s23M RC
(LB) (CG)

E.Sheringham Q(3)10s BYB

Sheringham
(LB) (CG)

Weybourne

W.Sheringham Q(9)15s Y B Y

Sheringham Shoal

Blakeney Overfalls Fl(2)R.5s Bell R

Cley (CG)

Blakeney Pt

BLAKENEY

Bar Q.Y YG

Stiffkey

S Race Q(6)+LFl.15s Bell Y B

E.Docking Fl.R.2.5s R

Blakeney Overfalls 5

The Brink

WELLS NEXT THE SEA
(LB) (CG) (P)

Wells Fairway

Wells Fairway RW Fl.5s

Stiffkey Overfalls

Bridgirdle R

Scolt Head I.

Docking Shoal
4 5
5

5
5
2

Burnham Flats
3 6
1 7

Thornham

BRANCASTER

S Inner Dowsing Q(6)+LFl.15s Bell Y B

Scott Patch VQ(3)5s Y B Y

Burnham Flats VQ(9)10s Bell Y B Y

Gore Middle
5

Woolpack Fl.R.10s R
1 4

Middle Bank

Old Lighthouse

HUNSTANTON
(CG)

North Well RW LFl.10s Whis

Lynn Knock Q.G G

N

53° N

05'
10'

30'
40'
50'
1E
10'
20'
30'

55'
50'

# The Havens

Any skipper going to Thornham, Brancaster or Overy Staithe, is likely to have craft (boat), craft (skill) and craft (knowledge) that will take him safely along the close inshore route between Sunk Sand and Middle Bank through the channel and on to the Bays and Gore Middle. The alternative, perhaps for Wells-next-the-Sea or Blakeney, is to take the northerly turn round the *Woolpack* (red can) for the Sledway and on to the Stiffkey Overfalls via the *Bridgirdle* (red can) for the *Wells Fairway* and the *Blakeney Bar* buoys.

All the havens except Wells (that is, Thornham, Brancaster, Burnham and Overy Staithe) are best suited to shoal craft, and only easily negotiated if you draw no more than around the metre mark. It is not merely that there is little water in the entrance channel; once inside, with much more than a metre's draught and more than seven or eight LOA, there will be hardly anywhere you can be placed so that you are safe, comfortable and within accessible range of the shoreside facilities.

For any skipper with serious intentions of cruising the smaller havens, I would suggest that for the first visit the local professionals and their expert knowledge should be called on (none of them is what you could call expensive) for advice and/or pilotage. In addition, Henry Irving's *The Tidal Havens of the Wash and Humber* (Imray) offers helpful reading.

## Thornham

Thornham, the most westerly haven and closest to the Wash, is also the smallest. There are three approaches to choose from. Those skippers with really good local knowledge, and an ability to smell out the water, will, when conditions permit, take a close-in course from South Sunk Sand and St Edmund's Point just round the corner into the Thornham channel.

Others will reach the narrow channel by Middle Bank and Gore Middle into the Bays. Since neither of these tricky short cuts is buoyed, any skipper contemplating their assault should choose only the most settled of fine weather, and ensure that he has plenty of sound ground tackle, just in case.

Thornham's head of navigation is as secluded as its channel is perplexing.

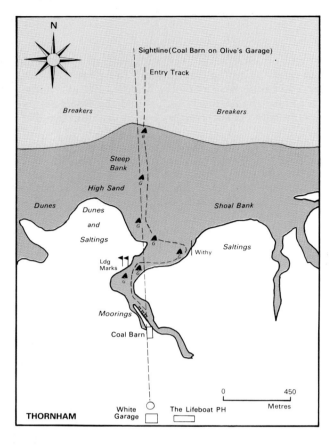

THORNHAM

The old lighthouse at Hunstanton: one of the few landmarks on the (symbolically and actually) bleak coastline of The Wash. The fogs and mists that are notorious (and regularly present around here) usually mean that you will only just be able to catch a glimpse of it

The third approach is for the more cautious and that takes you right outside to the *Woolpack* buoy and the deep water channel of the Sledway; heading thereafter into Brancaster Bay and then turning west for the Thornham channel.

The Admiralty *Pilot* is very stern on the North Norfolk coast, pointing out that harbour entrances can become mere masses of broken water with marks almost impossible to see. 'Conditions rapidly worsen when the ebb stream begins to run or if there is swell as a result of a previous gale.' Not the most encouraging of reports.

The approach channel to what is euphemistically called Thornham's Harbour crosses a broad sandy foreshore and is constantly changing in depth and direction. In good conditions, a vessel drawing 2·7m can reach Thornham Staithe, which is a mile above the entrance; but generally speaking any craft near even the 2–3m mark will experience difficulty except near calm springs.

The local fisherman do their best to keep the channel buoyed but the combination of the surrounding flatness and the plentitude of trees make it very difficult to identify anything.

There is also a near replica of the classic petrified forest to add further to the confusion. However, as with many small havens on the east and southwest coasts, once gained, they are to be valued as the fisherman's pearl.

There is nothing at all formal about Thornham. Even the local sailing directions, for which I am indebted to John Conder, skipper of the gaff cutter *Zhivago*, offers this charming leading line: 'Coal barge to Olive's garage'. Now; it is important to know that Olive's garage is next door to the Lifeboat, the pub that draws crowds by its reputation for good food and real ale. I for one cannot think of a more unlikely spot (for it is bleak and remote to a degree) to find made-on-the-spot gravad lax as a lunchtime snack. There are facilities in the village itself (a short walk inland) but many mariners never get further than the hostelry.

In his *Tidal Havens* guide, Henry Irving has this to say: 'The creek today has lost its bustle but it retains its beauty and aura of the past. For this reason alone it is worth a visit and it presents no serious problems in settled weather.' I find no reason to disagree with him.

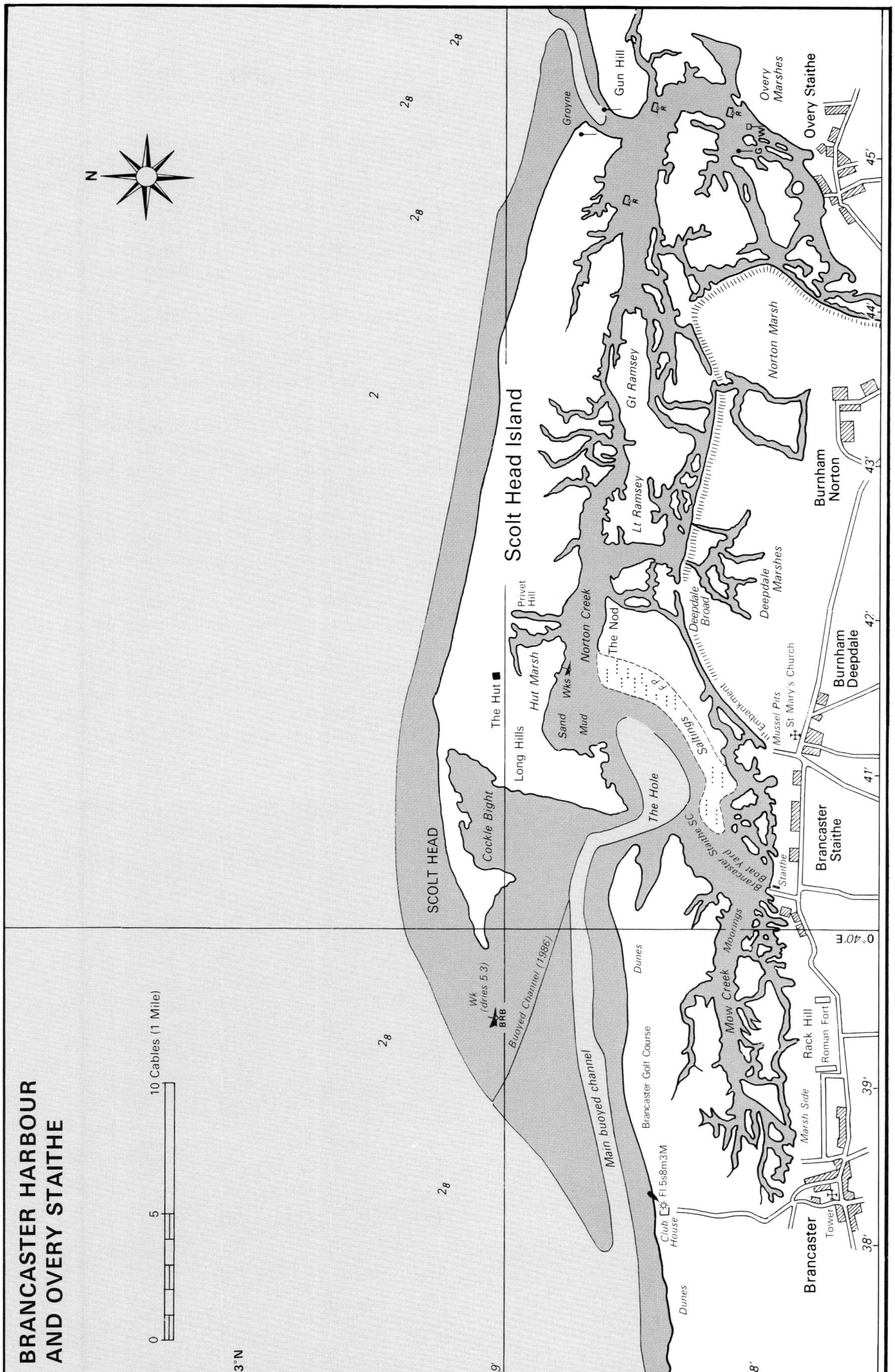

# BRANCASTER HARBOUR
# AND OVERY STAITHE

N

10 Cables (1 Mile)

0    5

53°N

59'

58'

2₈

2₈

2

2₈

2₈

2₈

2₈

SCOLT HEAD

Cockle Bight

Long Hills

The Hut ■

Sand

Mud

Wks

Hut Marsh

Privet Hill

Scolt Head Island

Gt Ramsey

Lt Ramsey

Norton Creek

The Nod

Deepdale Broad

Deepdale Marshes

Norton Marsh

Overy Marshes

Gun Hill

Groyne

Overy Staithe

45'

44'

43'

Burnham Norton

42'

Burnham Deepdale

St Mary's Church

Mussel Pits

Embankment

Saltings

The Hole

Wk
(dries 5.3)

BRB

Buoyed Channel (1996)

Main buoyed channel

Brancaster Golf Course

Dunes

Club ⬠ Fl 5s 8m 3M
House

Dunes

Brancaster

Tower

Marsh Side

Rack Hill

Roman Fort

Mow Creek

Moorings

Staithe

Brancaster Staithe

Brancaster Staithe SC

Boat Yard

41'

0.40'E

39'

38'

45

# Brancaster harbour and Brancaster staithe

To the east we come to a pair of harbours that are at one and the same time as close as Tweedledum and Tweedledee and yet as different as chalk and cheese: Brancaster Staithe and Burnham Overy Staithe.

The former is always known simply as Brancaster, but the latter is known by a variety of appellations, three being Burnham, Burnham Overy and Overy Staithe. Since there are many places called Burnham and Overy in the vicinity, it is best to stick to the full title, or you may find yourself trying to launch a 7m power boat from some miles inland.

The outstanding natural feature in the area is Scolt Head, a remarkably long sandhill. It is the most northerly point on this coast and affords protection for both the havens. Scolt Head is a nature reserve on which breed common and sandwich terns. Brancaster is approached from its west and Burnham from its east.

To reach Brancaster Staithe, the long entry has to be negotiated. The Admiralty *Pilot* gives its usual stern commentary: '... should only be used by those with local knowledge; the approach channel, between sandbanks which dry out for a mile, is constantly shifting in depth and direction. The channel buoys are difficult to see in moderate onshore winds, due to broken water, when the entrance should not be attempted.'

The champion of the area and author of *The Tidal Havens* guide, Henry Irving, puts the case slightly differently: 'Although the normal strictures about fog, darkness and heavy northerly weather hold true for Brancaster as for all the other harbours of north Norfolk, it is probably the least severe of them all.'

Instructions as proffered to me by the commanding character of the harbour, Mervyn Nudds, the master, take a different tack and are couched in an altogether contrasting tone: 'There are two channels. The buoys are all numbered. *Number One* buoy is west of the golf club; and the wreck channel *Number One* is northwest of the wreck, the *Vinna*.

'Going out over the bar, we have a green top mark buoy for the two channels. Moorings are available when they are not in use, or the owners are out visiting or on a long cruise. If not, I can always anchor one safe.'

You will have to go a long way to find mariners more sensitive, sensible and straight up and down than those of this coast; and among them, harbourmaster Nudds is known for his expertise, his friendly co-operative manner and his incorrigible attitude to all things of the sea. Any intending skipper would be well advised to book him as their pilot. His services as guide, philosopher and friend come in train.

There is much to attract the visitor to Brancaster. The Romans were here, as witness the site of the Branodunum fort on Rack Hill. It was the most important of their sea fort defences and a cavalry troop was stationed there.

The course (neither true, magnetic or clock, but golf pure and simple, except that golf is never either) of the Royal West Norfolk Golf Club is to be found between Mow Creek and its adjacent saltings and the North Sea approach channel.

Close by, on the open sand flats, windsurfing is all the rage. Although the golf course is protected by locked gates with monumental pillars, at least the sands are free and its clubhouse provides a useful landmark. Much of the area is also free for wildlife to breathe and breed, thanks to the control and administration of the National Trust, whose presence is well represented at their barn-like hut opposite the sailing club near the spreading foreshore. There is a great feeling of openness about the approach, the harbour and the village.

When approaching the Brancasters in anything like decent visibility, the outer buoyage, Scolt Head, the wreck *Vinna* and the Royal West Norfolk Golf Club, all important visual aids to navigating a successful entry, are easy to spot. Then come the closer markers: the port hand red bladder buoys; the beacon on the wreck; and the fixed light at the golf club.

Just to make life more challenging for the stranger, there are, in fact, two channels. However, all the buoys are numbered, the first *No.1* is west of the golf club; while the second, the other *No.1*, is NW of the wreck. Going out over the bar there is one topmark for the two channels. Visitors are made welcome to use the Brancaster Staithe Sailing Club. There are some local moorings available when owners are away cruising; but, in any event, Mervyn Nudds will always be ready to 'Anchor you up safe'. It is worth noting that there is a bye-law as follows: 'Vessels in the harbour must muffle their rigging.'

For all aspects of pilotage, and all the other ins and outs, a telephone call to Mr Nudds will give you a lot of information; and if you need more help than telephone instructions he will generally be able to arrange for one of the local fishermen to meet you on his normal return at tide time. It is well worthwhile making preliminary arrangements and, indeed a preparatory visit if at all possible. I would personally urge any skipper with a draught of more than 1·2m not to come for the first time by boat without having visited the shoresides well ahead and got advice and arranged for help.

No matter from which perspective you look at Brancaster ... its leaning masts 'n' marks are remarkable.

# Burnham Overy Staithe

Burnham Overy Staithe is very much a sequestered and confined community, with a tiny harbour and a very tight run in; indeed, its approach channel has been described as a mere tidal creek.

The approach is from the east side of Scolt Head, by the quite unmistakable gap between that island and the threateningly named Gun Hill. The authority is the Burnham Overy Harbour Trust, and the centre of all life is to be found at its small jetty overlooking the modest mooring area. Across the road is the Boathouse, a chandlery and boatyard facility run by one Peter Beck, who is the Cruising Association representative and boatman and also Auxiliary Coastguard. His place is a real seaman's Aladdin's cave.

The entrance is generally deemed to be more difficult than Brancaster's. Although it is not so long, it is more arduous since it changes even more frequently and, although buoyed, is of a complexity to confound even some of the local fishermen from time to time.

As at Brancaster, it is not too difficult to spot where you are because of the unique configuration of Scolt Head and Gun Hill, but after that it is a tortuous and confusing affair. The place is such a small paradise that it is easy to understand why they are trying to keep it secretly to themselves. However, once you are there, you will be made extremely welcome.

There is a red bladder buoy for the harbour entrance; and small yellow floats. There are also beacons and various posts that are markers to those with local knowledge or enough native wit to work them out. Visitors are advised not to try to enter the harbour in northerly winds, unless guided. There are a few swinging moorings.

The best plan for any visitor is to arrange a shoresides look at low water and fix a date with Mr Beck for pilotage. He is decidedly modest about the need for help and advice, saying only: 'Do not attempt to enter harbour with northerly winds unless guided.' Any visitor with a boat of more than three to four feet draught should consider pilotage obligatory for a first entry.

Nelson was born in one of the other Burnhams, nearby Burnham Thorpe, and the Overy locals have made much of that ever since he became famous. There is no evidence, however, that he ever came near the place. Indeed, it seems he showed little interest in the sea at all until he was rudely introduced to its ways courtesy of his uncle's man-o'-war.

Burnham Overy Staithe has a warm feeling about that is not usually associated with the North Sea's east coast, making it a charming harbour and one of the prettiest havens on this stretch of coast, rivalling those even of the remoter parts of Cornwall.

# Wells-next-the-Sea

The first time I visited Wells was under conditions vividly described in the Admiralty *Pilot's* strict directions: 'Vessels should never attempt to enter Wells Harbour at night, nor without local knowledge, especially with onshore winds.' To be fair, I was actually being towed in by the *Isabella*, a local whelking boat, after an unpleasant contretemps with crab-lines off Cromer. Even so, the rough and tumble experience across the double bar provided me with enough misgivings to accept every word the *Pilot* had to offer.

But there were compensations: one moment we were being tossed around at the end of a long rope from the ex-lifeboat; and the next were deep in a shadowy night of enchantment with the lights of the buoys flashing in fairy tale array against the thick darkness of the enveloping banks and trees, all of which lent an air of mystery to our near-silent journey.

All on a sudden, we were face to face with the raucous road and side shows that comprise the quay: bazaars and bingo; fish, chip and burger bars; pubs and snackeries; and lights and music all the way.

The men of Wells looked after me and sorted out *Valcon's* props and attendant problems without fuss or payment. Not one of those who helped would take a penny. and it took a lot of arm twisting before my original rescuers, Sonny and Alan, would accept a bottle of whisky. That, however, is typical of Wells-next-the-Sea.

Access is from an hour and a half before to an hour after HW. The Bar at the entrance is 3m maximum, and 'winds from the northwest can cause a heavy swell over it.' Those are the harbour master's words. I would describe those particular conditions more dramatically, but no matter which words you choose, they are to be avoided.

The old black fairway buoy was 'replaced' with a new red/white one when it seemed likely the old one would go missing. That was years ago and it is still in place. Everyone still finds the two so helpful that if the 'old' one ever does disappear it will probably be replaced.

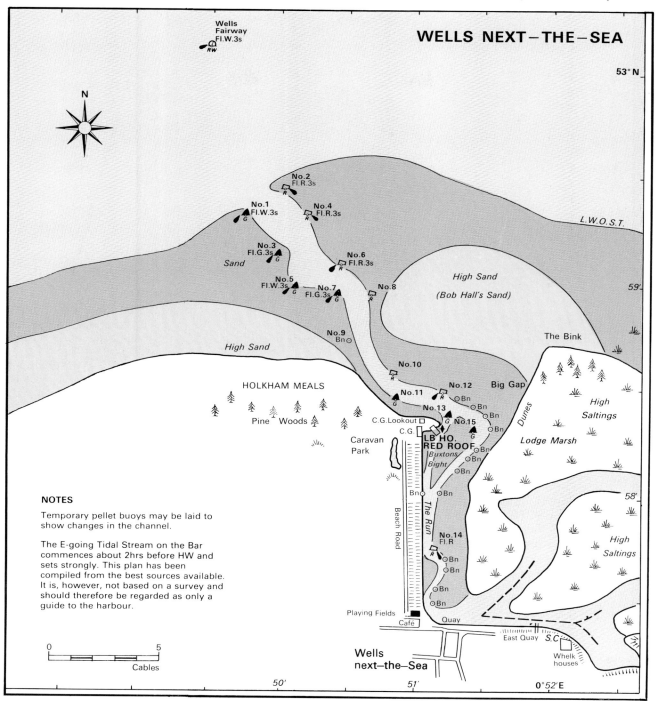

WELLS NEXT−THE−SEA

53° N

Wells
Fairway
Fl.W.3s

No.2
Fl.R.3s

No.1
Fl.W.3s

No.4
Fl.R.3s

No.3
Fl.G.3s

No.6
Fl.R.3s

Sand

No.5
Fl.W.3s

No.7
Fl.G.3s

No.8

High Sand

(Bob Hall's Sand)

L.W.O.S.T.

59'

No.9
Bn

High Sand

The Bink

No.10

No.12

Big Gap

Dunes

High

HOLKHAM MEALS

No.11

Bn

Saltings

Bn

No.13

Pine   Woods

C.G.Lookout

No.15

Bn

Lodge Marsh

C.G.

LB HO.

Bn

Caravan
Park

RED ROOF

Buxtons
Bight

Bn

Bn

58'

Bn

Beach Road

The Run

No.14
Fl.R

High

Bn

Saltings

Bn

Bn

NOTES

Temporary pellet buoys may be laid to
show changes in the channel.

The E-going Tidal Stream on the Bar
commences about 2hrs before HW and
sets strongly. This plan has been
compiled from the best sources available.
It is, however, not based on a survey and
should therefore be regarded as only a
guide to the harbour.

Bn

0                           5

Cables

Playing Fields

Café

Quay

Wells
next−the−Sea

East Quay   S.C.

Whelk
houses

50'

51'

0°52′E

It is vital that yachts should identify and approach the *Haven* buoy (or buoys if there are still two) otherwise there is a good chance of getting caught on the notorious Bob Hall's Sand. The most common problem is being blown on to the lee shore and, in spite of the reputation of Bob Hall (not to mention the bar) some skippers are still careless and these mishaps occur regularly.

Special caution: yachts are not to proceed east of the conspicuous silo without prior permission since there are extensive mussel lays which are extremely vulnerable to damage.

Wells-next-the-Sea is not well known. Indeed, on many occasions when I have telephoned friends from there, they have automatically jumped to the conclusion that I had been miraculously transported to Bath and Wells although I was known to be cruising the Norfolk coast at the time. It may be a commercial port but with a population of no more than 3000 it feels like a village. It is also described as a small sea town, a harbour and haven, and nary a soul would quarrel with that last, but for me it is quintessentially Wells: a place in its own right, and quite the friendliest place between Ramsgate and King's Lynn.

NO BOATS ARE TO BE LAUNCHED
FOR ANY PERIOD WITHOUT PRIOR
NOTICE TO THE HARBOUR MASTER
PAYMENT of DUES ~ ALL BOATS LAUNCHED TO
BE PAID TO THE HARBOUR MASTER EITHER
AT HIS HARBOUR OFFICE BETWEEN THE HOURS
OF 9&11 A.M. OR AT 30 MILL RD. WELLS-NEXT-THE-SEA
TEL · 710655 · DAILY OR PERIOD RATES
ALL MOORED BOATS MUST BEAR A NAME
OR MOORING NUMBER & EXHIBIT THEIR RECEIPTS
FOR BOAT FEES. LICENCE HOLDERS MAY BE
OBTAINED FROM THE HARBOUR MASTER
BY ORDER · WELLS HARBOUR COMMISSIONERS

Towards the smoke houses and the whelkers huts, the quieter
waters of Wells backwaters take over.

Wells and its worthies are deeply attached to their history, rooted to it but not bogged down in it, and while the flavour of the past has been well preserved, the community has kept up with the times. However, it is still something of a contradiction to discover that this quite busy port, with its bingo halls, an excellent and up to date caravan site, a plethora of television aerials, and a narrow shopping street of character and urban 'busyness', has no railway connection, and a public bus service that carries so few passengers it feels private and runs so infrequently that it barely justifies the claim 'service'.

The centre of Wells' 3–4 square miles must be its centrally placed and totally charming green with its nearby public houses and hotels, a real attraction on a blustery summer day, when it affords protection from all but the worst of winds and presents a traditional village aspect. But this centre is neither the heart nor the core of Wells. Like any well-proportioned photograph its focal point is right off-centre and in the case of Wells it is the quay. Old, well-used and much-loved, it is often busy with coasters and the fishing vessels that serve the adjacent whelk houses. It is no longer as thronged as it was in the days when vessels filled the haven and their crews burst the seams (and much more) of the 32 taverns the port then boasted. But there are still all the facilities, the bustle and the inherent dignity of a place alive with a continuing reliance on the harbour and the sea ... and the 8 inns that remain provide plenty of friendly entertainment and vitality.

Wells is dedicated to its quay, and little happens there that is not subject to the keen scrutiny and passionate interest of the many small groups that people it. There occurs hardly an event that is not closely observed, reported at length and discussed in detail; and what transpires in the morning, no matter how unobtrusive, inconsequential or guarded, come the evening will be broadcast and debated as a matter of some concern. The quay symbolises the town's dependence on the sea and the men who go down to it in little ships, small boats and penny numbers to wrench from it a hard-gotten and not always rewarding living. They are mainly whelkers, and for some of them there is a trip of up to 30 miles before they start at their pots, and another 30 when they have finished. It is a totemistic spot for a community in which families of the seagoing fishermen listen to their VHF radio monitors for news of the port's fleet of whelkers and shrimpers echoing, in contemporary terms, the age-old anxieties of those who wait and watch. Wells-next-the-Sea is one of the most intriguing, fascinating and appealing harbours on the east coast.

Wells quay is always a lively spot: afloat or shore sides.

Blakeney has many charms for the visitor, but only a few berths – and none at all for large craft.

## Blakeney and Morston Quay

Blakeney, a small fishing village on the Norfolk coast, has many attractive features. For the holidaymaker, tourist or rambler it is a headquarters for all kinds of excursions, and for the conservationist and bird watcher it is a special trust reserve of the National Trust. But for the mariner it is unique: being the first and last stop between the Wash ports and the haven of the River Yare at Great Yarmouth. Forty miles separate these two harbours, which could not be more different, and they are forty miles without a single refuge and little by way of coastal landmarks.

One of the Blakeney folk best qualified to assist, as well as being guide, philosopher, pilot and friend, is a character by the name of Stratton Long. He is the chief chandler in the place, running a stores that is a cross between a fisherman's hut and an Anglican Aladdin's Cave.

He is a boatbuilder extraordinaire, Blakeney boatman, lifeboat expert, unofficial harbourmaster, chandler, and, to use his own words 'general fiddler and diddler'. His business is Stratton Long Marine, known to one and all as Stratton's. It is not a place to venture if you are feeling one under the eight, for it is an experience to be lived up to.

It is difficult to decide whether entry to Blakeney is more twisty and turny by road or sea. There are two major landmarks: Blakeney church and the long, steeply shelved shingle bank that runs down to the sand dunes that mark the end of the Point.

Visibility on this part of the coast is not always reliable, so it is wise to be prepared to take regular soundings and not to try an entry until you have found the green and yellow buoy that is laid April to October and has a quick flashing light; the red bladder buoy; and the green wreck buoy. The wreck is of an old cod fishing smack. It can be a hazard up to half tide, and a constant reminder of threat at all times.

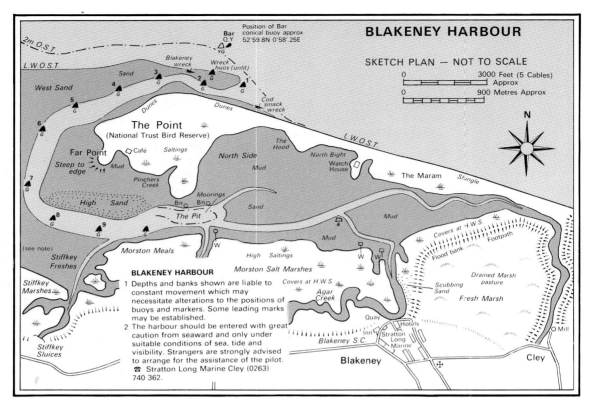

The channel is now well buoyed with marks that are all to be left to starboard when entering. However, as Stratton Long says: 'The entry is generally very difficult, for the sand bar is moving all the time; and if there is any northerly in the weather at all it will be extremely difficult and often dangerous.'

However, the entrance varies frequently and rapidly in position and depth. If you wish to experiment by making an unassisted entry, do so only under ideal conditions. And even so, visit shoresides first, and then you will be aware of the problems: finding the channel in the first place and then finding somewhere to lie once you are inside. If undeterred get local advice, at length and well in advance, and use the pilot. Stranded vessels have little chance, and it must be prudent to wait for settled weather and daylight, and it must be wisest of all to call there shoresides first and to arrange to be brought, at least for the first time.

The Roy Moreton Ferry Service (☎ Binham (032 875) 394) are prepared to offer visitors a pilot service provided they are not otherwise too busy to do so. They will also help in whatever way they can if you propose to take a 'biggish' boat up the quay; and by that they mean more than 9·0m LOA or a metre in draught.

The main channel leads past Stanley's Cockle Bight to the Pit and, once past Tibby Head, to Blakeney Channel and the quays. There are two quays; the Low Quay is the smaller of the two and is situated to the west of the larger one, but there is no official harbourmaster, Blakeney being one of the few remaining completely 'free' harbours in Britain.

Approaching from the road, there are some equally charming names to cherish: Cabbage Creek, Muckledyke, Stiffkey Freshes and Morston Meals; or, from the other direction, Bard Hill, the Skirts and Clay Eye. It is worth trying to stand back and view the flint buildings of the village from a good vantage point, but this is not easy as the streets are narrow and often busy.

Blakeney is one of those places where you get a strong whiff of its reality the minute you step off your boat (or get out of your car); nor does it disappoint you the longer you stay, repaying investigation by offering you jewels of art, architecture and people. Its only drawback is its popularity for visitors with cars. Happily, however, Blakeney is a place with a spirit and rhythm so all its own that it can survive all comers.

To stand on the quayside from tide to tide and watch the comings and goings of those who are earning their not much more than meagre livelihoods, as well as those who are spending their equally hard-earned leisure, is to experience something of the flavour of the days when Blakeney was a full-blown working harbour of substance and stature. Wool, grain and other exports were despatched to the ports of the Wash, Hull, Newcastle and London and as late as the 18th century, sailing vessels were still working Blakeney and its near neighbour Cley-next-the-Sea.

Blakeney is flanked by small communities with creeks. On the Wells-next-the-Sea side there is Morston, and on the Yarmouth end is Cley. Morston is little more than a quay and Cley is hardly a quay at all.

Morston Creek is the deepest and best channel associated with the Blakeney harbour complex, and as such, is in great demand and constant use by the professional boatmen who regularly take out parties to the National Trust bird sanctuary at the Point.

Visiting yachtsmen who understand the ways and needs of the boatmen are offered a friendly and helpful welcome, but woe betide those who expect to use a landing stage as if by right.

While the Morston Greens, Meals and Marshes are not to be compared to any of America's salt flats, there are still plenty of enthusiasts who use the area for land sailboarding.

Cley-next-the-Sea is an experience of quite another kind. If Morston is epitomised by its channel, creek and salt marshes, then Cley must be noted for its flint, both in the village itself and on the massive pebble ridge to be seen to full advantage down at Cley Eye.

The ridge is a splendid barrier to the encroachment of the North Sea and it is to be seen at its dramatic best when those waters spend their force furiously on its shelf.

Back in Cley village, there are many delights, from the major majesty of the old mill to the many minor ones to be seen in the facades of the cottages: some neat, some recently refurbished lavishly, and some as stark as they ever were. Most of Cley can be described as well-established, and even those shops and tea rooms that are not possessed of a long history look for all the world as if they are. Not to be missed are three equally esoteric establishments: the nationally famous pottery; the exotically stocked corner shop; and the not-quite-tucked-away smokery and fish shop, presided over by a Tolkien-like character.

Morston, Cley-next-the-Sea and Blakeney form a trio of communities that hang together with a unified will and spirit that face the rigours of the North Sea with a panache that is only equalled by the fortitude with which they face the demands of the touring multitudes. The locals know that they stand as much in threat from inundation by the one as they do from the other; but in true Norfolk tradition they calmly persevere, respecting both but deferring to neither.

# Cley to California

After Blakeney, the coast to Wells consists of low lying sands and marshes, backed by thick belts of fir trees that are a feature of these parts; and so begins the long slog from the great light of Cromer to the great dark of Yarmouth, with nary a bolt hole between. As Blakeney and Cley-next-the-Sea fall astern and we move eastward to the north of Sheringham, the coastline rises gently to a thickly wooded skyline of hills and cliffs. The small community of Sheringham lies in a hollow between the cliffs and hills. It nestles by the water's edge like a village in a merman's fairy tale. In the early summer sun with a slight haze, or an October moon, it can form a mysterious spectacle.

This sea-to-beach-state at Cley illustrates a frequent East Coast condition.

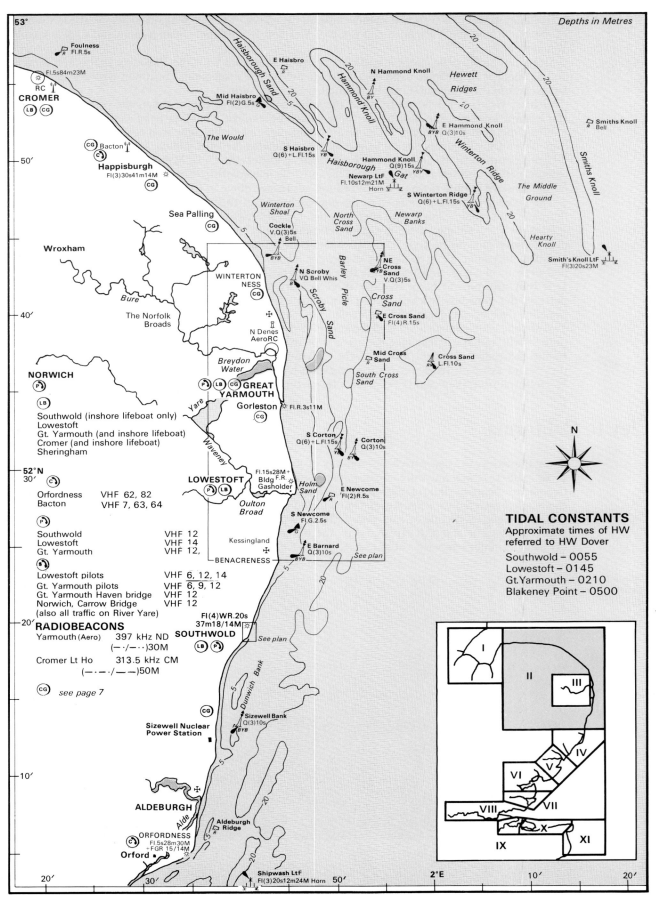

*Depths in Metres*

53°

Foulness
Fl.R.5s

Fl.5s84m23M
RC
**CROMER**
LB CG

CG Bacton
CG **Happisburgh**
Fl(3)30s41m14M
CG

**Sea Palling**
CG

**Wroxham**

**WINTERTON NESS**
CG

*Bure*

**The Norfolk Broads**

N Denes AeroRC

**NORWICH**
P
LB

Southwold (inshore lifeboat only)
Lowestoft
Gt. Yarmouth (and inshore lifeboat)
Cromer (and inshore lifeboat)
Sheringham

**52°N**
30'
C

Orfordness      VHF 62, 82
Bacton          VHF 7, 63, 64

P

Southwold       VHF 12
Lowestoft       VHF 14
Gt. Yarmouth    VHF 12,

Lowestoft pilots          VHF 6, 12, 14
Gt. Yarmouth pilots       VHF 6, 9, 12
Gt. Yarmouth Haven bridge VHF 12
Norwich, Carrow Bridge    VHF 12
(also all traffic on River Yare)

20'**RADIOBEACONS**
Yarmouth (Aero)   397 kHz ND
                  (− ·/− ··)30M

Cromer Lt Ho      313.5 kHz CM
                  (− · − ·/− −)50M

CG   *see page 7*

Breydon Water

*Yare*
P LB CG **GREAT YARMOUTH**
**Gorleston**
CG            Fl.R.3s11M

*Waveney*

**LOWESTOFT**
P LB
Fl.15s28M+ Bldg F.R. Gasholder

*Oulton Broad*

Kessingland

**BENACRENESS**

Fl(4)WR.20s
37m18/14M
**SOUTHWOLD**
See plan
LB P

*Dunwich Bank*

CG

Sizewell Bank
Q(3)10s
BYB

**Sizewell Nuclear Power Station**

10'

**ALDEBURGH**
*Alde*
Aldeburgh Ridge

C **ORFORDNESS**
Fl.5s28m30M
+FGR 15/14M
**Orford**

20'                30'

Shipwash LtF
Fl(3)20s12m24M Horn

50'                2°E

*Haisborough Sand*

E Haisbro
R

Mid Haisbro
Fl(2)G.5s

*The Would*

S Haisbro
Q(6)+L.Fl.15s
YB

*Haisborough Gat*

Newarp LtF
Fl.10s12m21M
Horn

*Winterton Shoal*

Cockle
V.Q(3)5s
Bell
BYB

N Scroby
VQ Bell Whis
B

*North Cross Sand*

*Scroby Sand*

*Barley Picle*

NE Cross Sand
V.Q(3)5s
BYB

*Cross Sand*

E Cross Sand
Fl(4)R.15s

Mid Cross Sand
R

*South Cross Sand*

Cross Sand
L.Fl.10s
RW

S Corton
Q(6)+L.Fl.15s

Corton
Q(3)10s

*Holm Sand*

E Newcome
Fl(2)R.5s
R

S Newcome
Fl.G.2.5s
G

E Barnard
Q(3)10s
BYB

*See plan*

N Hammond Knoll
BY

E Hammond Knoll
BYB    Q(3)10s

Smiths Knoll
R    Bell

*Hewett Ridges*

*Hammond Knoll*

Hammond Knoll
Q(9)15s
YBY

S Winterton Ridge
Q(6)+L.Fl.15s
YB

*Winterton Ridge*

*Newarp Banks*

*The Middle Ground*

*Hearty Knoll*

*Smiths Knoll*

Smith's Knoll LtF
Fl(3)20s23M

20

20

20

20

20

20

5

5

5

5

5

20

20

**TIDAL CONSTANTS**
Approximate times of HW
referred to HW Dover

Southwold − 0055
Lowestoft − 0145
Gt.Yarmouth − 0210
Blakeney Point − 0500

N

I
II    III
IV
V
VI    VII
VIII
X
IX    XI

My first boating experience off Sheringham was of a different order. Standing off about a couple of miles, so as to leave all the crab pots well to port, I noticed the marker of an isolated pot about two cables to starboard. 'Safe distance', I thought; but I was wrong for the line stretched ominously in front of our bows.

Too late I cut the engines and, Sod's law ruling yet again, I picked up the line around starboard prop. Full investigation showed that it was an already cut line. Later, taking avoiding action from an apparently unmanned coaster, I succeeded in wrapping most of the line round both props and the rudder. The tale had a happy ending in so far as the Whelkers of Wells rallied round to get me in and sort me out; but to this day I cannot see a crab pot marker without my anxiety level rising.

As the bulge of Norfolk moves out towards the most easterly point of England, the tendency is still generally towards a low-lying coastline; but within this overall view, some cliffs proper can be seen beginning to make their mark. Indeed, on either side of Cromer the cliffs rise steeply while the hinterland stands out conspicuously, being dramatically well-wooded. Where the cliffs begin to lose some of their grandeur towards the southeast of Cromer they are topped by bungalows and chalets that do nothing to improve the skyline. This marks the end of the two-mile expanse of cliffs, which, although they are not particularly tall, fall at a dramatically steep-to angle to the sea and in their entirety are beautifully sculptured. At one point, below an isolated white bungalow, one section of the cliffs is just like a massive replica of Old Father Time, with looming eyes, a hook nose and a V-shaped beard.

This represents perhaps the best cliff frontage and profile to be found between Flamborough and Beachy Head; indeed, it is also the last before the North Foreland except for the slow emergence of a short sequence by Caister-on-Sea. While still of miniature proportions, they offer an attractive frontage with modest spans that look almost primeval.

The area is a paradigm of disregarded, but not disgraced Britain; our natural heritage still alive, although so close to the assemblies of scattered and jumbled camps. It is no problem to conjure up images of those submarine forests that are to be found just off this coast, and to visualize the coastline itself as the long-suffering, silent and historic victim of those landslips and general eroding decay that have had their way as the sea has reclaimed, inch by inexorable inch, its own inheritance, the land. Next comes the full fall, as the low-lying house-peppered land starts a slow march down to Winterton Ness and its disused lighthouse, on a long promenade of sand that slowly slopes into the sea from its attractive undulating dunes.

Norfolk has its own version of California just to the north of Yarmouth. While its climate can never approach the Mediterranean style of the American state, it does manage to support pretty grass-covered banks that steeply shelve almost down to the water's edge. Here, they front lines of camps, beach huts, bungalows, chalets and other holiday homes, all proclaiming the move towards the centre of the fully matured tourist territory of Great Yarmouth.

# Great Yarmouth Haven

On the whole, my wholly unfavourable first impression of Great Yarmouth in 1975 remains unchanged. From seaward, the place displays a face of no appeal at all: a dejected countenance dominated and oppressed by the *mélange* of factories and power stations; the conglomeration of chimney stacks; and the silhouetted hump of the fairground's roller-coaster all real and symbolic monuments to Yarmouth's singular talents.

From the north, after the well known *Cockle* cardinal off Winterton Ness, the approach lies between the north shoals of Scroby and those off Caister: inside Scroby and outside Caister, straight down through Caister and Yarmouth Roads.

From the south, there is the choice of a straightforward inshore run from Lowestoft Roads, or an offshore approach followed by a cut in via the Holm Channel, NE after the Corton buoys: to the west of E Holm and to the east of Corton and S Corton. Both lead to Gorleston Road, situate immediately to the south of Yarmouth Haven entrance. From such a southerly position, at about half a mile off, the entrance shows as a long, low line in dark rust colour. A green silo shows to the right hand; a green and white silo is to the centre; and, just to west of north, the power station chimney shows prominently, and it is the most obvious landmark for the port.

From a scenic point of view, the coast to Great Yarmouth, from both the north and the south, tends to be somewhat boringly low-lying and featureless. Yarmouth itself stands out just like several sore thumbs; its piers, Great Amusement Park, towers, hotels, chimneys and Nelson's monument creating what might be euphemistically described as a miscellany. None of them, not even Nelson, is, however, easy to identify as a piece in its individual right.

The immediate entrance into the Haven, between the north and south piers, is difficult to identify exactly until you are very close, since both sides of the piers are the same dreary colour not only as one another but also as most of the background. So, a cautious approach is best until they are clearly recognised and fully open, when the old red brick lighthouse on the Brush, not one that can be called conspicuous, will lead you in on a near-westerly course.

To effect entry, substantial power may be needed if you are to make it on the ebb, for the rate can achieve anything up to 6 knots. Although there is complete access at all times, when there is any SE in the wind in excess of 3–4, entry against the ebb should not be attempted.

My first experience of Yarmouth's entrance was exciting but by no means enthralling: it was a combination of a 5/6 southeasterly with a spring tide on the ebb. Had it not been for current gale warnings and an already rising wind (with my next port of call northwards, namely Wells-next-the-Sea) I would never have tried. What the Admiralty *Pilot* says in no way overstates the case: 'Light-draught vessels may enter at most times, but high or low slack water is recommended. There is risk with a heavy sea in the entrance particularly during strong SE winds with an outgoing stream; under these conditions the roadstead is recommended for refuge'. The roadstead held no appeal as a refuge for me, and so I braved the mass of broken water, with, for ten minutes that seemed an hour, *Valcon* lurching in all three planes at once and apparently ready to capsize. It was I, of course, who was ready to founder; and the minute I had made the right angle turn to starboard into the river itself, I had recourse to the medicinal brandies.

## Great Yarmouth

After the Brush, a dramatic right angled near-blind turn to starboard, the Haven proper takes over with a wide and deep channel all the way up to the Haven Bridge. The vista that presents itself is one of tugs and rig supports vessels, as the slick oil spirit of Yarmouth materialises into a near solid ribbon.

Almost immediately after Brush Bend, on the port hand, you will find the fuel station, the RNLI and the pilot boats, wasp-like in orange and black with a yellow stripe. Most of the rest of the bank is taken up by the boats of the local professional fishermen. Just over half a mile up the Haven there is a cross-stream ferry to be negotiated.

The Haven Bridge, and the 'new' Breydon Bridge must be negotiated to reach the Broads; the Haven bridgemaster is on VHF channel 12 and the Breydon master is in contact with him. When closed, both bridges offer 2·8m headroom. Yachts are quite naturally expected to fit in with the bookings for commercial traffic, and they are usually permitted to wait at the Town Hall Quay. Occasionally they are given something resembling a smile; but things have changed very little since that first unhappy visit. On my latest, once *Valcon's* name had been espied, I was thrice visited by skippers who were anxious that I should broadcast their criticisms. Their complaint was that Yarmouth claimed to have a very welcoming stance to yachtsmen yet offered few facilities and proferred unco-operative, unfriendly service.

Great Yarmouth: frontage from seaward

Inside the entrance to Great Yarmouth Haven

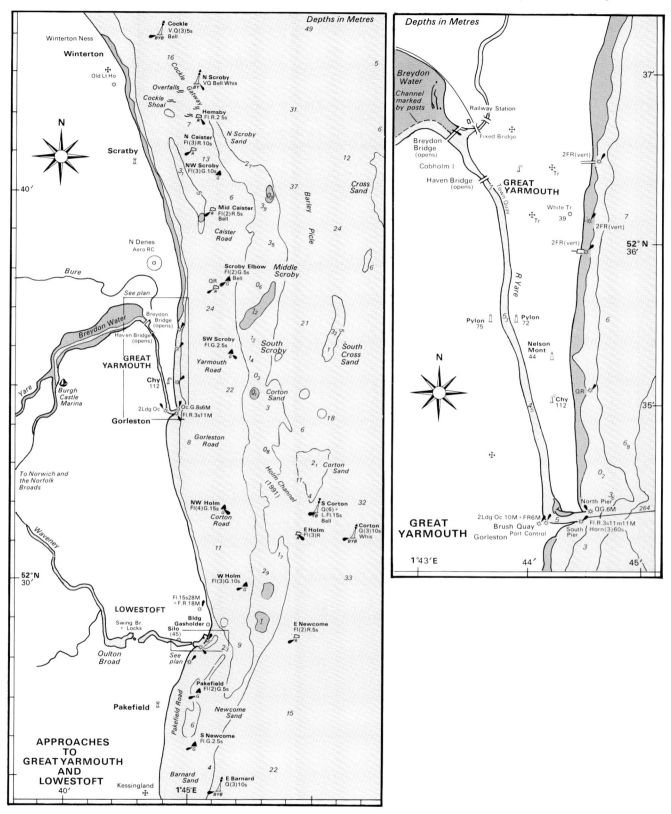

**Depths in Metres**
49

Cockle
V.Q(3)5s
Bell
BYB

Winterton Ness

**Winterton**

Old Lt Ho

5

16
Cockle Gatway

Overfalls

Cockle Shoal

N Scroby
VQ Bell Whis
BY

6

**Scratby**

31

Hemsby
Fl.R.2.5s
R

7

40′

N Caister
Fl(3)R.10s
R

N Scroby Sand

13

NW Scroby
Fl(3)G.10s
G

3₁

12

2₇

6

Cross Sand

Mid Caister
Fl(2)R.5s
Bell
R

3₉

0₂

37

Barley Picle

Bure

Caister Road

3₅

24

N Denes
Aero RC

Scroby Elbow
Fl(2)G.5s
Bell

*Middle Scroby*

QR
R

0₆

6

See plan

Breydon Bridge
(opens)

24

1₂

21

Haven Bridge
(opens)

**GREAT YARMOUTH**

SW Scroby
Fl.G.2.5s
G

1₂

3₂

5

South Scroby

South Cross Sand

1

**Burgh Castle Marina**

Chy
112

Yarmouth Road

1₄

Yare

22

0₃

0₁

Corton Sand

2 Ldg Oc

Oc.G.8s6M
Fl.R.3s11M

3

18

**Gorleston**

Gorleston Road

8

6

0₈

To Norwich and the Norfolk Broads

Holm Channel (1991)

2₁
Corton Sand

NW Holm
Fl(4)G.15s
G

S Corton
Q(6)+
L.Fl.15s
Bell
B

32

Corton Road

4

Corton
Q(3)10s
Whis
BYB

Waveney

11

E Holm
Fl(3)R
R

1₇

52°N
30′

W Holm
Fl(3)G.10s
G

2₉

33

Fl.15s28M
+F.R.18M

**LOWESTOFT**

Swing Br. + Locks

Bldg
Gasholder

E Newcome
Fl(2)R.5s
R

Oulton Broad

Silo
(45)

See plan

2₃

9

**Pakefield**
Fl(2)G.5s
G

Pakefield Road

**Pakefield**

6

Newcome Sand

15

S Newcome
Fl.G.2.5s
G

**APPROACHES TO GREAT YARMOUTH AND LOWESTOFT**

Barnard Sand

4

E Barnard
Q(3)10s
BYB

22

40′

Kessingland

1°45′E

---

Breydon Water

37′

Channel marked by posts

Railway Station

Fixed Bridge

Breydon Bridge
(opens)

Cobholm I

2FR(vert)

Tr

Haven Bridge
(opens)

**GREAT YARMOUTH**

Town Quay

White Tr
39

Tr

52°N
36′

2FR(vert)

7

2FR(vert)

Pylon
75

5

Pylon
72

R Yare

Nelson Mont
44

6

**N**

4₅

Chy
112

QR
R

35′

0₂

**GREAT YARMOUTH**

2 Ldg Oc.10M + FR6M

Brush Quay
Port Control

Gorleston

5

North Pier
QG.6M

3₆

264

Fl.R.3s11m11M
South Pier
Horn(3)60s

3

6₈

1°43′E

44′

45′

---

It is regrettable that it has not been seen fit to provide pleasing facilities for yachtsmen in this area, or even elsewhere in the Haven. It is not easy for a masted yacht to find a well-protected acceptable berth from which to taste the unique pleasures of the resort. Its appeal may not be universal, but the town has features that are worth exploring and, in the season, promotes a carnival way of life: cockles and rock; bangers and burgers; boat trips, birds and booze.

But as things stand, Yarmouth's main (and perhaps only) attraction must be the easy access it affords to the Norfolk Broads; and if Lowestoft were to get its act together at Mutford Lock, even this would disappear. All being well, the new Broads Authority will bring about much-needed changes. Once through the bridges, with Yarmouth astern and into classic Broads territory, be it north or south, you could not wish for a warmer welcome, friendlier officers or a more efficient service.

On occasion, you may find a berth where you can lie undisturbed for a few hours.

# Lowestoft

From the north, Lowestoft is probably best approached through Caister, Yarmouth and Gorleston Roads, even though you may have had no intention of calling at Great Yarmouth. On what is virtually a straight southerly course, you fall down past Holm into Corton and Lowestoft North Roads and on to a direct entry, and you can check your halfway progress from Yarmouth by the appearance of the unmistakable tower by Corton Roads Holiday Camp. A similarly plain approach marks the course from the south via Newcome and Pakefield, but see also below.

It is worth noting that the well-known red *East Newcome* stands outside the Lowestoft sandbanks and caution should be exercised if using it as a waypoint or entry marker for the harbour. I have jilled around the site more than once and now know that careful study of the chart and regular soundings are required – that is if you feel you must approach that way.

Lowestoft harbour is virtually impossible to miss, to overlook or to mistake, mainly because of its distinctive, rocket-like light towers at the entrance and the high-rise silos behind them. Just to the north of the entrance is the coast guard station. It is a prominent concrete building with the appearance of a luxury liner's wheelhouse. It looks reassuringly seaworthy.

Safe access can be had into the harbour at all times, but wind against tide, especially an ebb, makes for a rough five or ten minutes. Entry into the harbour is strictly regulated by traffic control lights.

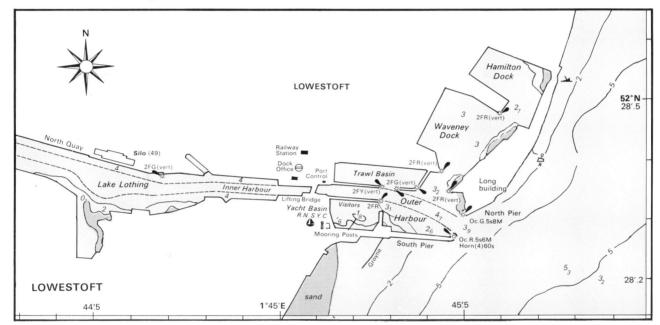

Lowestoft's twin space age rocket style lights form an unmistakable landmark on the south coast.

The bridge is raised regularly for commercial traffic and yachts use those occasions so as to disrupt the usually heavy road traffic as little as possible.

Royal Yacht Club and Royal Lifeboat cheek by jowl in the yacht basin. The locale is due for change, disruption and refurbishment.

It is worth checking with the harbour radio (VHF 14) for commercial shipping movements. This will also give you some idea of how long you might have to wait for the lights to come in your favour and allow you to get in. It can also inform you of the next opening of the bridge that permits you to 'cross the road' into Lake Lothing and make for the Inner Harbour … or even Mutford Lock; that is, if it happens to be 1400 on a Wednesday, and you have given prior notice of your intention to pass through. (For more information on this phenomenon, see below.)

Visitors' moorings are to be found in the South Basin, and the normal plan is to tie up to the North Wall at the Inner South Pier and await instructions from the Royal Norfolk and Suffolk Yacht Club's berthing officer who operates from a small office not far from the slip. The moorings were renowned throughout the North Sea cruising community for years because of their famous/infamous giant sausage fenders that will roller paint your hull with whatever oils, flotsam or other detritus happens to be floating in your vicinity.

I always think of the club as an amazing establishment: in spite of being a relic, redolent of those dear, dead Edwardian days well beyond recall, it is alert and alive with the kind of humming activity that is not usually associated with yacht clubs. Stringent regulations control your sartorial style in various rooms, and while they don't actually have a string quartet for your leisure and pleasure at afternoon tea, they should, for it would complete the *mise en scène*. But none of this in any way stands in the way of modern facilities and up to date services with a smile.

Mutford Lock is Lowestoft's head of navigation as well as the expensive gateway to the Broads.

There has been talk of a new marina development; the main idea being to extend the inner South Quay. This would provide leisure craft with moorings that are separate and safe from all docks traffic and with much improved protection from swell. There is also rumour that the old clubhouse would go in the general furore of a modern development scheme. However, we can all cease from mortal strife for a time still, since it appears that nothing will happen for at least four or five years. Long live the RN & SYC!

Once past the opening road bridge and through the inner harbour, you reach Lake Lothing. This is a favourite spot for large sailing yachts to undertake repairs and refurbishment. Not long ago, I was made welcome on board *Heartease*, one of the largest private yachts I have ever set foot on, as well as the famed *Young Endeavour* preparing for her epic cruise; and even as I write, Paul Getty's *Jezebel* million-plus floating folly is being refitted by Brooke Yachts.

At the head of Lake Lothing, the Cruising Club ('Long waiting list ... full for years') appears with its congregation of many pretty craft tucked away all neat'n'nice in the midst of the vast assembly of commerce, industry, wrecks, hulks and the general mess epitomised by the paper works storage. Nearby is the International Boatbuilding Training Centre, and the extraordinary shapes and colours of the many and various sizes of the survival capsules. Good photogenic stuff all round this area.

Charges for the use of Mutford Lock, which enables a speedy passage to the Broads at Oulton, are so inflated that they tend to prohibit its use by the general boating fraternity. Built over 150 years ago, it gloriously lays claim to gates that, just like Janus, face both ways, and stand, just as he does, ready to handle traffic from the end of the old or the beginning of the new; thus catering, as the official handout has it, for 'all states of the tide'. Face each way they certainly do. But as for catering for all states of the tide; well, they may be able actually to do that very thing, but in practice such provision never occurs. You pass through Mutford Lock by grace and favour of the port authority. For details please see below.

They don't even cater for more than a few hours of one day of each week (unless you want to disrupt the whole of the natural system as laid down by the authorities and pay through the nose.) For the ordinary cruising man, this means that access to the Broads through Lowestoft is so strictly limited (with regard to time and money) that most skippers would immediately revert to Great Yarmouth.

Lowestoft extends out to the most easterly point in the UK and is able to boast the most easterly pub in Britain. The town is a composite of the pretty old and the not so pretty new; and after many a sojourn in its well protected yacht harbour, I have come to review my first judgments on this town that mixes the trendy, the fashionable, the broken-down, the dull, the soiled and the stale, the ribald and the choice, with the gentry and the plebeian, the elite and the nondescript rubbing shoulders in one pseudo-egalitarian community. It is a curiosity affording entertainment and relaxation to the tourist, and at the same time being worthy of serious study by psychologist and sociologist.

Life in the harbour is different from the days when it was famous for its gangs of herring girls , but recent years have seen something of a revival of the port's fortunes, and fishing and commerce are both on an upward surge, as the development plans and the new buildings all show.

From the visiting yachtsman's point of view, it offers an excellently comprehensive range of boat gear, marine facilities and services run by staff who know what they are doing ... and don't overcharge. In these respects, Lowestoft cannot be bettered; and, bearing in mind that it is really easy of access and without attendant hazards, its strange blend of peculiarly charming and singularly charmless features must make it a port of call not to be missed.

This cannot be said with much conviction about any other harbour to the north until you reach Grimsby (up the Humber) or Blyth (on the way to Scotland).

# Southwold

From Lowestoft to Southwold the coastline is pretty uniform: slightly undulating and mainly featureless, with the occasional church, copse and splurge of greenery. Keeping about a mile off avoids any difficulty and takes you outside the Barnard shoal off Benacre Ness, but inside the buoy, and straight on to the S. *Newcome* and the *Pakefield* buoys. If the weather is poor, or you want to exercise full caution, the passage seaward of the *East Barnard* buoy is no more than two miles out. In good weather, there is no reason not to be as close in as you feel is comfortable since there is no upstanding hazard to take you unawares.

Whether approaching Southwold from the north or the south, the conspicuous lighthouse to the NE of the harbour entrance, and the water tower are the confirming visual aspects. There are two very good 'unofficial' leading marks from seaward in the form of the lighthouse and church in Southwold.

Lowestoft harbour.

Southwold harbour.

Southwold lighthouse.

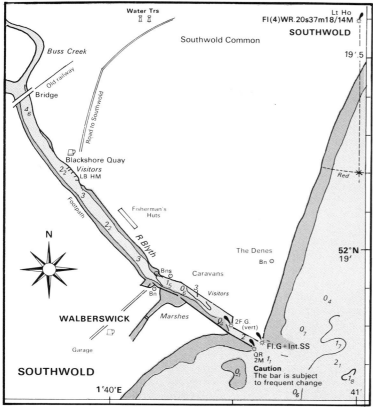

Southwold: looking upstream from
the end of the visitors' moorings,
showing the pontoons taken up by
'residents' or 'regulars'

When making for an entry, it is best to stand off about half to a quarter of a mile until you have fully opened the small piers (which have about 40m between them). The cross-streams can be strong and capriciously treacherous, so it is important to know exactly what they are doing and what you propose to do about entering. Offshore winds with an ebb tide can be very bad.

Southwold is a harbour where it is usually difficult to change your mind, or even manoeuvre at times, when you have once committed yourself to an entry. Past the piers, with the infamous Knuckle safely to the starboard side, the entrance waters widen to offer another welcome 20m or so with the 'Quay' and Old Trinity jetty on your starboard hand. 'Large' vessels can, by arrangement with the harbour master, be berthed at this quay. *Valcon* is not a 'large' vessel and so not eligible, but I have never been tempted by the appearance of that quay. I am sure it is all properly boatshape and Southwold fashion, but I have always found it of sinister aspect.

When I first visited Southwold in the late 70s, not only was it a strange Wild West kind of place but it also possessed an entry that was downright inhospitable to visitors. Between the piers, strangers would find it impossible to discern the channel, which, in any case, was unpredictable from tide to tide. There was a disreputable red flag permanently flown at the entrance, denoting 'entrance undesirable'. There were broken down jetties, huts, shacks and decaying hulls. The floating pontoons, which clearly found it difficult to live up to their description, were a miscellany of small unstable berths for pleasure craft (permanently private, but not always occupied), larger but hardly more stable catwalks, and piles for the few professional fishermen. A few unattractive berths were for those visitors who had chanced their all at the entrance and had actually made it to just below the bridge. In brief, confusion reigned; and the fact that the harbour master was also the supervisor of the caravan site seemed entirely fitting.

I remember that first visit clearly: the first thing I noticed through the binoculars was that torn and tattered flag on its unsteady pole. The Admiralty *Pilot* said briefly, 'A red flag, unreliable, means that entry is inadvisable.' The fact that it rhymed and nearly scanned was amusing but of little help or consolation; but since the wind, weather, tide and time were all in my favour I decided to risk an entry in the face of the crimson warning. After I had been there a day or two, I was instructed in the local lore and the reason for the red flag by the then harbourmaster and caravan supervisor. 'That self-same flag has been there for years. We leave it there all the time. It puts visitors off, and that's how we like it. But you should see what the charts say we've got. We're down for all kinds of things we've never heard of. That's always good for a laugh, that is.'

It is pleasant to be able to record that the situation has changed dramatically. The navigational aids are exactly what they are supposed to be, and the Admiralty has given the place a thorough survey. The visitors' pontoons are now quite splendid affairs, sound and new, with ladders and planks provided by the harbourmaster.

Moreover, the new shore groynes to the north of the piers apparently work well, so that the channel is no longer shifted tide by tide, but now tends to keep a central position. Even so, I have still found, once past the quay, that the best water tends towards the north of centre channel, with the southern edge tending to shoal.

Entry is made on 260° and craft of 1·8m are advised not to try to gain access earlier than an hour before low water, although there is now generally 2m in the entrance. But still, even after the improvements, changing your mind in the Southwold entrance is an extremely risky thing to do.

If you have found enough depth in the centre of the entrance channel, it is sensible to stay on that course and not be tempted by any apparent changes. An inspection of the area at low water will show some of the otherwise hidden hazards on each side. The Knuckle is worth close inspection, it is a disagreeable sight; and the hard sand/shingle bank which can often build up to a substantial drying height along the south side is another.

Most yachts will want to go to the refurbished visitors' moorings which start just below the large RNLI shed (also the HM's office) and continue up to the staging opposite the Harbour Inn. The moorings can actually accommodate 100 yachts, although I must say that at a first glance this appears to be about 80 more than is thinkable. Southwold, which is very popular with the foreign sailing fraternity, especially the Dutch, usually hosts 40 to 50 boats in an average week in the season; and visitors can find themselves rafted together up to 4 or 5 deep.

At low water springs, craft on the inside moorings will take the bottom, but on the outside there is a sharp drop to 6·0m or more. The harbour master will pilot you in if required. He is usually around at tide times to guide and assist you into a berth. At one time, as mentioned above, you needed your own planks; but under the new regime, together with a good water hose, they are now provided. However, you will need good strong warps; although the rise and fall is not more than 2·0m, there is a deal of power in the stream.

The Harbour Inn (which gets its deliveries from the Southwold Brewery by horse-drawn dray) is a classic of an old fashioned east coast hostelry. Its floors are uneven and prone to flooding; its timbers dark and unyielding and the staff can be similar unless and until you are elected to the chosen few; and its beer is of a quality to keep even east coast beer buff, Henry Irving, happy for at least a week. It does meals; but don't settle for anything other than fish and chips: they are not to be surpassed for leagues.

Next door to the pub, there is a small workshop for the convenience of the landlord. Happily, he is willing to help out with all sorts of repairs, or even plug you into his mains. That is, if your lead is long enough and you can gain his approval. He also runs an efficient private weather station.

Southwold itself is well distanced from the harbour by a road that offers an excellent walk but is pretty treacherous for motor traffic. It has a long history and is much livelier than nearby Aldeburgh which is twice its size. It is a pleasant walk from the moorings into the town which is famous for its two 'landmarks'. Their order of priority will depend upon your taste; they are the lighthouse and the brewery. The splendid old lighthouse is to be found right in the centre of the town and while it shows its age it is also manifestly well cared for.

There is a working bustle at Southwold, indicative of a truly busy place, that exposes the sham that is the 'business' of the other place. The town is remarkably well supplied with public conveniences and possesses a cross-section of contemporary life, from poorly patronised pseudo arts and crafts centres to one fish and chip shop that was so over-patronised that it seemed pointless to join the queue.

Nearer to the river mouth and the caravan park, the beach is bordered by a concrete apology for a promenade and a line of beach huts including those with names as incongruous as *Dodge City* and *High Chaparral*. Touristic and domestic accommodation is generally on the road at the back of sand dunes that are neither land nor sea scaped, just sparsely covered with gorse and sea grass.

Almost on the edge of the sea are a few outposts of what might once have been holiday homes. Bleak, with the kind of hospitality redolent of a Brontë father-figure, it takes little imagination to see them slowly disappearing under the waves like the dream home of a forsaken merman. They must provide fantastic experiences for anyone who can enjoy or even survive a winter in such splendid isolation.

Nearby, on the north side of the river, there are small huts from which the locals sell fresh fish that is landed from the boats before your very eyes. Once upon a time, fishy bargains were to be had at such locations, but those times have gone and you now pay the full going city rate. Nevertheless, the real fresh thing is so different from the pale imitations that flop on most of our townie fishmongers' stands that it seems, by comparison, to be half price, and nothing can beat the taste of sea-fresh fish at any price.

Although Southwold hosts a summer tourist brigade that has been consistently growing ever since Michael Palin's gentle satire gave it national TV prestige, it has not fallen victim to the dreaded faceless holiday strip ... resort amenities that seem to swallow so many of our coastal towns and villages. Southwold has retained its sense of identity, and there is silent witness to the spirit of the place all round Gun Hill by Southwold Common and Town Marshes.

However, it is not always sweetness and light in Southwold harbour. Some of the fishermen, happily a minority but a minority too many, retain old fashioned attitudes towards 'their' waters and grounds. More than once have I been disturbed by the manoeuvres of some clamorous midnight cowboy fishermen shouting and clouting boats. Indeed, one of them may still possess part of my treasured solid brass stern light. More than once I have been caught and rolled as if in a beam sea by their needless, heedless speed. So treasure this for the irony: on one occasion I was leaving Southwold at a modest three knots less than the traffic regulations when I was accosted from the bank by a trio of the very self same, gesticulating and bellowing, 'Slow down you bugger!'

# Walberswick

Across the River Blyth from the quay and caravan park at the entrance to Southwold Harbour is the village of Walberswick, an intriguing community that is as rich and remote as it is reserved and resolute against invasion and tourists.

From the north, the approach is via a ferry that looks back to the good old days when Dickens thought there was nothing better than a bloater from nearby Yarmouth. It is still hand propelled by an ancient mariner who looks so frail that he could be a candidate for Samuel Taylor Coleridge's original. In these days of inflation, it is a minor miracle that you can still be ferried across for pennies, and without need to defer to Charon or to bring a sop for Cerberus.

It is a peculiar community in many ways with most folk addressing themselves to retirement, isolation and privacy. Not entirely predictable in what at first seems the peace and quiet of a neighbourhood in aristocratic, is the assertive-to-aggressive defence of their territorial and riparian rights. You will not receive many unforced smiles, friendly words or even plain greetings when sauntering down the street, for it is not one of England's friendliest villages. Indeed, you are more likely to attract the scowl, the questioning gaze and the raised eyebrow for the community is very hot on security, giving sanctuary as it does to some of the UK's most famous and wealthy great and good.

That short trip across the ferry takes you into another world; one that could detain you for a lifetime. Most people I know who are addicted to Walberswick are also hot for Southwold; and that includes John Seymour who, in his *Companion Guide to East Anglia*, says: 'I cannot think of anything bad to say about Southwold.'

**BRANCASTER HARBOUR AND BRANCASTER STAITHE**

**Charts**
Imray Y9, C28
Admiralty 108

**Tides**
Immingham +0050, Dover −0430

**Authorities**
*Harbourmaster* M.N. Nudds, The Smithy, Brancaster Staithe, King's Lynn, Norfolk. ☎ Brancaster (0485) 210638
*Brancaster Boats* Mr Borthwick is available for help. He listens on VHF 'M' during tide times when sailing & board training courses are being held. ☎ (0485) 210236

**WELLS-NEXT-THE-SEA**

**Charts**
Imray Y9, C28
Admiralty 108

**Tides**
Bar +0020 Immingham, −0500 Dover
Quay +0100 Immingham.
*Wells Harbour Commissioners* Secretary, Mrs. C. Abel, Belmont Cottage, Burnt St, Wells-next-the-Sea, Norfolk.
☎ Fakenham (0328) 710497
*Harbourmaster* ☎ Fakenham (0328) 711744
VHF Ch 16, 14, 12, 8, 6, 37

**BURNHAM OVERY STAITHE**

**Charts**
Imray Y9

**Tides**
Immingham +0050, Dover −0430

**BLAKENEY HARBOUR**

**Charts**
Imray C28, C29
Admiralty 108

**Tides**
Immingham +0030 (The Point), +0050, (Quay), Dover −0500

**Pilot**
Stratton Long Marine, Blakeney, Holt, Norfolk NR25 7NQ
☎ Cley (0263) 740362

**GREAT YARMOUTH**

**Charts**
Imray C28, C29
Admiralty 1536, 1543

**Tides**
Lowestoft −0025, Dover −0210 (Haven Bridge − Lowestoft +0030)

**Authorities**
Port Superintendent 21 South Quay, Great Yarmouth.
*Port* VHF Ch 12, 16 (24 hours)
Haven Bridge VHF Ch 12
☎ Gt Yarmouth (0493) 855151 and 663476

**Traffic signals**
Fixed amber by day and no light by night: DO NOT ENTER.
1. Fl.5s: ebb depth of water 4·25m
2. Fl.5s: ebb depth of water 4·5m
3. Fl.10s: ebb depth of water 5·0m
4. Fl.10s: flooding
Less than 1 knot – Amber Lt
More than 1 knot – Mauve Lt

**Leading lights at Brush Quay**
*Front* Oc.3s6m10M
*Rear* F.R.20m6M and Oc.6s7m10M

**Haven Bridge**
*Northbound traffic*
Blue flag or F Bl over F W light on SE buttress exhibited 5 minutes before the bridge due to open.
*Southbound Traffic*
Red flag or F R over F W light on NW buttress exhibited 5 minutes before bridge due to open.

# LOWESTOFT HARBOUR

**Charts**
Imray C28, C29
Admiralty 1536, 1543

**Tides**
Dover −0145

**Radio**
VHF Ch 14, 16 (24 hours).
Docks manager ☎ Lowestoft (0502) 572286
Bridge master ☎ Lowestoft (0502) 574946

**Local regulations**
1. There is a flashing white harbour departure signal light situated below the Oc red light on the S pier lighthouse. When this light is flashing vessels may proceed to sea, but no vessel shall enter the harbour. At all other times vessels may enter but no vessel shall proceed to sea.
2. The outer and inner harbours are connected by a channel crossed by a bridge which carries the main A12 trunk road. This bridge may be opened to shipping at any time and yachts and small craft may also pass through the channel at such times provided prior notice is given to the dock and harbourmaster or bridge operator. Apart from this, provided at least one hour's notice is given, yachts may pass through the channel at the following times:
*Summer* (May to September inclusive)
Mon to Sat 0700, 0930, 1900, 2100 hours
Sunday 0700, 0930, 1400, 1900, 2100 hours
*Winter* (October to April inclusive)
Mon to Sat 0700, 0930, 1900, 2200 hours
Sunday 0800, 0930, 1400, 1900, 2100 hours
3. The regulations controlling the passage of all vessels and small craft through the bridge channel is as follows:
'No vessels shall approach to within 150 yards of the bridge until such time as a green light is exhibited on the N wall of the entrance channel. Whilst such light is exhibited, vessels may, as the case may be enter or leave the inner harbour through the entrance channel.'

4. The inner harbour and Oulton Broad are connected by Mutford Lock, Mutford Lock is operated by Associated British Ports. The maximum size of the craft that can use the lock is LOA 24m, beam 5·4m. The lock is only manned on a part-time basis as follows:
   a. Subject to 48 hours' notice to the docks manager's office every Wednesday at from 1300 to 1600 hours (excluding Bank Holidays).
   b. Subject to 48 hours' notice payment of an additional charge and availability of staff at any other time.
There is a swing bridge at Mutford Lock also operated by Associated British Ports and the arrangements for operating this bridge are the same as for the lock.
The clearance beneath this bridge is 2·1m MHWS or 4·0m MLWS.
5. Trawlers using Lowestoft Harbour sail mainly between 0730 and 0830 hours daily and arrive mainly between the following times:
Mon to Wed inclusive 1200–1245 hours
Thurs 2200–2245 hours
Sat 1100–1130 hours
Sun 0700–0800 hours

Yachts and small craft are advised when possible not to enter or leave the harbour during these times to avoid congestion.

Mariners are also reminded that Lowestoft Harbour radio operates a 24 hour service on VHF. Vessels with VHF radio should at all times contact Lowestoft Harbour radio for instructions before entering harbour or leaving their berth.

Vessels without VHF when entering harbour should proceed with utmost caution. Vessels without VHF when berthed in the harbour and wanting to leave should contact the port control either by telephone 2286 (telephone from the yacht club), or in person.

Harbour dues are payable in respect of all vessels entering the harbour at any point between the seaward entrance and Mutford Lock, both points inclusive. Such dues are payable in respect of each voyage undertaken to or from Lowestoft Harbour limits, which stretch from the sea to Mutford Lock. To 8m £4.00 per day; to 12m £5.00; to 18m £6.00.

**Mutford Lock**
In addition to the harbour dues, charges are applicable on each occasion a vessel passes through Mutford Lock: to 4m £8.00; to 6m £12.00; over 6m £16.00: For the opening of the road bridge to allow the passage of vessels: £8.00 per vessel per opening.
*Hours of opening*
Wednesday 1300 to 1600 hours on 48 hours' prior notice. Charges are also made in respect of passengers and for the opening of the swing bridge to allow the passage of vessels.

**Clubs**
Lowestoft Cruising Club has comprehensive facilities accessible from the club's walk-on, walk-off floating moorings at Lake Lothing. Access is through the bridge or from the Royal Norfolk and Suffolk Yacht Club moorings in the outer harbour.

Waveney and Oulton Broad Yacht Club is an inland club, situated on Oulton Broad. Water access is via Great Yarmouth or Lowestoft (via Mutford Lock, which does not open every day).

Royal Norfolk and Suffolk Yacht Club (☎ Lowestoft (0502) 566726) has a small number of bedrooms available: 4 at £11.00 per night and 2 at £13.00 per night per person, all twins. Breakfast: Continental £2.00; full English £5.00. They publish a most useful guide containing general information for visiting yachts.

## BUOYAGE
### Approaches to Lowestoft and Gt. Yarmouth

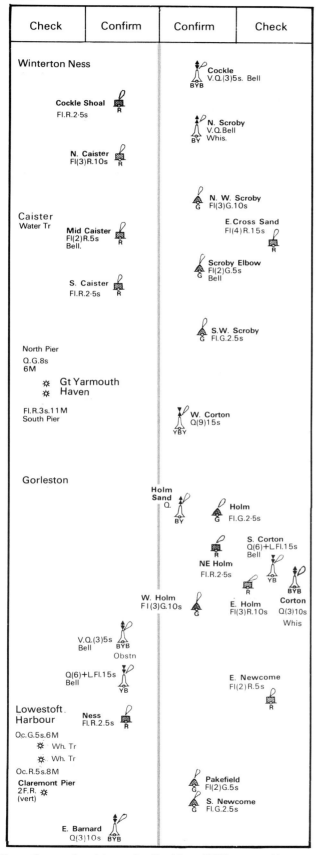

| Check | Confirm | Confirm | Check |
|-------|---------|---------|-------|

Winterton Ness

Cockle Shoal
Fl.R.2·5s

N. Caister
Fl(3)R.10s

Caister
Water Tr

Mid Caister
Fl(2)R.5s
Bell.

S. Caister
Fl.R.2·5s

North Pier
Q.G.8s
6M

Gt Yarmouth
Haven

Fl.R.3s.11M
South Pier

Gorleston

Cockle
V.Q.(3)5s. Bell
BYB

N. Scroby
V.Q.Bell
BY  Whis.

N. W. Scroby
G  Fl(3)G.10s

E.Cross Sand
Fl(4)R.15s
R

Scroby Elbow
Fl(2)G.5s
G  Bell

S.W. Scroby
G  Fl.G.2.5s

W. Corton
Q(9)15s
YBY

Holm
Sand
Q.
BY

Holm
G  Fl.G.2·5s

S. Corton
Q(6)+L.Fl.15s
Bell

NE Holm
Fl.R.2·5s

R

YB

Corton
BYB  Q(3)10s

W. Holm
Fl(3)G.10s

G

E. Holm
Fl(3)R.10s

Whis

V.Q.(3)5s
Bell  BYB
Obstn

Q(6)+L.Fl.15s
Bell  YB

E. Newcome
Fl(2)R.5s
R

Lowestoft
Harbour

Ness
Fl.R.2.5s  R

Oc.G.5s.6M
☀ Wh. Tr
☀ Wh. Tr
Oc.R.5s.8M

Claremont Pier
2F.R. ☀
(vert)

Pakefield
G  Fl(2)G.5s

S. Newcome
G  Fl.G.2.5s

E. Barnard
Q(3)10s  BYB

From the north: pick up the Cockles off Winterton Ness.
From the south: pick up E. Barnard off Benacre Ness.

## SOUTHWOLD HARBOUR
**Charts**
Imray C28, C29
Admiralty 2695
**Tides**
Lowestoft +0035, Dover −0055
**Harbourmaster**
*Radio* VHF Ch 12.
☎ Southwold (0502) 724712
**Trinity House Pilot**
Harbourmaster VHF Ch 12

# III. THE NORFOLK BROADS

The word 'broad' has far more meanings than its antonym 'narrow'; but when in the plural, they both at least deal with waterways. An East Anglia Broad is a large piece of water or lake-like expansion formed by the widening of a river; and that is what we are dealing with here; except and notwithstanding that many of the dikes and little broads are shallow in the extreme and so unbroad that they deserve to be designated narrows.

The Norfolk Broads fall naturally into two geographical areas: North and South, with each being possessed of a *genius loci* all its own, and each being approached by its own entrance. However, some would say there is a most important difference: while the North Broads can be entered through what is known as the front door, namely Great Yarmouth, the South Broads enjoy only the back door access afforded by Lowestoft and Mutford Lock'n'Bridge. It is difficult to know which offers the better deal.

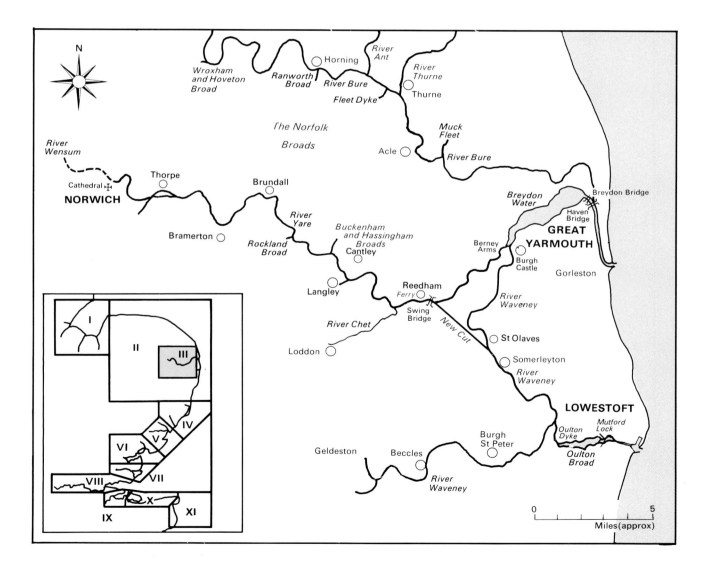

# The North Broads

Situate at the apex of the Rivers Yare and Waveney, at the mouth of Breydon Water, the Berney Arms is a much used staging post. The small community consists of the pub, the telephone kiosk, and the shop. There is also one other major feature: the windmill. These ancient and old-fashioned (but suddenly, now extremely fashionable) power sources can be seen all over Norfolk; and one of the most famous is to be found at Breydon.

Sadly, Broads windmills are mainly in various states and stages of decay; and it is only infrequently that you can find one in anything like decent condition. However, the Berney windmill carries the stamp that marks it out as an ancient monument in the care of the Secretary of State for the Environment. Its 21·0m height makes it stand out as a spectacular example of the genre. Unhappily, it is also a salutary reminder of so much of what we have lost; not only in aesthetic terms but also as sensible and danger-free engines of power.

Next door, the Berney Arms doesn't even try to compete with the grandeur of the monument, although it is itself quite old and occupies a site that probably makes it unique as a pub in the UK, for it cannot be reached by road; only on foot or by boat.

# Breydon Water

Different from most of the actual Broads, which were originally peat diggings, Breydon Water is the natural former sea estuary of the local rivers, before they finally united to rush through the Yare at Yarmouth. At low water, it is mainly one large mud flat, but at any state of the tide it is an impressive spread. Nearly four miles long and over a mile wide, it is to be compared to an inland sea, although the tourist board PR team likes to promote is as a lake. Consisting of some 2000 acres of wetness that always look dramatic, it is surrounded by open country leaving it exposed to the elements. There is a wide channel well marked by posts up to the Berney Arms, but the four miles defy any such disciplining or confining, being pretty impressive in their own right except that the area is much more frequently gloomy than it is pretty. Rough waters can be experienced; and wind against tide even in these 'sheltered' inland waters can make conditions dangerous for standard Broads cruisers.

The waters are more often grey than blue, but in early morning light, when you are steaming nor-easterly into a low rising sun, they can appear as if possessed of a singular spell and a curious air of mystery. I vividly remember once sharing the delight of Breydon Water only with *Valcon*. No boat, no fisherman, no sound other than of our sails. The place was abandoned except for an array of immobile cormorants and shags. In their remarkable, eccentric wing-drying postures they had perched on the channel markers and were displaying more haughty grandeur than the emblems of a Roman legion, which they uncannily resembled. The notion was all the more potent since we were no more than a cable or so from the old Roman fort of Gariannonum.

Nowadays, clearly numbered stakes mark the channel in standard red and green, and there are plenty of warnings to skippers not to deviate. Nevertheless, lots of boats still manage to find the sticky bottom and have to wait for a pluck (if in luck) or a decent tide to wash them off.

And all that is in spite of the recommendations that have been issued in the brochures for at least 25 years:

'Keep strictly in the channel, don't cut corners outside the line of posts even at high water. Don't follow the other fellow who thinks he knows a 'short cut', we've seen three cruisers 'on the putty' for 12 hours because the leader thought he knew. Keep at least 6·0m inside the line of posts.

Before crossing Breydon have your anchor (or mud weight) ready to drop and the rope secured to a cleat, then in the event of engine trouble you will not drift between the posts onto the mud. If you have to anchor, leave room in the channel for coastal vessels to pass.'

As one of the Broads Inspectors (a grand body of persons, these) once said to me: 'On one occasion there were 20 boats all stuck on the mud down the sides of the channel. The deep water channel between them was completely empty. There wasn't a boat in sight where they should have been. It looked like some strange layout for a maritime board game with all the boats poised like watery chessmen before the first move has been made. Talk about a gambit: an opening move that sacrifices a piece!'

It is true that we are now well and truly inland, and the influence of the tides is not the same as in the North Sea or next the Haven Bridge; but throughout the Broads you will find you can make a substantial saving in time and fuel (Henry Ford: 'Time is money!') and at the same time have smoother and more hassle-free trips if you make sure that the tides work in your favour. Tide tables are available at most of the mooring points.

The Norfolk Broads: an example
of the craft that you are likely to
encounter

The mud spit at the junction just before the Berney·Arms extends well out into the river and since there can be as little as 1·2m of water it is only sensible to have decided well in advance which route you are going to take. The starboard turn leads to the Berney Arms on the River Yare and to the first of the many windmills that, sad to say, for the most part are literally littered all over the place; and the port to Burgh Castle on the River Waveney.

## Breydon and Haven Bridges

Not long ago, there was only the Haven bridge between Breydon and the sea. Now there is the new Breydon bridge. The watch listens (as does the Haven bridge) on VHF 16 and 12. They are more than co-operative with visiting skippers: freely offering advice about the best times to arrive and depart for north or southward bent boats; explaining reasons for delays; and giving good notice regarding the exact moment of opening.

The famous Haven Bridge

... where, from time to time, you are allowed through.

Great Yarmouth Haven: The
Town Hall Quay, just south of the
Haven Bridge

*Above*. The well
known no longer
'new' Breydon
Bridge.

I have even heard them calling up some of the more dilatory and tardy boats so they don't miss their chance; and all without rancour. Oh that the same could be said of 'Grate' Yarmouth's Haven bridge; but this is Broads country, and that makes a difference.

Hire boats are not permitted beyond the confluence of the Rivers Bure and Yare; well above the Haven Bridge where the tides are too strong for holiday craft. In fact, there is enough to keep newcomers and novices alike well and truly occupied with the navigation from Breydon into the Bure.

## Navigating through Yarmouth

### GENERAL CAUTION
Passage through Yarmouth needs careful pilotage and correct timing.

The best known spots in Yarmouth on the River Bure are the popular Great Yarmouth yacht station and the Port of Yarmouth Marina. The best time for passing through or mooring there is at slack low water; this is about one and a quarter hours after low water and lasts for about half an hour. The tide turns in the Yare (and in Breydon Water) about an hour before the Bure.

There are two tricky aspects to Yarmouth: navigational and boat handling. The major navigational problem is one of logistics: the draught and height of the vessel meeting the demands of water depth and bridge heights. When there is too much water, you cannot get under the bridges; and when there is not enough water, you touch bottom. Fortunately, most cruisers using the Broads don't have more than a 3m draught. Boat handling skills are needed particularly when passing through and mooring up with a strong tide running. The question therefore is one of headroom under the bridges and strength of current.

If you are coming from the North Broads (the Bure) and wish to cross Breydon Water, you should time your arrival at the yacht station for slack low water. This will allow you to pass through the bridges without difficulty and give you the best of the flood tide to carry you across Breydon.

If you are coming from the South Broads (Breydon Water) you should also time your arrival to coincide with slack low water. This will bring you across Breydon before the flood starts in earnest and you can wait at the yacht station for the tide to turn to take you up the Bure.

However, with sufficiently powerful engines it is possible to make the passage through Yarmouth up to two hours or more after low water and, but only from the south, up to an hour before low water. Trying at other times will only mean a delay of hours waiting for sufficient clearance under the two fixed bridges.

Mooring in Yarmouth can also require extra special care and attention. If you are coming from Breydon, you should do so on the last of the ebb in the Bure. This will enable you to moor easily while facing the current upstream. If you are coming down the Bure, it is best to time your arrival to meet the young flood and use it as your brake. If, however, you are approaching the yacht station and the tide is still running with you, it is essential to go below it and turn (well before the bridges though) so that you can stem the tide to moor. There is a shoal patch almost opposite the yacht station and you can turn there, directing your bows towards the mud. No harm will befall should you touch; in fact that will help turn the boat for you.

Approaching from Breydon, after rounding the large dolphin and leaving it to port, Vauxhall is the first bridge on the Bure. It has 2·5m headroom at MHW. You should keep to the centre, if anything tending a little to starboard because of shoaling to port. Next is the new road bridge with 2·1m headroom at MHW.

Final cautionary note: the dangers of going up or coming down the River Bure at full flood or full ebb either to pass through or to stop cannot be overstated. It is dangerous to oneself and all other users of the river.

# The River Bure

Great Yarmouth has all the facilities any cruising family could want; and a great deal more that are of interest only to a few. In itself it may not be the most quiet and peaceful mooring station on the East Coast, but it does permit access to many berths that are. However, in order to reach any of these, you have to travel a few miles up the River Bure.

You don't get the ethos of the Broads nor have to come to terms with them quite so quickly on the North Broads as you do on the South; and there is much to help you on your way out of Yarmouth. For a few miles going upstream you will find that the banks are clearly marked with black and white posts to help you keep to the channel and in good water; and after a short five up the Bure, you encounter the 'first and last' pub, the Stracey Arms. It is a useful mooring station to get everything in order, whether you are waiting for the tide into Yarmouth or have just left it on the first stage of the great North Broads adventure.

After the village of Stokesby, a few windmills and pubs and Muck Fleet on the starboard hand (not to be navigated) you reach Acle Dike, ten miles from Yarmouth, and with its Hermitage Inn, promisingly redolent of the essence of the Broads. Acle also has a bridge where there are lots of facilities. It is one of the most popular spots on the river, with plenty of mooring spaces, but some of those immediately next the bank can be quite shallow. If, on the way back, you feel at all hesitant about tackling the task of taking your boat into Yarmouth yourself, you can phone Yarmouth from here to arrange a tow. Most anxious folk, however, join up with one or two more experienced boats and hope for the best.

The next place of interest is Upton Dike. It has a slight bar at the mouth and carries an average depth of over 0·1m. Upton village has much to interest those with a taste for the spiritual as well as the spirituous.

# The River Thurne

Another offshoot is next: the River Thurne. One of the most famous (some would say infamous) points of interest is the bridge at Potter Heigham, some three miles from the mouth. But first there is the tiny village of Thurne itself and then the delightfully named Womack Water and Ludham Dike. They are all worth a visit, but you will need to be careful about navigating the narrows.

The famous Potter Heigham bridge needs care not only because of its restricted headroom (2·0m at the centre) but also due to the width and curve of the arch itself; and, just to make matters more complicated, when there is any wind about, there can be a tunnel/funnel effect enough to disturb the passage of slow moving modest draught vessels. Newcomers should make use of the professional help that is always available free of charge to hire boat users. Apart from its bridge, Potter H is nothing but charming.

Just after the village of Martham (to starboard) is Candle Dike (to port) which leads to Hickling Broad. At first, there is a misleadingly wide stretch of water called Heigham Sound. Only its narrow channel is navigable, however. Then comes a fork: to starboard is Meadow Dike which leads on to Horsey Mere (yes, yet another one) and through the (Waxham) New Cut to Bridge Farm.

At this point you are really in the heart of National Trust and Broads principality. Life is real, life is earnest; for the dedicated conservationists: in every bush hides a bird if not a bird watcher. Only small craft can turn easily below the bridge in the Cut. Facilities can be obtained back at the Staithe at the east end of Horsey, and anchoring is permitted.

Hickling is a large broad, extending to some 300 acres. It is quite exposed, with little high ground around and little more than 0·6m of water for much of its extent. It is navigable only within the marked channels and is also very much nature country. Among other forms of life, it is blessed with the famous Hickling sponge weed. There are some moorings at the Pleasure Boat Inn.

The last stretch of the River Thurne after Candle Dike leads past the well known swing ferry bridges and directly to Martham Broad (small) and the quiet village of West Somerton, where you can moor by the banks. For seagoing folk, it is only a few minutes' walk from Somerton or Horsey Mere to Winterton Ness.

## Bure again

Back on the Bure, it is not long before you pass the remains of St Benedict's (Benet's) Abbey and reach the South Walsham Fleet Dike and the associated Broads which are renowned as being amongst the prettiest, and are certainly a miniature delight not to be missed.

## The River Ant

Soon after Fleet Dike, on the opposite bank, comes the River Ant. This is the narrowest of the three North Broads rivers, and the one that offers the quietest experiences, twisting routes and channels and remote havens in beautiful scenery.

Just inside the mouth is to be found Mill Brig Reach, often known as Little Duffers. Not far ahead, after a dramatic 'S' bend is Ludham Bridge (2·5m at MHW). Small beer and similar stores can be obtained here.

Above Ludham Bridge, the river meanders in a northeasterly direction and the scenery becomes even more attractive as you cruise through wooded banks, meadows and reed beds with the occasional ruined windmill to add sombre dignity to the locations. Boat progress is more than likely to be well suited to the landscape: slow and easy.

The small village of Irstead comes just before Barton Broad. This broad is special in two respects: first, others are approached via a dike, whereas this one has its river running right through it; and second, according to local lore, Nelson learned to sail here. A left turn, away from the main channel, will take you to the Old Lime Kiln Dike by the village of Neatishead where there is a staithe. The village centre with the usual facilities, is only minutes away.

## Sutton and Stalham

At the west head of the main channel is the small village of Barton Turf; another quiet staithe with modest facilities. The easterly channel is the main course of the Ant, and this leads to another parting of the ways at Big Bog.

To starboard is Sutton Broad, now navigationally no more than its dike channel, but still a most pleasing place, with an attractive mooring. Sutton is believed to have been habitable and hospitable since the days of the Anglo Saxons in the AD 500s. It is possible to sit on deck at night and be convinced nothing has changed. To port is Stalham Dike. Stalham possesses far fewer moorings than one would expect bearing in mind the many facilities it has to offer.

## Ant End

Above and beyond Big Bog, the River Ant twists and turns before passing the mill at Hunsett and then moving on to Wayford Bridge, where there is an eponymous village. There are facilities and moorings, and above the bridge the North Walsham and Dilham Canal is (almost: take care) navigable for just over two miles to the first lock at Honing. It is shallow, and to be navigated only by those with an obsession for cruising every last dishcloth-full of water. For the rest of us, Tonnage Bridge (the first one in the canal) is the head of navigation of River Ant and its bits and pieces.

## More Bure

After the diminutive charms of the Ant, the Bure, itself no expansive waterway, appears by comparison to be vast. Its next port of call is the Ranworth Dam (misnomer for Dike) that leads to Malthouse Broad. The dredging was completed only as recently as 20 years ago, and the staithe has been popular ever since, suffering from the same kind of weekend congestion as Yarmouth, IoW. Its facilities are modest but the location is first rate and anchoring is most pleasant. Ranworth Broad proper is chained off and is a bird sanctuary. Another quiet spot nearby, for bird watchers is the tiny mouth of Cockshoot Broad.

Next come bends and more bends, and round each you are likely to find stunning examples of *dolce vita* architecture. This is Horning country, where the village is divided into two parts: Upper and Lower Street. This place is often described as the prettiest on the Broads. It is a popular spot for visitors by road and river alike. However, its appeal must be restricted to those who have a penchant for socialising in style and at length.

The Swan Hotel, with its grand timber and stucco facade, occupies the prime position on the sweeping bend of the river. It reigns supreme over all it surveys both up and downstream. A similar attitude is to be found in the skippers of the commercial trip boats: some of them Southern Comfort type riverboats, but with crews that are seemingly unaware of any old world southern courtesy to man, woman or boat. Visiting skippers be warned.

Between Horning and Wroxham, there are three broads to visit. First, Little Hoveton, which, as its name suggests, is a modest affair. Some of it is very shallow, but anchoring is pleasant. The inner broad is private and chained off. Second is Salhouse Broad, another small water, but navigable with care; and with plenty of trees to provide a good shade for Broads' summers.

Third is probably the best known, Wroxham Broad; a much larger lake, being nearly a mile long and 250 yards wide, giving it an expanse of 80 acres of water. It is the headquarters of the Norfolk Broads Yacht Club. Anchoring and fishing are allowed for a fee. There is little rise and fall of water here, so there is no anxiety about getting hung up, afloat or shoresides since the whole area is a thoroughly relaxing one; especially away from its socialising centre – and even more so out of season.

The dreamy picture book look by Coltishall.

## And so to Wroxham and Hoveton

And so to the hub of it all. It was here, at the end of the 19th century, that boat hiring on the Broads was born. Ever since, this has been the heart and heartland of Broads cruising. Hoveton is famous for its shopping centre, catering more and more these days for gongoozlies and sightseers; while Wroxham has two claims to fame. The first is its insistence on the possession of the world's largest village stores; and the second is the world's most bumped into bridge. The road bridge is known far and wide in Broads cruising circles. It has hardly more than 2·0m headroom and is responsible for more headaches and bruised bumpheads than any other on the circuit. It is no doubt the proximity of so many hostelries and a general ambience of festive conviviality that distracts the minds of skippers and crew alike.

Although unquestionably popular, it is not extreme in the manner of Horning, although the changeover days for hire craft can be pretty grim. All the shifting from cars to boats and vice versa can make life hectic even for the would-be bystander who may only want to play Pooh Sticks, somewhat perilously, from the bridge.

There are all the facilities you can want (and probably a few you can live without) together with some very pretty stretches of river. The Hotel Wroxham is one of the few in this neck of the Broads that does not cast you from its moorings if you do not immediately book in half a dozen hands for dinner. The rise and fall is negligible.

Upstream of Wroxham Bridge, Belaugh is halfway to Coltishall. The river is unostentatiously pleasant and Belaugh has a few facilities and a splendid church. Coltishall is an attractive, straggling village often referred to as the gateway to Broadland. Moorings are available, and the village centre is a few minutes walk away. This is the veritable head of navigation of the Bure, although it rises much further away at Melton Constable.

You cannot get further away from Yarmouth on the Bure, and nothing could be further from it in appearance or atmosphere; nor could you be further away from Norwich, in entirely different senses. But they, and all the fascinating bits and pieces in between, all combine to create that unique feature of East Anglia, the Norfolk Broads.

## Lowestoft

On the one hand, there is no doubt at all that Lowestoft is not only the door with 'Welcome' on the mat but also has by far the better entrance; being accessible at all times and with no attendant hazard, features not met further north until Grimsby. It can also boast an excellent yacht club and all the facilities that any cruising man, woman or child may crave, desire or pine for.

## Mutford Lock

On the other hand, the passage from Lowestoft into the South Broads is restricted, if not indeed inhibited and impeded by the notorious lock and bridge at Mutford. The lock, built at Oulton 150 years ago, proudly boasts gates that face each way and can open 'at all states of the tide'. Today, this is something of an empty claim since it makes no difference which way they are facing. They still open only once a week.

Skippers are asked to give at least 48 hours notice to the dock master's office before they will be permitted to pass through between 1300 and 1600 hours on a Wednesday excluding Bank Holidays. The discipline of notice, time and day is not the only one to deter: the prices have reached heights attainable only by the very rich. It will cost you something over £44·00 to go in and out with nothing bigger than a 21' cruiser and that doesn't include the daily harbour dues of £3.40 (under 25'), £4·25 (under 35') and £5·10 (35'–60').

For years, schemes and stratagems to bring together all the interested contingents and factions have been mooted so that lock and bridge could be brought more into use. In spite of the obvious appeal (whether being convenience, finance, utility or just plain merit) so far it has all been to no avail; and the current view from the Lowestoft harbour office is, 'It has all been in the air for some time now, and it is still all in the air if not perhaps all over the place.'

However, Mutt and Jeff affairs apart, Lowestoft must be an attractive starting point for the South Broads. Shoresides it is an intriguing place: it has the most easterly pub in Britain but not the best beer. It is a mixture of old and new (some very ancient, some very novel); noisy ribaldry and gentle gentry; beer swilling, swelling and swallowing plebs, and brandy and soda blue bloods; as well as some of the best and the worst food in all England. It is worth knowing that you can buy fish caught that night at the dock. And for those with a yen for *la vie sportive*, it offers some pretty heavy surf bathing in steeply crashing breakers on a close and shelving shore.

Yachtsmen usually find a berth in the South Basin, where the dominating feature in every way used to be the nostalgic ambience of the Royal Norfolk and Suffolk Yacht Club: a genuine and charismatic relic, redolent of those dear dead days beyond recall, when royals sailed, afternoon tea was taken with a string quartet and serving crews were paid to stand and serve and know their place. A pearl not to be missed even at any price; and their visitors' fees were never one new pence behind the modern cost of living.

## Oulton Broad

So, with Lowestoft's eccentricities, Lake Lothing's singularities and Mutford's marvels left behind, what lies ahead? First is one of the best known and largest of these lake-like expansions known as Broads: Oulton Broad. It covers about 130 acres and apart from one or two clearly obvious shoal patches it is all navigable.

It is also one of the busiest of the lakeland centres, managing to combine some the charms of rurality with access to enough socialising to satisfy even the most convivial of crew members. All facilities are close to hand, with plenty of places to moor; and, of course, all the attractions of Lowestoft are nearby. However, no serious cruising or sailing can be undertaken within its confines, although it is a pleasant enough spot for young persons' water sports.

Oulton Broad is connected to the rest of the Broads by the short stretch of waterway known as Oulton Dyke, which is one of the busiest 'roads' on the Broads. It is not really suitable for mooring, although it is pleasantly situated apparently in the middle of vast marshes. The only serious drawback is the lack of decent access through Mutford Lock and the bridges.

## The River Waveney to Beccles, Geldeston and Bungay

The Dyke leads to the first major river to be encountered, the River Waveney. At the junction you can turn to port or starboard: the short reach of the first will take you to Beccles, while the second will lead you on to what will be a long expedition to Norwich and all stations in between.

The River Waveney is tidal as far as Beccles, which is 28 miles above its mouth, and is accessible to craft with no more than six feet draught. On the way, the first edifice to catch the eye is St Mary's Church, with an eponymous reach and staithe. Mooring is not easy here, but that is no problem since it is no distance to Burgh St Peter, on the west bank near the junction that leads to Oulton Broad. Close by is the Waveney River Centre and its associated hostelry, the Waveney Inn. There is a large mooring basin, plenty of riverside moorings, a shop, restaurant and boatyard. Quite large craft are to be found moored and cruising here.

A little further on, by Castle Mill and Reach, there is a much quieter spot for those who want peace rather than a piece of the action; but care must be taken not to be caught out by thinking there is always deep water at the banksides. Reeds frequently disguise silt and a foul bottom.

The environs change little for the run into Beccles, where there are all round services and facilities, plenty of corporation utilities, deep water moorings and a 5 mph speed limit. The A146 crosses the river here, and this means that air draught is restricted to 2m at the very best of 'low' (which is never very low) water. Craft of up to 1·8m will have little difficulty with regard to water draught. There is no strong tidal effect at this point on the river, and a rise and fall about 0·9m. Beccles is a busy but nevertheless quite charming spot.

It is difficult to imagine that Beccles was once a famous fishing port. It is the kind of place where you will want to spend a few days meandering. In a small café, I overheard, 'We came here on holiday and just fell in love with the place. So, as soon as we could, we moved and bought a house here.' I know they were not alone in what they felt, nor in what they had done.

Smaller craft can navigate for a further four miles to the derelict lock at Geldeston. In fact, it is a pleasant trip by dinghy through the Barsham marshes, with plenty of hostelries en route. This is an amiable village, much visited by artists, tourists and anglers, all of whom have a positive bent for gongoozling.

It is possible, with light craft capable of portage, to go still further up the river, for the Waveney actually goes as far as Bungay; but Beccles is the head of navigation for all intents and purposes.

# The River Yare to Reedham

Meanwhile, back at Oulton Dyke, we take the turn to the right, and follow the channel for a mile or two of easy if not demandingly scenic waterway. First port of call is Somerleyton, famous for its swing bridge (2·5m clearance when closed) and Ripplecraft's boatyard, where Christopher Cockerell developed the hovercraft. It is a small bubbling community, where everyone knows or wants to know who is who and what is what. A nice enough spot for a couple of nights, although not over-blessed with sophisticated mooring arrangements, and with bankside depths no better than a metre. It is wise to exercise caution near the piers for the current can run uncommonly briskly at this point.

Next comes the small community of St Olaves which sits by the junction of the river and Haddiscoe New Cut. At one time, its bridge used to open, but was replaced by the present fixed one in 1961. It permits an air draught of 7·0m. The village offers basic boating and domestic facilities, but little in the way of grand moorings, and the banksides can have no more than a metre of water. A metre is also just about the size of rise and fall of tide; but, unexpectedly, there are one or two spots, especially near the bridge, where local currents are much endowed with eddies.

The River Waveney continues to Burgh Castle, where it joins the River Yare at the confluence with Breydon Water. From St Olaves to Burgh Castle and the Berney Arms, which is approachable only by water or rail, is only four miles. The other choice is that of the 'new' Haddiscoe Cut which will take you to the swing bridge just below Reedham a few miles up the river from Breydon Water.

So, leaving behind the Ferry House, Duke's Head, Crown and the other charms of Somerleyton and Olaves, we move on to the novel experience of Haddiscoe New Cut. This straight section was dug as part of the Lowestoft to Norwich navigation, and considerably shortens the journey from Norwich to Beccles as well as avoiding the strongish tides that can be encountered by Breydon Water.

Just after the New Cut joins the Yare (watch out for shoal patches on the spits and coasters round the bends) you reach Reedham, extremely well protected by the railway bridge below and the chain ferry above. The bridge is something of an antiquity and is operated by characters (and gentlemen) who are of an old fashioned spirit, enjoying nothing more than swinging their beloved bridge. Eminently capable, they believe in the personal touch, and will do anything they can to help waterborne navigators, be they regular coaster skippers or first-time cruisers.

There is a large sign telling when the bridge will next open, and, in addition, there are flag signals: No flag – Bridge open; One red flag – Bridge will open soon; Two red flags – Bridge will not open. Recent causes of the bridge not opening were being struck by lightning and overcome by an autumn heatwave. On such occasions a keeper will come out personally to signal and shout the news with relish.

The famous chain ferry upstream of the village is also extraordinary, usually busy with its perpetual loads of holidaymakers in, on and around motor cars. It is more than wise to wait upon the movements of this monster, for its pleasure is to grind slowly and, like the wheels of God, to grind exceeding small. It crosses with all the puissance of an African Queen and just as inexorably as well. I have never seen anyone actually mown down by it, but it still looks like the king of the river.

# Reedham

Between the two sits the village of Reedham. I think it is a splendid place and always try to make sure I have a few days to spare whenever I am near. Although it is a tourist-busy spot with comprehensive facilities, it somehow manages to absorb us all without losing its quiet charm.

Part of the village is at sea level, on the waterfront, and part on the high rise behind. No visitor should leave without taking a walk up any of the short hill-lanes to the upper village, where you will find an almost separate community consisting of exceptional people and places. Wherever you should chance to wander, you will hear the mellow melodious tones of mannerly Norfolk calmly inhibiting or absorbing the brash voices of sightseers.

In fact, Reedham is divided, like Caesar's Gaul, into three parts: the horticulture, husbandry and locals' shops of the top village by Witton Green; the boating-cum-tourist *mélange* of the waterfront; and those relics of the industrial revolution, the railway station and chain ferry.

While everyday shopping needs can be met on the waterfront, it is worth the short walk up the hill to Lidstone's store, which has been revamped and expanded into something spacious and gracious. In addition, it is well-stocked with fresh goods. Next door is the ancient Red Brick House, with, from time to time, a red-as-bricks keeper of its portals.

Reedham is a favourite port of call by land and water; by foot, motor or sail.

Reedham's diminutive ferry: where the skipper's courtesy to other craft is often the cause of local road traffic jams.

Only a few paces away is an equally red brick and stone decorated classic Methodist chapel, built in 1881. Immediately next door, modest and retiring, is Blanche's, one of the best miniature eating places in the country. They have only a few tables and one kind of service: man and wife personal. Their notice reads, 'This is a small restaurant so booking is essential.' Not only is all their food freshly excellent with delectable puddings, but their value-for-money-rating is almost unknown these days, especially in a tourist-dense neck of the woods. Blanche's deserves to be renowned.

Nor should any cruising man fail to visit the Sanderson Marine Craft boatyard. They are boatbuilders of the old school trying to survive in the new school without losing skills or integrity. While they are no longer building wooden boats, they are always happy to while away the moments talking wood'n'boat, and indeed taking your booking for a holiday hire boat which is nowadays their main business. They all have a sense of humour that can take you unawares; and their charges are almost as old-fashioned as their craftsmanship. It is a family business and they will be as pleased to take you as a client as you will be pleased with the bill they will present.

I always make Reedham my first stop whenever I am in these parts. It is accommodating, relaxing and entirely symptomatic of the best of the Broads.

# The Chet to Loddon

After Reedham, the tiny River Chet a few cables up on the port hand leads to the tiny haven of Loddon. By the junction of the rivers is the famous Hardley Cross (AD 1676) on the bank. It marks the lower boundary of the city of Norwich and stands as a reminder of all the ancient disputes between Norwich and Yarmouth; and not forgetting those that still persist. It is said to have been the place where the officials met to resolve their annual differences.

It is a fine and easy place to visit in a shoal draught craft, always accessible for craft say around 1·0m, but at 2·0m, you must needs await spring tides and work them properly. The Chet can also be tricky for craft with LOA of more than 10·0m, for it is narrow and has some very tight bends. It is not always possible to see what is coming round the corner and turning is hopeless. In addition, there are the Hardley marshes to beware of: they used to be well drained but now they flood, and cross currents can be set up. In spite of these obstacles however, the town of Loddon is worth the hassle, for it a small treasure of a place.

# Back on the Yare to Brundall and Surlingham

Hardley Dike, just downstream of Cantley, is a miniature rivulet. Extremely pretty, it is marked by a long line of masts beyond an entrance bearing a forbidding notice of foreboding: 'Hardley Dike. No facilities. Difficult to turn. 3 mph.' Clearly territorial rights are exercised strongly in this neck of most attractive backwoods and waters.

In keeping with the picturesque ambience just before you get to the Cantley Bends, there is a small reminder of riparian undertakings at their proud best. There is a modest group of private boat berths on the bank, backed by verdant gardens that in turn front a classic red brick country cottage. Setting off the scene stand a Victorian street lamp standard and a lion rampant in white stone.

Next is something else, being the landscape blot of the Cantley sugar beet factory that dominates the surroundings: smell, sight and sound, it has the lot. Nor is it alone in ugliness: there could hardly be a greater contrast between the cared for spruceness of Hardley Dike and the sad remnants of once splendid windmill and other derelict farm buildings. In the sugar beet season, the near-nauseating odours advertise its presence more effectively that any placard ever could.

There is another side; for the stark, unsugary style of British Sugar PLC does serve one aesthetic purpose, rendering the unattractive exterior of the next door pub almost pleasing by comparison. Situate right on the bend, it is a dark red brick tiled edifice with the predictable appellation 'The Red House'. It occupies a magnificent site, commanding views up and down the river. Surrounded by a court of minor establishments, it is utterly devoted to the fast food syndrome.

After this near grandiose spread, there is the relief of Langley Dike, a shallow quiet spot with easy mooring at the entrance, and an entirely ungrand legend indicating the presence of the appropriately named Wherry hostelry.

Rockland Broad is a miniature affair consisting of the Fleet and Short Reach. It is liable to silting, and there is not a lot of water to be found anywhere around. There is a 3 mph limit and a pub at the head of the navigation. Canoeing is not permitted in the reaches since the area is a nature reserve. You will meet lots of barnacle and Canada geese and grebe – and, of course, the omnipresent coot & co. Unlimited.

The most popular spot in the area is by the site of Buckenham ferry, for which there a large sign but no sight. The reason is the Beauchamp Arms that will hove into view as a relatively mini mansion, heralded by the masts of the Buckenham Sailing Club where there is a small lay-by and a large hard standing boat park. The Beauchamp also has a useful lay-by and a neat stretch of good moorings put down to strong grass. However, they do not drain as efficiently or as quickly as they might and you may have to have recourse to wellies. Nearby, there is plenty of good fishing and good pub grub; and you don't have to catch your own for it to be fresh.

Rockland Broad and the Dikes are mainly remote encounters; quite different from Brundall, which is the next big port on the agenda. But before it takes over, the Strumpshaw Steam Museum is not to be missed. In particular, its old chimney and weathered brick outbuildings are magnificent.

The first proper hint of Brundall is the imposing edifice of Coldham Hall, an old pub with moorings that are good and free. Its environs are made up of a large marquee, small waterside boathouses, modest wooden buildings and trim sailing craft. Next door are boatbuilders W. J. Breach & Sons and the Coldham Hall boatyard. Nearby, a black and yellow board shows the flow of the tide, for the motions of the North Sea, distant as they may seem from this inland retreat, still reach effectively though not disturbingly up here.

Brundall itself, afloat or shoresides, is a sophisticated and urban, if not entirely urbane locale, extremely well suited to its preoccupation with expensive bungalow sites, mooring plots and GRP cruisers, the best known of which are the famous Brooms. Nor can you miss the large notice advertising Brundall Marina: 'Private moorings berths available, and the nearby massive picture of a heron on a board.

Brundall does not have one focal essence; it has two. One is generated by the majority of the buildings which are waterside homes, with their near-permanently fixed living sculptures of ducks. Technicolour ducks in various kinds of china, pot or clay, flying up walls may be the unacceptable sign of kitsch; but ducks on the front lawn (no back parlour insults here), apparently tethered like geese for *foie gras*, hint at the upwardly mobiles.

The second comes, not flying, but floating. Sooner or later you will encounter the Brooms, afleet, in harness or just plain solo. Except that Brooms do not tend to come plain, penny or otherwise. They are very much tuppence coloured prospects and seem very much at their ease when rounding the downstream corner approach to their birthplace and Valhalla, Brundall. The big bend is dominated by a film location-type mansion which fittingly overlooks and seems to bless the expensive craft that pass beneath. Brundall has plenty of everything, including the very best of *la dolce expensi vita*, and knows how to value it and charge for it accordingly.

Central to Brundall, and just off the fairway, is the long, low red brick building of the fuel station, supermarket and chandlery. They offer a vast range of goods and goodies and provide excellent service with a smile. Sometimes, boaters' antics can provoke the raised eyebrow but seldom the raised voice and never the frosty reception. It is a pleasure to be assisted by ladies and gentlemen whose welcome is as warm as their patience is perpetual.

Close by is Surlingham. It is situate on a pleasant stretch of the river near two sharp bends and the Ferry House Inn. It has a small broad, most of which is too shallow for navigation, but there is a channel that leads to Bargate Water. The surrounding property is owned by the Norfolk Naturalists' Trust. Some sunken wrecks have been marked in their time. The island offers a dramatic contrast to the village with its almost untouched but certainly unbuilt upon natural glory. The route is through the soft underbelly of Brundall, as it were, coming out on the other side near to Coldham Hall.

There is one more hostelry before the last leg and that is the Ferry House, with stern-to moorings that require the mud-bag-anchor treatment. It is not quite Mediterranean in climate, but the mooring and the tides are quite on a par.

# Bramerton Woods End to Norwich

A little further up the river comes one of the prettiest, sleepiest settings on the river: Bramerton Woods End. The first views of it come complete with manse-like mansions in the hills; and, at the water's edge, 'desirable properties in rural surroundings'. The houses seem to get better year by year.

It is tranquil, with sandy hills and trees. People tend to keep their own counsel on this stretch with the result that no one comes calling unless invited. It is a particularly attractive and popular spot with usually enough room along the free parish staithe for all those who want to stay, since most people seem to moor a little further along, to be that much nearer the convivial local only a few cables upstream. Apart from the one pub and the open grassed spaces, wild life, wooded hills and cruisers, there is little else for miles.

Then comes a mini marina with an intriguing assortment of craft from midget runabouts to large seagoing vessels, power boats and all kinds of genuine sailing vessels. Next door are the contrasts of the dark and sinister shapes from the commercial barge yard and a dainty cottage complete with rose-bedecked door. Opposing it all is a popular picnic site with easy road access, ensuring a constant flow of single person propelled floats of all kinds – many quite unimaginable but nevertheless there, if not in the flesh then in the plastic.

We are now not far from Norwich. But before its pleasures are to be enjoyed there are two impediments and one attraction to be negotiated. The attraction is the tiny community of Thorpe separated from the main drag by the New Cut which was dug so that the railway could cross the river twice without the need for bridges. It consists of a small, nearly self-contained boating community with plenty of facilities and charm, both quaint and vulgar. It is popular with those smaller boats who can negotiate its narrow street without difficulty so it not always possible to get a berth for more than a very short stay. Sadly, Thorpian pleasures are denied to all except those who can drop their overall height to 1·8m.

After Thorpe's small twinned bridges Norwich proclaims itself, or is proclaimed, by seeking fingers of pylons and towering power chimneys and the legend, 'Welcome to Norwich. A fine city. Yacht station ½ mile Ahead.'

The impediments are in fact more bridges: yet another railway bridge; the Carrow road bridge; and the new fixed bridge (with 10·7m clearance) that is part of the city bypass system at Postwick.

Operative bridge masters keep a listening watch on VHF Ch 12, but while the keepers are more than efficient and user friendly, the system itself is not. The British Rail bridge is the offender: openings are now regulated by what are known in the authorised jargon as 'windows of opportunity'. Men and boats alike are made to wait upon what seem to be the caprices of BR hands on, humanoid or computeroid. It is worth a call on VHF, well ahead of your approach, to check the next opening times or you could be in for a long wait. You could anyway, because the bridges are prone to sticking, and BR can't seem to crack that one as yet.

Carrow Bridge is an impressive sight when it is lifting, especially at rush hour. Its traffic signals are: Red flag – downstream right of way; Blue flag – upstream right of way. The bridge can be contacted on VHF Ch 12, as can the coasters on the Yare and the pleasure cruiser *Regal Lady* when she plies from Norwich to Brundall. It seems silly that there is no radio contact between the road and railway bridge keepers. The keeper at Carrow is co-operative and will open almost on the second of any agreed plan.

While waiting, most probably by Colman's, it is worth noting that their riverside factory buildings have overhangs that can seriously damage the health of masts and rigging. If you have to wait here, do not miss the opportunity to monitor the radio traffic of the Carrow and Trowse Bridge men. Their exchanges rival many a music hall duo.

Nevertheless, the keepers do the best they can to mitigate the worst excesses of the system, and there is a notice in the office at Carrow Bridge: 'By law, vessels have priority over road traffic, and the council is liable to a penalty if a vessel is detained by the bridge being closed.' Nice one!

Visitors can find a secure berth upstream of Carrow, just round the bend and the turning bay for the commercial coasters that frequently come to Norwich. You are then surrounded by the massive structures of the station, the hotel and Foundry Bridge. When I first brought *Valcon* to Norwich in the late 1970's, men were hard at work de-tiling roofs along a short stretch of this part of the river. When I last visited in the early 1990s men were still de-tiling roofs along the same stretch.

*Above*. Norwich has a fairly depressing approach for such a fine city.
*Above right*. Norwich: Carrow road bridge.

Norwich: rail bridge

# Norwich: A fine city

This will be the head of navigation for many, since the headroom is restricted to 2·4m at best; remember, the river is still tidal at this point. However, the restriction is no deprivation since the yacht station just upstream of the bridge is a liability to the reputation of Norwich. It has none of the benefits that one has come to require of a marina facility operated for gain.

A berth just below the Foundry Bridge on the starboard hand puts you almost in the middle of Norwich. Close by is the recently redesigned and refurbished railway station. It is splendid in its refound, restored glory; making it even more sickening that the yacht station is still as grotty as ever. The city fathers have decided to advertise the virtues and magnetism of Norwich by erecting on the roadside at each entrance the same legend: 'NORWICH: A FINE CITY', and it is treated as the capital of East Anglia.

Although the riverside siting of these is unsightly, and although there are still those who refuse to accept the place as the capital of East Anglia, I, for one, can find nothing to criticise in such claims. The custodians and guardians have transported their city into the 20th century with a balanced mixture of restored old edifices and heritage-aware new ones that produces an architecture that is both tasteful and functional. In particular, the many red brick features of Norwich are splendiferous to behold, and come in so many shapes and sizes that eyes, mind and spirit need almost a full cruising holiday to occupy them.

Not only are there the predictable facilities you would expect from a city of the size and status of Norfolk; but there are also many useful contacts for seagoing yachtsmen that you would certainly not expect to come across so far inland.

It is possible to go further upstream on the River Yare. In fact, its source is in East Dereham, some 12 miles north of Norwich. When it reaches the city, it is joined at Trowse by the Wensum before it flows through the centre on its way to the sea.

## The Waveney and the Yare to Breydon

If we follow it, retracing our wakes, we get back to the point where we left the Haddiscoe New Cut. Here you have a choice of routes to reach Breydon Water. One takes you along the River Waveney from St Olaves to Burgh Castle, some four miles or so; and the other from Reedham along the River Yare to the Berney Arms, about the same distance.

The Waveney has little to offer en route except the quiet of tall reeds and banks with hardly anything to see but the odd windmill and the high ground on which stands Burgh castle. There are plenty of mooring and cruising facilities, but the paramount attraction must be the remains of the old five acre Roman fort of Gariannonum with its walls amazingly well preserved after nearly 2000 years.

The trip from Reedham is altogether different: the Waveney is a small fry leisure waterway while the Yare is a heavily used commercial river. On the Waveney you should be on the lookout for the kind of life that is found in *The Wind In The Willows*; while on the Yare you need to be on the *qui vive* for 400 ton coasters plying their trade, and just to help confuse the issue, you may also come across one of the classic wherries in full sail. The stretch is not without its hazards, as the notice boards proclaim: 'No mooring'; 'Submerged rocks and piles'; 'Danger of being hit by coasters'. Happily, all the professionals more than understand the ways of leisure craft, whether in the hands of wise and cautious skippers or cowboy neophytes.

At the junction with Breydon Water, we find a typical Broads picture postcard holiday snap scene: a windmill and a pub; and whatever your boating experience or your kind of craft, sooner or later you are likely to end up sampling the wares of the Berney Arms; everyone does, if only the once. It is the staging station between North and South Broads, as well as being the gateway to the North Sea via Great Yarmouth. 'We'll spend a night here and foray into Breydon Water at the crack of dawn.' That's what everyone says; but most are still sleeping it off when the sun is well past the yardarm. For some people, the Broads means only boats; for some it means only birds; but for many it means boats, birds, booze and the holiday of a lifetime.

### GENERAL CAUTION

There is a rise and fall of tide throughout the Broads from 0·6m to 1·8m dependent upon how far you are from Yarmouth. Always allow sufficient slack on your ropes: getting hung up is no fun on your boat or on your nerves.

# IV. THE ORE & ALDE AND THE DEBEN

## Approaches

Leaving astern Southwold's water tower, its church, its old lighthouse and pier that sticks out like a long black finger, and making southward for the Ore, there are some points to note.

First, the most outstanding landmarks: recent developments with regard to the A,B and C (and no doubt ultimately D to Z) Sizewell power stations make them conspicuously unmistakable. The Orfordness light always has been.

Second, prevailing sea conditions: both Dunwich and Sizewell Banks can play up with frequently troubled waters, and there can be a nasty short sharp chop off Orfordness, even when the rest of the area is more or less calm.

Since my first wary essays round the area, I have been able to establish personally that there is a safe water passage, close in, all the way round from Southwold to Orford Haven. However, a wary watch must be kept not just for the standard crab pot markers and their gear, but also for the massive array of some that are laid with cable lengths just on or just below the surface.

Also to be watched out for, although for very different reasons, are the light brown 'cliffs' of Dunwich and their sparse, indeed scarcely grassy, banks. Steam past them slowly and reverentially, for immediately below your keel may well be the remains of our early ancestors, their forests, churches, castles, their feudal domains and their walled cities. Ever since the natural disasters of the 13th and 14th centuries much of the history, heritage and residuals of the domain of Dunwich have been dispersed over this sea bed. Sadly, it is extremely unlikely that much will ever be traced in the frequently inclement conditions, and the murky waters that often restrict visibility to a few feet.

The exact location of the ancient sunken city of Dunwich is about a quarter of a mile out to sea in seven fathoms in Dunwich Bay, between the Dunwich Bank and the Dunwich Cliffs. During the time of Henry II (1154–1189) the city of Dunwich was probably in its prime. One 18th century historian credits the city with 52 churches, chapels, religious houses and hospitals, one king's palace, one bishop's seat, one mayor's mansion, one mint, as many top-ships as churches, and no fewer windmills. Its forest extended to a point seven miles southwest of the city and probably stretched many more miles to the east before falling victim to the sea. It was surrounded by a great wall within which were set massive brazen gates.

Today, there is little to remind anyone of that past glory and pride: a history going back to the times before the Druids. It seems, somewhat sadly, that it will not be long before all that is left of even the present modern, condensed Dunwich, moved inland centuries ago, will be memories and legends. The cliffs crumble and fall casualty and sacrifice to the inexorable demands of the harshly elemental North Sea.

Aldeburgh is demandingly eye-catching from seaward, with its variegated houses hugging the waterline in one colourful, charming and rustic array. They add the final scenic touches to a model illustration of our domesticated coasts at their very best.

Even more eye-catching is the 28·0m tall white tower at Orfordness. Its light may no longer burn as bright as it used to, nor does it any longer occupy the prime place it once had in coastal navigation, but it is still a significant symbol and important landmark for all East Coast yachtsmen. Londoners may believe that Watford Gap marks the beginning of rule and reign by North England savages; but all coastal cruising folk know that the light at Orfordness marks the end of the North Sea at its most threatening, and the beginning of the solace and succour of calmer waters.

Before reaching the Ore and the Alde, it is quite intriguing to look across the flatland to Havergate Island. You can easily see the castle ruins, yet while you still have miles to travel and corners to turn before you reach it, the river itself is only cables from the shore.

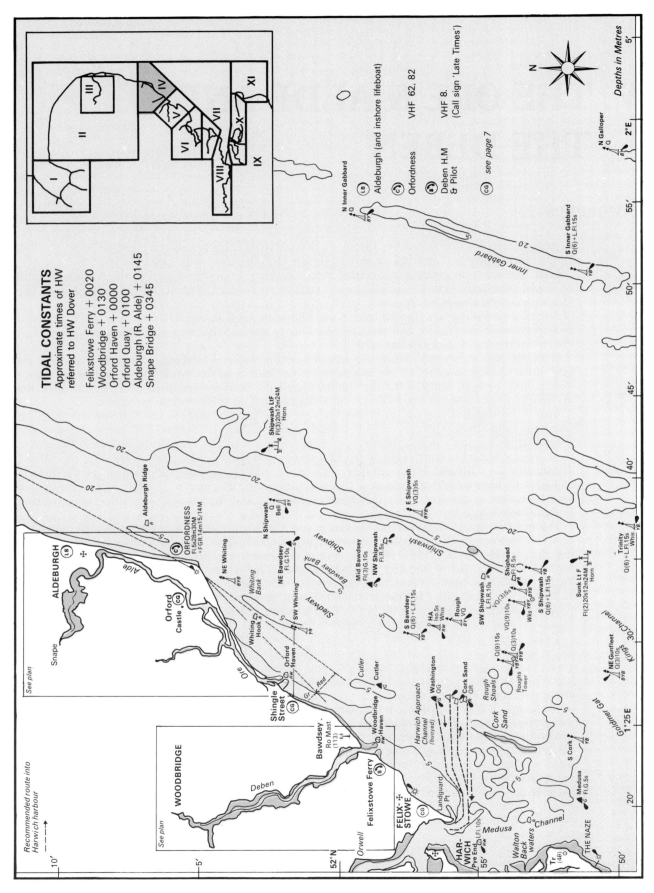

**TIDAL CONSTANTS**
Approximate times of HW
referred to HW Dover

Felixstowe Ferry +0020
Woodbridge +0130
Orford Haven +0000
Orford Quay +0100
Aldeburgh (R. Alde) +0145
Snape Bridge +0345

Depths in Metres

*Recommended route into*
*Harwich harbour*

WOODBRIDGE

ALDEBURGH

Orfordness, where you can steam in so close, you can almost touch
the light; which must be one of the best known on the east coast.

# The River Ore

## Entrance

Down the road apiece, the Deben has a notorious bar but if anything, I have found that the
entrance to the Ore tends to be even more difficult than that of the Deben. First impressions,
however, suggest that it is not so manifestly intimidating on bad days. There are specific reasons
for my worry about the Ore entrance.

First: although the Woodbridge Haven buoy is not one of the easiest to spot, the Orford Haven
buoy is frequently so heeled over by the local races that it is only too vexatiously simple to lose it
against the undistinguished shoreline in what are often disturbed waters. Not until you have
identified it and have begun to move into position to try an entry will you be able to make use of
the Martello tower and the cluster of cottages that is known as Shingle Street.

Second: there is no official pilot. There is, of course, the CG station at Shingle Street, with
occasional watch-auxiliary; but in essence there is just the single buoy and the one leading mark.
True, there are quite a few 'leading lines' that will bring you safely in, but these require 'local
knowledge' at a level denied to most visitors. In any case, they all depend upon getting a 'just
open' view between (say) 'the third chimney' and (say) 'a conspicuous clump of trees.' And that is
if you can see any or all of these in what is often misty visibility.

Third: the Admiralty *Pilot* reinforces it all by saying, 'A dangerous place except in settled fine
weather. A mistake with a strong onshore wind would probably mean the loss of the boat.' And
again, somewhat unhelpfully in view of the above mentioned info, 'Entrance to Orford Haven
should not be attempted by strangers without the assistance of a pilot.'

The channel and bar tend to change frequently; perhaps not dramatically but regularly and
often. So, the best plan, certainly for a first engagement, must be to wait for settled conditions
and to time your approach for about an hour after the flood tide has started, unless, of course you
draw in excess of 1·5m, when you wait until nearer high water according to draught. It will then
be possible to interpret the surface water signs which clearly delineate the deeps from the banks.
The best water still tends to be towards the west on entering, and a careful, slow approach
between north and south shoals, when the shingle is still uncovered, will enable you to make a
slow and cautious but fairly safe and sound way in. Do not be not be misled by the apparently
tempting channel which seems to exist just to the north of the tiny separated out shingle isle.
Whatever the weather at the time of your entry, it is important to keep an eye on, and a good
clearance from, North Weir Point since the rush of the stream around the sand and shingle spit
can be powerfully confusing to look at or to negotiate.

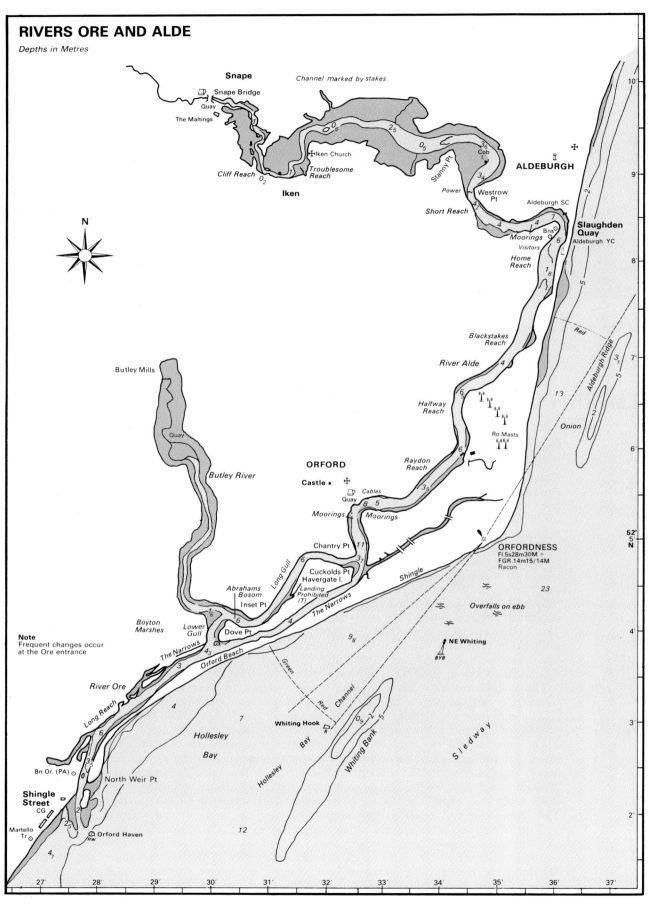

# RIVERS ORE AND ALDE

*Depths in Metres*

Snape

Snape Bridge

Quay

The Maltings

Channel marked by stakes.

Iken Church

Cliff Reach

*Troublesome Reach*

Iken

Stanny Pt

Power

Westrow Pt

Short Reach

Cob I.

**ALDEBURGH**

Aldeburgh SC

**Slaughden Quay**

Aldeburgh YC

*Moorings*

Bns

*Visitors*

*Home Reach*

Red

*Blackstakes Reach*

Aldeburgh Ridge

Butley Mills

*River Alde*

Quay

*Halfway Reach*

Ro Masts

Onion

*Butley River*

**ORFORD**

Castle

*Cables*

Quay

*Raydon Reach*

*Moorings*

*Moorings*

**ORFORDNESS**
Fl.5s28m30M
FGR.14m15/14M
Racon

Chantry Pt

*Long Gull*

Cuckolds Pt
Havergate I.

*Landing Prohibited (T)*

*The Narrows*

*Shingle*

*Overfalls on ebb*

Abrahams Bosom

Inset Pt

**Note**
Frequent changes occur
at the Ore entrance

*Boyton Marshes*

Lower Gull

Dove Pt

NE Whiting
BYB

*The Narrows*

Orford Beach

*Green*

*River Ore*

*Long Reach*

*Red Channel*

*Hollesley Bay*

Whiting Hook

*S l e d w a y*

Bn Or. (PA)

North Weir Pt

*Hollesley*

*Whiting Bank*

**Shingle Street**
CG

*Bay*

Martello Tr

Orford Haven
RW

*Top* There is a lot that has changed a little over decades if not centuries in King's Lynn.
*Left* The bridge at Fosdyke can be a thing of dread and threat… although (*above*) the spirituous liquors at the nearby hostelry may help you see it in many different lights.

*Above* Much has changed at Denver since the lock was a haven and a retreat for frogs, swans and peacocks.

*Above right* Even when Blakeney quay is, as it often is, fully occupied, it is never 'busy'.

*Opposite* The guillotine at Denver, while French in style, is a dramatic reminder of the early works of the imported Dutch.

*Below* Brancaster epitomises the Spirit of the East: it is not far from Bracing Skeggy.

*Above* Wells-next-the-Sea is also Wells-next-the-quiet-inland-waters; and they are frequently a welcome relief after crossing the famous bar.
*Opposite* The cathedral at Ely imposingly overlooks everything for miles around; including the marina known as Babylon.
*Below* Thornham is a classic among the few and far between small havens of the East Coast.

*Top* Blakeney: at tide time, the height of convenience.
*Left* Norwich: 'A Fine City'.
*Right* Lowestoft: the bridge-gateway to the Broads.

*Above* The remains of the AD1216 priory
of St Olaves.
*Right and below* Mills abound; such as this
example at Horsey…this is at Wroxham.
*Hoseasons Ltd*

*Top* Great Yarmouth: the imposing architecture under which it is seldom easy to moor. *Kim Hollamby*

*Top right* Berney: the best-known mill on the Broads.

*Above* Lowestoft; where there is always a tremendous contrast in craft.

*Right* Southwold Fisherman's Reading Room, where the figurehead's not for burning.

*Above* Aldeburgh: sea, sand and hinterland with river.
*Lance Cooper*

*Below* Orford: sea, sand and hinterland with river...plus Ness.
*Colloryan*

*Above* Waldringfield now has a new pleasure-boat pontoon…not in picture.

*Below* Woodbridge: for mooring in the river, it's Catch Me If You Can.

The longstanding 'classic' advice, is to keep the black topmark of the famous (position fixed) conspicuous grey chimney almost in line with the orange diamond topmark of the famous (position approximate) beacon. The chimney should generally be kept slightly open to the west; but nothing can be guaranteed to keep you dead to rights from winter to winter, although this does offer an entrance that tends almost dead to north. The important thing is to obtain the special local chart as soon as possible after Easter.

The old Imray pilot says: 'When strong winds and a rough sea prevail, entry should not be attempted. Entry against the ebb is not recommended and is possible only in quiet weather for yachts having plenty of power. Local knowledge under these conditions is essential'. I can endorse all of that, having once had to sweat it out to Southwold, due to an entrance that was demonstrably 'impossible', and that with no more than a Force 4 against a spring ebb. The entrance is particularly bad with a strong wind from the east, and at its worst when it is ESE.

There is a solitary beacon shoresides which is intended to be used in transit with the offing buoy to give a course into the entrance. I have tried this approach three times, twice being followed by foreign visitors who recognised *Valcon* from using earlier editions of this pilot guide, and on each time have had to head dramatically off course to the SW in order to keep the water. In balance, it must be favourite to wait for settled conditions and try an entry at about half tide when it is probably easiest to read the surface of the water. The rising flood will be with you, more or less towards the mouth proper, and that will help should you hesitate, touch or find bottom.

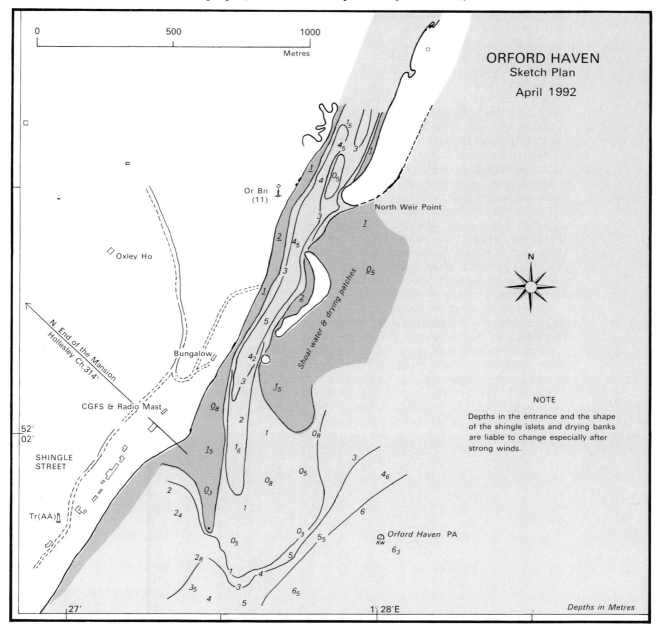

ORFORD HAVEN
Sketch Plan
April 1992

NOTE

Depths in the entrance and the shape of the shingle islets and drying banks are liable to change especially after strong winds.

# Mouth to Orford

Once inside, having hung on tight as you went round the bend, the river settles down almost immediately. On my very first entry into the Ore, unpiloted and paranoid, I was rewarded by the sight of three seals basking on the port mud spit. I cut the engines and gave them a gentle happy/self-congratulatory wave; but they were to be neither wooed nor impressed.

Just after North Weir Point, by the not very distinguishable orange Ore beacon on the west bank, there are some isolated drying patches (almost small islands). The way to avoid them is, once the solid bank proper of North Weir Point has grown fully out of the sand and shingle fingers, to move over to the east of centre, and so continue upstream in deep water. Once that manoeuvre has been successfully adopted and completed, the Ore should present no further problem,provided you remember that good ground tackle is needed for any anchorage and treat the mud flats-and-banks and saltings with the respect that any East Coast river deserves. It is the rate of the stream that is the really threatening thing to watch out for. Then at last you can start to enjoy some of the finest river scenery in England.

Right up Long Reach to Dove Point, on Havergate Island, there is a good 2m in mid channel. The NW bank tends to be vague and shallow, while the SE is all shingle and steep-to virtually up to Havergate Island.

The oyster-famous Butley River is the first watering hole of note. It is to be found on the port hand, after Flybury Point and Lower Gull; that is, a couple of cables after from the red and white buoy marking Dove Point's spit. Don't be tempted to cut corners; Boyton Marshes reach out well into the Butley at the bend. The Butley River affords the first possible anchorage: dependant upon draught, you can go up to a mile or so, near Ferry Cottage, Gedgrave cliff and the ruins of the old jetty, but always on the lookout for the oyster beds with their markers, stakes or legends, especially to port.

This is the first anchorage that can be used without constant anxiety about ground tackle. Some folk have it that there is a secure anchorage by Flybury Point, but I have found the power of the of the middle ebb is such to require a continual watch, something that can be circumvented by going further upstream or just that bit further into the creek. There is another anchorage just after the Butley entrance at the back of Dove Point, by Abraham or Abram's Bosom/Besum/Bosum/Bosun according to taste. It is also susceptible to strong streams and eddies. The Butley is straightforward, provided care is exercised with due regard to the obvious pitfalls of shallows, foul banks and oyster beds.

Out of the Butley, Long Gulls leads to Short Gull, Horse Hard and, opposite Chantry, Cuckold's Point at the most northerly point of Havergate Island. This is the longer way round the island; the shorter, more direct, route lies to starboard after Dove Point, where the Narrows and Main Reach rejoin the former just by the end of Havergate. Long Gull carries more water generally, but apart from a shoal patch (1·5m) by Long Reach there is no shortage of depth and little to choose between them. The final anchorage in the Ore is just below Orford Quay in more than 4m, but it is close to the moorings and tends to be a busy area.

My favourite spot in the river is just off Cuckold's Point by Havergate Island. It is well sheltered and just far enough away from Orford not to make it too popular. Havergate Island is a bird sanctuary, and landing is strictly prohibited.

There is another side to the area: the practice of strange military antics and manoeuvres that derive from the ministry building in the name of defence; and indeed, in general, the east bank is an inhospitable perilous place: Landing Prohibited. 'This is a prohibited place within the meaning of the Official Secrets Act: Unauthorised persons entering the area may be arrested and prosecuted.' Nor are its official occupants very keen on yachtsmen with or without field glasses ... and being a bird watcher is no justification.

Cuckolds Point: enigmatic appellation notwithstanding, an excellent anchorage.

In spite of this constraint I have spent many happy indolent hours, off Havengore and behind binoculars, in my regular quest for avocets, but have never been fortunate enough to see one. The uninhabited island of 70 acres is noted for its colony of those curiously beaked birds, previously believed to have disappeared from the UK around 1824. The sandy island wilderness, which is in the care of the Royal Society for the Protection of Birds, is also host to godwits and curlew pipers. I saw not one of those either.

Across the other side of the river, it is a pleasant morning walk on the 'mainland' bank to Orford, where the village possesses all kinds of cultural joys: castle, church, plebeian pub, elitist 'hotel', fish smoker and keep.

# Orford

Reaching Orford's unique form of civilisation by boat requires a little study. Access to the town quay is predictably best at HW; but with care, both quay and surrounding waters can be approached at almost any state of the tide. There is very little room for either manoeuvring or parking at the quay, so any visit must be made with all the proper circumspection.

There are moorings, but they are all private (with a long waiting list) and there is none specially set aside for visitors. For use of the moorings or the quay, contact the harbourmaster: Ralph Brinkley, East View, Quay Street, Orford, Suffolk. ☎ Orford (0394) 450481. The HM is not always immediately accessible, but diligence and application together with a request via the Bostock's Old Warehouse chandlery will usually prevail.

Facilities for yachts are neither comprehensive nor sophisticated. Diesel and fuel can be had by can via the jetty, where there is also a standpipe water tap. Minor repairs can be arranged, but this is not the place to break down or decide on a major overhaul. There are scrubbing posts, a small slipway and modest mobile crane.

A special treat and warm welcome is to be had at the Old Warehouse on the quay, a chandlery and restaurant run by Charles Jackson and Jean Bostock. If you want to know anything about boating on the Orwell, just call in. If you want chandlery, they have it; if you want food and drink, they have that too; and, in addition, they have some of the best views in Suffolk, especially if you just happen to be gazing at them through a rosé haze (Mateus or otherwise) after a lazy meal on their restaurant balcony. You can telephone them on Orford (0394) 450210. The same premises are the headquarters of Orford Marine Services who offer to meet all your practical/technical boating needs.

From the river, Orford offers a variety of vistas.

*Above*: The Ore part of the River Ore and Alde: looking downstream from the miniature quay and jetty at Orford. So long as you ignore the Ministry of Defence (or whatever euphemism you prefer) and its goings on, you could almost be in a previous century. The village is a spot to treasure
*Left*: The River Ore: Orford is a place of very special, indeed unique, qualities, it is remote, quiet and filled with its own idiosyncratic character. It is, therefore, entirely in keeping with such an ethos, that the water stand-pipe should be as it is. It is a downright symbol of the *genius loci* of a village that never lost its birthright

An additionally extra happy contact in the area, and one who is ready to do anything he can to help for all and sundry boaters, is the Royal Cruising Club representative, Major Clem Lister, Walnut Corner, Ferry Road, Orford IP12 2NR. ☎ Orford (0394) 450653.

Major Lister, together with Commander Prior, prepares each year a chart of the entrance to the river. This is promulgated in conjunction with the Old Warehouse, from whom copies can be obtained in time for each season.

Orford is neither quaint nor *outré*; but it is undeniably *recherché* and as such well worth a row from any of the river anchorages. It has a long, wide avenue that leads from the quay to the historic castle and church; and on each side of the continental style approach there are walls, cottages, gates, doors and gardens (not to mention cats and dogs) that just cry out for observation and inspection. There are the usual friendly and informal amenities of a small country village, with one special to the locality: a smoked fish shop not only of distinction but also of excellence. Orford is also one those places where, not all that long ago, it was still an active practice for the majority to be convinced of the need to watch the wall my darling while the gentlemen go by! To this day, there is a hint of curtain twitching and quick door closing when there are strangers about. Indeed, in many ways it is not very different from Staithes way up in the north above Whitby.

# The River Alde

Just above Orford, the River Ore suddenly becomes the River Alde for no reason that I have been able to discover; in just the same way as there is mystery about the Yorkshire Ouse changing to the River Ure at one sharp bend. But then again, there is also mystery about the derivation of Cuckold's Point and Abram's Bosom; and for that matter I am not sure whether it is only the one Cuckold or not, but this to err on the generous side.

## Aldeburgh

Aldeburgh's Slaughden Quay is the undoubted Mecca. You don't have to make a long pilgrimage but you must remember that access is best at top of tide. At Slaughden, The Man, and also Cruising Association boatman, is Mr R. F. Upsom. He it is who must be obeyed and he it is will keep you right. He is to be found at the quayside; usually not far from the notice whose runs do read, 'Dogs and owners please use your wits. The quay is not a place for meditation'. In a way, the same must be said for the Ore and the Alde for the bottom is perverse in its shelving.

There are better-than-basic facilities, and the boating fraternity is approachable and helpful. Between them, Russell Upson and Peter Wilson of the Aldeburgh Boatyard Co. will fit you in with what you want; and if they can't they will either know a man who can or send you where you can get it for yourself.

My first foray into the Alde River section of the river(s) was from the anchorage at Cuckold's Point in a small Avon dinghy complete with oars and something approaching the smallest extant seagull. First up to Orford Quay, then the MOD establishments, past Town, King's and Lantern marshes, past Halfway Reach and Blackstakes, predictably with no stake black or otherwise, and finally into Home Reach by Sudbourne marshes.

With a slight following wind and the tide in my favour it was a most agreeable trip; and it was just about lunchtime when I dragged the dinghy up the hard at Slaughden quay. The wind had picked up slightly, but it had done nothing but help me; and I had neither the common sense nor in those days the experience to think that it could be a hindrance on the way back.

I returned to launch the Avon at the turn of the tide, looking forward to being an Easy Ebby Rider on the way back. No way! When I reached Slaughden quay the tide was OK, but the wind had become stiffish. As soon as I saw the waves roughing up the dinghies on the hard and the wind roughing up the water into frequent white horses (good title for a book I have always thought), it was clear I was in for a rough trip.

Just to launch the Avon took too much time and energy, and by the time I was just out of hailing distance of the quay I was exhausted; so that when the Seagull was swamped for the third time, it was no longer able to be started – or I was not able to start it. I tried rowing, but found it impossible to do more than hold my own. The ebbing tide was with me all right, but the wind, now in its fives and sixes, was not, and the lightweight dinghy stood no chance. Nor did I, with the wind and spray against me; and the rain, for by now there was that as well.

Fortunately, fate was on my side that time, and dead on cue, along came a yacht with folk who not only recognised my plight but immediately did something about it. They could not get close to me because of the danger of grounding, but they stood off in mid stream until I managed to manoeuvre myself near enough for a line; and soon we were both under way. I was hauled on board and treated to rum and coffee and it seemed minutes only before I was back on board *Valcon*, in the anchorage so sheltered that hardly a ripple disturbed the surface; while round the bend and out of Havergate's lee, the water was as turbulent as ever.

Aldeburgh itself is a place apart: exclusive to a degree (bachelor's not master's); fashionable but *démodé*; elect without ever achieving a select status; above its station but below the salt; genteel without gentility; lacking in true grit; and forever on the make: socially, culturally and financially. Situate so close to Britten's beloved Snape Maltings, it is ironic that Aldeburgh should seem to have neither unison nor harmony. Aldeburgh attracts the epithet 'mixed-up'; and a typical example is the contiguity, the very cheek by jowlness, of the privileged and esoteric yacht club and the not very couth pub where the bar has a vast ceiling from which hangs a display of portable urinals otherwise known as chamber pots. To be there, as I once was, in the company of a not very comic comedian on stilts is to suffer something akin to a WMC Ladies' Night gone wrong. Metaphorically, in season, every day is a flag day with the locals the exclusive beneficiaries.

It is the leaden echo flip side of the Orford coin. In Orford, there is a definite sensation that worldly things are never quite with you; and for sure, the Orford world of the flesh and the devil will never pursue you for a quick handout or try you for a fall-guy and a fast buck.

# Aldeburgh to Snape

After Aldeburgh, the Alde continues until it reaches its head of navigation at Snape Maltings. I have both heard and read (consistently on both counts) that Slaughden Quay, the first port of call after Orford, is accessible at all states of the tide for craft drawing up to 1·5m. Or, if not actually accessible in the full meaning of the word, then that you can at least stay afloat. This aberration continues to 'hold water' as it were, in spite of it manifestly not being the case; as I have verified with *Valcon's* long, straight and extremely stout keel. So the alternative for those wishing to stay in the area is an (experimental) anchorage upriver of the Horse and downstream of Aldeburgh itself; namely, before the moorings near the Martello tower. Should this be of appeal, do take all the local advice you can get if you draw more than a metre, since my experience has been that the bed of the Alde is not to be trusted as it can shelve dramatically from 5m to less than 1·5m in no more than 2m.

If you want to anchor out of touch, right out of any dredged channel and be disturbed by nothing but the sound of lappings and lapwings, then the upper reaches of the Alde will be your

The Ore and Alde: one of the most attractive anchorages in the country; you are seldom likely to be bothered by neighbours of any kind (except wild life that is) at this peaceful haven by Iken Cliff.

Elysian cruising fields. Those skippers and crew who find themselves at anchor above Westrow Point and near the difficult-to-discern Cob Island, do not do so by chance. To find your way from concealed pole to lost perch takes dedication of a high order, and once you start on the long turn to the westward after the Cob Island stakes have been identified and left to port, you are, by modern cruising standards, in almost uncharted territory. The domain becomes not only rustic and rural but also runs the gamut from wild to sylvan: the reaches called Collier's, Stanny, Mansion, Bagnall's and Church broadly drift and meander between the extensive marshes of Hazlewood and Iken until they present you, penultimately, with their own version of classic troublesome reaches. Last before Snape, where the channel really does become utterly vague and indistinct, near Cliff reach, are two of my favourite end of the world anchorages: the Oaks and Iken cliffs.

## Snape Maltings

It is sad that there is no longer a local pilot to help out with these teasing reaches. Anyone with a mind set on getting to Snape, which is well above Aldeburgh and with a channel that is not clearly indicated either by moorings or good withies and posts, should do so first in the ship's tender near low water. To be able to observe the critical twists and turns that make up the course of the channel under unstressed conditions must be a wise precaution. I have been shown the way but still find it more convoluted and misleading than Conyer, and its course is much longer. Although there is physically less when you get there; in quality it is an exceptional venue of irresistible appeal to Britten fans; and others will proclaim, and frequently chant to boot, the delights of the local hostelry.

Craft of under 2m should make the trip on a good rising tide, intending to reach the head of navigation at the old quayside about half an hour before high water. Just in time to take the mud, and spend an enjoyable time and tide in the Plough and Sail.

Devotees of these solitary and hidden delights belong to a small section of the boating fraternity that wants nothing to do with mains water or power; is all for getting the last cable out of the lightest of airs; and has no time for inflatable dinghies, especially those fitted with oversize outboards. True, theirs is probably a fanciful, romantic and whimsical way of life, but what is sure is that it belongs in a disappearing world. However, this little corner of the East Coast rivers world is likely to linger on in yesteryear for many years to come; with Sizewell being the biggest blot and threat on the waterscape.

The Ore and Alde make a strange combination of riverbed-fellows. There is no doubt that they offer something quite different in the cruising experience and possess many unique qualities. On a sunny day, it is difficult to imagine a more picturesque, idyllic riparian scene; and on a typically British grey late autumn evening, the MoD edifices, together with the distant lighthouse flashing to seaward, and Orford's church and castle on a pale skyline, its *genius loci* is still charged, but in quite another key. Give it a try; and take your counsel from those who linger by Orford's jetty and Aldeburgh's quay. It comes from the wisdom of generations.

# The Deben

## Approaches

The coast from Orford Haven to the Deben is mainly one of low shingle beaches with little variation and only Martello towers for landmarks. It is only a short leg to the Woodbridge Haven buoy which stands off the River Deben, where the grim Bawdsey Manor with its conspicuous radio tower standing on the NE banks and Martello towers T and U on the SW mark the approach to keep watch over the entrance.

The normal approach is first to pick up the Woodbridge Haven buoy, which is easier to spot than it used to be, and then take it slowly until the green bar buoy is spotted. In spite of its radar reflector, it can be difficult to identify and can easily be taken for a crab pot marker, especially since the waters are frequently troubled. In poor weather it may be necessary to be on top of it before you actually see it. It can get pulled down by the tide, and in bad weather is difficult to spot, let alone confirm.

Until the *Haven* and the *Bar* buoys have been identified, strangers should not attempt to enter. In particular a rough southeast wind on an ebb tide will make conditions almost impossible. (Trying the Ore and the Alde as an alternative to the Deben at any time would be foolhardy, the best plan being to move to the cover of Harwich.) In good weather, you should pick up the two entrance buoys straightaway. Martello towers T and U feature on the west bank together with some old groynes; and Bawdsey Manor with the nearby conspicuous radio tower are on the east bank.

## Deben entrance

The entry is currently straightforward: the single green buoy and then the two leading marks for the bar channel which are: front – red and white triangle; rear – all red square. The theory is that you line them up exactly and follow that course straight for the shore until, just in the nick of time, you make a sharp turn to starboard with the stream carrying you in. On my unaccompanied approaches to the Deben I have found that the best water requires you to keep just to port of the leading line. The notorious bar shifts fairly often, and if there has been a really big blow, it can change overnight. In summer, the buoy and leading beacons don't need to be moved; but since the banks often change substantially through the winter, it is best to wait for settled weather and check it out before trying for an entry, or to use the pilot.

The shingle shore is steep and the channel is close so close that only a few years ago, when there were leading marks near the Felixstowe Ferry crossing, it was virtually impossible to line them up without going ashore to do so. You will still find that holidaymaking children may hold out their hands to offer you sweets as you steam so near. In 1982 the channel, which can be less than a cable wide, ran virtually north/south. In 1984 the channel broke through the Knoll to run virtually at right angles.

At the beginning of the 1992 season, the bars, banks and braes had so extended themselves that the actual (as opposed to apparent) entrance channel was something of a dog leg: requiring you to keep easterly after you have passed to the north of the Haven buoy, clipping the Green Bar buoy just to the south until the leading marks come into line. Robert Brinkley (please see below) prepares a chart of the entrance each year. He makes a charge of 50p which is donated to the RNLI, and in 1991, he was able to contribute over £30.00.

Generally speaking, it is safe to enter the Deben (if 'safe' is ever the word, that is) with 1·5m draught around one hour each side of low water. About two hours after, the broken water areas are plain to see, and while this usually shows quite clearly the relative positions of the channel and the bar, this is not entirely reliable, especially for a first time visitor. The Bar usually carries 1m at spring ebb low water, and there is a very fast rise of tide at the bar on the new flood with a likelihood of nearly 2m an hour after low water. Strangers are strongly advised not to enter before half tide.

I cannot speak too highly of the help I have had in the past from Charlie Brinkley, who was harbour master and pilot for many a year. I should never have survived my first entries into the Deben without his advice and assistance. He and his colleagues did all they could to make sure I got in safely and was found a decent mooring or, in later days, sent up river to one of the better anchorages. The small fee charged for their wise and friendly services in no way really recompenses him for the aggro that is caused by the (almost unpredictable) shifts in the bars and the channels.

I strongly recommend strangers to wait for calm, settled weather or to use the pilot before entering the river for the first time. The charts on p. 96 show how dramatically the bar and the channel can change.

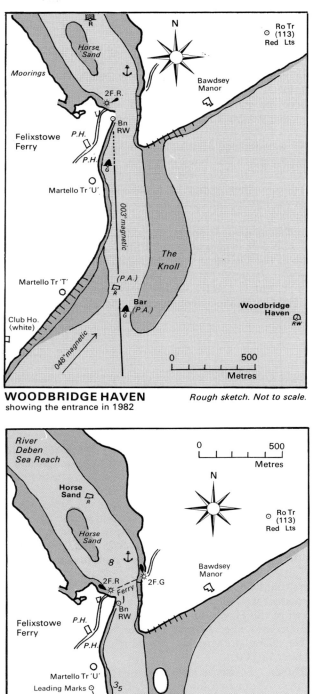

**WOODBRIDGE HAVEN**
showing the entrance in 1982 — *Rough sketch. Not to scale.*

**WOODBRIDGE HAVEN**
showing the entrance in 1991 — *Rough sketch. Not to scale.*

# BUOYAGE
## River Deben from Woodbridge Haven Buoy

| Check | Confirm | Confirm | Check |
|---|---|---|---|
| **Woodbridge** | | Granary Reach | |
| | No. 24 R | | |
| | No. 22 R | | |
| | No. 20 R | | |
| | No. 18 R | | |
| | No. 16 R | | No. 13 G |
| | | Methersgate Reach | No. 11 G |
| | | | No. 9 G |
| **Martlesham Creek** | No. 14 R | | No. 7 G |
| | | | Methersgate Quay |
| | No. 12 R | | No. 5 G |
| | No. 10 R | Waldringfield Reach | |
| | No. 8 R | | |
| | | | No. 3 G |
| **Waldringfield** | | Pilots Reach | |
| | | | No. 1 G |
| | No. 6 R | | |
| | No. 4 R | | |
| | No. 2A R | Ramsholt Reach | |
| | No. 2 R | Green Reach | Prettyman's Pt |
| | | Blackstakes Reach | Ramsholt Arms Inn |
| | Horse Sand R | Sea Reach | |
| | 2F.R. ☼ | | 2F.G ☼ |
| | Fl.R ☼ | | Bawdsey Manor Ro Tr |
| **Felixstowe Ferry** | | | Bar G |
| | Woodbridge Haven RW | | |

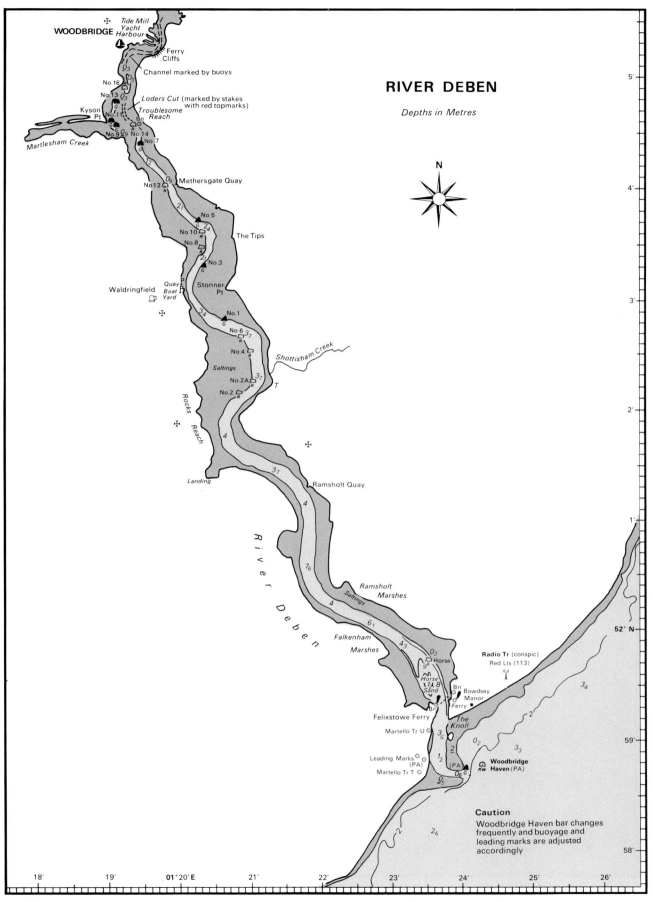

WOODBRIDGE
Tide Mill Yacht Harbour
Ferry Cliffs
Channel marked by buoys

**RIVER DEBEN**

*Depths in Metres*

No.16
No.13
Loders Cut (marked by stakes with red topmarks)
Kyson Pt
No.11
Troublesome Reach
Bn
No.9
No.14
No.7
Martlesham Creek

N

No12
Methersgate Quay
No 5
No.10
The Tips
No.8
No.3
Stonner Pt
Quay
Boat Yard
Waldringfield
No.1
No 6
No.4
Shottisham Creek
Saltings
No 2A
T
No.2

Rocks Reach

Landing
Ramsholt Quay

River Deben

Ramsholt Marshes
Saltings
Falkenham Marshes
Horse
Radio Tr (conspic)
Red Lts (113)
Horse Sand
Bn
Bawdsey Manor
Ferry
Felixstowe Ferry
The Knoll
Martello Tr U
Leading Marks (PA)
(PA)
Woodbridge Haven (PA)
Martello Tr T

52° N
59'
58'

**Caution**
Woodbridge Haven bar changes
frequently and buoyage and
leading marks are adjusted
accordingly

18'   19'   01°20' E   21'   22'   23'   24'   25'   26'

# Felixstowe/Bawdsey Ferry

Once inside, past the hospitable Felixstowe Ferry Sailing Club on the west shore, there is usually a hustle and bustle of one kind or another: fishermen, leisure craft and one of the ferry boats (*Late Times, Odd Times* or *Our Times!*) plying across. In addition, any wind against tide confrontation in this crowded area can create a rough and tumble of water enough to confuse your progress more than somewhat.

The moorings have been expanded and now are absolutely packed together at what must surely be saturation point. There are still a few places to anchor and sometimes a free swinging mooring, and for these you take advice and instruction from those on duty ashore. You need to be fairly self- sufficient to maintain a stay at Felixstowe Ferry. All shops are in Old Felixstowe, 1.5 miles away, but there is a bus service. Social life centres on the pubs, the café and the fresh fish stall, but local charm, character and friendliness are unrestricted. It is a splendid spot for photography, and boasts a climate for which Skegness coined the concept 'bracing'. A bit of the East Coast at its best.

Once past the tumble of sea over the bar and the tumult just within, there is one last hazard to be negotiated before the river settles down. That is the Horse Sand. It is well marked by a red can buoy, but it seems to the stranger that the indicated channel must be doubtful since it is so close to the Bawdsey shore, and I remember feeling very ill at ease the first time Charlie Brinkley led me that way. There is, of course, plenty of water both abeam and below provided you do not have to play silly games with boats not following the rules of the road. With a good spring tide, you will swiftly pass Horse and be carried into the broader reaches of what quickly becomes a classic East Coast river: low-lying banks, far-reaching mud flats, frequent saltings, and a narrow channel in the middle of a broad expanse of shoal waters.

Felixstowe Ferry

# Ramsholt and Prettyman's Point

The first sign of organised hospitality comes with the small community of Ramsholt. The old quay was once a thriving trading post for barges, but it is now virtually untended and uncared for. Hardly used, it must stand as a prime candidate for refurbishment into Port Deben Marina, complete with yachtsmen's residences; perish the thought, but it will happen. Approaching Ramsholt, along the aptly-named Green Reach you come to Falkenham Creek, where some folk anchor but I have always shied off, not being sure of the bottom. The river then becomes crowded with moorings, and the fairway is not really obvious until you are in the middle of it. Flood and ebb move fast enough here to make it hard work for small outboards to make much progress against the stream.

There is a hypothesis of long standing, somewhat in keeping with the 'Here be dragons' legends and syndrome, that there is a boatman hereabouts who waits in attendance. I have still to come knowingly face to face with him. His presence is of some import since there is always a great demand for crew and visitors to get ashore and the services of a powerful launch are clearly at a premium. And for why this Gaderene need to rush ashore? The answer lies at the doors of the Ramsholt Arms Inn, which has a superb location and specialises in glorious sunsets. Over the years it has collected signs that prohibit all kinds of things from dogs to picnicking.

Vacant moorings can be had by Ramsholt jetty, but they are in great demand. Just a few cables upstream are to be found the attractive alternatives: the Deben anchorages. Two have very good holding ground and are particularly well protected, and consequently are very popular. They are: a) the west side of Hemley Bay (just off Kirton Creek to the north) and b) along the stretch known as the Rocks, just off Prettyman's Point. Both can become uncomfortable enough to be untenable when a strong wind is gusting against a spring ebb; but even then, a judicial move (made ahead of need) up or down stream, as deemed appropriate according to the prevailing conditions, usually achieves a substantial amelioration.

Prettyman's Point, only seriously crowded at weekends in the season, has a slender strip of firm sandy beach, a tree-covered slope that drops steeply to the shoreline and plenty of pathways and shrubbery. The river bank and saltings offer a variety of colour, pattern and texture rich enough to delight even the most picky painter. There is also a profusion of wild life, with a number of resident swans; and when there are not too many humans around, the hymns of the larks can be breathtaking. Most of the area is redolent of primitive Nigerian bush and jungle, while the rest mixes rock pools, saltings and almost untouched rural chaos with what are never more than modest essays into agriculture.

There is a really good walk to the Ramsholt Arms, where you are overlooked by the strangely shaped church tower that is supposed to have been in its day notorious as a smugglers' staging post, trafficking station and house of ill fame. Of an evening, you will be unlucky not to hear at least one nightingale singing on the way there ... and on the way back, it is not entirely impossible that the mermaids will sing to you.

There are one or two patches towards the upstream end where the holding quality is not absolutely first rate, and trial and error will sort that out. In the downstream section there are some foul patches, mainly in the area near the extremely useful drying creek that is usable only during spring tides.

The River Deben: one of the most attractive and least abused anchorages on the East Coast. This is known as Prettyman's Point or The Rocks according to your perception of life. Both elements are there and care is needed in anchoring, for there are some foul patches just offshore by the grounded barge.

The Ramsholt Arms is a favourite stopping off point for most
Deben travellers ...

# Waldringfield

Next, on the port hand opposite Stonner Point, comes the maze of moorings that denotes Waldringfield. This is a busy attractive spot, with an excellent boatyard and general stores that is as different as chalk from cheese (they sell both) when it comes to the usual run of street corner generals. The pub is not to be overlooked. It is the renowned Maybush, with its display of cartoons personally signed by Sailor Giles.

A phone call, in advance of a visit, to Waldringfield (047336) 260 will put you into touch with one Mr Brown whose patch it is. He is a most co-operative, approachable and affable gent who will see you well served. Anchor to port downstream of the moorings, just after and opposite green *No.1*, or pick up a vacant mooring buoy and go ashore to the boatyard or the Maybush.

He may be able to fix you up with a deepwater or half-tide mooring; but this is not as sure as death and taxes, for the river has become increasingly busy, as witness the plethora of mooring buoys that extends from Waldringfield's tip to toe. Vacant ones in particular can easily mislead newcomers about the direction of the fairway since many of them are red. It is unusual for buoys to have to be identified and negotiated in extremely restricted channels, but there is little room for manoeuvre here and none at all for error. The channel bends, twists and turns; is none too wide at best; and all around are shoaling banks of solid East Coast mud.

There has been onshore development, bringing the place into today's commercial league of tourism. Waldringfield now sports a new feature: day trips on the Deben – on the good ship MV *Jahan*, embarking from a new jetty that extends helpfully into the river. It all looks neat, tidy and efficient; not a bit like the old Waldringfield image.

Bye-laws are posted on the beach, informing all and sundry of what they must not do. One prohibition in particular shows how far our national weakness with regard to silly rules and regulations will let officialdom go: 'No digging for worms on the foreshore'. The river frontage

... although there is usually a shortage of vacant moorings.

still proliferates with its mix and match of the old and the new and the classic beach bungalows still cling stubbornly not only to their last square feet of sandy fringe benefit but also no doubt to their dwindling last days. But they still offer discrete testimony to the concept that some things do not change: these miniature holiday mansions are all variegated replicas of a *fin de siècle* archetype, spanning the style spectrum from the plainly plebeian to the luxuriously eccentric.

## Hams and Tips to Woodbridge

In about a mile, on the east bank there are the pleasant features of the Hams and the Tips; both ideal spots for a break and a picnic. The anchorage around here is about the furthest upriver you will be able to stay afloat even at springs in about 2m. From here on, the only hazard is one of running out of water; the channel upstream begins to deviate, and craft drawing more than 2m should not attempt to proceed past Methersgate Quay until after half tide. Running out of water, either by being too early on the tide, or by ignoring or clipping the first rate buoyage, is the only hazard up to Woodbridge. It is worth noting that the buoyage can, in the strong winds and harsh streams that can frequent the Deben, get dragged off station, However, joy of joys, the bottom is good-old-soft-gooey mud and no harm will befall. This stretch of the Deben is now even busier than ever, with the ribbon development of moorings reaching downstream to Methersgate quay almost non-stop from above Woodbridge.

East Coast rivers are famous for their 'troublesome reaches' and the Deben is no outsider. It comes just before Kyson quay and Martlesham creek and, in fact, is no real trouble at all. The creek is a preferred choice for many locals who want just to pop out of Woodbridge itself on a tide for fish, beer or pipe, but there is little water and the project needs to be approached with caution. A low water dinghy inspection is best. The general area is headed by most attractive scenery and properties well kept by zealous riparians, especially the miniature headland opposite Kyson Point.

It is well trimmed, barbered and presented, all smartly green and tree clad right down to the last metre by the riverside. Strength to their lawn mowing elbows.

Much more likely than Troublesome Reach to cause aggro is the tempting short route known as Loders Cut, marked by three red beacons at beginning, middle and end. Shoal craft use it frequently and quite happily, and while some locals say it is good for 2m craft at HW springs, I have not been prompted to try it.

# Woodbridge

Woodbridge Water at the top of the tide always tends to be a busy, popular place. Approaching on the last leg, the waterway, but not the channel itself, broadens out and opens up as it bears you towards the church and the boathouses. The main landmarks are undoubtedly attractive, with the restored and refurbished Tide Mill (dating back to 1170) presiding over all; while the tiny, colourful rotunda of the band box bandstand (dating back no time at all) shows itself sweetly to be in the Cake Decoration school of architecture. All of which is as it should be since it is immediately next to the traditionally classic-looking cricket pavilion style headquarters of the Deben Yacht Club. You can almost hear the thwack of willow on leather and taste the cucumber sandwiches.

From here on, the track is not always easy to spot, for both the channel and its many moorings are, on the tide, often filled with craft jilling around not only to little apparent purpose but also with inadequate indications of their intentions. Either that or they are swinging whimsically to their buoys. Woodbridge mariners tend to navigate intuitively, and woe betide those who are not on the native wavelength. It is particularly important to obey the buoyage through the Woodbridge fairways, because the narrow, deep-water-channel is by no means obvious. The area is congested with moorings and there are seldom any vacant. It is virtually impossible to find a really safe spot to anchor.

Negotiating the reds round the tight corners of the Bends soon brings the Tide Mill Yacht Harbour into view, with the flatland of town and harbour to port and the wooded hills that hide Little Sutton Hoo to port: a splendid haven. The Tide Mill marina, now run by a new skipper Nigel Kember, is not the only place where you can moor at Woodbridge, but I recommend it as the most sensible for a first time visitor. From there, you can use the dinghy to visit the local yards downstream; the limited but extremely peaceful mooring facilities just upstream; and further examine rural Suffolk as the creek finally gets near the famous Sutton Hoo site.

I spent a winter aboard *Valcon* in the Tide Mill Yacht Harbour, and while I was well looked after, indeed from time to time actually cosseted, by all kinds of persons, the quality of life would have been improved if the marina facilities had been more up-to-date, but see below.

## Woodbridge town

It is only a short walk into the centre of Woodbridge from the marina. The town is old and looks it; and now the bypass takes most of the heavy traffic, it feels it. The first record of settlement goes back to the 10th century, but there are finds that date back to the Neolithic Age, 2500 to 1700BC; old enough for me. To walk around its streets can be to gain the impression of a small market town with its spiritual home in the 1830s, though not averse to a slice of the pie of today's prosperity. Nowhere can that be seen to better effect that at the main cross of Quay Street and The Strand, where stands the Crown Inn. Once a 17th century coaching inn, it has been appropriately modernised in the style of Trust House Forte. So has the service.

Although the town of Woodbridge suffers frequently from visitation from our flying cousins from over the water, the airborne Americans, roaring noisily whether on the ground or in the skies immediately above, there are parts the US does not reach, and there, Woodbridge is still essentially East Anglian. Except for Saturdays (or especially on Saturdays, according to taste) Woodbridge is an excellent place to explore. It is particularly good on bookshops, fresh fish and deli's.

And while on the subject of food, although I have no intention of letting this become a cruising man's guide to good pubs or eating houses, there is a special case for the inclusion of an extra special eating house in the square. It is the French restaurant, Le Provençal. (☎ Woodbridge (0394) 385726). Like Blanche's at Reedham on the Broads, it is important to book a place (Saturdays very well ahead) since it is a one man and his wife with girl establishment, and once you are at your table, it is yours for the night. Dining at Le Provençal is sensational, and their 'bouquet' of vegetables unforgettable. Happily their prices are less exotic. While the cuisine is not exclusively nor even especially provençal, the food is uniquely delicious, served in vast quantities and not to be missed.

# RIVER ORE AND ALDE

**Charts**
Imray Y15 and C28
Admiralty 2052 (entrance only), 2695
See also the annually produced chart/plan of Orford Haven produced by The Old Warehouse Chandlery, Orford. ☎ (0394) 450210

**Tides**
Entrance: Harwich −0025, Dover 0000

## ORFORD

**Tides**
Quay: Harwich +0030, Dover +0100
*Harbourmaster*
Ralph Brinkley, East View, Quay Street, Orford, Suffolk. ☎ Orford (0394) 450481.

## SNAPE MALTINGS

**Tides**
Harwich +0200, Orfordness +0345, Dover +0345

## ALDEBURGH

**Tides**
Harwich +0115, Dover +0145

**Moorings**
Contact the Harbourmaster:
Russell Upson, Slaughden Quay, Aldeburgh. ☎ Aldeburgh (0728) 452896.

**Boatyards**
*Aldeburgh Boatyard Co. Ltd*, Fort Green, Aldeburgh ☎ Aldeburgh (0728) 452019. Contact Peter Wilson
*Aldeburgh Yacht Club*, The Clubhouse, Slaughden Quay, Aldeburgh. ☎ Aldeburgh (0728) 452562
*Slaughden Sailing Club* The Clubhouse, Slaughden Quay, Aldeburgh

## DEBEN ENTRANCE AND FELIXSTOWE/BAWDSEY FERRY

**Charts**
Imray Y15, Y16, C28
Admiralty 2693, 2052
An annually produced chart/plan of Woodbridge Haven is produced by the Tidemill Yacht Harbour.

**Tides**
Harwich −0015, Dover +0020

**Harbourmaster and pilot**
Robert Brinkley, Fisherman's Haul Cottage, Felixstowe Ferrry, Suffolk, who is also an auxiliary coastguard and now runs the ferry. The bush telegraph has it that they respond to the telephone, radio, dipped burgee, 'G' flag, or even a bucket in the rigging. ☎ Felixstowe (0394) 270853.
Launch: *Late Times*, VHF Ch 8.

**Radio**
Harbourmaster, Aux. CGs and local fishermen all use VHF Ch 8.

**Moorings and slip**
Mr. Moore, Felixstowe Ferry Boatyard ☎ Felixstowe (0394) 282173.
*Scrubbing posts and anchoring* Harbourmaster.

# WOODBRIDGE

**Tides**
Harwich +0040, Dover +0130

**Marinas and boatyards**
*Frank Knights (Shipwrights) Ltd*, ☎ Woodbridge (0394) 382318. A traditional site by the river, a traditional master and a traditional service. Andy Seedhouse Boat Sales. Woodbridge (0394) 386213. If no one else does or has what you want, there is a good chance that you will find the answer here; although he maintains that he does sell new gear, it is the vast range of his other goods that I have always found keeps me riveted there.
*Tide Mill Yacht Harbour*, ☎ Woodbridge (0394) 385745. Things are on the move here: a new sill, a dredged basin, new piles, fully floating pontoons and more shower blocks are all functioning. Indeed, many craft can now stay afloat during the low water period. There is water and electricity and diesel, but petrol must be obtained elsewhere. VHF marina channel.
*Sailmakers* Suffolk Sails, Quayside Buildings, Woodbridge, Suffolk. ☎ Woodbridge (0394) 386323.
*Small Craft Deliveries Ltd*, ☎ Woodbridge (0394) 382600, 24 hours. Their idea of 'small craft' may not be yours or mine (they cope with vessels up to 1500 tons world wide) but the rest of what they do (books, charts, Admiralty 'A' agents, navigation equipment as well as clothing across the road) is all of the highest possible standard for the cruising man.

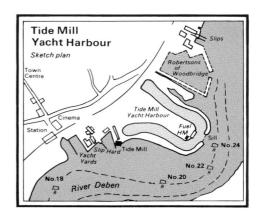

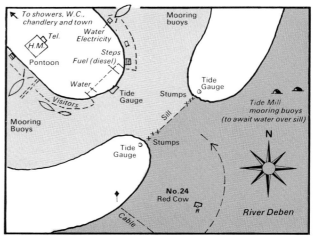

**TIDE MILL YACHT HARBOUR ENTRANCE**

# V. THE ORWELL, STOUR AND WALTON BACKWATERS

## Approaches

It is only a short leg from the Woodbridge Haven buoy, the last two Martello towers (T and U) and grim Bawdsey Manor with its conspicuous radio tower to Landguard Point, the entrance to Harwich. During the progress, there are gentle alterations and quiet contrasts to enjoy: cliffs, grassy banks, low shingle beaches and a facade of multicoloured huts; with tanks, towers, churches, a pier and a few more Martello towers also to be spotted.

Here and there, the natural frontage is broken by a facade of beach huts in a splendid technicolour array. From shoresides, however, they are less than gay and sport little connection with Joseph's coat, for many are dressed in drab seaside-resort green, with terminal wood rot at their feet and noxious rubbish bins to the rear.

You need to stand out about a mile offshore. Thereafter, a route more or less parallel to the shoreline takes you across Felixstowe and Wadgate Ledges, where there are shallows close to the *Wadgate* green buoy itself. Avoiding the drying areas of Andrews Spit, off Landguard Point and to the north of green *Beach End*, you should arrive at a point halfway between *Platters* south cardinal mark and green *Rolling Ground*; the latter well named, for that very phenomenon can really seem to occur in the troubled waters that can exist in this area. After this, you are required to cross the shipping lane at ninety degrees and take up an entry course on the south side of the main buoyed channel, in never less than about 4m, as shown on the chart. This is the standard recommended track for yachts. A return to the main channel is restricted until you are past Shotley Spit.

Craft approaching from the south will have arrived via either the east or the west of Cork Sand. The easterly approach by the Roughs picks up the buoyed channel somewhere between the red *Cork* and *Cork Sand* and then proceeds almost due westerly on to Pitching Ground, for there is no escape, and so into the haven ports area. The westerly approach uses the Medusa Channel, meeting the shipping channel between *Landguard* north cardinal mark and red *Cliff Foot*.

## The Haven Ports

Harwich, Felixstowe Container Port and Parkeston Quays provide as much to delight the eye as marvel at; they must rank as a positive wonderland for a photographer. They combine in fact into one of the busiest ports in the UK, with a host of speedy tugs and pilot cutters in the harbour. Their masters are always well prepared to spot yachts, errant or otherwise, in advance of any difficulty, but all cruising skippers must be particularly vigilant when negotiating this port area. The official harbour launch *Valentine* is on station at summer weekends to advise, assist and discipline leisure craft if necessary. You can call them on VHF Ch 71.

The large ferries bound for the continent contrast dramatically with the Trinity House light vessels at their moorings just off Shotley Gate. Seen in their seldom disturbed berths, it is difficult to imagine how their majestic forms and masterful turrets could ever be menaced by the coastal waters of the North Sea.

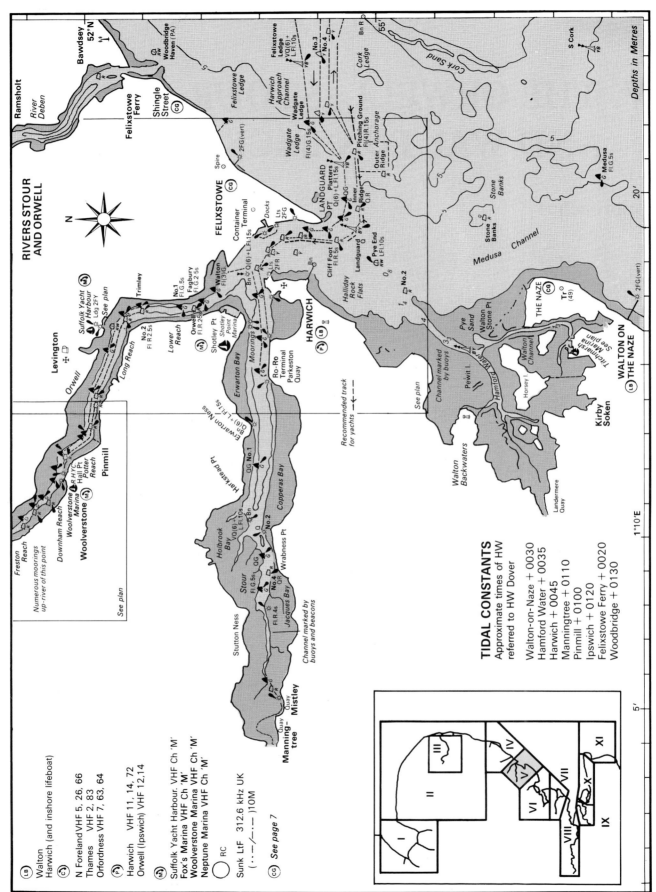

RIVERS STOUR AND ORWELL

TIDAL CONSTANTS

Approximate times of HW
referred to HW Dover

Walton-on-Naze + 0030
Hamford Water + 0035
Harwich + 0045
Manningtree + 0110
Pinmill + 0100
Ipswich + 0120
Felixstowe Ferry + 0020
Woodbridge + 0130

Walton Harwich (and inshore lifeboat)

N Foreland VHF 5, 26, 66
Thames      VHF 2, 83
Orfordness VHF 7, 63, 64

Harwich   VHF 11, 14, 72
Orwell (Ipswich) VHF 12,14

Suffolk Yacht Harbour. VHF Ch 'M'
Fox's Marina VHF Ch 'M'
Woolverstone Marina VHF Ch 'M'
Neptune Marina VHF Ch 'M'

Sunk LtF   312.6 kHz UK
(·· –/–·· –·· )10M

See page 7

# The Orwell

## Shotley Point Marina

Before actually entering the Orwell, there is the new development of the marina facility by the junction of the Stour and Orwell at Shotley Point to be noted. It is situate at the tip of Shotley peninsula.

The marina offers the following advice to visitors for approach and locking: 'ENTRANCE CHANNEL: Yachts approaching from seaward must keep to the track recommended by the Harwich Harbour Board as published in their guide, until reaching the Shotley Spit beacon (YB) then steer west until the piles marking the outer channel limits are reached. From there the channel is controlled by an Inogon light mounted on the east side of the lock buttress which indicated when a vessel is on the correct bearing. A vertical black stripe indicates the correct track and a broad arrow indicates direction in which to alter course to come back on track. On arrival at the lock approach there are some waiting pontoons with access bridge to the shore at the lock buttress on the port side. Passage through the lock is controlled by red (no go) and green (go) lights operated by the lockmaster. He can be contacted on VHF Ch 37 (Ch 'M'). At all times please comply with the lockmaster's instructions over the public address speaker.

THE LOCK: Vessels using the lock should provide fenders port and starboard and mooring lines to attach to the cleats on the floating fenders which rise and fall with the water level in the lock barrel and are mounted on each lock wall. The cycle when the lock is being worked takes about five minutes after all boats have been secured. Be prepared for some turbulence in the lock as the penstocks are opened, vessels need to be well secured to the floating fenders as there is a strong surge usually towards the inner mitre gates. Please advise the Lockmaster of the name and length of your boat as you pass through and new arrivals or visitors are asked to pay a call on the marina control tower after they have secured at their berth. The lockmaster will direct visitors to a berth.'

The marina was opened in 1988 by Lord Lewin, Admiral of the Fleet, with a ritual entrance of the sailing barge *Ethel Ada*, to be the centrepiece of the Classic Boat Centre. This marina-based leisure facility has a capacity of 350 berths in a locked basin that affords access at all states of the tide. From there it is no distance at all to the River Orwell proper which is entered between points with names on which to ponder: Bloody Point and Fagbury Hill.

# More Orwell

The Orwell is not a very long river, being no more than 10 miles from its entrance to Ipswich Docks; but is does pack an enormous variety into its short course. The inexorable progress of its commercial traffic contrasts markedly with the serenity of its peacefully changing scenery which shows a variety of trees, smaller greenery and mixed veg. The banks of the river grow in stature until, at times, they are quite substantial. Novel on the East Coast, this.

The lower reach of the river has marshes on each side backed by wooded hills which shortly march directly down to the river, establishing the Orwell as different from anything to the south almost until the Dart.

The standard buoyage has been well designed and maintained. It is frequent enough even for poorest East Coast visibility throughout the channel which is no more than 2½ cables wide at some points and is dredged to 5·8m right up to Ipswich. For most of the time, it is possible to see the way ahead well and clear; and with such a deep channel, often straight, it is permissible for even first-time visitors to let eyes wander over the attractions of the passing scene. I find it odd that Messrs Edwards and McKnight, both experts in these areas, seem not to be impressed by it.

Full fathom five is not what the river carries; neither is there coral from bones nor pearls from eyes; but of the Orwell in very truth it can be said, 'Nothing of him that doth fade, But doth suffer a sea-change, Into something rich and strange'. Of all the areas covered by this volume, this is the one that has altered more than any other; indeed, it has been transformed, and nothing that has not been for good. Not only are there now more marinas than there were before, but two of the three that have been there some time have themselves been refurbished in accord with what is happening around them.

As for anchorages in the river, the first comes well after Shotley Point Marina on the port hand. It is towards the west bank, above Fagbury Point and green *No.1* to the east and, off the Shotley Marshes, looking to the villages of Shotley and Shotley Street shoresides. Lots of folk use it quite happily, but I prefer to go a little further upstream, where there are two more. Both are on the

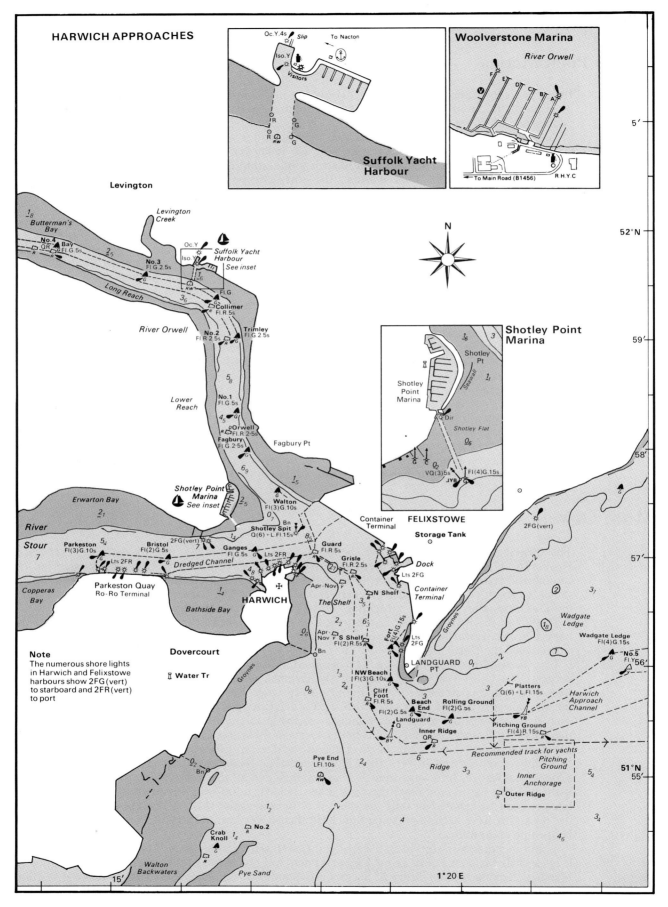

**HARWICH APPROACHES**

**Suffolk Yacht Harbour**

Oc.Y.4s · Slip · To Nacton
Iso.Y · Visitors
R · G · RW · G

**Woolverstone Marina**

*River Orwell*

F · E · D · CT · B · A
V
To Main Road (B1456) · R.H.Y.C

5′

Levington

Butterman's Bay
No.4 Bay QR G Fl.G.5s
*Levington Creek*

Oc.Y · Iso.Y · *Suffolk Yacht Harbour See inset*

52°N

No.3 Fl.G.2.5s
*Long Reach*
RW
Collimer Fl.R.5s
No.2 Fl.R.2.5s
Trimley Fl.G.2.5s
*River Orwell*
Fl.G

59′

N

**Shotley Point Marina**

Shotley Pt
Shotley Point Marina
Seawall
Dir
VQ(3)5s · Q2 · JYB · Fl(4)G.15s
*Shotley Flat*

FELIXSTOWE
Storage Tank

58′

*Lower Reach*
No.1 Fl.G.5s
Orwell Fl.R.2.5s
Fagbury Fl.G.2.5s
Fagbury Pt

Shotley Point Marina *See inset*
Walton Fl(3)G.10s
Shotley Spit Q(6)+L.Fl.15s
Bn

Container Terminal

2FG(vert)

57′

Erwarton Bay
River Stour
Parkeston Fl(3)G.10s
Bristol Fl(2)G.5s
Lts 2FR
Ganges Fl.G.5s · Lts 2FR
2FG(vert)
Guard Fl.R.5s
Grisle Fl.R.2.5s
Guard
*Dredged Channel*
Apr-Nov
Dock Lts 2FG
Container Terminal

Copperas Bay
Parkeston Quay Ro-Ro Terminal
Bathside Bay
**HARWICH**
The Shelf
N Shelf
Apr-Nov S Shelf Fl(2)R.5s
Fort Fl(4)G.15s
Lts 2FG

Wadgate Ledge
(2)
(1)
Wadgate Ledge Fl(4)G.15s
No.5 Fl.Y

56′

**Note**
The numerous shore lights in Harwich and Felixstowe harbours show 2FG(vert) to starboard and 2FR(vert) to port

Dovercourt
Water Tr

NW Beach Fl(3)G.10s
Cliff Foot Fl.R.5s
Beach End Fl(2)G.5s
Landguard
LANDGUARD PT
Rolling Ground Fl(2)G.5s
Platters Q(6)+L.Fl.15s
Pitching Ground Fl(4)R.15s
Harwich Approach Channel

Inner Ridge QR
*Recommended track for yachts*
Pitching Ground
Inner Anchorage

51°N
55′

Pye End LFl.10s
RW
Ridge
Outer Ridge

Crab Knoll
No.2

Walton Backwaters
Pye Sand

15′
1°20′E

# BUOYAGE
## River Orwell: from Shotley Spit

continued

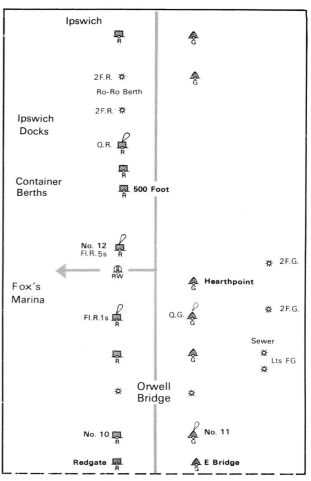

Continued from top left

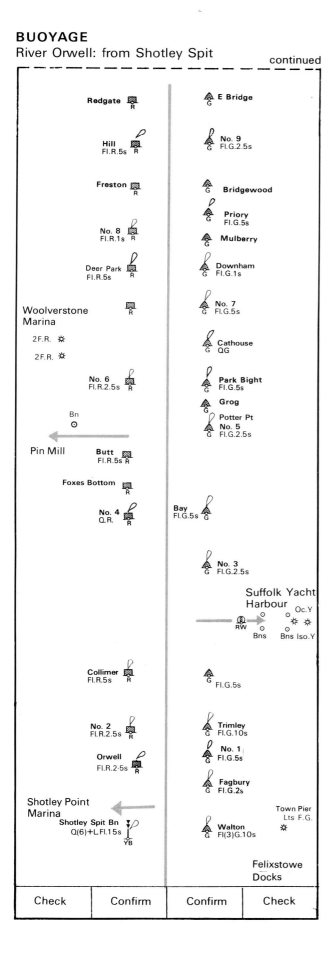

| Check | Confirm | Confirm | Check |
|-------|---------|---------|-------|

port hand; the first, a quite restricted area, is near the red *No.2* below Collimer Point old hard and tide gauge and the second, a much longer stretch, towards what is now the south bank of the river, near the north mile marks, green *Bay*, and red *Foxes Bottom*. It is essential to be well clear of the main channel which is used by big ships. Anchor lights are equally essential in all places of course; but in some places they are more equally essential than others. These are some of those places.

## Suffolk Yacht Harbour

Suffolk Yacht Harbour has now had to surrender to Shotley Point Marina its claim to fame as the first of the welcoming hosts on the Orwell. It is a well protected facility, so much so that you see little of it, apart from masts, until you have fully opened up its entrance. The approach channel, a straight run in at right angles to the fairway, is well marked and dredged and lies just past *Collimer* on the SE side, starboard hand going up river. Craft under 1·5m have access at all times through the channel that is now dredged to 1·5m LWS. Deeper draught vessels will have to wait accordingly. Reception, consisting of two 9·0m pontoons, is dead ahead on entering; that is, to the east of the fuel bay which is just inside the entrance.

Inside, you will find that many recent changes have made a stop here a pleasure, for cruising amenities are all up to date, thanks to their recent alterations and refurbishment. Because of this and their established personal attention to yachtsmen's needs, Suffolk Yacht Harbour has an EC-wide reputation and is usually busy. Permanent berths are at a premium. Power and water are now available at all jetties. There is a new shower and toilet block, a well stocked chandlery and a small general grocery shop. The Haven Ports Yacht Club lightship clubhouse, recently brillianted bright red, is known throughout the cruising fraternity worldwide. I have been shown its picture in France taken by a Dutchman; in Spain taken by a Frenchman; and in Ibiza taken by a German. They all mentioned the excellence of the food, and that kind of publicity speaks for itself.

## Pin Mill

However, there are places where change is not the keynote, and is completely without enchantment; neither for hosts nor guests. Such a spot is Pin Mill, the Thames bargee's idea of the 'Great Mooring in the Sky', the 'Haven' called 'Heaven' or is it the other way round?

Some Pin Mill folk were hurt, some put out and some made angry by what I originally wrote of the place. Some were moved to question whether or not I had actually visited the place. Clearly, I had not made clear the fascination, curious but authentic, that the place holds for me, and for most people who visit it. It is true that I am neither in the mould of the Ancient Mariner nor of the class of Maurice 'Swatchways' Griffiths; so my feelings about this locale will not be in accord with those who have been brought up on traditions and word of mouth going back decades if not centuries.

But I can speak as I find. First, here are the defects as per the canons of those who like awarding marks or coming first: Pin Mill will never win silver anchors, gold stars or any other prestigious prizes for being the best kept boat berth in the UK. It is not the kind of neat'n'nice village to feature in *Country Life* nor is it a scandal site for the sore eyes of the *Daily Star*. Neither will it achieve fame and fortune from vast sales of calendars and postcards of German tourists standing largely in front of rose-strewn doors. It doesn't even possess a single picturesque craftsman, with or without cider, straw and clay pipe, making model barges in birch or Spanish oak.

So; what is the good news? Pin Mill is solid and substantial. It is an abode where gravel from the boulders of epochs has fused with the bed of the vigorous river by its portals to create not only a symbolically concrete-hard-fact of riparian life but also a hard for all men, all boats and all seasons. Its inhabitants come from that stock that knows the value of things, yet often underprice and undersell them to admiring guests. They also know that too swift arrives as tardy as too slow; and can see no reason why the passing of the past in places elsewhere should forecast the demise of the present or threaten the future of any or all of its livelihood. Pin Mill will surely never try to emulate Shotley Point Marina nor Port Solent, and there is its strength: it cares little for the current gusts of change and will quietly wait for them to die away before it does. Pin Mill is *sui generis*; and likes itself quite a lot that way.

With regard to facts, figures and facilities, Pin Mill is not without detail. The Ipswich Port Authority's representative, the official designation for the non-existent post of Pin Mill harbourmaster, is Tony Ward, of Ward's chandlery and moorings. Harbourmaster he may not be, but master of the harbour and hard task master he certainly is.

Pin Mill

His headquarters are at the top of that hard. The end of its concrete run is marked by a red can. Access isn't seriously restricted by tides, but landing can be difficult one hour each side of LW. Swinging moorings are available, and during the summer about half a dozen are reserved, and all clearly marked, for visitors. There are possibilities of anchoring, and the prudent skipper takes advantage of Tony Ward's presence and expert local knowledge before thinking of dropping anything permanent. Mrs Ward will also serve, minister and advise from the small but well stocked and stacked chandlery, marked in the lane by the fuel pumps.

Most boating facilities are to hand: in addition to Orwell Yacht Services, there is F. A. Webb, the yacht and boatbuilder who specialises in repairing Thames sailing barges; and King's boatbuilders, (Harry King and Sons, contact Geoff King). Pin Mill Sailing Club looks after all kinds of interests and is a good and friendly contact for visitors (they have showers as well). There is no post office or shop, although Webb's do carry a supply of groceries and possess an off licence. Most village services are found in the ½ mile distant Chelmondiston (and if you want to be ahead of the yuppies, you must try calling it Chelmo). Pin Mill is a traditional, quiet anchorage where all the best in East Coast hospitality is to be found at the Butt and Oyster. This characterful and atmospheric pub has not yet found itself in the pages of *Michelin* or Egon Ronay, but it is legendary among sailing folk, and that is probably an accolade with more kudos and bite; or is it bight?

Character and characters abound all round: from the boldly brazen blurb advertising the talented presence of a floating tattoo artist to the strutting Ladies Bountiful who walk their dogs whilst still driving their cars, to the jeopardy of both. But sadly, the scene is played against the inescapable backdrop of barges that have seen better days and a wooden half submerged structure that in silhouette on a murky evening stands like a gibbet at the ready.

Classically and traditionally, Pin Mill is the quiet centre of it all where you may hear the still small voice, and this may be so, indeed is, for many of the 365; but come the weekends in the season and Pin Mill comes on heat with aggressive drivers who lose their cool when they discover that they cannot come and go like crazy in the restricted channels, be they afloat or ashore.

## The RHYC and Woolverstone Marina

After Pin Mill come two contrasts: the esoteric Royal Harwich Yacht Club and the exoteric Woolverstone Marina; the first hazily redolent of its founding and the second now in the hands of the marina-voracious, near-omnipresent MDL.

The Royal Harwich is an eminent club to which access is restricted not by sills, tides, times or winds but by less perceptible, more elusive shibboleths. It possesses a few moorings and members of other yacht clubs are welcome. They publish a most useful guide to local facilities for visiting yachtsmen.

The RHYC is very close to the next station up the river: Woolverstone Marina which has both swinging moorings and pontoon berths. It is on the port hand, between and opposite *Cathouse* and green *No.7*. Its final approach, heralded by a long line of beautifully maintained racing craft, leads to the visitors' berths on the outer pontoons, and its entrances and exits are marked by red and green beacons: the former downstream, the latter upstream. The outside pontoon berths are situated at what are known as the hammer heads because of their shape. A little further upstream are more berths for visitors immediately round the top port corner. Some person is usually in attendance. There are comprehensive boating and domestic services, with pantry, a well-stocked grocery shop and an equally well-stocked off-licence.

The down to earth/river, somewhat brusque if not harsh, business manner of the marina has the mien of hard-at-it, busy efficiency, and is in marked contrast with the refined and delicate aristocratically laid back style of the marquises and marquees of its downstream but not downmarket neighbour. It is always a cause for sadness when enthusiasm for business deals seems to overwhelm any desire for kindly kinship or friendly contact.

# More Orwell

The buoyage can be a bit difficult to spot above *Cathouse*, with a number of greens being difficult to isolate from their confusing backgrounds, especially with incipient mist. However, a reasonable middle of the road track is to make for the middle arch of the 'new' road bridge with its air draught of 40m. Look out for blind green *No.11*, just before the bridge, where there is a dog leg. In poor visibility it is easy to make an error, since some of the buoys are numberless.

Almost immediately after Woolverstone, towards the NE bank, by the unmarked green buoy between *Prior* and *Mulberry*, there is a green beacon that tells of a small broken down jetty, dangerous pipes and stakes, and slightly further upstream there are some standard diamond beacon cautionaries. While on the SW side, in Downham Reach, is the red *Deer Park* buoy, but it is no longer little dears but big cows that make the running shoresides on the gracious grazing of the splendid park. By red *No.8*, on either side the river lie, not fields of barley or indeed of rye, but other grasses for different lasses; while in contrast, are castles, red brick halls and palaces. Then to change the ambience utterly and abruptly there is a hostelry at neighbouring Freston where you can put the boot in; put your foot in the door; or get your feet under the table. It is called the Boot Inn.

Mighty big ships navigate the Orwell by day and by night.

The new motorway bridge presents many aspects as you progress up river.

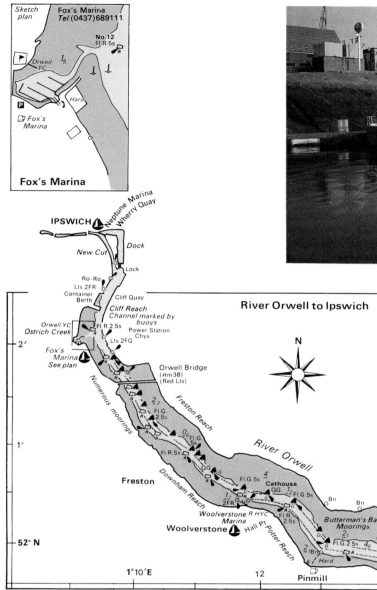

No matter how many times it may have changed hands, it is still known as Fox's.

# Fox's and Double's

Fox's Marina can now correctly be called Fox's again; although for most on the river it was never properly anything else. The last of the river marinas, not far upstream from the 'new' road bridge, it is easily spotted on the port hand by the red *No.12*. The approach channel has now been dredged to take vessels up to 2m at all states of the tide. The facilities are comprehensive, and now there is the benefit of mains power and water and a new loo and shower block. General expansion has been the order of the day, but the old order of well-organised, fast and friendly service has not changed; nor have their bills yet escalated out of sight. It is charmingly tucked away, if that is how you can describe a marina with 100 berths, in a quiet corner that gives immediate access to a pub and a shop in which it is worth spending both time and money.

Not long ago, it was almost impossible to find a 'chance' berth, but now there are over 100, and chances are better. Over the years, it has 'suffered' all kinds of sea changes. It has been known variously as Fox's, Ipswich, Oyster and other sobriquets; it has been part and parcel of all kinds of big-bang financial wheeling/dealing; but it has never ceased to improve its skills, its services, its facilities, its facade and its image. It is a welcoming and efficient place.

Malcolm Westmoreland is the presiding genius. There are now power and water on all pontoons; new toilets, showers, chandlery and yacht spray centre (always one of their specials). Diesel and gas are always available.

It is also possible to approach the Ostrich Yacht Club who maintain premises north of the marina. Shoresides and waterfronts can be well sussed out from the road bridge while en route for shopping in case you have in mind to play guest. They also have their moorings in the river.

Doubles, the quaintly named stores, is proud to have been established in 1929; but their service is of the grand kind that goes back to Napoleon and Dickens. Indeed, Browning would have found his wishes granted here, for in his poem *Shop* he wrote: 'I want to know a butcher paints. A baker rhymes for his pursuit, Candle-stick-maker much acquaints His soul with song, or haply, mute, Blows out his brains upon the flute'.

I don't know about selling blunderbusses, blowing out brains, nor finding Flute the bellows-mender at home, but you never know your luck at Doubles, for this is what they say of themselves: 'We are within walking distance from the marina and specialise in provisioning yachts with all general grocery, fresh fruit and vegetables and off-licence requirements. Free delivery service'. Open 364 days a year, they encourage you to 'Ask for what you want. You never know it might be hidden away'. Topsy emulators, they have just growed into something bigger, brighter and busier year after year.

I visited the much older Ostrich (1612) the first time I came here, and cannot forget the joy with which I read the following: 'I Thomas Pimper, drank 2 cups of Sack with my friend J. Hotlip 8th May 1698 in this house and 6 cups this day April 1702.' Nearly 300 years on, sack butting has to be on its way out as the Ostrich makes inexorable upwardly mobile moves.

At one time, Fox's was virtually the head of navigation except for those daring eccentrics who fancied their somewhat doubtful chances in the Cut. Now there are marina facilities in Ipswich Dock, at Wherry Quay and Neptune Marina, so a foray almost into the centre of the city can be achieved by boat.

# Ipswich

It is possible to navigate to Ipswich at all states of the tide. The lock is 91m by 15·2m and is manned 24 hours; but the lock crew is mustered only between 2 hours before and 1 hour after HW. Yachts are asked to navigate at levels between the river and the wet dock, as and when these occur. That can vary from as much as 2½ hours around tide time, to no level being achieved at all. Harbour staff will instruct.

There is something legendary about the locking times that yachtsmen are supposed to use. I was given the above information verbatim from the lock master; but in the port authority's handbook, yachtsmen are asked to use the locking facilities only from 1 hour before until HW Ipswich. It is clearly wise to take advice before arriving. There is a waiting pontoon outside the lock.

Ipswich Dock was once a Mecca denied to all but a few privileged yachtsmen. Things have now improved dramatically, and a great deal of the dockland area has been given over to leisure and pleasure; some of it is, predictably, up for grabs. But already completed are the differing but equally attractive premises of the consular building and the deli/cious/cate/ssen food bazaar known as Mortimers. Both are appealing from the outside, but the latter has an unique magnet inside for all gastronomic connoisseurs.

Two marina facilities are but part of the Ipswich new look: Neptune Marina is to be found outside what used to be Whitmore's, one of the famed chandlers of the East Coast and a severe loss to yachtsmen, for it changed into a snooker hall with talk of a wine bar. Neptune is a new berthing facility with floating pontoons for boats to a maximum of 12m LOA x 4m beam with minimum alongside depth of 2·5m. Electricity, water and, a new ploy up here, telephone points. When wishing to berth here, contact the Orwell Navigation Service (Ipswich Port Radio) VHF Ch 16 and 14 when at *No.9* buoy to check approach and admission through wet dock.

For outside locking times, Neptune Marina has established waiting buoys (bright orange) just below the road bridge at Freston Reach. Once inside the lock, mooring is bow or stern to, using port and starboard securing lines. Pick up at buoy and make fast line as tightly as possible. Ensure that the vessel has two quarter lines to the pontoon. Normally the level will drop about 1m after mooring up. Glasspool and Swann are the skippers.

More new buildings and refurbishment have made this area by the really attractive old custom house quite unrecognisable. Not even Prince Charles would be likely to suggest that what has happened to the old malt kiln can be described in carbuncle terms. In any event, it is a treat and a delight for yachtsmen to find an alongside quay stretch offering electricity, water, showers and more; with berthing for over 45m LOA and 2·5m draught (although all bigger sailing vessels are restricted by the 40m air draught of the (new) Orwell road bridge. John Beard is The Man; and he will see you right.

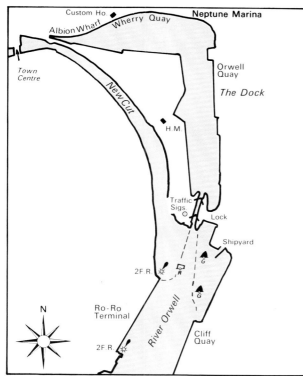

**IPSWICH DOCKS**

Ipswich Docks with its architecture old and new now offers
hospitality and comprehensive services to visiting yachtsmen.

## BUOYAGE
### Approaches to Harwich

| Check | Confirm | Confirm | Check |
|---|---|---|---|

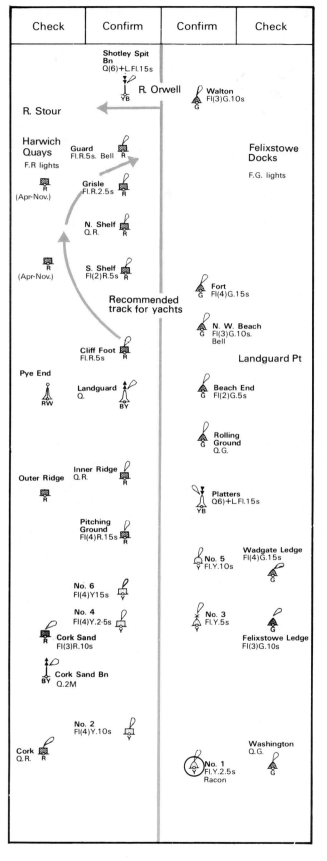

Shotley Spit
Bn
Q(6)+L.Fl.15s

R. Orwell
YB

Walton
Fl(3)G.10s
G

R. Stour

Harwich
Quays

F.R lights

Guard
Fl.R.5s. Bell
R

Felixstowe
Docks

F.G. lights

R
(Apr-Nov.)

Grisle
Fl.R.2.5s
R

N. Shelf
Q.R.
R

(Apr-Nov.)

S. Shelf
Fl(2)R.5s
R

Fort
Fl(4)G.15s
G

Recommended
track for yachts

N. W. Beach
Fl(3)G.10s.
Bell
G

Cliff Foot
Fl.R.5s
R

Landguard Pt

Pye End
RW

Landguard
Q.
BY

Beach End
Fl(2)G.5s
G

Rolling
Ground
Q.G.
G

Outer Ridge
R

Inner Ridge
Q.R.
R

Platters
Q6)+L.Fl.15s
YB

Pitching
Ground
Fl(4)R.15s
R

Wadgate Ledge
Fl(4)G.15s

No. 5
Fl.Y.10s
Y

G

No. 6
Fl(4)Y15s
Y

No. 4
Fl(4)Y.2.5s
Y

No. 3
Fl.Y.5s
Y

G

Cork Sand
Fl(3)R.10s
R

Felixstowe Ledge
Fl(3)G.10s

Cork Sand Bn
Q.2M
BY

No. 2
Fl(4)Y.10s
Y

Washington
Q.G.

Cork
Q.R.
R

No. 1
Fl.Y.2.5s
Racon
Y

G

## BUOYAGE
### River Stour: from Shotley Spit

| Check | Confirm | Confirm | Check |
|---|---|---|---|

Channel continues to Manningtree

Mistley

2F.R.
Baltic Wf

No. 15
Fl(2)G.5s
G

No.14
R

No. 13
Q.G.
G

No. 12
Q.R.
R

No. 11
G

No. 10
Fl.R.
R

No. 9
G

No. 8
R

No. 7
Q.G.
G

No. 6
Bn
Fl.R.4s

No.5
Fl.G.5s
G

No. 4
Q.R.
R

No. 3
Q.G.
G

Bn
No. 2
Q.
BY

Bn
V.Q(6)FL.Fl.10s

Erwarton
Ness

No. 1
Q.G.
G

Bn
Q(6)+L.Fl.15s
YB

Parkeston Quay

lights show 2F.R.

Parkeston
Fl(3)G.10s
G

Bristol
Fl(2)G.5s
G

Shotley Pier

2F.G.

Harwich

Ganges
Fl(2)G.5s
G

Harwich Harbour
Lights 2 F.R.

Shotley Spit
Q(6)+L.Fl.15s
YB

Guard
Fl.R.5s
Bell
R

# The River Stour

Overall, the river extends for 35 miles between Harwich and its (now weeded-up) source. The 25 miles above Manningtree are acknowledged by many authorities on such matters as being some of the most beautiful in England, if not the world. They certainly had their appeal for some painters' eyes, having been immortalised by Constable and Gainsborough. They are no doubt the ones I should have concentrated on, humping my canoe from one mini navigable stretch to another.

As it is, I am unconvinced, and aware only that the ten miles from Harwich to Manningtree cannot even squeeze into the picturesque division being, in the main, such a bleak and featureless vista. There are a few hills around and the Holbrook Royal Hospital School stands out conspicuously but without aesthetic appeal. Opposite is the drabness of Wrabness and, further upstream on the same bankside, the almost twinned villages of Mistley and Manningtree. Mistley is quite properly known for its Thames barges; while Manningtree lays claim to fame as being the headquarters of one Matthew Hopkins, Witchfinder General, who in his day sent to their deaths more than 400 persons for supposedly dabbling in witchcraft.

The Admiralty *Pilot* says of the Stour: '... flows into Harwich Harbour from W, provides communication with Mistley and Manningtree, 8 miles above Harwich. Its banks are from ¾ to 1 mile wide, but the navigable channel is reduced to a width from 1 to 3 cables by drying mud flats extending from the banks; these mud flats are intersected by creeks. There are dredged depths of 7·2m off Harwich, thence the depth decreases irregularly as the river is ascended. The channel winds but is well marked. There is only about 0·5m when nearing Mistley.'

Those who passionately plead the charms of Mistley, Manningtree and the Stour at large are members of the same kind of brigade that cannot bear to look realistically at Pin Mill. Their wishes being indeed father, mother and midwife to the thought, their justification and verification are to be found lurking deep in the wish fulfillment well of their own passionate imaginings.

Anchorages, form a major attraction for anyone who is going to exploit the River Stour; and this is where it can be said to come into its own tiny corner of the East Coast world. Before considering these anchorages, a cautionary word: the Stour is neither a predictable nor a professionally dredged river, and is little used by anything approaching the epithet 'big ship'. The consequence is that visitors are likely to find the bottom one way or another, sooner or later during sojourns in the river. If you have in mind to anchor more than just once, you should have the kind of stout East Coast boat that will feel at home in shoal waters and be able to take the ground, while under way or at anchor, without problems.

With that in mind, let us turn to the first of these anchorages, though by no means the most attractive, but a happy choice because of its reasonable access to a landing place and then on to civilisation in the form of the village of Erwarton. It lies off the eponymously named Ness, near the remains of the old quay. Safe non-grounding water for 2m craft is delineated by the distance off of the south cardinal mark. Landing is not without its problems and a certain amount of strength and agile guile will serve you well. Stout foot gear is advised.

The next choices come with the generality of mud flats in the Holbrook Bay vicinity. Perhaps the best known is the safe, well protected spot just above Wrabness Point, where 2m craft should stay afloat throughout low water, and access can be made at all times. The village is achieved only after something of an uncompromising uphill walk.

On the other side of the river, between Harkstead Point and Stutton Ness, sounding like locations from *Heartbreak House* or *Nightmare Abbey*, are the channels of Holbrook Bay. 2m craft can reach the *Holbrook* south cardinal mark at all states of the tide. After that, it is a case of spending a tide or two in the tender working out which of the channels, pools or ditches takes your fancy. Landing is possible at Holbrook Creek Head, once you have found your way by grace and favour of the withied troughs. It is one of the most pleasant places on the river, and there are safe anchorages up the creeks for two to three cables, more or less par for the gutway course as we move into the more southerly of the East Coast rivers, and this kind of cruising becomes less extraordinary.

As for the rest, only the peace and quite compensates for the narrow and tortuous channel that wends its way through the broad stretches of the river from there to the barrier at Cattawade. Mistley and Manningtree can be approached at high water, preferably on spring tides, with the buoyed channel being strictly observed with an additional eye on the sounder. Commercial vessels navigate to Mistley, but that doesn't mean that anybody can.

Perhaps the most interesting and rewarding parts of the river are those to be found near Shotley, where the Stour joins the Orwell. There are thriving combinations of business if not merchant venturers, pleasure seekers, princes of commerce and all the liege lords of sea-traffic, as well as all the other impressive trappings of the famed Haven Ports. Certainly, they are the liveliest; and, near the new marina, the ones in most demand.

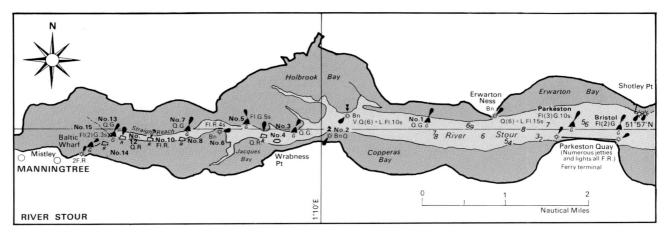

In conclusion: the Stour is no place for those in search of sophistication or comprehensive facilities; nor for that matter for those who want no more than a safe and relatively comfortable berth. It is, in essence, a private chapter in an obscure book, suited best to those who are used to taking and suffering pains, but who still remain susceptible to the very real pleasures of shoal draught art and craft. The fact that I am not a fully paid up, card carrying member, will, in the long run I am sure, redound only to my loss.

# The Walton Backwaters

## Approach

This multitude of quiet anchorages behind Walton-on-the-Naze and near the haven ports of Harwich and Felixstowe have become increasingly popular over the years. But it is still possible to find near-secluded anchorages where you will not be accosted by the rest of the boating world demanding its rights, nor woken at unearthly hours by the noisome vroom-vroom-broom-broom of some British skipper pretending to be German driving a cruiser.

The approach from the south majors on picking up the tower at Walton-on-the-Naze, crossing Naze Ledge and using the Medusa channel leaving *Stone Banks* to starboard. You then look out for the notorious *Pye Ender*. Although it has been renewed in the past few years, and is now maintained by Big Brother, it is still never very easy to identify.

In general, it is just not sensible for strangers to be navigating around the Halliday Rock Flats and Pennyhole Bay at anything worse than half tide. You won't be able to get into the Backwaters before this time, and you will only risk finding the bottom fairly frequently. Should you ever make the trip to the Backwaters from Haven Ports area, it is worth knowing that a wind against tide configuration will expose you to the peaks and troughs of a quite unpleasant beam sea.

The only sailing directions I had to follow on my first visit went something like this: 'From the *Stone Banks* buoy a course of 345 to 350 should bring into line three conspicuous white building blocks. When the lower of the disused Dovercourt Lights is in line, the *Pye End* buoy will lie between the two left hand ones. However, this very same background can also confuse the issue.'

I spent ages sorting out the multiplicity of possible candidates for white buildings before rejecting that method as being quite unproductive for strangers. I returned to the chart and the good old hand bearing.

I shall not readily forget that first attempt. First, as a novice skipper, I was becoming rapidly exhausted by having to contend and bargain with 101 spotted dinghies, all racing like mad. Then, in spite of all my work with white buildings, directions, charts and compasses I still could lay neither hand nor eye upon the wretched *Pye End* buoy. I jilled around for another quarter hour knowing I had to be at least somewhere near the right spot. In the end I felt forced to admit defeat, for by now the tide was ebbing and I had visions of a forced night's vigil on The Stone.

So, reluctantly, because I lacked the confidence to be other, I steamed up to some nearby fishermen in a couple of boats that had been there for at least half an hour. I hailed the four fishermen: 'Where can I find the *Pye End* buoy?'

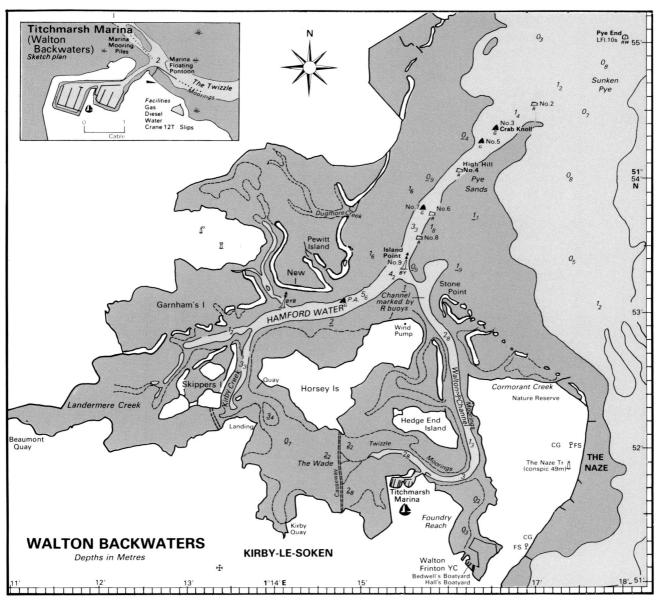

**Titchmarsh Marina**
(Walton Backwaters)
*Sketch plan*

Marina
Mooring
Piles

2 — Marina
Floating
Pontoon

The Twizzle
Moorings

Facilities
Gas
Diesel
Water
Crane 12T  Slips

0                    1
Cable

N

Pye End
LFl.10s  RW  55'

Sunken
Pye

No.2
R

No.3
Crab Knoll

No.5
G

High Hill
No.4
R
Pye
Sands

No.7
G  No.6
R

No.8
R

Island
Point
No.9
BY

Stone
Point

Channel
marked by
R buoys

Dugmore Creek

Pewitt
Island

New

Garnham's I

HAMFORD WATER

P.A.

Wind
Pump

Cormorant Creek
Nature Reserve

Walton Channel
Moorings

Skippers I

Kirby Creek

Quay

Horsey Is

Landermere Creek

Landing

Beaumont
Quay

The Wade

Twizzle

Hedge End
Island

Moorings

CG  FS

The Naze Tr
(conspic 49m)

THE
NAZE

Causeway

Kirby
Quay

Titchmarsh
Marina

Foundry
Reach

CG
FS

**WALTON BACKWATERS**
*Depths in Metres*

**KIRBY-LE-SOKEN**

Walton
Frinton YC
Bedwell's Boatyard
Hall's Boatyard

11'        12'        13'        1°14' E        15'        17'        18'  51'

Fishermen? Not on your life; or if so not that day. They nudged the two boats only slightly apart to expose and display a gleaming one-eyed red and white monster: the *Pye End* buoy. Their faces were a delight to behold; and mine must have been a sight to see: all during the time that I had been baffled, stymied and foiled in my search for the wretched buoy, they had been quietly replacing it after service.

It has been renewed, revamped and very slightly increased in size, and is now the responsibility of Trinity House. In bright sunlight it winks at you from all of two miles away. But its notoriety will still live in legend.

Years and many *Pye End*-probes later, I now know that there is no serious hazard in the area and a calm scrutiny usually 'unearths' it without fuss. In any case, you can always lay the flattering unction to your soul that it is easier to see it on the way out and so not feel too bad about following a local boat in to the channel. Nowadays, Decca and its successors make the search an entirely different kind of exercise, and the saga of *Pye* is reaching its end.

## Entrance

It is a generally southwesterly run into the backwaters from the *Pye End* buoy, with the buoyed channel being entered between Crabnowe Spit and the northerly fingertip end of the extensive Pye Sand. Indeed, once it and all the other drying areas have been covered, you find yourself in a vast sea with only the narrowest of channels to take you to Island Point where the routes round the island divide.

*119*

I have always tended to the northerly when making my way to the first Backwaters 'gate' of *No. 2* red and green *Crab Knoll*, and have found as much water there as in the channel itself. This cannot be said if you deviate too far to the south.

Once you are in the channel proper (and it does not begin to feel that way until past the tighter gate of red 6 and green 7) the way is then clear and plain sailing all the way up to Island Point, Stone Point, The Twizzle or the Backwaters themselves. The buoys are easily observed, the starboard beacons after Stone Point being withies of good quality, leading right up to the beginning of the permanently laid moorings. The two lines of moorings clearly indicate the main channel.

The Island Point north cardinal marks the Junction; and it is here the cry goes up, 'All Change', for the parting of the ways around Horsey island. Just to starboard but more or less straight ahead lies the main Hamford Water route between acre after acre of saltings and mud flats and the vast capriciously drying areas to the north and, to the south, the down to real earth solid Horsey island. To port is the much used main Walton Channel, and we will look that way first.

Its first landmark, Stone Point, is a popular leisure spot for anchoring and landing. The shingle/sand is clean and steep to and the holding quality for substantial ground tackle is good. Do take proper soundings and lay out the appropriate scope; many folk get taken short by Stone. Others lay off so far that the congregation from time to time extends across the fairway; with not many anchor balls in sight – and once I was completely fooled by a white fender displayed in the rigging.

Off The Point, by Stone Creek near Stone Marsh, are the last places where it is possible to anchor before you move into the major fairway of Walton Channel and then on to Twizzle Creek where are so many moorings; so many discarded and broken pieces of ground tackle; and so many troublesome foul reaches that there is space for neither boat nor anchor to stay in safety. Upon entering Walton Creek, there are two red canned withies to mark the channel, just after Stone Point and by Stone Creek.

## To Walton Mere

The channel runs in a generally southerly direction between the Naze to the east and Hedge-end Island to the west. When wind and tide are both set fair, the fairway, just to the east of southerly, is shown very clearly by the attitudes of the swinging boats; but under inclement conditions the boats do nothing but confuse the stranger. There is a speed limit of 8 knots.

In about a mile or so, Twizzle Creek reaches a junction. There is a substantial turn to starboard and the west, en route for the Wade, the vast drying area by Horsey Mere to the south of Horsey Island and the north of the mainland. This leaves behind, dead ahead and dead dry for much of its time, that tiny creek or gutway known as Foundry Reach that leads to the fount of all Naze knowledge, the Walton and Frinton Yacht Club. Its clubhouse extension is draped with neat net curtains, and the dining room is usually all laid in impeccable style; reminiscent of those best of Brits who in the days of Empire used to dress for dinner in isolated pairs in the jungle.

At high water it is possible to reach the yacht club landing, to water up, take an aperitif, make a meal of trout or just have a snack/chat. The yacht club undertakes the mainly thankless task of furnishing and maintaining the blind buoys in the channel into the town, where there is only 1m in the entrance at LWS.

The adjacent quay is extremely well kept and has beacons to show the entry. They should be closely observed and complied with. The town is very close and nearby are possible short and long term moorings.

Bedwell's administer the moorings that are held in the attractive locked pound where there are bow posts and stern buoys. Craft of 1·8m have access for about an hour each side of high water for the 10–12 days around spring tides. However, there is no guarantee, for sometimes the water does not reach even the 1·5m mark. Berths may be allocated to visitors upon application to the boatyard, which is usually open from 1000 to 1600. It is best to telephone well ahead.

At the Town Quay there is also a small top-of-the-tide hard landing with a (typically territorially) imperative notice from the trustees regarding the mandatory removal and obligatory impounding of boats that do or refrain from doing this or that. It is packed with boats, and nearby can be seen at the walls and gates the sturdy defenses against the flood.

The general tract of some dry land, mud and saltings sometimes known as Walton Mere, is not one devoted to the touring cruising industry, so it just as well to call personally well ahead of any boating visit to see for yourself what is what, and make any necessary arrangements. The buildings are singularly appealing, with some showing of decay, decline and deterioration. But all is as it should be in this best of all possible worlds, for neither the jarring sights nor the cacophonous sounds of the twentieth century will blind the eyeball or deafen the eardrum when you take a stroll round the mud flats in the mini hinterland. I was once accosted when landing from the dinghy by a Charles Dickens Greatly Expecting type of youth with the classic phrase, 'Watch your boat for a bob, sir?'

For all boatyard information, you should contact Frank Halls and Son, Mill Lane, Walton-on-the-Naze. ☎ Frinton-on-Sea (0255) 675596; Bedwell and Co., The Bend, Mill Lane, Walton-on-the-Naze. ☎ Frinton-on-Sea (0255) 675873.

## The Twizzle and Titchmarsh

If not rushing up the creek, or making straightway for one of the Backwater anchorages and looking for something just a little less remote, my first preference is for one of the most amenable spots on the East Coast, Titchmarsh Marina, that agreeable spread at the head waters of the Twizzle. It is very much a low key affair, with the whole setup organised in a non frenetic, pleasant and efficient manner. To judge it by its manner and ethos, you would never form the opinion that it is one of the largest marinas on the East Coast, more than 400 berths inside and 100 outside. In spite of its size, it has kept its quiet charm well and at no sacrifice to efficiency.

Generally speaking, visitors take up berths outside on the sturdy, well maintained pontoons before the entrance. It is also possible for small craft to moor on the inside of these pontoons. Past the entrance, to the westward, there are mooring piles.

The channel to the inner moorings is usually accessible for 1·5m craft at all times, but at low water springs, together with unfavourable winds and bad barometers, there can as little as 0·5m. Exceptionally it can reduce to a trickle.

The marina, like its namesake owner, is available and friendly to almost everyone almost all the time. Strictly speaking the HM keeps office hours, but he is usually around and about; and living on site he is used to a certain lack of formal etiquette when yachtsmen find themselves in trouble. But, no matter what, you will never be denied an East Coast welcome. All in all a splendid spot for the cruising man, novice or sophisticate. Telephone the boss at Frinton (0255) 672185).

Stone Point offers a most attractive welcome by the Walton Backwaters and the Twizzle.

*121*

All boating facilities are available at short notice, and most are on the spot, but for comestibles and other domestics you take the pleasant (except for the rubbish tip) walk to shop and pub via the marina lane to the main road; under half an hour dependent on age, ability and attitude. From time to time you can buy not yet landed fish at the end of the pontoon without having to pay through the nose for it. Further west lies the causeway which you must cross to reach Horsey Mere and the islands of the Backwaters if you are to approach from this side, and we shall be looking at that area from the other approach too.

There is another interesting walk along the sea wall past Colonel's Hard and Caravan Hard into the tourist town of Walton-on-the-Naze. From seaward and also from the Walton Channel, I formed a pleasing impression of Walton, but a close shoresides encounter reveals it to leave a lot to be desired. It is usually crowded far beyond the needs and sense of the leisure industry; is short on important facilities like public lavatories and working telephones; and specialises in shoddy goods. The Backwaters are best beheld without resort or reference to Walton.

## Classic Backwaters

So; back to Island Point for the other route, into Hamford Water, that leads to Landermere and Kirby Creeks where there is a perspective of an altogether different nature. In toto, there are ten low-lying islands in the Hamford Water group with a combined area of little more than five square miles. Many of them are separated by difficult to see narrow channels and confusingly reed-covered meres. While there is good grazing in places, and here and there the isolated brick farmhouse, much of the area is marshlands visited only by wild life. The Essex Naturalists' Society uses Skipper's Island. The sinister Mirador and the many notices invite everyone to 'Keep Off'.

Horsey Island, too, has its own special designation with a notice board proclaiming 'HERE BE WITCHES'. It was a long time before the penny dropped. It was the country of Arthur Ransome's *Secret Water*, a young people's adventure story published in 1939. Horsey Island was Swallow Island and my anchorage was Goblin Creek. The small landing opposite was Witch's Quay; and Horsey Mere was the Red Sea. It is intriguing to discover that his sketch maps are as relevant today as they were before the war.

I remember it as a really quiet spot, particularly in the evenings. More than once I was entertained by the sounds of grey mullet as they nuzzled and nibbled at *Valcon's* hull.

No sooner had they left me to the stillness of that secret place than another visitation took place. A wide spread of floating islets of grey-green phosphorescence covered the surface of the water. It stretched from side to side of the wide channel. The islets moved slowly towards me like an armada of water-borne wills-o'-the-wisp.

Once I got accustomed to the sight, I dropped small pebbles into the glowing swarms. The reward was a show of lights rising and falling like milky sparks in a watery way. It could have been a diminutive St Elmo's Fire.

My mind slowly emptied as I plopped stone after stone into the luminous sheen. I began to feel almost at one with those Jack o' the marine lanterns. I know there is a scientific explanation for that phosphorescence, but I still prefer my own perception of that night's show of sheer natural magic.

There are what are perhaps best described as 'accessible landing places' at a number of points. The ones most useful for shopping at Thorpe-le-Soken are Landermere and Beaumont Quays, both so well inland and drying to over three metres that accurate tidal timings are of the essence; for Kirby-le-Soken it is to Kirby Quay to which you must wander through the gutway that will surely tantalise and may even defeat you; and on the 'mainland' opposite the southeast corner of Skipper's.

The many creeks that surround Horsey Island should be explored by dinghy. Not only is it most enjoyable and relaxing on its own account, but after half tide through to low water it presents an opportunity to inspect the gutways when whims and deviations are at their most apparent. After which you can judge which are of the greatest appeal and where you can take your boat without menace. Most are peaceful and well protected, although Hamford Water itself can get rough in a brisk a northeasterly. It should be noted that the causeway is quite impassable at low water.

So what are the main choices? The first of the true Backwater Ditches usually to attract interest is to be found by the green buoy about five cables up Hamford Water. A low water exploration is a must because of the old 'training wall-embankments'. Between Pewit Island, one of the many that proliferate on the East Coast, and New Island, the waters offer a few pleasant holes for those diligent enough to search them out. You will almost certainly be left in peace and it is a good place from which to watch the world go by. You are not likely to be able to get away until well after half tide.

Walton on the Naze is an unusual place with its hard
and clubhouse creating contrasting perspectives at
the head of the gutway.

Next is the more substantial waterway between Pewit and New to the east and Garnham's and Bramble to the west. After the west cardinal marker, for about a mile the tortuous northerly channel will allow access even at low water to craft of 1·5m, so long as due and constant attention to soundings and surface water signs has been paid. This is still used by biggish commercial boats, but there are some offshoots that offer a safe and secure anchorage. Once again, this tends to be a solitary spot.

Next come the two favourite visitors' channels for anchoring: Landermere and Kirby Creeks. There are moorings in both and clearly marked oyster layings in the latter. Sometimes it is possible to use an available mooring, but do be prepared to be moved along at any hour, for the indigens and other holders have a habit of coming and going at quite unexpected hours. As, for that matter, does the HM Customs launch. You may think you are all alone, but that is not always the case. They are both good spots from which to make excursions into Horsey Mere and the Causeway, where the musselling is rewarding.

I have never spent an unhappy hour in the Walton Backwaters. They offer a choice of berthing or anchoring in well protected conditions; the places likely to attract visitors are in the main all accessible at half tide or better; there are equal opportunities for full blown revelling, mild socialising or almost completely disappearing into utter seclusion; and better than basic facilities are all within easy striking distance with attractive walks. In addition, there are hundreds of miles of cruising waters literally on their watershed doorstep.

## HARWICH/FELIXSTOWE
Access at all times.
**Charts**
Imray C28, Y16
Admiralty 1491, 2052, 2693
**Tides**
Standard port. Dover +0045
**Radio**
VHF Ch 11, 14, 71, 16 (24 hours)
**Authorities**
*Harwich Haven Authority* ☎ Harwich (0255) 243030
*Harwich Haven Operations* ☎ Harwich (0255) 243000
**Marinas and boatyards**
*Shotley Point Marina* Shotley Gate, Ipswich IP9 1QJ ☎ (0473) 788982 *Radio* VHF Ch 80 and 37
*Suffolk Yacht Harbour* Stratton Hall, Levington, Ipswich IP10 0LN ☎ Nacton (0473) 659465 and 659240 *Radio* VHF Radio Ch 'M'
*Jack Ward & Son* Orwell Yacht Services, Pin Mill, Ipswich, Suffolk IP9 1JN ☎ Woolverstone (0473) 780276
*Royal Harwich Yacht Club* Cat House Hard, Woolverstone, Ipswich IP9 1AT ☎ Woolverstone (0473) 780206 (office), 780219 (members)
*Woolverstone Marina* MDL, Woolverstone, Ipswich, Suffolk IP9 1AS ☎ Woolverstone (0473) 780206 and 780354 *Radio* VHF Ch 'M'
*Fox's Marina* The Strand, Wherstead, Ipswich ☎ Ipswich (0473) 689111 *Radio* VHF Ch 'M'

## IPSWICH
Commercial port and harbour.
**Charts**
Imray Y16
Admiralty 2693
**Tides**
+0020 Harwich, Dover +0120
**Radio**
VHF Ch 12, 14, 16 (24 hours)
☎ Ipswich (0473) 231010)
*Locking signals*:
*Day* Ball at masthead south end of west pier head – Proceed outward.
Ball & flag at masthead – Proceed inward.
Ball at yardarm - Dock closed.

*Night* Light on mast at south end of west pier head for inward bound vessels.
Light on pole at north end of east pier head for outward bound vessels.
Green light – Vessels to enter lock.
Red light – Lock closed.
**Marinas and boatyards**
*Neptune Marina* Wherry Quay. Ipswich Port Authority refers to them as port agents, and say prebooking for visitors' berths is necessary through them. ☎ Ipswich (0473) 230109. *Radio* monitors VHF Ch 14 and 'M'; works 'M'

## RIVER STOUR
**Charts**
Imray Y16
Admiralty 1594, 2693
**Tides**
Harwich +0030 (Manningtree), Dover +0110

# VI. THE COLNE AND THE BLACKWATER

## Coastal approaches

The Knoll is the key to the entrance to the cruising grounds of the Blackwater and the Colne. These two rivers share some of the most pleasurable leisurable cruising grounds on the East Coast. Treated together, they afford splendid contrasts and contrasting splendours; and the Imray *Y17* chart *River Colne to the Blackwater and Crouch*, recognises their connections.

Moving down from the Haven Ports towards the *Knoll* cardinal marker, for the Colne, the Blackwater, the Crouch and/or the Roach there are frequent towers to be observed along the coast, but there is one tower that stands out from all the rest. It is distanced from them geographically and stylistically. It is the tower of the Naze.

Twenty four metres high and mounted on a promontory that is itself twenty three metres above sea level, the Naze tower makes an excellent land-mark and also a reminder that the ledge it overlooks reaches out shallowly for about a mile towards the green buoy marking the Medusa Channel, with its overtones of doom-laden myths. The tower is much easier to spot than the *Medusa*, even on radar; although, once, after tedious adjustments, I did manage to get an echo from it at more than a mile.

En route for Colne Point, there is no hazard a mile offshore and enough to entertain the crew even in the lightest of airs. To seaward there is Gunfleet Sand and the disappearing remains of the old lighthouse and beacon. Shoresides, the coast undulates gently and is punctuated by diminutive cliffs that neither threaten vertigo nor peter out into crumbling miniatures. There is a generous smattering of sandy beaches, many of which almost hummock into full-blown dunes, and a sufficiency of hills and trees to give a nicely contrasting prospect. This stretch also contains those twinned opposites Clacton and Frinton, both styles 'on-the-sea', each with their contrasting architecture: contemporary brutish vies with decaying baroque, as does the Victorian yellow-glazed brickwork with the faded greens-and-blues of 1930's pantiles; the concrete shades of pseudo-Bauhaus villas match the pale greys, browns and fawns of once-aspiring Edwardian maisonettes; while for miles high-rise towers compete with Martello towers, water towers and Fawlty Grand Hotel-type towers.

## Close approaches

The most usual approaches to the Colne and the Blackwater are down from the Wallet or through the Wallet/Swin Spitway. From the Wallet, you then pick up the *Knoll* north cardinal and leave it to starboard, or the *North Eagle* and leave it to port. The thing not to do is to get them confused and set a course between them. From the Spitway, you make for the *Knoll* and, immediately after, the *Eagle*. In each case, the next step is to 'gate' the green *Colne Bar* and *North West Knoll* and move on accordingly: more or less northerly towards red *Inner Bench Head* for the Colne; or the green *Bench Head* for the Blackwater.

However, there are some alternatives for shallow draught boats; and if you draw no more than 1·2m, have a good forecast and a rising spring tide, you may feel like exploring them. The best known is the Ray Sand Channel which connects the Crouch and the Blackwater by cutting off Buxey Sand and saving the haul around the Spitway. After that, there are variations: crossing the Whitaker Spit; negotiating the miniature channel by the Knoll and Batchelors Spit; and missing out Bench Head to skirt the old target by Mersea Flat or Cocum Hills when coming from the Blackwater. This latter cuts off the same kind of corner spit in exactly the same way as does the short cut into the Hamble from upstream. However, there are ample markers in the Hamble, but here you need to keep your eye on the sounder for between Mersea Flat and Bench Head there are inconspicuous hazards.

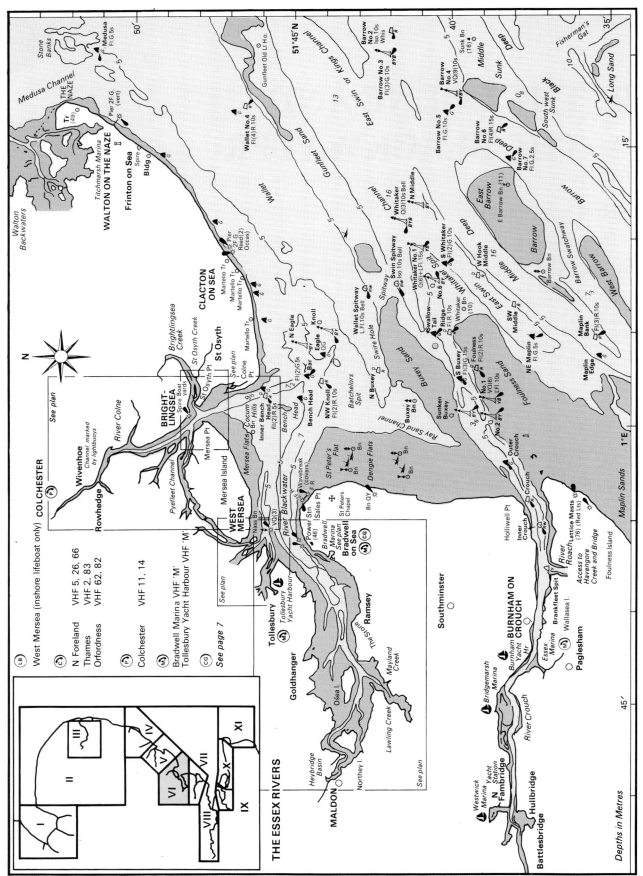

# THE ESSEX RIVERS

**COLCHESTER**

Wivenhoe *Channel marked by lightbuoys*

Rowhedge

**West Mersea** (inshore lifeboat only)

| | |
|---|---|
| N Foreland | VHF 5, 26, 66 |
| Thames | VHF 2, 83 |
| Orfordness | VHF 62, 82 |
| Colchester | VHF 11, 14 |

Bradwell Marina VHF 'M'
Tollesbury Yacht Harbour VHF 'M'

*See page 7*

**BRIGHT-LINGSEA**

**WEST MERSEA**

**Bradwell on Sea**

Tollesbury
Tollesbury Yacht Harbour

Goldhanger

Ramsey

Southminster

**BURNHAM ON CROUCH**
Burnham Yacht Hr

Paglesham

**MALDON**

Heybridge Basin

*See plan*

**Fambridge**
N Station

Westwick Marina Yacht Station

Bridgemarsh Marina

Essex Marina

**Hullbridge**

**Battlesbridge**

*Depths in Metres*

**WALTON ON THE NAZE**

**Frinton on Sea**

**CLACTON ON SEA**

**St Osyth**

Brightlingsea Creek

St Osyth Creek

River Colne

St Osyth Pt

River Blackwater

Mersea Island

Osea I.

Northey I.

Mayland Creek

Lawling Creek

The Stone

Wallasea I.

Brankfleet Spit

River Crouch

River Roach

Lattice Masts (76) (Red Lts)

Access to Havengore Creek and Bridge

Foulness Island

Holliwell Pt

Inner Crouch

Outer Crouch

Maplin Sands

Maplin Edge

NE Maplin Fl.G.5s

Maplin Bank Fl(3)R.10s

SW Middle

S Buxey Fl(3)G.15s

Sunken Buxey

Ray Sand Channel

Dengie Flats

St Peter's Flat

St Peters Chapel

Sales Pt

Power Stn (46)

Bradwell Marina

Nass Bn VQ(3)

Mersea Pt

Mersea Flats

Cocum Hills

Inner Bench Head Fl(2)R.5s

Bench Head Fl(2)R.5s

Bench

NW Knoll Fl(2)R.10s

N Knoll

Eagle

Bar Fl(2)G.5s

N Eagle

Knoll

Colne Pt

Martello Tr

Pier 2F.G Reed(2)

Pier 2F.G (vert)

Stone Banks

Medusa Fl.G.5s

Medusa Channel

THE NAZE

Tr (49)

Titchmarsh Marina

Spire Bldg

Walton Backwaters

Wallet

Wallet No.4 Fl(4)R.10s

Swire Hole

Wallet Spitway L.Fl.10s Bell

Swin Spitway Iso.10s Bell

Spitway

Whitaker Ql(6)+LFl.15s

Whitaker No.1 Ql(6)+LFl.15s

S Whitaker Fl(2)G.10s

N Middle

Whitaker 16 Ql(3)10s Bell

No.6 Bn

Swallow Q

Ridge Fl.10s

No.1 VQ(6)+ LFl.10s

Foulness Fl(2)R.10s

S Foulness Fl(2)R.10s

Foulness Sand

Buxey Sand

Batchelors Spit

N Buxey

Buxey No.2

Outer Crouch

Gunfleet Old Lt Ho.

Gunfleet Sand

East Swin or King's Channel

Middle Deep

Black Deep

Barrow Deep

West Barrow

East Barrow

Barrow Swatchway

Barrow Bn

E Barrow Bn (11)

Middle

W Hook Middle 16

SW Middle

S Whitaker

Barrow No.2 Iso.10s Whis

Barrow No.3 Fl(3)G.10s

Barrow No.4 VQ(9)10s

Barrow No.5 Fl.G.10s

Barrow No.6 Fl(4)R.15s

Barrow No.7 Fl.G.2.5s

Sunk Bn (16)

Sunk

Fisherman's Gat

Long Sand

South west Sunk

51°45'N

50'

40

35'

15'

45'

5

1°E

There is also the sometime vaunted short cut across the Colne Bar to the north of the Eagle bank and its attendant marker the *North Eagle*. Careful study of the charts and a survey of the area from the dinghy at low water will show that the bottom is likely to be encountered in all kinds of unexpected spots since the Colne Bar is an unshapely collection of holes and bumps which shift frequently and unpredictably. Such research will, I am sure, put off all but the reckless.

Mostly, these by-ways and non-high-ways take you over entirely or partially drying sands and I have been in the process of being shown the way, the truth and the lights by some 'locals with special knowledge' when they themselves have lost the track. I am not condemning. Their skills were far in excess of mine. Merely emphasising how difficult these channels are: even those who have navigated them once or twice before must do so with caution unless they are to be caught unawares. Some professional fishermen know their exits and their entrances and only need you to wring out a wet dishcloth for them to cross the bar. Their pilotage often seems nothing less than miraculous; but the rest of us are no more than mortal.

I do not think that strangers on passage should try to use these channels at all. They are best kept for relaxed exploration, in fine weather with rising tides in your favour, and never at night. They are indeed a challenge for those who want to search out every last swatchway, but on passage they seldom save enough time to justify the anxieties. Such 'short' cuts, here or in the Wash, are seldom worth the attendant risks. They are excellent for days out in a substantial dinghy with a powerful outboard, when channel exploration, fishing and sightseeing can all be happily and safely combined.

Here are Ms. Driscoll's views on the area: ' Going back to the estuary, the Knoll Buoy nearly lost its light in 1931. Trinity House used to maintain the light on behalf of Colchester Corporation, and in that year they raised their charges. Colchester authorities were worried because it was paid from the rates, and this light only benefitted a small proportion of their ratepayers. Then Kent & Essex Sea Fisheries Committee and others organised a protest, and the light was saved. It was a lit buoy much needed on that stretch of coast. I can well remember when the Wallet Spitway Buoy had neither light nor bell on it, and the difference this made when both were fitted in October 1961. Even the Swin Spitway light only dates from February 1936. It was put there as a result of a campaign organised by the late E.G. Martin, a yachtsman who had spent a winter as a mate of a trading sailing barge and discovered how much a light was needed. The Big Guns at Trinity House had ignored previous requests from coastal seamen for a light to be put on this buoy. When Brightlingsea was a naval base in the 1914–18 war, a light was put on the buoy but was removed after the base was closed in 1924. The present Spitway has changed its channel since I first came barging. The one we use now is a low-way discovered by the Colne ballast barges, which had echo sounders well before any other barge-type craft had them, which is how it was discovered that there was more water in this low-way than in the official Spitway channel. Skipper Tom Baker of Redoubtable once told me that before the war the channel was in yet another place, and that he had tried it one day and found water there.'

To close the subject, I monitored a fascinating exchange on VHF Ch 16 that went like this.
'I am *Desire*. You are *Beagle*. Come in *Beagle*'
'*Desire, Desire, Desire. Beagle, Beagle, Beagle*. This is Caroline, *Desire. Beagle* over.'
'I am *Desire*. You are *Beagle*. *Desire* to *Beagle*. I am about to cross your bows well ahead of you. I see *Beagle* that you are actually on the Ray Sand. Is that so *Beagle*? I am *Desire*. Over'
'*Desire, Desire, Desire. Beagle, Beagle, Beagle*. This is Caroline, *Desire*. I don't think Anthony knows exactly where we are. This is Caroline, *Desire*. I suppose if you say we are on the Ray Sand I expect we must be, *Desire*. This is Caroline, *Desire. Beagle* over.'
'I am *Desire*. You are *Beagle*. You are on the Ray Sand and I shall cross your bows, Roger? *Desire* over and out.'
'*Desire, Desire, Desire. Beagle, Beagle, Beagle*. This is Caroline. *Desire, Desire, Desire*. This is *Beagle, Beagle, Beagle* over and out.'
I can report that there is no error because my tape recorder was at the ready for the weather forecast; and all on VHF Ch 16; as I said, unbelievable!

# The River Colne

Once the *Colne Bar* buoy has been identified, the channel right up to Mersea Stone and Brightlingsea will be easy to identify. Watch out for the substantial tidal set across the entrance. It is worth keeping an eye on your wake with the *Bar* buoy astern to make sure you aren't drifting off. There is shoal water to each side, so it is best to maintain a central course in the channel. The beacons marking Colne Point, Mersea Stone and the measured half mile are all clear to see. Some very small fishing pots and markers are to be met in the channel.

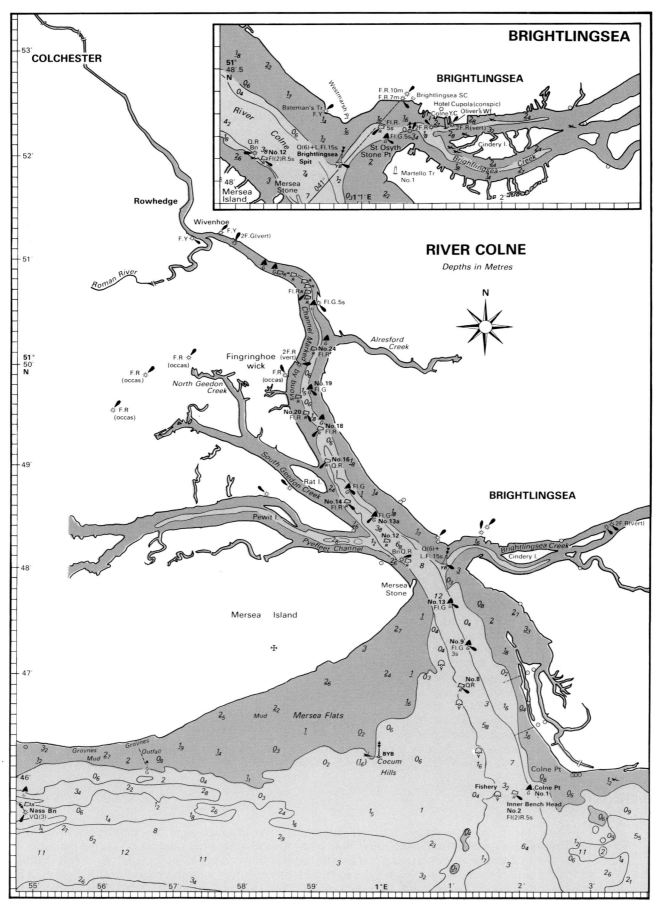

**COLCHESTER**

53'

**BRIGHTLINGSEA**

**BRIGHTLINGSEA**

51°
48'.5
N

River

Westmarsh Pt

F.R.10m
F.R.7m

Brightlingsea SC
Hotel Cupola (conspic)
Colne Y.C   Oliver's Wf

Bateman's Tr
F.Y

Colne

4₂

St Osyth
Stone Pt

2F.R (vert)

Cindery I.

52'

Q.R
Bn   No.12
Fl(2)R.5s

Q(6)+L.Fl.15s
**Brightlingsea Spit**

Brightlingsea Creek

48'
Mersea
Island

Mersea
Stone

Martello Tr
No.1

041°

0₃1°1'E

**Rowhedge**

Wivenhoe

F.Y

F.Y   2F.G (vert)

51'

Roman River

**RIVER COLNE**

*Depths in Metres*

N

Fl.R.R

Fl.G.5s

Alresford Creek

F.R
(occas)

F.R
(occas)

**Fingringhoe
wick**

2F.R
(vert)

**No.24**
Fl.R

North Geedon
Creek

F.R
(occas)

F.R
(occas)

**No.19**
Fl.G

51°
50'
N

**No.20**
Fl.R

**No.18**
Fl.R

**No.16**
Q.R

South Geedon Creek

**BRIGHTLINGSEA**

49'

Rat I.

Fl.G

**No.14**
Fl.R

**No.13a**
Fl.G

Pewit I.

Pyefleet Channel

BnQ.R

2F R(vert)

Brightlingsea Creek

Cindery I.

Q(6)+
L.Fl.15s

48'

Mersea
Stone

**No.13**
Fl.G

**No.9**
Fl.G
3s

Mersea   Island

**No.8**
Q.R

47'

Mersea Flats

Mud

**BYB**
Cocum
Hills

Groynes
Mud

Groynes
Outfall

Colne Pt

**Fishery**

**Colne Pt
No.1**

46'

Nass Bn
VQ(3)

**Inner Bench Head
No.2**
Fl(2)R.5s

55'   56'   57'   58'   59'   **1°E**   1'   2'   3'

# BUOYAGE
## The River Colne and its approaches

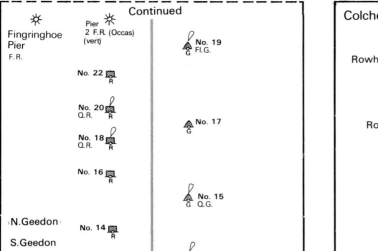

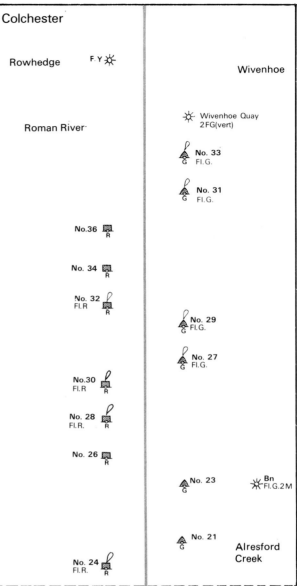

| Check | Confirm | Confirm | Check |
|---|---|---|---|

From the Wallet or the Spitway, pick up the Knoll Lightbuoy

For the Ray Sand Channel See text page 125

The Colne's first offer of hospitality is Brightlingsea.
It also plays host to a variety of ships, from
commercial big visitors to modest safety boat
indigens.

The Colne's front door may be said to stand between the St Osyth Stone Point Martello tower to
the east and Mersea Stone, the extremity of Mersea Island, to the west. Rising some 32 miles away
in the northwest of Essex, it is no more than a muddy trickle above Colchester at low water. Its 11
miles of tideway run down to the sea through extensive mud flats, saltings and detached banks.
Although not bleak, there is little relief to be found in this low-lying plateau; and its real appeal is
to be found not in its scenery but in its communities. The first of these, a small harbour of no
more than 6000 souls, is known by a really happy accolade.

# Brightlingsea

Brightlingsea may be small, but it is a thrivingly busy place. Like Topsy it is just growing, and at the same time is also getting busier. The approach into the harbour is problem free if you note that it has little more than a metre at low water. So access is restricted to an hour and a half or so after low water if you want to be on the safe side.

Otherwise there is no difficulty in gaining the main harbour itself. From the river, you leave green *No.13* to starboard to avoid the spit off the south of the entrance, and then leave the cardinal to port to avoid the broader spit above it. There are red/white leading marks: both have red centres with white/grey strip/stripes. It is not particularly easy to differentiate them from their backgrounds, but close to their right is a noticeable triangle belonging to the yacht club station. There are also F.R leading lights.

After leaving *Brightlingsea Spit* south cardinal buoy astern, keep well close to the moorings and the buoys (the first of which is lit) and watch out for the odd withy. The inner entry is a slow waltz to starboard until you are past the fishing fleet to starboard, when the visitors' moorings which will not before have been immediately obvious, will come into view, although there is not a super-abundance of them.

Visitors go between one of the first four piles where boats are tied fore and aft. Since it is not easy to identify which line is which, it is a good idea to jill around by the big fishing boat moorings or the Colne Yacht Club pontoon until you have some idea of your bearings. Take advice if they are full. If you are a biggish boat it may not be easy to find a home, but there is just a chance you may be allowed to tie up alongside one of the fishermen.

When looking for a mooring on the piles, keep to the centre lanes and the Cindery Island (northerly) side. The far lane, which is to starboard when entering, does not carry enough water for boats with more than 1·5m draught. A good plan is to take the north side on the way down, then turn and come up the centre channel. If you have entered on a rising tide you will also have the advantage of stemming it while you inspect the trots.

Brightlingsea is a complex experience: at one and the same time
fast and furious; yet curiously delicate and docile.

I have always found Brightlingsea reminiscent of Yarmouth Isle of Wight, except that in Yarmouth there is always a gaggle of harbour staff to watch you in and give you instruction. For those who do not like being regimented, Brightlingsea will be a relief, for there is none of that. The visitor is left mainly to his own devices with the HM approaching only to extract the proper dues. You will discover that it is much easier for the HM to find you than it is for you to find him.

There is a boatman who operates from the yacht club jetty. When he does so a flag is flown from the flagstaff on the jetty. The service is from Friday evening to Sunday evening (and for parties he will arrange to run a last boat as late as 2300). He is also the local safety boat and listens on VHF Ch 16. His call sign is *Colne Ranger*. There is also a boat service from Brightlingsea hard to Stone Point. It is licensed to operate within a one mile radius, and for a small consideration the boatmen will pick you up and drop you at your boat. They stress that they are not a ferry!

There is water at the YC jetty and the key is held by the barman at the club. It is possible to anchor in the north channel but this is not popular with the HM, who ought to be consulted in the first place or you may find yourself with a problem. During the week there are barges that carry sand in that channel (riding light essential) and there is the additional complication of the new wharf building developments. However, the sand barges are not permitted to work up the creek from Friday evening to Monday morning.

The Brightlingsea Harbour Commissioners' laws proclaim the following:

'You are advised that your anchored vessel could cause unnecessary difficulty to the navigation of the larger craft using Brightlingsea Creek. Anchoring north of moorings 1–9 in the outer reach of the creek or in the north low water channel east of the public causeway is not recommended at any time. Visitors' moorings are available in the south channel.' ☎ Harbour master: Brightlingsea (020 630) 2200/2283.

To the east of Cindery Island, there are creeks, but they carry so little water and are so tortuous that there is little point in trying to negotiate them in spite of the romantically tempting name of 'the Pincushion'. Cindery Island itself has a spit out to the west that extends for a very long way; many strangers find themselves stranded even with flat rubber-bottomed dinghies, which are pigs to haul on mud.

# Colne again

Outside in the river again, immediately opposite the entrance to Brightlingsea, there is a sound anchorage between Mersea Stone and the lit red can that marks the wreck. This is Ms. Driscoll's letter on the subject: ' The wreck which you mention off East Mersea is not the steamer Lowland, mined during the 2nd World War, but the Lowlands built Sunderland 1888, which went on the mud about 1918, being put there when she was about to sink. To date I haven't been able to establish the exact year when she was put there but it was between the end of 1917 and the autumn of 1921, which narrows it down. It's a long story that I won't tell you here or this letter, already long, will get totally out of hand.'

This anchorage suffers from no disadvantage but neither does it possess the charms of the one round the corner in the popular waters of Pyefleet Creek. In this area, an extremely busy one, you will come across all kinds of traffic from the most unstable of youthful dinghies and the most acrobatic of windsurfers to stubborn small coasters apparently ignoring everything, but in fact not missing a trick.

# Pyefleet Creek

There is an old-world feel to this area that is strewn with working boats, nets and huts. This was the first proper anchorage I ever found in *Valcon* and I stayed there for much longer than I had intended. I even risked running out of gas and water (there is no facility here) just because of its quiet, spell-binding magnetism. It has a *genius loci* all of its own. When the setting sun threw its rays on the fishermen's huts, the steeply slanted angles made them into monuments of picturesque decay and a real inspiration to the imagination. In the overhead brightness of high noon, it was unhappily obvious that, in the absence of the magic of long shadows, they possessed no more than the spirit of a broken-down shambles; but they were not built for midday inspection. It was really at night, when their textures were chased in and out of relief by a cloud-caught moon that huts and boats and nets became transformed into history made manifest and grew in stature until they were dramatic emblems of centuries of local tradition. It is one of the most charming anchorages on the East Coast, of enduring appeal to most East Coast yachtsmen, many of whom happen to be pagan.

Pagan? Worth a mention since the place is not without its call, of an entirely different ilk, for land-bound others too. Sightseeing Christians and Touring Pilgrims make the long shoresides trip to what is no more, to be realistic, than the dull edifice of an isolated place of worship, now past its use and prime. Many come from as far as Horbury Bridge on the Aire and Calder Navigation near Wakefield where the Reverend Sabine Baring-Gould started his sombre ministry in those classic midnight-oil mills and deep hued waters that give the north its gloomy, looming satanic reputation.

It seems fitting that such a man as the Reverend should choose this part of the world in which to have six of his many children. In the middle of the nineteenth century there can have been little doubt how appropriate it might have seemed for local fishermen to be treated to his mellow tones encouraging them with such of his works 'Through the Night of Doubt and Sorrow', 'Now the Day is Over' and 'Onward Christian Soldiers'. Perhaps he even called them to leave their nets and become fishers of men. Others turn more readily to other kinds of life, as symbolised by the Dog and Pheasant nearby.

# More Colne

If Pyefleet isn't far enough away from the rough and tumble for your taste, there is a possible navigation round Rat Island. The lower channel takes you in sight of the north and South Geedon Creeks and Fingringhoe Marsh. The whole area is restricted: when it is not active as a killing field, it comes into its own as a nature reserve. Steps should be taken to allow responsible navigators in the these westerly creeks. In my experience, the presence of yachtsmen usually does nothing but improve the conditions of the wild life in the area.

Further up, on the starboard hand comes Alresford Creek. The green *No.21* marks the limit of low water navigation for craft drawing more than 1·5m and very little is gained from going up from Pyefleet. The channel is well buoyed, but since it is extremely narrow it is important to follow the laid out track exactly. No more than slight deviations will have you churning up the silt-soft mud of the river bed.

The creek allows craft in for a couple of cables at tide time, and there is good dinghy access and landing further in. Unless you are deeply into the ways of swatch and shoal, it is perhaps better not to try to anchor in the creek itself but to use the stretch between the two greens *Nos.19* and *21*. You must keep well clear of the channel of course; hoist a good anchor light; and and be prepared to find the soft bottom.

*Valcon* seldom reaches more than seven knots so there is always a wry smile when I pass a speed limit notice, as here, prohibiting anything in excess of eight knots. The channel is particularly well buoyed upstream with lots of reds and a few greens; but because of the magical mystery tour that lies ahead I would so much more like to give the instruction: 'Follow the yellow brick road' to 'Somewhere over the rainbow.' And why?

## Wivenhoe

The reason is Wivenhoe. At first glimpse, this tiny port is a busy big ship stop. Second sights and later thoughts confirm this impression; but with the qualifying criterion that it is, in addition, something quite other.

But before looking more closely into that, let us get there. It is important not to deviate from the centre of the channel when you are getting close to Wivenhoe because the banks on both sides are host to a variety of obstructions and some wreckage. By the sand/gravel working on the port bank, the channel itself is on the extreme port hand and very close to.

Otherwise the approach is central and generally straightforward with the Wivenhoe Sailing Club moorings appearing to starboard. There is sometimes a visitor's mooring to be found on the E side of the channel. Occasionally the upstream head of the swinging mooring buoys is left unoccupied and reserved for a visitor. I have yet to find it vacant.

Wivenhoe is, from time to time, and now increasingly so, not only extremely busy with its own and visiting yachts, but also very occupied with the great deal of commercial traffic passing through to Rowhedge or on to Colchester at the head of the navigation, as well as calling at Wivenhoe itself. At high water therefore, it behooves skippers to make sure a really efficient traffic watch is being kept. You can get some useful assistance from the harbour radio officer will who be pleased to inform you of the traffic he knows of and expects in the river.

And now to the nub of it all: the small non-commercial quayside that makes Wivenhoe the wonder that it is. It is nowadays such a popular spot that seldom indeed will you be able to find a vacant berth. If you are lucky enough to do so, you will moor up bows on (there is insufficient

Wivenhoe: quite large coasters use the Colne to Wivenhoe, Rowhedge and Colchester

water at the edge to moor up stern to) and will need a ladder or plank to get ashore. There is little sign of any improvement or even simple repair work, so the riverside moorings are not being enhanced. This is no doubt all part of a dark plot on the part of the indigens to keep Wivenhoe quiet, but it must be hoped that the waterfront will not be allowed to drift into decay.

To arrive at Wivenhoe by water is to come close to a sympathetic encounter with part of our maritime heritage that is resolutely wed to part of our riparian history; in spite of the fact that BBC Radio 4 refers to it bluntly as a port. These two aspects are firmly held in the hands of time while indigens, guests and visitors alike try to keep one foothold there, another in the present while trying not to overbalance on the brink of the future. The shopkeepers have a cavalier if not eccentric attitude to opening (bad mark) and closing (bad mark cancelled) times.

This is all symbolically presented in concrete form in the eye-catching cluster of stylishly modernised houses which contrast so clearly with their neighbours, a clutch of older cottages in an excellent state of repair and decoration. There is a public house blessed with an exterior of charm and character and an interior suffused with warmth and welcome.

You will frequently see an assembly of wooden boats moored bows-on to the jetty, and, as if directing the whole scene to suit their own special vision, a coterie of painters, complete with stools, easels, shawls … and straw hats, absorbed as if preserving a vision of a world that was about to be devastated. They may have a mission.

I hope that, while the details may change over the next few years, the essence will linger. This intriguing riverside village is known to the Admiralty as a sub-port of Colchester.

# Rowhedge

Next up the river on the port hand comes the small village of Rowhedge. It has some shops, a pub or two, a few hundred feet of wharf space, and a traditional boatyard. It is always good to find a boatyard working in the traditional manner. Do visit Brown's. They will be pleased to see you; but don't just drop in for they are very busy working on RNLI boats as well as yachts.

Just upstream of the boatyard is Rowhedge's public quay. In spite of the presence of a first rate hostelry, that quay is not as hospitable as it looks. Most of the Colne is soft mud; and much of the ground by that tempting quay is also soft mud but there is a shelving collection of concrete blocks, bricks and other impedimenta that makes it an unpleasant spot. Even if you manage to bottom without disaster, you are likely to dry out in a most uncomfortable manner.

Slightly further up river on the port hand there is another spot that seems to invite mooring lines: right on the corner towards the end of the village. The corner is in fact one of the last places to moor: coasters have been known, more than once, to swing too far, too fast and so do serious damage not only to the boats but also to the corner itself. It is best to arrange any trip to Rowhedge to be a top of the tide visit, leaving well before the ebb starts to run out on you.

There is no hazard going up river, where, indeed, the waterway is floodlit whenever appropriate for traffic. It is accessible to 1·5m craft from about two hours before high water. The Colne offers four main choices on: an anchorage in Pyefleet Creek; a berth at Brightlingsea; a perch at lotus land Wivenhoe; or, here and now just upstream, a mud patch at Colchester.

# Colchester

Over the years, Colchester has had something of a poor press for the yachting world. I have found it a most hospitable spot, with plenty of services and a most helpful and friendly harbour staff.

The quay master of the visitor's stretch is known as 'Big John', and not even Robin Hood's diminutive model could help you more. When he is not tree felling (or humping, pumping and jumping), he is around and about on his stretch of the quayside ready to assist. He owns the longest and most efficient water pipe system I have ever come across on the East Coast.

The mud is so malleable here, that it takes only a single tide for you to make a better 'ole of your own and so have a settled, level berth for the rest of your stay. Not only are all facilities within walking distance, but Colchester is a real visitors' special.

The port services about 100 big ships a month but the staff are equally happy to deal with the enquiries of a small cruising man. The water hose at the quayside is one of the most efficient and largest capacity that I have come across. The only slight obstacle to look out for is the possibility of the channel in the harbour itself being dredged and the consequent presence of dredgers and their chains.

The Colne is not the longest river in the world, being no more than fifteen miles at most; nor is it the most beautiful, but it does possess splendid anchorages and attractive ports of call. It is a river to be neither missed nor rushed. Give yourself time to enjoy it.

Ms. Driscoll's letter says this: 'At Colchester, the general rule is that nothing going away moves until on the high water, so going up on the ebb is extremely unwise, apart from the tide pushing your head away at each bend as it strikes your port bow.'

# The Blackwater

## Close approaches

As described at the beginning of the chapter, you reach the river from the Wallet or the Spitway. The surrounding coastline has few high-rise attractions, and it is from plain ground that the chimneys of Bradwell power station rise. From miles away they are impossible to miss, being the most noticeable landmark in the area, and usually grimly silhouetted against a background of classic unrelenting North Sea grey. Dominating the skyline, a ghastly warning to any marine conservationist or bird watcher, they continually bring to my mind those 'vast and trunkless legs of stone that stand in the desert', of which Ozymandias, King of Kings, said, 'Look on my works, ye mighty, and despair!' And we do; we do.

The navigation of the Knoll and Eagle to Bench Head, after which it is deemed that the Blackwater proper begins, is without difficulty. It usually feels a long haul from the Knoll to the Nass, with very little to threaten or to inspire. Nor is there much to look at or to see except perhaps to keep an eye out for the odd constructions, with red tops and lights, resembling concrete barges that go to make up the wavebreak off Sales Point. The actual entrance lies between Mersea Flats to the north and St Peter's Flats to the south; both areas that live up (or should it be down?) to their names, since they offer no contrast in contour or scenery. Indeed, there is nothing but the deep and regular water channel, atypically deep and regular for the East Coast, to the Nass beacon: probably as well known and significant on the East Coast as is the Chichester beacon on the south. From then on there is Shinglehead Point to starboard, and Bradwell to port.

Accordingly, getting into the Blackwater is about as straightforward as any East Coast river ever can be, and once inside it is clear it is another river not to be missed. Although, in fact, many people may be forgiven for not knowing much about it, since even those well informed gentlemen on inland waterways, Edwards and McKnight, refer to it only in passing, concentrating on the Chelmer and Blackwater Navigation; which with a depth of 0·75m and headroom of 2·0m must be a near non-starter, and no more than second fiddle to the river itself.

Nor, once discovered, is it a river to be rushed, for it too has its unique attractions. One is the air of contradiction that invests the area. Idiosyncratically, while all that is grounded or land based seems to be looking back, not in heady anger but in heavy nostalgia, life afloat is a forward looking affair, with much that is vigorous, business based and progressive. Some of the most intriguing attractions are Mersea, Osea Island, Heybridge Basin and Maldon; and while this last is the drying head of the navigation, it is still nowhere near the source which is over 30 miles distant.

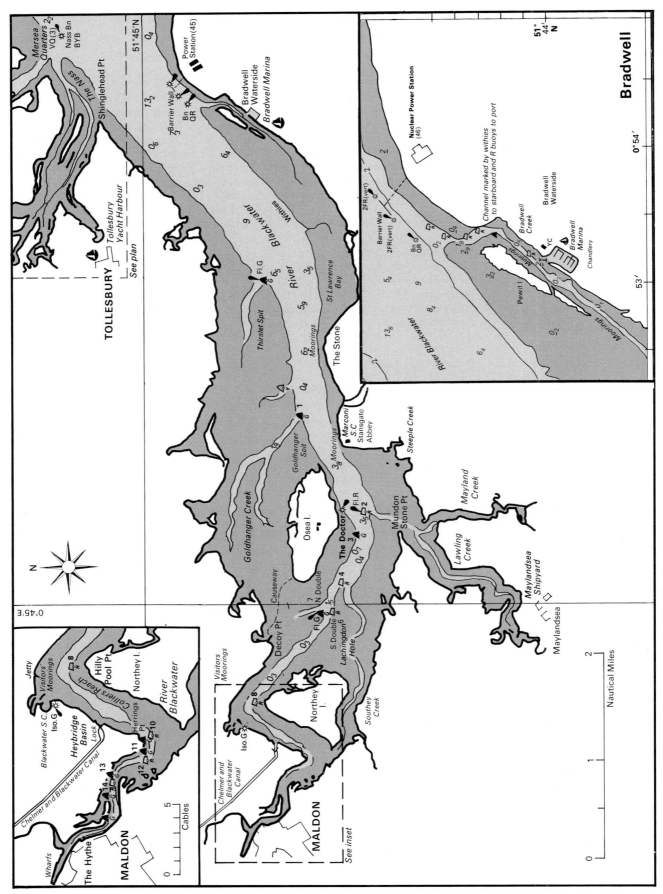

**Bradwell**

Mersea Quarters
VQ(3) 2
Nass Bn
BYB

51°45'N

The Nass

Shinglehead Pt

Tollesbury Yacht Harbour

TOLLESBURY

*See plan*

Power Station(45)

Barrier Wall
Bn QR 3

Bradwell Waterside
Bradwell Marina

*Blackwater River*

Withies

FI.G

Thirslet Spit

St Lawrence Bay

The Stone

Moorings

Goldhanger Spit

Goldhanger Creek

Moorings

Marconi S.C
Stansgate Abbey

Steeple Creek

Osea I.

Causeway

Decoy Pt

The Doctor
FI.R
G R

Mundon Stone Pt

Mayland Creek

Lawling Creek

FI.G
N Double
S Double R

Lachingdon Hole

Maylandsea Shipyard

Maylandsea

Southey Creek

Visitors Moorings

Northey I.

Iso.G

Chelmer and Blackwater Canal

MALDON

*See inset*

N

0°45'E

Jetty
Visitors Moorings

Blackwater S.C.
Iso.G

Heybridge Basin
Lock

Hilly Pool Pt

Northey I.

*River Blackwater*

Collier's Reach

Herrings Pt

Chelmer and Blackwater Canal

The Hythe

Wharfs

MALDON

Cables
0   5

Nautical Miles
0   1   2

**Bradwell**

51°44'N

Nuclear Power Station (46)

2FR(vert)

Barrier Wall
2FR(vert)

Bn QR

Bradwell Creek

Bradwell Waterside

Moorings

Pewit I.

Bradwell Marina
Chandlery

*River Blackwater*

Moorings

Channel marked by withies to starboard and R buoys to port

0°54'

53'

For 1·5m craft, access to the Nass beacon is problem free at all states of the tide; and once that uniquely slender, unmitred cardinal has been identified, the cry goes up: where now; right, left or centre?

# Mersea

To starboard, are those classic fleets, islands and marshes that go to make up the very popular area of West Mersea, the Quarters and Tollesbury. The channels tend to the narrow, the shallow and the tortuous. Mercutio might well have been talking of one of them instead of his fatal wound when he said: 'No, 'tis not so deep as a well, nor so wide as a church door; but 'tis enough, 'twill serve'. And serve they do, through the maze of oyster beds and moorings that, in their own discrete ways are all marked as territorial reservations. Indeed, some are staked out as in the old movies gold rush claims; and guarded with as much fervour but without recourse to fire arms although that restraint was not always respected in the past when vandalism, bed-rock plundering and smuggling were all prevalent.

There are channels and marshy banks to be explored by the hour if not the day around here; and all best done by the dinghy for there are oyster beds in profusion. The main channels are those round Sunken Island that lead (but only ultimo ultimately) to the hamlets of Salcott and Virley, which sound like a better class act from a palace of varieties.

The others are the Ray and Strood at the back of Mersea, which just like the back of Wight in the south coasts's Solent gets little publicity and hardly a dozen floating visits a year. The lower end of Ray is not one for strangers to navigate in the mother vessel for the moorings are crowded and tight; and that is without further mention of the oyster beds, as omnipresent as the Reverend Sabine Baring-Gould's everlasting arms. I would urge first time visitors to take a berth at one of the two nearby marina facilities and search out moorings and anchorages by dinghy. In such ways are the most appropriate places for one's own boat discovered; good relationships developed; and the interests of nature, the working community, and all other locals and strangers are all served.

Visitors to the starboard aspect will also want to make their ways past the Nass beacon, through the well buoyed Mersea Quarters northward of the Nass and so into the confined but manifest channels that lead to South Channel and from there on in the direction of the very head of the gutway where stands Old Hall Farm, approached eponymously by Old Hall Creek. But this is rushing ahead where it is actually impossible to rush, and such tracks to the Hall should only be made by visitors in the tender, or by taking the truly muddy rural route by foot from the yacht harbour which will be most folks' intended destination.

Back to the Quarters and westward for Tollesbury. After the last of the outside Nass standard reds, *No.6*, the first of the inside Nass reds is labelled *T1*. While the channel is only modestly wide, it is well marked with black bottomed, white topped red and green Barrels. Visitors need to keep their eyes open and their speed down however, for there is no space at all for grand manoeuvres and not a lot for correcting errors.

Towards the end of South Channel, the headland of Shinglehead Point becomes very noticeable, which it is not from the main channels of the Blackwater; and important goal-marks in the form of white houses, with their near-butterfly roof formations, are unmistakable. Once inside and pointed northeasterly, you move directly towards Tollesbury Fleet. No pomp, no panoply nor spectacular show will mark your arrival or delay your progress, but you will nevertheless be slowed down if not indeed stopped in your tracks by the appearance of the water/landscape as it opens up before you, enough to arrest even the world weary. The scene is a paradigm of inland waterways and a classic expression of Blackwater/backwater saltings and East Coast scenery at their flat best. Chestnut browns and bronzed siennas surround you in all shapes and shades, tints and textures, while small islands and headlands point fingers of green to search out and show the shallow creeks and channels.

The laid moorings show the track up South Channel leaving Cob Island to starboard, and on the port hand are oyster layings, some not very distinctly marked by withies. Last on the menu is the port turn into the diminutive Woodrolfe Creek for the silled entrance into the Tollesbury Yacht Harbour. For those with a wish to search out the less orthodox, there is also another channel, to the north; but goose pimples has always made me chicken out of swanning up past the Great Cob that way.

Tollesbury is tucked away with a well protected marina.

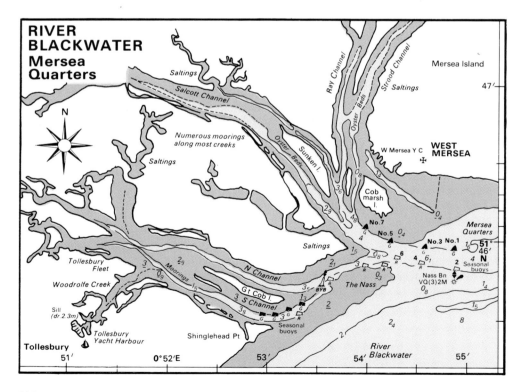

# Tollesbury Marina

This is the establishment's view of itself:

'Tollesbury Marina, which is owned and administered by Woodrolfe Boatyard, is situated at the head of Woodrolfe Creek on the site of the old shipyard. About seven acres of saltings have been excavated to provide a safe and sheltered harbour for over 240 yachts with up to 2·1m draught lying afloat. Surrounded by fields and trees, the harbour is pleasantly situated, and is only ten minutes walk away from charming Tollesbury village and good shopping facilities.

The marina has a sill or bar at the entrance, and access is dependent on the height of the tide over the sill. Dependent upon weather conditions, access is available from two hours either side of HSW and one hour either side of HSW.

Mean High Water depth over the sill is about 2·3m; i.e. up to 2·7m or more at HWS and 1·5m at HWN. Nearly all through the summer, there is 1·8m or more at neaps. This period has what are known locally as 'Bird Tides': springs and neaps are more evenly spread with the water rarely covering the saltings. This permits the birds to nest with little fear of their eggs being washed away.

Fresh water, and electricity are available on the pontoons and full facilities are offered to visitors at the Tollesbury Cruising Club. These include showers, bath, laundry, restaurant, bar, covered heated swimming pool and two hard tennis courts.

The boatyard has 3 slipways for vessels up to 30 tons with cranage. There are large areas of hardstanding and workshops for repairs with direct gas supplies and a well stocked chandlery.

The marina offers the following advice to visitors approaching from the River Blackwater: Leave the Nass Beacon to port. After passing two red buoys to port, steer WSW and enter Tollesbury Channel marked by buoys (red port). Pass between No.3 red and No.4 east cardinal and steer to leave No.5 green buoy (marking southern end of Great Cob Island) to starboard. Steer keeping to the centre of the South Channel, (marked with withies), passing close either side of any boats on moorings leaving Little Cob Island to starboard. After passing five mooring buoys of Woodrolfe Boatyard, enter Woodrolfe Creeks and keep the centre of the channel. (Tide mark at entrance to Woodrolfe Creek will indicate depth of water on harbour sill.) The yard harbour entrance will be seen just south of the prominent white buildings or Woodrolfe Boatyard. Craft should not enter Woodrolfe Creek until the tide gauge shows enough water to clear the sill. Anchor clear of the channel or pick up a Woodrolfe Boatyard (WB) mooring if awaiting the tide. Do not raft up more than two abreast. If the moorings are taken, craft should anchor clear of moorings and the centre of the channel, in the north or South Channels of Tollesbury Fleet.'

There is never an air of noisy commotion in the marina's precincts. It is a site that is well protected from the clamour of society as well as nature, and the Tollesbury Cruising Club, while happy to welcome visitors, is also happy to keep it that way. For those whose enthusiasm might have been fired by the thought of the covered heated swimming pool, it must be noted that while the description is exact in every detail, you will find it a cooling rather a warming experience. Whereas rather the opposite will probably be the case is you succumb to the lure of the clubhouse and restaurant where they have an awe-inspiringly long menu and wine list. On the ablutionary front, there are showers for all – and, luxury for some, namely, a bath for ladies. There is also a washing machine and dryer; not inexpensive but a first rate facility.

The village is not far away, and the pleasant but above all intriguing walk will take you within sight of three chandlers and the parish council open air swimming pool. The ancient buildings of the waterside are set off well by the comprehensive use of weatherboarding, and there are many occasions when you can stand and think yourself straight into one of the old masters. Closer to the village there begins a strange and fascinating combination of a modern industrial estate intent upon presenting an olde-worlde, craft-based image and a genuine olde-worlde, craft-based village intent on being with it.

It offers good shopping opportunities, with a most excellent butcher and grocer who carries a large selection of 'deli' and other esoteric eats; in fact a most unlikely range for the corner shop of a remote and tiny village. Don't miss 'Marjorie's: Fish and Fashion'.

# More Blackwater

Gently to port after the Nass beacon, to the southwest that is, lies the deep water channel that will lead into the River Blackwater proper and towards the apparently inescapable power station. You will probably find some big ships almost spoiling at anchor in the main channel between Shinglehead Point and the power station. The big ships are unmistakably clear and plain to make out. The barrier wall of the power station is not, and its perspective changes so that it too appears to be another large vessel. In the end, of course, it explains itself and becomes a useful marker for Bradwell Creek. There is a beacon at the river 'outlet' of the creek that leads to Bradwell Marina which can be easily seen once you are past the barrier wall.

## Bradwell Marina

The marina channel is well marked by red buoys, some of which are sea-changed beer cans. There is one not particularly well cared for green cone that is often on its side and half submerged, perhaps from too much fraternising with the reds. There are starboard hand withies. The marina entrance channel itself tends to port of middle. There is a small spit to starboard when you first

Tollesbury Marina.

The approach to Bradwell Waterside is mainly redolent of the old part of the village; where tradition reigns.

Bradwell Marina

turn in. You will need better than half tide if you draw more than 1·5m. If in doubt, call the marina on Channel M. They will help whether you are merely passing by or have been a berth holder for some time.

Predictably, there is tremendous rivalry between the two 'neighbourly' marinas, so it is only ethical and evenhanded that Bradwell should be allowed its personal statement: 'Bradwell Marina is ideally placed for the East Coast sailor with the Blackwater estuary 'on the doorstep' and being within easy reach of the other Essex rivers and well placed for cruising the Dutch and Belgian coasts.

The yacht basin itself is sheltered on all sides by sea walls. Deeper draught vessels must exercise caution at low water, especially during spring tides, as the navigable channel in Bradwell Creek becomes narrow at low water and there is a bar at the entrance to the creek. Visiting yachts are welcome and on arrival should berth at the visitors' berths (marked by a notice board) at the end of 'A' pontoon and then report to the conspicuous blue and white tower. After office hours a night watchman will assign you a berth.

The marina basin provides berths for nearly 300 yachts, with a maximum length of 15m. There are freshwater stand pipes and electricity on each pontoon. The Bradwell Cruising Club overlooks the marina basin and comprises a club room and bar, changing and toilet facilities. Berth-holders can join the club on payment of a small entrance fee and annual subscription. Temporary membership is extended to visiting yachtsmen.

There are plenty of facilities, either at the marina or in the small village of Bradwell Waterside. Many yachts also use Bradwell Creek itself and they can be seen for a long way up the river. I have been made more than welcome at Bradwell Marina many times and oft; and recent changes have served only to improve the general atmosphere. The club serves first-rate meals at down to earth prices (7 days a week customers willing) and table service and a reasonable wine list make even being weatherbound an attractive proposition.

# Back in the river

Leaving Bradwell Creek, it looks tempting to cut the corner by the beacon, but it is right on the spit and must be fully rounded. Further up river the low water level is marked by withies. Since many of them are submerged at high water, it is not good to go too near the sides, unless one of the regular East Coast fogs demands you pick them up for navigating.

The entrance to the shallow St Lawrence Creek is two miles SW of Bradwell power station and is marked by a small red buoy. It nearly fully joins Bradwell Creek and is a nice hidey hole for getting out of the main channel on the less broadly muddied side.; while just across the water, on the starboard side, Thirslet Creek can be identified by the unusual beacon buoy that marks its spit.

Many yachts have been caught out by the fact that the banks and their extensive spits stretch further out into the river than you might think. Make sure that you don't set a course that lines up *Thirslet* beacon and the green *Goldhanger* buoy when proceeding to or from the power station. Instead, keep the south power station block. If you are at all unsure, it is better to keep to the south shoreline, with an eye open for the withies which also mark far-reaching oyster layings. Both Thirslet and Goldhanger Creeks provide quiet anchorages just within their entrances. Neither offers a spectacle of natural splendour, but both have elements of barren grandeur and furnish silence and seclusion.

By using the dinghy and stout wet gear boots you can find numerous landings at all these creeks and plenty of quiet country walks to the not too distant local communities. Ordnance Survey Pathfinders are useful guides.

Upstream on the port hand comes the Stone by Ramsey Wick, where there is an extremely popular leisure area, as witness the plethora of moorings belonging to the local sailing clubs, and the shoresides miscellany of short order holiday accommodation.

Shortly after a striking white hut, there is a fixed navigation flown by the Marconi Sailing Club. Round the corner to the southwest is an open view of Stansgate Abbey, which, from the anchorage at Osea Island, makes a splendid sight in the changing lights of the passing days and months.

Osea Island was known to the Romans and inhabited in Saxon times by a fishermen and three serfs who guarded 60 sheep. After 1066 it was given to a nephew of William the Conqueror. In 1903, one Mr. F.N. 'Brewer' Charrington bought it to build 'Temperance Town', but his plans came to nought. He did however turn his own home on the island into a 'retreat for gentlefolk who had fallen into the drink habit.' In the Second World War it was used by the navy, but more recently it has gone back to private ownership.

I for one have questions to ask about the new private usage, having always found the island to present something of an enigma. I have never felt that I have in any way pierced the mysterious ambience that veils the cryptic and, I sometimes ponder, perhaps clandestine events that may occur behind the blind windows of the sombre edifice that is its only permanent, hospitable gesture to chance visitors. For example, there are apparently temporary denizens of a secretive nature who propel, from time to time, unusual vehicles that move in unearthly ways their wonders to perform. I have spent many half hours trying to solve the riddle of their noises, shapes and sizes. In the end, all I knew was that one of them flew like a bird. We need to know.

I find Osea Island endlessly appealing not only because of the enigma and its but fascinating, chequered history, ancient and modern; but also because of its splendidly situated anchorage, just below the pier. You just need to keep an eye on the soundings and make sure you don't meet the nearby Barnacle. There are other pleasing anchorages not far away: Lawling Creek, also just inside Mayland Creek and, for shoal craft with a notion for shallows, the miniature Steeple Creek; just out of the main channel in Cooper's creek, opposite the *Doctor* buoy; and near the entrance to Southey Creek, in Latchingdon Hole, which is the farthest point upstream where craft can lay afloat through the tides.

## Maylandsea

Opposite Osea Island is Lawling Creek and its offshoot, Mayland Creek. The red can (*No.2*) buoy marks the main river channel at the furthest extension of the spit off *Mundon* Stone Point, while a yellow buoy, marked Mundon, is laid just off the Spit. Dan, Webb and Feesey maintain a red and orange deep water mooring at the entrance, just before Pigeon Creek.

Lawling Creek leads to Maylandsea, when Dan, Webb & Feesey have completed their pontoon facilities, and the channel up to them and through the moorings is now plain and clear. Strangers should follow the line of moored craft up Lawling Creek, keeping close to the 'C' (not C Charlie, but C Channel) numbers as they progress. Those with more than average draught will find there are big boats to offer guidance about the deep water channel. For 1·5m craft, access across the

Mundon Bar and up to the pontoons is about half tide. Visitors go to the last, 'the Big Black', pontoon. While still remote-feeling, the place is no longer out of touch with contemporary cruising needs. For example, it has a comprehensively stocked chandlery, and recent expansions and improvements have made it a most attractive weekend retreat.

Shoresides, the truth will out: it is something of a strange if not actually weird place. Not without charm and attraction, but definitely unusual. Its services are all up to scratch and 'go bananas' is a quite unbelievable tutty-fruity affair that is not to be missed. For the carless, Mr. Whent runs a brilliant personal taxi service, 'Maylandsea to Maldon? No sweat; no time at all.' One of the places to which he could take you is the scrap dealer who operates only five minutes away from the creek. His cave, pad and patch with all the stuff'n'gear is straight from an unholy alliance of Sinbad, Long John Silver and Steptoe.

# Back in the Black

Going up river, strict pilotage rules become essential as the channel not only narrows but also wanders at whim, but in the still confusingly broad waters of the flats. The red can buoy at Hilly Pool Point (*No.8*) is not easy to spot against the moorings and shoreline but the Blackwater Sailing Club flagstaff is a good mark after the green *North Double* buoy. The plentiful speed limit buoys also tend to give some indication of the channel. However, there are, in addition, dinghies and other small craft in the area to add even more colour to what is generally a fairly confusing panorama.

## Heybridge Basin

After *No.8* buoy, the river turns dramatically to port and shortly leads to the lock basin at Heybridge. There is a large mooring buoy up river of the entrance of the lock, but the holding ground is good immediately opposite. Although the lock is not usually operated except for about an hour before and after high water, the keeper does have his eye on the river most of the time and will call you to the approach so that you can tie up to the staging as soon as possible. The cross river channel to the lock entrance is a dog leg and marked with withies.

The Heybridge Basin on the old Chelmer and Blackwater Canal is a delight.

Heybridge is still having something of a hey, high and holiday in its renewed popularity with cruising folk, and it is not always possible to get a berth on demand or chance. It is sensible to phone ahead of time.

Heybridge Basin is a splendid spot: it is attractive in most of the usual postcard ways, but it also a one off. The only other lock I know that is anything remotely like it is West Stockwith on the River Trent, all that way up in the frozen north. There is no shop, but there are two pubs; and if you are interested in people as well as places, there will be no shortage of interest, intrigue and entertainment. You will be well looked after by all. Sadly, there is no really regular bus service to the basin: sometimes it arrives and sometimes it departs, but one is well advised to consult the operators at length before planning a trip to Maldon. Otherwise it is a long but quite pleasant walk along the canal bank to Heybridge and then into the town. The canal is no longer what you would call navigable by anything much more substantial than a canoe.

# Maldon

A berth can sometimes be achieved in Maldon by going up with the tide. With anything more than 1·5m it would be best to go for Maldon only on springs: there will be little time to jill around trying to find a berth or a staging. Perhaps the best plan is to stay over a tide or two at Heybridge, which is after all no hardship. You can then take local advice and make local contacts for a modus operandi on your approach to Maldon. This may seem tedious, but it can save the skipper's blushes and a hasty retreat after having been foiled by those locals who will welcome only working barges over 100 years old.

If you draw more than 1·8m or more, you will need to take care (and as much local advice as you can get) before trying to get into Maldon. There is never more than 3m at the best spring tides in Maldon and neaps can be down to less than 1·5m by the jetties; although there is about 0·5m more in the channel itself. For most yachts it is a case of coming and going immediately upon the tide or finding a spot to tie up without too much fuss, bother or time wasting. It is worth remembering that the harbour master deals only with commerce; yachts are the province of the river bailiff. Dan, Webb and Feesey will advise you about the best course of action.

Here is Ms. Driscoll on the area: 'When you speak of the Blackwater you talk of port hand buoy No. 8 at Hilly Pool. This was extremely difficult to spot at night, but one skipper I sailed with discovered that if you lined up the lights on the entrances of the two toilet blocks at Mill Beach Holiday Camp this meant that you would spot the buoy without too much trouble. The Blackwater Yacht Club used to have a light on its roof which was supposed to be a navigational aid. But it was a white light and so looked just like a shore light. It stayed on for some time, and then went out for the same length of time, so that you then lost it. So as a navigational aid I always considered that it had its drawbacks.

Now Heybridge Basin used to have a little shop by the lock ('Old Ship' side) and down the Lock Hill and round the corner was a sizeable double-fronted shop, Pam's Stores, and a small butcher's shop. I wish I'd read your book before my last visit in June this year (when I was not looking for shops and so did not notice whether they were there or not) or I'd have checked up on this. The bus service is as you describe. The canal is said to be the shallowest one in England. Brown & Son at Chelmsford used to have cargoes of timber up from the Basin by special craft built for the canal. In the Basin, too, used to lay Dutch and Danish eel boats when Kuitjen's live eel business was situated there.

I can't see any mention of the dreaded 'Northey Road', a causeway connecting Northey with the shore at low water. I've got stuck across this causeway in fog and others have damaged their propellers on it. (The River Bailiff is not chimerical incidentally.) As you pass the Basin, bound up to Maldon you see Herring Point to starboard and also three very large concrete blocks. Late in 1961 the Maldon ballast firm of A. J. Brush Ltd., put a Scotch crane here, hoping to load craft here instead of at Maldon, but for a variety of reasons it was not a success and the crane was removed. So the locals still call this place 'the crane', and this is why. Just past the crane, if too early on the tide, you suddenly run out of water and grind to a halt. There's plenty of water until you get to this point, and then it shoals out rapidly so you have to wait for the tide to flow a bit more before you can get to Maldon. Once at Maldon, beware of 'Purbeck Point', a gravel spit running out at the entrance to Heybridge Creek and named for the motor ship which regularly grounded there in the early 1960s (her skipper was always trying to get away before there was enough water under her). There have been proposals to deepen the channel by dredging the valuable gravel from the bed of the river, but nothing ever seems to come of these ideas.'

## RIVER COLNE

**Charts**

Imray Y17
Admiralty 3741

**Tides**

Sheerness -0040 at Brightlingsea. Dover +0100 approx.

## BRIGHTLINGSEA

Harbourmaster, Peter Coupland, said recently that although they had been busier with leisure craft than ever before, they are still very proud of the fact that they have never turned anybody away.

## WIVENHOE

Accessible for no more than +/-0200 HW.

It is hoped that in the near future the HM office at Wivenhoe will be sited within sight if not sound of the new flood barrier.

## COLCHESTER

**Radio**

VHF Ch 14, 11, 68. Office hours or from 2 hrs before to 1 hr after HW.

☎ Harbour Master: Colchester (0206) 827316.

## RIVER BLACKWATER

**Charts**

Imray Y17
Admiralty 3741

**Tides**

Sheerness +0005 (at Maldon), Dover +0100, depending upon exact place in river below Osea Island.

**Marinas and boatyards**

*Tollesbury Marina* ☎ Maldon (0621) 869202/868471

*Bradwell Marina* ☎ Maldon (0621) 76235/76391

*Dan, Webb and Feesey* Maylandsea Shipyard: ☎ Maldon (0621) 740264/741267

Maldon Shipways: ☎ Maldon (0621) 854280/856829

**Authorities**

*Maldon Harbourmaster* Responsible for cargoes and the buoyage down to Heybridge Basin. ☎ Maldon (0621) 853110

*Maldon River Bailiff* Responsible for boats and their dues. ☎ Maldon (0621) 854477/856487 or in emergency 853759

*Heybridge Basin Lock keeper* ☎ Maldon (0621) 853506

Tollesbury is tucked away next door to totally rural and quite undisturbed settings.

## BUOYAGE

### River Blackwater and its approaches

| Check | Confirm | Confirm | Check |
|---|---|---|---|
| | | Maldon | |
| | | G | |
| | | G | |
| No. 14 R | | No. 13 G | |
| No. 12 R | | No. 11 G | |
| | | | Herrings Pt |
| No. 10 R | | No. 9 G | Heybridge Basin |
| Northey Island | No. 8 R | Y.C. Flag Staff Iso.G.5s.2M | |
| | S. Double No. 6 R | N. Double No. 7 Fl.G.3s G | |
| | No. 4 Southey Creek R | | |
| | | No. 3 The Doctor G | Osea I. |
| Lawling Creek | No. 2 Fl.R.3s R | Pier 2F.G.(vert) | |
| | Marconi S.C. F. | | Goldhanger Creek |
| Bradwell Marina buoyage and withies (see text) | | No. 1 Goldhanger Spit G | |
| | | Thirslet Spit Fl(3)G.10s G | |
| | Bradwell Bn Q.R. | | Tollesbury Fleet and Marina |
| Power Station | 2F.R.(vert) | | Mersea Quarters and South Channel Seasonal buoyage |
| Barrier Wall | 2F.R.(vert) | | |
| St Peters Chapel | | Nass Bn V.Q (3) 5s. | Outfall |
| | | Bench Head G Fl.G.5s | |
| | N. W. Knoll Fl(2)R.10s R | Colne Bar G | R. Colne |
| | | Eagle Q.G. G | N. Eagle BY |
| | Knoll Q. BY | | |

# VII. THE CROUCH, THE ROACH AND HAVENGORE

## The Crouch

### Approaches

Unless you are a local, creeping through the Ray Sand Channel from Bench Head or the Colne Bar, your main navigational aids will be the red and white Swin Spitway; the red and black Whitaker beacon and/or some of the many Whitaker buoys. Once you have confirmed the ones for your track, provided you take care to follow the route indicated by the River Crouch buoyage, there is no hazard to Burnham-on-Crouch. Visitors should note that the better water has, in the past, always seemed to tend southerly in the river. Make sure that you keep an eye on the sounder when near the *Sunken Buxey* and the *Buxey Nos. 1* and *2* in case you need to tend to the north.

An Essex landfall will be neither inspiring nor dramatic, merely a slow growth from shallow waters to grey, low-lying flats. Maplin, Foulness and Buxey offer little of what is usually understood by the words 'land' or 'sand'. In any case, there is a good chance that they will be shrouded by one of the area's regular mists so that there will be nothing to see ... and virtually nothing to look at even when you can see. That is, unless you can find charm in a vista that consists in the main of muddy wastes broken only by sewer outfalls, pylons and factory chimneys, with spasms of beach huts and bathing shacks, and cars and caravans with umbilically attached carports.

As and when the coastline does emerge, it will do so as a muddy waste, broken only by sewer outfalls, pylons, factory chimneys and spasm after spasm of bathing huts, caravans. It does seem sad that we could not have left the area to creatures who would have been able to put it to better use than we have. I suppose we must lay the flattering unction to our souls that there is, not quite yet anyway, a hyper/jumbo airport.

Nor was it of any consolation, on my first visit, to read: 'CAUTION FIRING AREA Experimental firing is frequently carried out off the Maplin and Foulness Sands. While this is in progress, no vessel may enter, or remain in the area'. Firing itself is surely bad enough, but what about that 'experimental firing'? However, that was not the end. It went on. 'Obstructions to navigation, sometimes submerged, may be encountered within the area. Beacons of no navigational significance, with or without lights, may also be erected'. None of that endeared the place to me.

It is a good, long haul from the *Whitaker* buoy to Holliwell and Foulness Points and then there are still four more miles to Burnham. I always find that the long finger of Holliwell Point takes a long time to form itself into anything recognisable and substantial. The first sign of man's blessed building programme comes with a military style, concrete lookout/pill-box to the north; and to the south, all the paraphernalia of the Foulness Firing Range and Great Shell Corner.

En route, the only other visual relief, if it may properly be so described, comes from the occasional shed-like, wooden-clad, single-storey construction insufficiently substantial for a bungalow and too characterless for a cottage. Two or three of these neglected near-dwellings make the place look like a film location, where, sagas of death by drowning and madness at sea were enacted. The characters might yet return to haunt their salt-encrusted walls and repossess them as sympathetic shells for crab-like human hermits.

Two miles or so below Burnham, comes Nase Point, facing Ness Hole. Since it extends pretty far out, it is not a place to cut corners if turning into the Roach. It is not alone: off Wallasea Ness, on the west bank of the River Roach, comes Brankfleet Spit. It is marked by a permanent yellow spherical buoy carrying a radar reflector. It also should be well rounded when making for The Roach from the west, particularly after NE winds when it can be blown back on to the spit it marks. The spit itself is a slender finger searching out the Crouch for a good way. It is worth a nod and wink at low water springs.

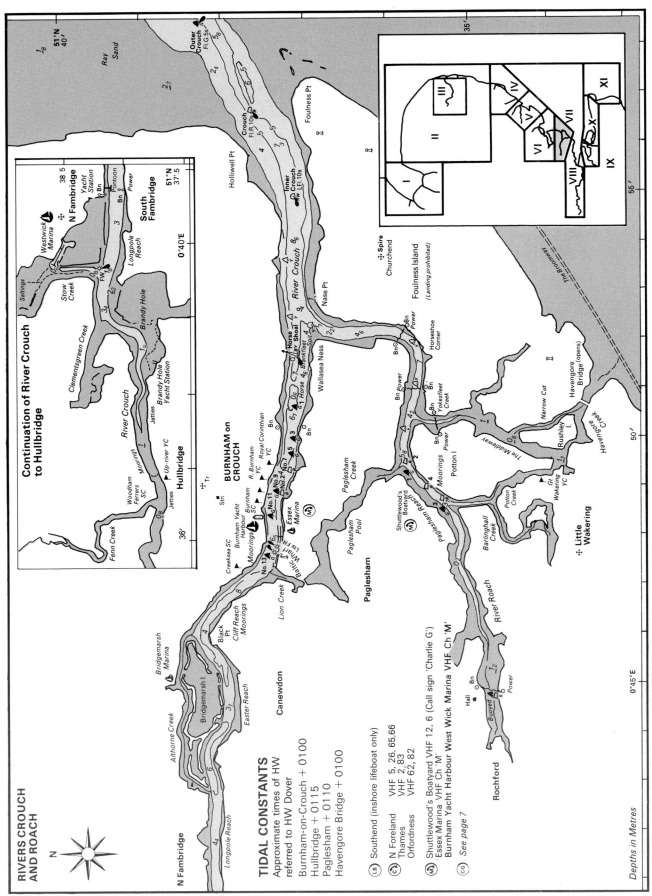

**RIVERS CROUCH AND ROACH**

**Continuation of River Crouch to Hullbridge**

**TIDAL CONSTANTS**
Approximate times of HW referred to HW Dover
Burnham-on-Crouch + 0100
Hullbridge + 0115
Paglesham + 0110
Havengore Bridge + 0100

(LB) Southend (inshore lifeboat only)

(C) N Foreland    VHF 5, 26, 65,66
Thames    VHF 2, 83
Orfordness    VHF 62, 82

(M) Shuttlewood's Boatyard VHF 12, 6 (Call sign 'Charlie G')
Essex Marina VHF Ch 'M'
Burnham Yacht Harbour West Wick Marina VHF Ch 'M'

(CG) See page 7

Depths in Metres

Just upstream of Wallasea Ness, is the commencement of the Horse Shoal, now marked not only at the west end by the upstream green *No.1* but also by a north cardinal marker. Leisure craft can progress closeish to the banks on either side of Horse in a least depth of 4m while The Horse itself has no more than 0·6m. It is followed by the four dramatically striking spheres of the recognisable yellow buoys that mark the power cable.

They are not to be taken for one of the yellow racing buoys, many of which are taken up in the winter, that are extremely easy to spot both in the Crouch and in the Roach, where they make good courses from spit to spit. The last leg is marked by the much improved buoyage delineating the fairway into Burnham.

# Burnham-on-Crouch

Burnham-on-Crouch is often called Britain's 'foremost' yachting centre. Many Yorkshire racing/yachting types who have learned their sailing skills under conditions more arduous than those usually encountered on the Crouch would, however, be sure to challenge any such claim to superiority that came from these waters. Be that as it may, there is no argument about it being very busy, but the river is no longer as crowded with moorings as it used to be, thanks to the most recent development, the Burnham Yacht Harbour.

The other marina is across the river: the long and well established and now refurbished facility of Essex Marina at Wallasea Island. Since dredging, drying out has been mastered and the new pontoons offer up to 10m at some berths at LWS. There are comprehensive boating facilities, two pubs and an hotel with restaurant where discos and flashing lights are a late night feature. Once the festivities die down, the late night/early morning fishermen usually arrive to prowl the pontoons – and not always in silence even at 0300. Waiting in external attendance by the litter bins and the food outlets is a fleet of feral cats. Domestic shopping and chandlery are basic.

If you favour a swinging mooring for a visit, the usual plan is to take the first convenient buoy, then go ashore for advice and instruction. This can come from the boatyards or the clubs. Another way it to phone the Crouch Harbour Authority harbourmaster before your visit. The authority maintains a launch that cruise/patrols the river Wednesday, Saturday and Sunday, keeping a listening watch on VHF Ch 16.

Shoresides, you will find all shopping requirements catered for in Burnham-on-Crouch; which, once basic needs have been met becomes an acquired and delicate taste, appealing to those with a penchant for the expensive and the extravagant. In fact, the place is such a high temple to the fruits of the affluent society that, when priests and acolytes ritually foregather as they do at the height of the season, even Rolls-Royces have to suffer the indignity of being rafted two deep in the High Street.

Some of the intriguing, attractive craft to be found on the Crouch

The River Crouch.

For many people, it is the clubs and the racing that form the main attractions of Burnham-on-Crouch. There are certainly ideal conditions for racing, with most of the ten miles to the Whitaker likened to the open sea with little to diminish the winds from the estuary. There are merits from the cruising point of view as well. In particular, you can stay afloat right up to Stow Creek and so use the stretch as a viable staging post. From the water, there is indeed much to extol on the Crouch.

# Up the Crouch

Some cruising men still insist there are good anchorages to be found both above and below Burnham. There may well have been long ago, in the days when there were good ferries. Now it is prudent to anchor only well above Burnham, and certainly no nearer than Cliff Reach. With the Baltic Wharf commercial traffic in addition to all the leisure craft, Burnham is just too busy for any anchorage to be a sensible proposition.

If quieter aspects are what you seek, there are plenty of inducements up the river. One of which is the sheer romance of the names: Lion Creek, Brandy Hole, Landsend Point and more. The first really handsome site upstream is Cliff Reach; an attractive anchorage where the modest rise of its cliffs, nowhere more than 15m, helps distract the mind and in part compensate for the monotony of much of the environs. On my last visit, at a very low water springs, I discovered some foul patches when searching close to the bank, so it is as well not to approach too near and to keep a good watch. It is only just over a mile up from the *NW Fairway* buoy, immediately after which the mud spit to starboard is clearly designated by the moorings. There are moorings to port as well, but the channel is plain to see. There are additional opportunities to drop the hook with care in Easter Reach, on the Upper Raypits south side, between Black Point and Landsend Point.

## Bridgemarsh Island

Just upstream, and across the river from Black Point is the east entrance to Althorne Creek. First impressions suggest a nascent creek, little more than a mature dyke and not very hospitable. Closer inspection determines differently, to reveal it to be not only well marked but also inviting.

Westwick Marina: quietly situated off Stow Creek behind the River Crouch. The place is fairly remote, the scenery is gently pretty and the people are friendly. There are facilities nearby, including a smashing pub; so what more could you ask if storm-bound – or just not bound anywhere at all?

And the inviting is the result of the efforts, enterprise and aspirations of John and Ray Walker to establish an 'X Marks the Spot A1 Place' where they run an informally tight little ship of an enterprise, called modestly enough, Bridgemarsh Island Marina. The entrance round the bight now carries 1·5m at LWS thus allowing most leisure craft access at most states of the tide, and quite similar to such places as Bradwell and Westwick. Through the creek there is a very fast tide that cleanses, scours and flushes so there is no problem of silting, though initially the pontoons needed dredging to prevent the boats on the floating pontoons taking the bottom at low water.

BI Marina is a particular, personalised operation. There is none of the anonymity of the G&T GRP boat parks. I first met the Walkers with their traditional old Dutch schooner on the slip from which John passionately declaimed, 'We own the river from our moorings to the jetty, but nobody ever mentions us. So far as the magazines, pilots, guides and all that lot, we might as well not be here. Though we have been here now for years and years. As I said to one editor, 'What if somebody had a heart attack just off the island? They could land here. There's a telephone. The ambulance could get right to the slipway. But they wouldn't know. They'd have a corpse on their hands, wouldn't they?' It could definitely save a life.'

There is a five minute walk up the lane to the hinterland for Althorne station, which has single line trains at better than hourly intervals. Bridgemarsh Island itself consists mainly of saltings with most of it covered most of the time. Landing is prohibited and since some of its 'banks' are dangerous to approach, it can hardly be described as a prime attraction of an island. Some mud spits are marked by withies. In spite of what John and Ray say, there are signs of silt at the west end of Althorne Creek. Between Shortpole Reach and Stow Creek there are many unpleasant obstructions on the north bank; they are all clearly marked by withies which are fully visible most of the time, but it is no place to go in search of a bankside mooring at HW when they are not all obvious.

## North Fambridge and Stow Creek

By the time you reach North Fambridge the moorings have become extensive, but it is possible to anchor in Longpole Reach well below and away from the moorings. It is worth seeking advice on good spots from the North Fambridge Yacht Station (see below). On the north shore, there is a white hut which was once a lepers' holiday hospital; while the North Fambridge Y.C. house, was, more predictably, the ferryman's boathouse. It has been raised a metre to prevent flooding and there has not been a ferry service for some time.

The North Fambridge Yacht Station started life as recently as 1981, but its attitudes to service and courtesy go back much further. They have now installed a new pontoon access to the river and established the additional service of a launch taxi for yachtsmen on Friday night to Sunday night. They are also undertaking comprehensive improvements and extensions which will provide fingers out into the river, and half tide mud berths.

It is an extremely pleasant spot with unusually vivid dawns, nebulous dusks, and intense sunsets. It is an excellent place for keen photographers and painters.

Excellent also is Stow Creek just round the corner on the north bank. There is a pile tide marker that seems as if it must mark the centre of the channel so far out is it from the bank; but then, the mud spit reaches out no less far. You can leave it close to starboard upon entering. Starboard withies mark the channel in Stow Creek and then into Westwick Marina which is to starboard at the 'head' of the creek. At the entrance to the creek, a water tower at the top of the hill when in line with the entrance beacon will mark the track of the channel. There is no hazard in the area and the limiting factor is draught; if you draw more than 1·5m it is better not to approach Stow Creek until two hours after low water.

Westwick Marina was established ten years before its NFYS sister, in 1971. There are continuing improvements here as well, as new pontoons, mains water and power are installed with all the skills, expertise and materials that an (ex) aficionado of the building trade, haulage and tin plate recovery trade can create. They can usually accommodate visitors, for whom there is spacious car parking, although groups need to make prior arrangements. But whatever the state of their business or work load you can still be sure of a warm and enthusiastic welcome. You will notice that the pontoons are swept every morning and that the thoughtfully designed loos are spotless. It is no exaggeration to describe Westwick as immaculate and efficient; but with none of the clinical anonymity that often accompanied those qualities. It is a place of character and characters, with the overall ambience of a boating preserve. It is in fact something of a sanctuary for a number of ducks and one china goose that are symbolic of the proliferation of local wild life.

Local life of an entirely different calibre must be tasted at The Ferry Boat. Dearly departed the ferry may be, but local life, soul and party all proceed apace in this truly amazing pub.

North Fambridge, where the single line trains cross at the station, is less than a mile distant. There is a post office and a pub in the village. For really first rate shopping you should go to the 'new village' of Woodham Ferrers; and in any case, its design, layout and some of its architecture make it well worth a visit in its own right.

## Head of Crouch

Further upstream is the unapproachable but nicely named Clementsgreen Creek to the north. There is nothing there for boats, except the possibility of an anchorage just inside the wide entrance. Leaving the creek and its extensive spit on the starboard hand, the river runs into Brandy Hole Reach, where, in the proximity of the far-reaching saltings, the Yacht Station maintains its deep-water moorings; and where, in Brandy Hole Bay you find a pleasant anchorage. Please to take instruction from club members before dropping your hook. The area is quite charming and the local yachtsmen most welcoming, provided you don't want to stay too long, for there is a waiting list and congestion here as elsewhere. After which come Hullbridge and Battlesbridge.

For those who must go every inch of the way, it is possible to reach the basic 'source' of the Crouch at Battlesbridge on the top of springs provided you don't draw more than 2m. The navigation of this stretch is tortuous and narrow and also littered with moorings. I generally look upon Stow Creek as the virtual head of navigation, but that is mainly because I don't fancy unshipping the dinghy or facing a row ashore. Kindly note, outboards are not well liked and noisy ones are despised.

I have taken *Valcon* up to Battlesbridge, and while that was an exacting and tedious passage because of *Valcon's* strong twin-screwed objections to being in less 2·5m, it did allow me to remark the attractions of the river as its banks inexorably closed in on me. There are lots of moorings, no major marks and little to show the true nature of the deep course. Shallow river water reading expertise is called for.

I felt it necessary to turn round, not the easiest of manoeuvres either, and leave immediately since I was not convinced I would happily lie anywhere at low water. It also meant going down on the ebb which is another activity I don't care for in a restricted waterway that I don't know. I like the stretch, but now return only by grace and favour of local shoal draught craft.

Here is what Ms. Driscoll has to offer: 'Land Water, incidentally, can also be found at Maldon, especially in the stretch between the bridge and Heybridge Creek, and I shouldn't wonder if it isn't also at Battlesbridge, just below the bridge (we used to go to Mathews' Mill there with grain, and it was an extremely awkward place to get alongside but I won't burden you with this). The Crouch is an area of extremely strong tides. We used to go to Creeksea Jetty, which was across the tide, and keeping alongside there on the ebb was a problem.'

One of the great things about the Crouch is that if you don't feel like going upstream for a quiet day's cruise, you can go downstream and turn into the Roach for an equally non-threatening trip.

*Above* Woodbridge on the Deben, with boatyards and its famous Tide Mill. *Lance Cooper*

*Below* Felixstowe Docks: most of the vast expanse is denied to pleasure craft. *Colloryan*

*Above opposite* Shotley Point Marina: where mooring is designer style and state of the art. *Shotley Point Marina*
*Below opposite* Wivenhoe: where mooring still needs ancient arts and crafts...and a subtle touch of guile.

*Above and below* The Blackwater can usually be relied on to provide peace and quiet for those who want to get away...while those with an eye on socialising will find a welcome at Bradwell Marina.
*Right* The riverside at Maldon is still almost as traditional as that at Pin Mill.

*Above* The faces of the Crouch may change with the times, but the river is still peerless among piers.

*Below and above opposite* The Roach can be a place of passive, silent beauty, with many hidden charms...but it also has its bleaker more exposed moments...while (*below opposite*) Tilbury is Tilbury, full stop.

*Above (by Kim Hollamby) and opposite* The Thames Barrier was completed some time ago…while Canary Wharf suffers from a shortage of gnomes.
*Below* Chelsea Bridge after Football and/or Boat Race Fever? *Keith Pritchard*

*Above* The entrance to St Katharine's Dock just below Tower Bridge.

*Above right* A favourite watering point (or staging post) just below Rochester Bridge on the River Medway.

*Below* The new Marina at South Dock is closer to the Medway than you might think, being run by the same charismatic stable as the marina at Hoo.

*Above* At the head of Conyer Creek, there is room only for those who run a tight ship.

*Above* Harty Ferry, in the East Swale by the entrance to Faversham Creek, is one of the most favourite and haunted spots in the area.

*Right* Ramsgate: all things to all men, but never inexpensive at the price.

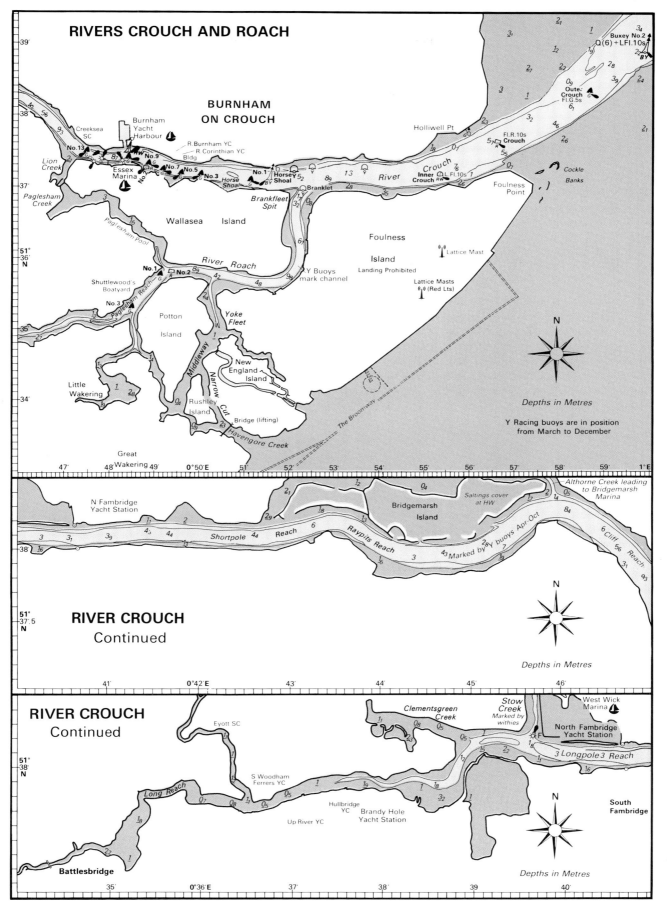

## RIVERS CROUCH AND ROACH

39'

**BURNHAM
ON CROUCH**

38'

Creeksea
SC
Burnham
Yacht
Harbour
No.13
R.Burnham YC
R.Corinthian YC
Bldg
HW
No.9
Lion
Creek
No.7 No.5
Essex
Marina
No.3
Horse
Shoal
No.1
Horsey
Shoal
Branklet

37'

Paglesham
Creek
Wallasea    Island
Brankfleet
Spit

Holliwell Pt
Fl.R.10s
Crouch
River    Crouch
Inner
Crouch   L Fl.10s
Foulness
Point

Cockle
Banks

51°
36'
N
Paglesham Pool
River    Roach

Foulness

Island
Landing Prohibited

Lattice Mast

Lattice Masts
(Red Lts)

No.1 No.2
Shuttlewood's
Boatyard
No.3   Paglesham Reach
Y Buoys
mark channel

Potton

Island
Yoke
Fleet

35'

Little
Wakering
Middleway
Narrow Cut
New
England
Island

N

34'

Rushley
Island
Bridge (lifting)

*Depths in Metres*

*Y Racing buoys are in position
from March to December*

Great
Wakering   Havengore Creek

47'   48'   49'   0°50'E   51'   52'   53'   54'   55'   56'   57'   58'   59'   1°E

Buxey No.2
Q(6)+LFl.10s
Oute:
Crouch
Fl.G.5s

---

## RIVER CROUCH
### Continued

51°
37'.5
N

N Fambridge
Yacht Station
Shortpole    Reach
Raypits Reach
Marked by Y buoys Apr-Oct
Bridgemarsh
Island
Saltings cover
at HW
Althorne Creek leading
to Bridgemarsh
Marina
Cliff Reach

38'

N

*Depths in Metres*

41'   0°42'E   43'   44'   45'   46'

---

## RIVER CROUCH
### Continued

51°
38'
N

Eyott SC
Clementsgreen
Creek
Stow
Creek
Marked by
withies
West Wick
Marina
North Fambridge
Yacht Station
Longpole   Reach

S Woodham
Ferrers YC
Long Reach
Hullbridge
YC
Brandy Hole
Yacht Station
Up River YC
South
Fambridge

N

**Battlesbridge**

*Depths in Metres*

35'   0°36'E   37'   38'   39'   40'

## BUOYAGE
### The River Crouch and its approaches

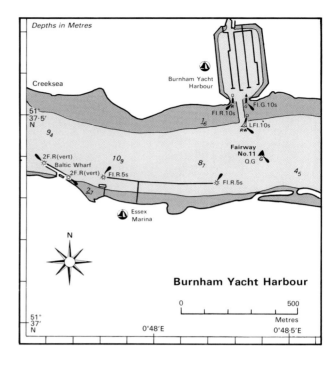

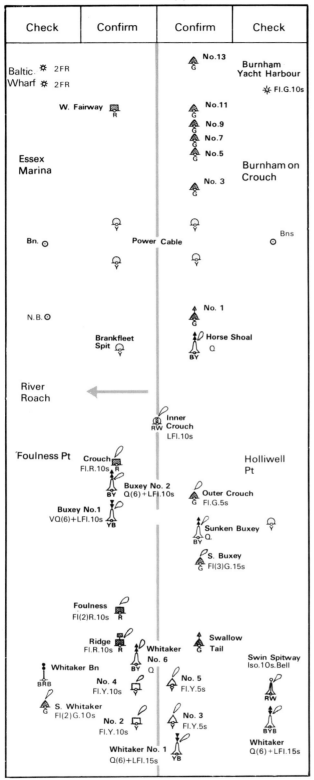

| Check | Confirm | Confirm | Check |
|---|---|---|---|
| | | No.13 | Burnham Yacht Harbour |
| Baltic. ✳ 2FR | | | |
| Wharf ✳ 2FR | | | ✳ Fl.G.10s |
| W. Fairway | | No.11 | |
| | | No.9 | |
| | | No.7 | |
| Essex | | No.5 | Burnham on Crouch |
| Marina | | | |
| | | No. 3 | |
| | | | |
| Bn. ⊙ | Power Cable | | Bns ⊙ |
| | | | |
| N.B. ⊙ | | No. 1 | |
| | Brankfleet Spit | Horse Shoal Q BY | |
| River Roach ⟵ | | | |
| | | Inner Crouch RW LFl.10s | |
| Foulness Pt | Crouch Fl.R.10s R | | Holliwell Pt |
| | Buxey No. 2 BY Q(6)+LFl.10s | Outer Crouch G Fl.G.5s | |
| | Buxey No.1 VQ(6)+LFl.10s YB | | |
| | | Sunken Buxey BY Q. | |
| | | S. Buxey G Fl(3)G.15s | |
| | Foulness Fl(2)R.10s R | | |
| | Ridge Fl.R.10s R | Swallow Tail G | |
| | Whitaker No. 6 BY Q | | Swin Spitway Iso.10s.Bell |
| Whitaker Bn BRB | No. 4 Fl.Y.10s | No. 5 Fl.Y.5s | RW |
| S. Whitaker G Fl(2)G.10s | No. 2 Fl.Y.10s | No. 3 Fl.Y.5s | Whitaker Q(6)+LFl.15s BYB |
| | Whitaker No. 1 Q(6)+LFl.15s YB | | |

From the Wallet, the East Swin or the Kings Channel, pick up the Whitaker lightbuoy.

In addition to the above, yellow racing buoys are established in the Rivers Crouch and Roach during the season.

# The River Roach

## Entrances

There are two ways into the Roach and they could hardly be more different. The first is from the River Crouch, entering between Brankfleet, the spit that extends from Wallasea Ness on the west bank, and Nase Point on the east; while the second is across Maplin Sands and the Broomway through Havengore Creek and under the eponyfamous lifting bridge.

As mentioned in the section on the Crouch, it is important to respect the yellow buoy off Wallasea and to keep to a central channel when entering the Roach since Brankfleet Spit and Nase Point both extend well out into the river from their respective roots. Cutting corners here is a fool's game. Keep an eye on the sounder until well into Quay Reach, since the depths vary quite a lot quite quickly.

For example, there is the deep Ness Hole followed by a small half bar. Better water follows for a time but only to become shoal again before finally developing into a channel proper well after Crow Corner in Quay Reach. Thereafter, you carry plenty of water until Paglesham Reach, that is, well past Shuttlewoods Eastend Boatyard. The yellow racing buoys that abound in the Crouch and the Roach, marking the spit ends and turns, are a most useful adjunct for the cruising stranger.

## Anchorages

There is a proliferation of anchorages in the Roach. To start with, there are good places just in the entrance to the Roach: one just past Brankfleet Spit towards the west bank; another on the other side in Quay Reach, but past the quay that does its best not to resemble one, towards the east bank; and and a third tucked in the corner by Whitehouse Hole. The Roach is used by coasters and barges bound for Rochford, and their courses are strictly limited by draught. The rules must be strictly observed: keep as far away out of the fairway as possible, and always employ a good riding light.

There is also an appealing anchorage, remote from all connections, in Yoke Fleet, where just after the entrance there is good water. You need to be careful when negotiating the turn into the entrance, for the channel is very narrow and tortuous. Any prospective hook-dropper would be well advised to cruise by at dead low water and inspect with care, for the actual detail of the contours is worth imprinting on the brain.

There are also pleasing anchorages in Paglesham Reach, above Barlingness and well past the moorings; and in the West Reach by Potton Island, clear of the moorings and before Barlinghall Creek. For those who are prepared to take the ground, Paglesham Pool is possible, and Barlinghall Creek absolutely delightful. They should both be inspected through the glasses before a final choice is made as there are one or two undesirable spots. An exploratory low water foray makes all things clear.

An anchorage between Barling Point and Potton Island is the alternative to a mooring by the boatyard. Near the big fishing boats there is well protected good holding ground where you will stay afloat. It is a fairly remote but very attractive spot.

## Roach Reaches and Creeks

Potton Point, just after Devil's Reach, is a place to look out for. If you can arrange it, it is worth inspecting at low water since the spits and the narrowness of the channel must be seen to be believed. Past the point, plentiful withies mark both banks and the entrance to Paglesham Pool.

Next come four standard buoys from the entrance to the pool up to Barlingness: greens *1* and *3*, reds *2* and *4*; and they lead you right up to Shuttlewoods Reach. There has been a boatyard at East End since 1840 and it has been known by its present name since 1890. Moorings are often available from the boatyard which is a thriving business. The master and his men will all be much more than helpful once you have shown your goodwill and established your bona fides.

Indeed, I remember one autumn, I used one of their buoys to moor for a few days hoping for some late sunny pictures. When I arrived, I had been steaming non-stop for 14 hours and was feeling shattered, so I was more than grateful when Mr. Norris, the boatyard's charismatic number one, told me on VHF that if I jilled around for a few minutes he would be across to help me pick up a buoy and make fast. There was already a fierce tide rip and a brisk wind was getting ready to blow even brisker. As good as his word, he came alongside and I was all tied up in less than five minutes.

Next morning, when the hooligan wind was really blowing, Mr. Norris came on board again: 'We couldn't see any sign of life on board, so we thought we'd better see if you were still alive. I'll ferry you back if you like; you'll never make it in that silly inflatable of yours.' Service of that calibre is beyond a hard cash price.

There is a long history of oysters, floods and smuggling hereabouts, and it takes only one evening quietly at anchor in Barlinghall Creek to believe every single word that comes you way in the pub, which like the small stores, is only a short walk from the boatyard slipway.

Every other trip must be done on the tides, since all other places dry out. A visit to the Rochford end of the Roach will show the river to have only a narrow channel. In spite of its commercial use, you must exercise caution if you are not to stray from the channel. There is little in the way of attractive scenery. There are two buoys that appear somewhat unexpectedly on the scene near the end of the navigation: a red and a green that mark a submarine cable. There is little to fire the spirit at Rochford and if you propose to visit you must be prepared to take the ground almost straightway. It is not a trip to be recommended, except in a tender, day-boat or dinge. That also applies of course equally well, or ill according to your point of view, to a number of the creeks of the Roach. Those 'navigable by tender only' are Shelford Creek, Paglesham Creek, Little Wakering Creek, Fleethead Creek, Bartonhall Creek, and the upper part of Barlinghall Creek. With the exception of Bartonhall, which is not a prime candidate, they are fine for a day spent messing about in boats with children. Their foremost and singular attributes are their remoteness and usually unchallenged privacy. Paglesham Pool is a possible port of call with the mother craft, but only in the entrance since the bottom is very shortly foul. That leaves Barlinghall with it lower reaches to take my prize for the most appealing and sheltered venue in the Roach. It is, of course, removed from all contact with 'civilisation', but anyone who is cruising this area should from the outset have wanted to get away from it all.

The other, navigable 'creeks' are not serious candidates for pottering, but afford access to Havengore and a passage into the Thames, thus saving the long haul round the Whitaker. They are: Yoke Fleet, the Middleway, Narrow Cut and Potton Creek. They should all be used near high water, preferably on a rising spring, and are to be navigated with precision. There is no need to promulgate advice for each one separately for they are all susceptible of the same procedures: keep one eye on the sounder, the other on the banks and the third on the stretch just in front. In other words, treat all the stretches as shoal and make sure you have plenty of power available, and some in reserve.

There are one or two particulars: the entrance to Yoke Fleet, by Potton Point, is extra difficult for there is a projecting spit at the west side and an extensive mud flat at the east. Generally the water starts off by being towards the west bank but gradually makes a central (more or less!) course. After a mile, Shelford Creek will be seen to port, to be followed by another opening at the now dammed-off New England Creek. Neither of these is of any interest to yachtsmen. Shortly after, the Middleway splits and the turning to port is Narrow Cut to Havengore. The other passage round Rushley Island, with Potton on the other side, also takes you to Havengore but will involve you in some nasty twists and turns if you are not to get firmly stuck on the mud by the southern end of Potton Island.

There are plenty of moorings at the home of the Wakering Yacht Club complete with boatyard and pontoons but unless you know exactly where you are and what you are doing it will be almost impossible to find the channel without touching bottom once or twice. This could involve you in an unwanted delay if you have in mind to catch a tide through the bridge. This passage must be negotiated if you are going to come through from Barlingness. On that route there is a hard that should not be approached at anything less than an hour or so before high water. That is found by Great Potton, where there is also the swing bridge just before Wakering. The bridge keeper will probably be at his post ready and raring to go for he is a bright and considerate master who takes a delight in getting his bridge working. You must keep well to the centre here for there is an extensive shoaling mud patch on the Wakering side.

Whichever approach you use to Havengore itself, do remember that the tides are eccentric and can race through the creeks at a cracking pace. You need to be confident of your power and your ground tackle; otherwise you will be better employed staying in Yoke Fleet or Paglesham Reach.

# Havengore and the new bridge

The new bascule bridge lifts in 90 seconds, as opposed to the seven minutes for the old one. Here are the details as provided by the Procurement Executive Ministry of Defence Proof and Experimental Establishment:

'1. The new Havengore Bridge is fitted with a boom to the underside of the Bascule thus preventing free passage when the bridge is not manned.

2. The bridge will be raised for a vessel 2 hours before and after predicted high tide every day of the year (except Christmas Day) during daylight hours, providing the Range is not firing (indicated by red flags).

3. Daylight is defined as half an hour before sunrise or half an hour after sunset in winter and one hour before and after in summer. Winter and summer being defined as when the clocks change to and from BST.

4. The Range is seldom active at weekends or public holidays. Persons wishing to discover if the Range will be firing may telephone Southend (0702) 292271 extension 3211 or ask by calling 'SHOE BASE' on the marine net Ch 16 during working hours. A forecast of activity can be given some days ahead. During silent hours the telephone number only will advise on bridge opening for the period up to the next working day.

5. The Bridge Keeper does not have the authority to say whether the bridge will open on future days but will know about today. He can be found on the same number extension 3436 or as 'SHOE BRIDGE' on marine Ch 16.'

There is a passage to and from the River Roach across the Maplin Sands, crossing the Shoeburyness gunnery range, through the 'new' Havengore bascule lifting bridge. Although the occasional commercial vessel still tries its luck in an attempt to save time and fuel, the passage is only suitable for craft drawing no more than 1·5m and then only on the top of springs....and then only in fine, settled weather. There is a local saying: 'If the Broomway doesn't get you, the mud spits will!'

It is difficult to get definitive information about the Havengore route. For example, I have interviewed skippers with 1·1m draught who have pronounced it to be 'OK'. In the main they had very fast motor cruisers that, if anything, drew less and not more than 3'6". I traced one skipper whose draught was 1·4m and he said, 'Oh no! that was far too iffy every to try again'. I also heard around and about of boats of 1·8m that had been through but to this day I have not been able to trace one of the. I think the point is straightforward: if the conditions are fine and settled,; if there is a biggish spring tide; if your boat falls into the appropriate draught; and generally speaking if you know what you are doing, then the Havengore route will be worth trying.

However, it is worth noting that Shuttlewoods boatyard at East End, would have none of *Valcon* crossing the Broomway once they knew she drew more than 1·5m under way; and that the bridge keeper at Havengore said, 'On a 5·5m tide, the maximum draught is 0·8m; on a 6m tide, 1·8m boats have been known to get through and others have foundered but you must know what you are doing....and exactly where you are'. Quite clearly, basic maths has little relevance to the navigation of the Broomway. It would appear that no one who has any acquaintance at all with its whims and ways is ready to risk a thing when the vagaries of the tide are the controlling factors.

It is not a trip to make just out of idle curiosity nor for the pleasure of a 'different' day out. It is one for those whose boats meet the necessary requirements and who need to save the time by going that way in safety.

As mentioned earlier, the sands around here are not without their hazards. The Admiralty *Pilot* says: 'Firing takes place from Shoeburyness 51°32'N 0°48'E. Experimental firing is frequently carried out in all conditions of weather and tide in the sea...' The Imray *Pilot's Guide to the Thames Estuary* said: 'Traffic in and out of the creek is entirely controlled by firing practice. Facilities are granted to proceed during firing by permission of the Officer Commanding Shoeburyness Garrison, and every consideration is given in this respect'. Nothing has changed, and the bridge keeper and the range planning officer will do all they can to co-operate. Obviously, firing takes precedence, so the range planning officer or the bridge keeper should be contacted at the very least 24 hours before you want to go through. As the bridge keeper says: 'We all try to co-operate as much as possible, but you would be amazed how many people just turn up, thinking they can get through at any time never mind the firing. Me. I'd be worried stiff once I heard those bangs'.

The range planning officer can be contacted during office hours Monday to Friday; and the bridge keeper is in attendance from two hours before to two hours after high water, sunrise to sunset. Passage is not allowed through the bridge at night. Generally speaking it is best to try for a weekend when there is usually no firing. Occasionally there is firing at night. Red flags are displayed on Havengore Bridge and at frequent intervals along the sea wall between Shoeburyness and Foulness Point, also on the south bank of the River Crouch and the east bank of the River

Roach when firing is in progress or is about to take place. Passage is prohibited when flags are displayed and approach is dangerous, especially from seaward.

It used to take the keeper 7–8 minutes to open the bridge once he had pressed the last button in the over-all process; and before he did that he had to close the road barrier by hand and operate the traffic light. There was never any way in which you could get through 'at the drop of a hat'. You had to be properly prepared since the ebb and flow through the bridge are very strong; frequently taking strangers by surprise and pinning them against the bridge.

A surprising factor to many visitors is that the tidal streams run in both directions for each tide; before the Broomway is covered, the flood comes from the Roach, running southeast; once it is covered, it comes from the estuary and runs northwest. The reverse occurs on the ebb, and these changes happen about 1½ hours each side of high water. The tide itself stands no more than 2–3 minutes and sometimes not at all.

On leaving the creek for the Broomway (or Broomroad, the highest ridge of the drying sands, along which traffic passes, and sometimes referred to as the military road) the channel is roughly a dog-leg; port, starboard, port. The general approach from seaward is to pick up the *East Shoebury* buoy and then set a course for the red and white (vertical) can buoy that is the current major replacement. Then you will see a line of small buoys to be left to port when making the last approach to the bridge. On the way out, deeper draught boats go on to just north of the *Blacktail Spit* buoy, while shallow ones can make for the South Shoebury. All passages must be close to high water.

Shuttlewoods advise anyone with more than 1·2m not to try the Havengore route. I like to give the last, classic words to the bridge keeper who put it this way: 'You need to know where you are, where you are going, what you are doing and how to get out of it if need be. Many boats find bottom on their way out. The buoyage is not perfect, although Wakering do try to replace and maintain as much as they can – especially the red cans. If you do touch, go astern immediately. If you do that pretty smartish and come back straight in you stand a chance of having a decent day on this side of the bridge at least. Too many try to thrash on over what they think might be just a tiny hill, or treat it as they would a maze; then they bash about on the hard sand, dry out and much later come back complaining to me that they've had a hard time. I sometimes wish I had the authority to keep them on the safe side but I haven't.'

## RIVERS CROUCH AND ROACH

**Charts**
Imray Y17
Admiralty 3750

## BURNHAM-ON-CROUCH

**Tides**
-0030 Sheerness, Dover +0100 at entrance.
**Authority**
*Crouch Harbour Authority* ☎ Maldon (0621) 783602 or Tillingham (0621 87) 747. There is an answerphone service on the first number; or Douglas Sanders ☎ (0621) 740944; or Ron Pike ☎ (0621) 782869
**Marinas and boatyards**
*Burnham Yacht Harbour* ☎ (0621) 782150
*Essex Marina* ☎ Southend on Sea (0702) 258531 VHF Ch M (0900-1700)
*Bridgemarsh Island Marina* ☎ Maldon (0621) 740414
*North Fambridge Yacht Station* ☎ Maldon (0621) 740370
*Westwick Marina* ☎ Maldon (0621) 741268

## RIVER ROACH

**Marinas and boatyards**
*Shuttlewood's Boatyard* Southend on Sea ☎ (0702) 258226
VHF Ch 12, 6 (*Charlie G*).

## HAVENGORE BASCULE LIFTING BRIDGE

*Operations Officer*
☎ Shoeburyness (0702) 292271 Ext 3211
Bridge keeper. Ext 3436
(+/-2 hours HW sunrise to sunset)

# VIII. THE THAMES

## By way of introduction

Until I encountered Father Thames, I thought an estuary no large piece of water. Rather, I envisaged it as a fairly narrow affair, a river mouth say, like the Humber at Spurn Head. Certainly, no broad expanse in which land was out of sight in all directions.

Reality is another matter. The Admiralty *Pilot*, in its usual somewhat prosaic manner defines the Thames Estuary as follows:

From the Naze (51°52′N 1°27′E) SW to
Shoeburyness (51°31′N 0°47′E) S to
Garrison Point (51°27′N 0°45′E) E to
North Foreland (51°23′N 1°27′E) N to the Naze

The seaward limits of the Port of London Authority are bounded as follows:

Foulness Point (51°37′N 0°57′E),
Gunfleet Old Lighthouse (51°46′N 1°20′E),
near Tongue Sand Tower (51°26′N 1°25′E),
Warden Point (51°25′N 0°54′E)

The Cruising Association *Handbook* says this: 'The estuary is notorious for its short, steep seas when the wind is against the tide, and the worst seas occur with northeasterly winds. It is much encumbered with shoals which are subject to frequent changes.' Chambers's *Twentieth Century Dictionary* defines an estuary in these words 'Tidal mouth of a large river' and the Latin reference is to 'aestuarium/aestus: burning, boiling, commotion, tide'. Putting the two concepts together gives you some idea of the magnitude of the singular experience that is known as the Thames Estuary.

The Thames has a fantastic history and its banks are literally crowded with great and small monuments to our heritage. All in all, it is certainly a candidate for the title, World's Most Famous River. It rises in Inglesham, Gloucestershire and from there, through its 44 locks down to the mouth of the estuary by Shoeburyness, the river runs for nearly 200 statute miles. It has been navigable since ancient times and has a very long tradition of pleasure cruising. At London Bridge, the Thames is still quite obviously a river. You can see easily from one bank to the other and the distance between them is no more than 240m. At Woolwich, hardly any distance down the river, it is already much wider at 450m; and by the time you are down river as far as Gravesend it has grown to 1300m, nearly a mile. Any cruising man ought to look upon the tidal waters of the Thames below the comparative safety of St Katharine's Dock as a fully operational, major seaway – and take the corresponding precautions.

In my view, the Thames below Tower Bridge is a major seaway. I never approach it without making preparations to befit this powerful and substantial reach. Moreover, its strong tidal flow can be even more disturbed by the many kinds of commercial shipping which always seem on the move. Further down, the estuary is really a big sea in its own right, with its own whims and eccentricities. It also possesses its own laws and disciplines, and woe betide any skipper who thinks they can be flaunted. Its five hundred square miles of watery expanse are enough to make any crossing a challenge.

## From the Medway

There are several ways of approaching the Thames. Perhaps the easiest is directly from the Medway, via the estuary's soft underbelly as it were. This popular river offers the only easy, safe havens between St Katharine's and Ramsgate. Heading London-wards from here brings you past Sheerness, past the wreck of the ammunition carrier, *Montgomery* and past the usual conglomerate of big ships in the anchorages awaiting the tide. The approach is then by Nore Sand through its Swatchway along the south bank by Yantlet Flats. I have always found it difficult to pick out London Stone or the entrance to Yantlet Creek. For me, this side of the river is perhaps best

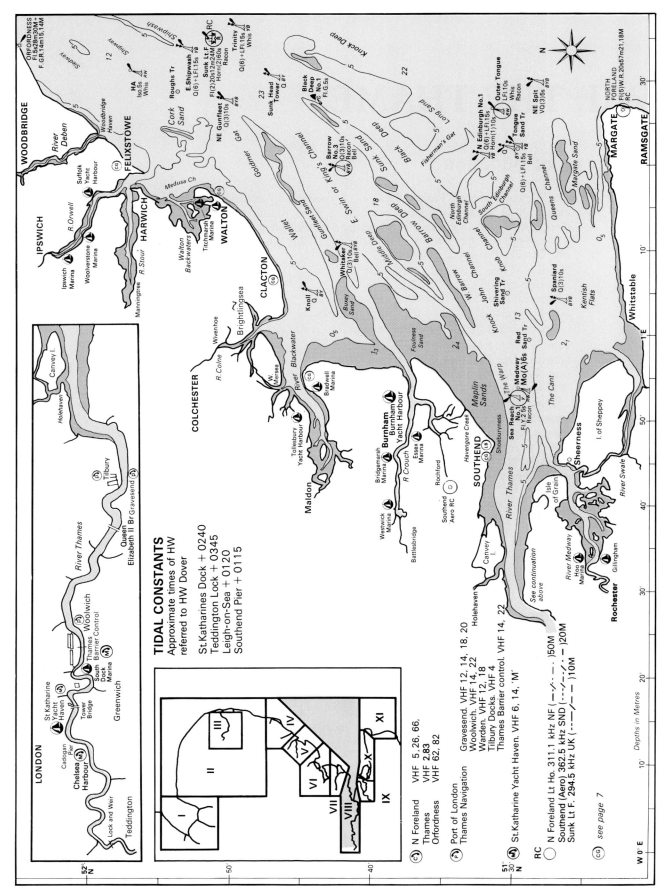

**TIDAL CONSTANTS**
Approximate times of HW
referred to HW Dover

St.Katharines Dock + 0240
Teddington Lock + 0345
Leigh-on-Sea + 0120
Southend Pier + 0115

Port of London
Thames Navigation

Gravesend. VHF 12, 14, 18, 20
Woolwich. VHF 14, 22
Warden. VHF 12, 18
Tilbury Docks. VHF 4
Thames Barrier control. VHF 14, 22

Ⓟ N Foreland    VHF 5, 26, 66,
   Thames          VHF 2, 83
   Orfordness      VHF 62, 82

Ⓜ St.Katharine Yacht Haven. VHF 6, 14, 'M'

RC   ◯ N Foreland Lt Ho. 311.1 kHz NF (—·/·—··—)50M
         Southend (Aero) 362.5 kHz SND (···/—·/·—·)20M
         Sunk Lt F. 294.5 kHz UK (··—/—·—)10M

Ⓒ ◯ *see page 7*

*Depths in Metres*

banished to the relative obscurity of mud flats, saltings and marsh gas. Nevertheless, I have met skippers who speak well of Yantlet Creek, and there are even one or two who are proud to tell how they have found hook-dropping spots to stay afloat at all states of the tide. It is like a Medway creek insofar as it is dominated by the vertical excrescences of the power stations and the oil refinery; but in all other respects it is like any other near-inaccessible East Coast mud flat ditchway. The plaintive cries of the birds are my lasting impression.

# From seaward southerly

Coming from seaward, on a southerly approach through the South and Gore Channels, past Whitstable and the Isle of Sheppey to the *Montgomery*, is a fairly straightforward piece of pilotage, but it can, nevertheless, quite frequently make severe demands upon seamanship. Many times have I thought myself chicken-hearted after being chided by some outspoken, courageous, non-voyaging skipper when I decided that a force 4/5 wind against the tide was too much of a good thing for a crossing from Ramsgate to Harwich. It was only after a number of such tough passages that I met up with three round-the-world sailors – at quite different times – to discover they shared the same view of the estuary: it can furnish some of the nastiest waters in the world. Nothing shakes the cautious attitude with which I approach an estuary passage; and I would urge all readers to take a similar view.

While cruising the East Coast and the estuary waters, I have been involved with too many incidents of boats that got 'caught out' – simply because the skipper had underestimated how rough and tough this estuary with its apparently safe, home coastal waters can be. Even the 'overland' route via the Kentish Flats and past the old Wansum outlet near Reculvers can make the tidal mouth seem more associated with those mythical monsters, Cyclops, Scylla and Charybdis than the good-old-friendly Father Thames that everyone knows and loves from day trips through the city or from the alcoholic warmth of the Victoria–to–Brighton buffet car.

There are some romantic-sounding names that can work like a magnet; names like Copperas Channel, Pan Sand Hole, Southeast Mouse, Deep Knock John and Gunfleet Old Lighthouse and some people can be tempted to visit them all; but in fact they are all possessed of the same turbid waters and sandy bottoms that go to create the grey and usually forbidding surface that is typical and symbolic of the Thames Estuary – and, for that matter, most of the coastal waters of the west side of North Sea.

# From seaward northerly

## Sea Reach

Most cruising skippers will be making for a berth further up river, and the most popular venues are found at St Katharine's Dock and further upstream. However, long before comes the stretch officially known as Sea Reach. It continues like a seaway until the *No.1* buoy marking Mucking, with its marshes and flats.

Approaching from the northern side of the estuary, you meet its first marker, Sea Reach No 1, between Maplin Sands and the Cant; and a pretty bleak area it is. From here right up to *Sea Reach No.7* there is little to rivet the eye ashore until you can pick out the usually dim and misty outline of Shoeburyness. Then comes Southend with its repaired one and a half mile pier. Plans for a marina are still said to be in the pipeline for hereabouts, but as Crown property is involved, they are so hedged around with red tape, that nothing is likely to materialise for many a year. In settled weather, it is possible to tie up at the end of the pier, or you can anchor just off for easy dinghy access to the various services that Southend has to offer.

Next, however, comes something of a change with those erst communities of Leigh-on-Sea, Canvey Island and Holehaven. On my first visit to the area I was completely put off by noticing on the chart, just by Canvey Island, 'Chapman Explosive Anchorage'. Of course, I knew of Bad Holding and Foul Ground, but the idea of an Explosive Anchorage was too much. For skippers emboldened by a stout craft that can take the bottom and who have an interest in creeping in and out of holes, havens and creeks, there are some classic 'better oles' to be found in the area of the Yantlet Channel by Canvey Island.

# Leigh-on-Sea and Holehaven

Leigh-on-Sea and Hadleigh Ray are favourites with those who know the waters; these have yacht clubs and plenty of facilities within easy reach. Holehaven, Benfleet, Small Gains and Tewkes Creeks are also in favour with those who possess a goodly portion of that telling factor local knowledge. Benfleet, Essex, Island and Leigh-on-Sea are all clubs that have moorings in the vicinity. Halcon Marine at The Point, Canvey Island, also has moorings, but none available for visitors.

Leigh-on-Sea is approached via Ray Gut, marked by the green Leigh (also known as Low Way) just to the westward of Southend Pier. This leads in its own inimitable fashion through Marsh End and Leigh Sands to the all-change-junction for Hadleigh Creek (also known as Ray) and Leigh Creek. Although the creek is buoyed, the moorings are probably the surest way of guiding yourself in; if that is what you have to do. A far better way is to thumb a following ride with a sister vessel near the top of a tide. There is deepish water in Hadleigh Creek and this tends to make Hadleigh and the nearby stretch to Smallgains Creek perhaps more popular than Leigh, thus explaining the multiplicity of buoys, beacons, marks and markers as well the plethora of moorings. However, there is a very good anchorage in the vicinity, so long as you avoid the few low spots that are to be found. It is true that when the tide is over the sandbanks, conditions can cause rocking and tolling of craft; but for the best part of 6–7 hours of each tide, it is a comfortable spot.

Water is less as you move up to Benfleet bridge through the narrow buoyed channel. I have never found conditions quite right to be able to get *Valcon* there or to Smallgains and its Island YC at Creek Head even for a quick visit. Benfleet Yacht Club will afford you a warm welcome, and there is the possibility of a berth at the slip or by their barge. In the clubhouse there are showers, drink and some food. If you want to visit; give them a ring beforehand and it is possible that someone will be able to meet you to guide you in. ☎ Benfleet (0268) 792278.

Holehaven is the well—named facility that created the eponymous community. There is usually a chance of getting a mooring or making an anchorage within the creek. It is best to consult the master or another local expert at the jetty around high water, and take instruction. Perhaps the main reason for calling here is the classic 'olde worlde' pub, The Lobster Smack; where 'Fings Ain't Changed From Wot Vey Used Ter Be'.

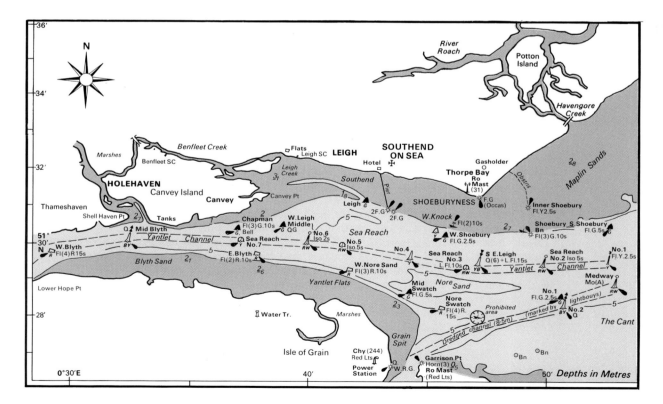

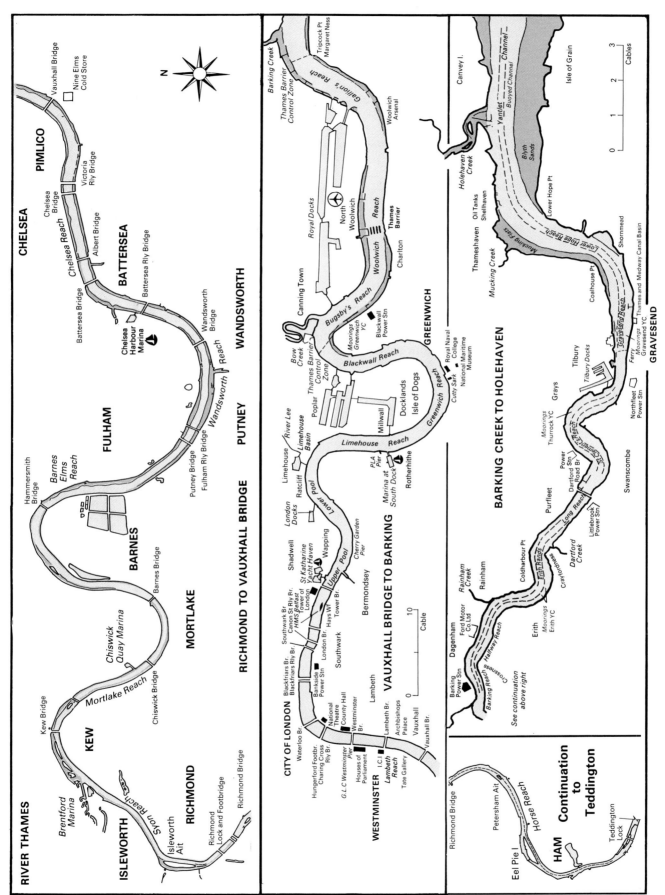

**RIVER THAMES**

N

Nine Elms
Cold Store
Vauxhall Bridge

**CHELSEA**

**PIMLICO**

Chelsea
Bridge
Victoria
Rly Bridge
Albert Bridge

*Chelsea Reach*

**BATTERSEA**

Battersea Bridge
Battersea Rly Bridge

Chelsea
Harbour
Marina

Wandsworth
Bridge

**FULHAM**

*Barnes
Elms
Reach*

Hammersmith
Bridge

Putney Bridge
Fulham Rly Bridge

*Wandsworth Reach*

**WANDSWORTH**

**PUTNEY**

**BARNES**

Barnes Bridge

**MORTLAKE**

Chiswick
Quay Marina

Chiswick Bridge

*Mortlake Reach*

Kew Bridge

**KEW**

*Syon Reach*

**ISLEWORTH**

*Brentford
Marina*

Isleworth
Ait

Richmond
Lock and Footbridge

**RICHMOND**

Richmond Bridge

**RICHMOND TO VAUXHALL BRIDGE**

**CITY OF LONDON**

Blackfriars Br.
Blackfriars Rly Br.
Southwark Br
Canon St Rly Br.
HMS Belfast
Tower of
London
London Br.
Hays Wf
Tower Br.

Shadwell

*River Lee*

Limehouse

Ratcliff

St Katharine
Yacht Haven

Wapping

*London
Docks*

*Upper Pool*

*Lower Pool*

Cherry Garden
Pier

Bermondsey

Southwark

Lambeth

Waterloo Br.

National
Theatre
County Hall

Hungerford Footbr.
Charing Cross
Rly Br.

Westminster
Pier

G.L.C Westminster
Houses of
Parliament

Westminster
Br.

**WESTMINSTER**

Lambeth Br.
Archbishops
Palace

**Lambeth
Reach**

I.C.I

Vauxhall
Br.

Tate Gallery

Vauxhall

**VAUXHALL BRIDGE TO BARKING**

0                    10

Cable

**Bow
Creek**

Canning Town

*Thames Barrier
Control Zone*

Poplar

*Thames Barrier
Control Zone*

Royal Docks

North
Woolwich

*Woolwich Reach*

Woolwich
Arsenal

**Thames
Barrier**

Charlton

*Bugsby's Reach*

Moorings
Greenwich
YC
Blackwall
Power Stn

Blackwall Reach

**GREENWICH**

Docklands

Isle of Dogs

Millwall

Royal Naval
College
Cutty Sark
National Maritime
Museum

*Greenwich Reach*

Limehouse
Basin

*Limehouse Reach*

PLA
Pier

Marina at
South Dock

Rotherhithe

**Gallion's Reach**

Barking Creek
Tripcock Pt
Margaret Ness

**BARKING CREEK TO HOLEHAVEN**

**Dagenham**

Ford Motor
Co.Ltd

Barking
Power Stn

*Barking Reach*

*Crossness*

*Halfway Reach*

Rainham

*Rainham
Creek*

Erith

Moorings
Erith YC

Coldharbour Pt

*Erith Reach*

Crayfordness

*Dartford
Creek*

Purfleet

*Long Reach*

Littlebrook
Power Stn

Dartford Stn
Road Br.

Power

Swanscombe

*Fiddler's Reach*

*St Clement's Reach*

Northfleet
Power Stn

Grays

Moorings
Thurrock YC

Tilbury

Tilbury Docks

*Gravesend Reach*

Ferry
Moorings
Gravesend YC
Thames and Medway Canal Basin

**GRAVESEND**

Canvey I.

Thameshaven
Oil Tanks
Shellhaven

*Mucking Creek*

*Lower Hope Reach*

Lower Hope Pt

Shornmead

Coalhouse Pt

*Mucking Flats*

*Holehaven
Creek*

*Blyth
Sands*

*Yantlet Channel*

*Buoyed Channel*

Isle of Grain

0        1        2        3

Cables

*See continuation
above right*

**Continuation
to
Teddington**

Richmond Bridge

Petersham Ait

Eel Pie I

*Horse Reach*

**HAM**

Teddington
Lock

Holehaven itself is not easy to spot, but nearby in the river there are very powerful traffic lights (white single and white group) which operate when large tankers are manoeuvring near their berths. Indeed, it is very busy with work boats working and tug boats tugging throughout the year.

For those keen on anchorages, there are some to be found in Ray Gut and Hadleigh Bay, for Leigh; but you will need to ask around. In addition it might not be impossible to find a resting place in Holehaven if the authorities and friends afloat will connive to inch you in.

There is no doubt that both of these places are packed with interest and redolent of our history and heritage, and any yachtsman thinking of paying a visit should have a good reason for calling in; should prepare himself for the occasion by researching the charts and tide times; and should also drop by shoresides to make contact and arrange for a welcome ... if not indeed a pilot.

And in this respect you can do no better than try one John Duce, a much travelled local operator who is expert in engines, maintenance, boats and all the 'bovver' that goes to make up the cruising life. Even if you have no deal to negotiate or business to transact, you will find it your worth your while to fix a meet just for the company, the crack and the conviviality. You can call him on ☎ (0268) 793203.

# Gravesend to Woolwich

Opposite the Tilbury Docks buildup is the not very well known resort of Gravesend. Here you can ease into the basin of the now disused Thames and Medway Canal from 2hrs before high water. The lock is unmanned at other times. About 300m above the Canal Basin is the landing at the causeway. Facilities, with a few moorings, abound in the vicinity, including the customs house, yacht club and the Thames Navigation Service.

The onset of Tilbury marks the beginning of the heavy commercial aspect of the river, and all leisure craft are well advised to keep away from the busy container port. Along Lower Hope Reach, small craft are advised to keep to the south on ebbs and the north on floods; and it is important to remember the floating pipeline that reaches out from the shore between *Muckings 5* and *7*.

As one would expect, the buoyage is excellent right up to Tilbury, where it stops, but any hazards upstream are not due to a lack of buoys because the navigation is well marked by shoresides beacons for all the legs and stretches. No; hazards there are but not navigational: they are encounters, if not engagements, with the huge heaps of debris, garbage and litter that accumulate and drift down the river. They consist of all the nasties you can imagine. Serious threats are lengths of rope and nylon/plastic sheet and, at the other end of the spectrum, hugely rafted oil/water logged/clogged sleepers. They look somewhat akin to sleeping crocodiles: they are half submerged and just as well camouflaged. It is probably worth all the complications and the hassle of even having a crew, just for someone to keep a debris watch.

This may seem something of an exaggeration in a 'peaceful' river like the Thames, but some of the big ships, as well as the police, customs, pilots and the like, can move so much water in their progress that their bow waves and stern wakes can require the exclusive, full-time attention of the

*Opposite.*
Tower Bridge: closed or open, it must rank as one of the most impressive sights on the river. Few pleasure craft need the bridge to be lifted; but if you can't get your timing right or feel you would just like to see it work, be prepared to dip deeply into your purse. A recent price was over £1,000

A typical police launch on the Thames.

skipper for a long time. I remember, on one occasion near Coalhouse Point, being overtaken by a Russian ship. Its wash was so tremendous that I nearly surfed along it a couple of times. The natural surging and resurging from the banks was still continuing when I had to contend with a small collection of coasters and yachts working in both directions: coasters wanting to overtake but not going quite fast enough unless I cut down, and the yachts doing their best to manoeuvre under sail as if they had the 'SAIL' right of way willy nilly.

The chances are that you will also be accosted by other traffic: the police and/or the customs. Provided you are on lawful business or pleasure, it is always encouraging to discover that these officers get around much more than one might expect. (I recall in the middle of winter being visited early in the morning at an anchorage up the Deben by a customs man who greeted me with: 'Didn't see you here yesterday morning sir; just wondered if you were all right?')

On my first trip up the Thames, my first visitor was from a police launch. I had noticed it had been ambling along behind for a while, so gave them a call on VHF. The launch was alongside and a River Police officer jumped on like boarding a bus. No Fuss. We chatted about this and that, partaking of the inevitable cup of tea, but it wasn't long before we got down to the day's agenda: checking the serial numbers on *Valcon's* gear. It was all put so politely, that it seemed impossible I might have been the target of their investigations. 'We like to know who's passing through our patch and what they've got on board. If some of it should later sadly turn up on another vessel, we know where it belongs, don't we?' As I said, not a hint I might be a crook. When the police vessel came to pick off their man, I noticed there was a customs launch almost in tow. Clearly, they were in cahoots; and a good thing too.

In spite of the attractive sounding names of St Clement's or Fiddler's Reach and Erith Rands, there is little to attract hereabouts, for the area tends towards the busier and dirtier aspects of river life. In addition, there are certain particulars that require special attention. Craft in the measured mile on Dartford Long Reach may fly International Flag 'A'. Keep well clear since they will be on speed trials. The rifle range at Purfleet can be active, and a red flag shows when firing is in progress.

For the yachtsman, more interesting features come further up. However, there are items of note to entertain on the way – the new Dartford road bridge which has closed the river to tall ships (Hm 54 m), the enormous trumpet-shaped vents mark infamous Dartford Tunnel, Henry Ford's factory at Dagenham, and Barking Creek's imposing guillotine gated entrance. Then comes Gallion's Reach, with its locked entrances for Queen Victoria, Royal Albert and King George V Docks. This once-busy area is now coming to life in new form. Already home to the London City

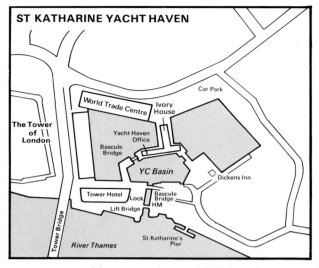

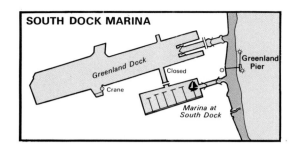

Airport, and a multiplicity of modern development built and unbuilt, it is anticipated that 'The Royal's' will finally house at least one marina, with the Albert Basin currently favourite as a venue.

Gallion soon gives way to the wide, long Woolwich reach, and this holds two obstacles for the mariner. The more noticeable is the striking Thames Flood Control Barrier. I can never look at it without its nine hooded piers reminding me of the ceremonial garb of some gargantuan cardinal. However, there is nothing mystical about its workings. The Thames Barrier Navigation Centre controls all traffic movements. Vessels are required to make contact on VHF Ch 14 when passing Crayfordness or Tower Bridge. Permission to pass will be given once the vessel is at Margaretness or Blackwall.

Less noticeable, and therefore more hazardous are the ferries that ply from Woolwich. The area is just as grim and grotty as it was over forty years ago when I 'served' in the arsenal. In those days, I was masquerading as a WO3 in the Royal Artillery attached to the Education Corps, but was really beginning to discover how to educate myself. The good old Woolwich free ferry had a certain charm; and it was not a case of 'Je ne sais quoi.' It was the undoubted possibility of 'Picking Up a Bit of Stuff' only slightly more euphemistically referred to as 'Getting On and Getting Off': the title of a book in which I was, so many years later, to describe what was often a usually maladroit procedure.

# The Isle of Dogs to St Katharine's Dock

So, round the loop in the river which encompasses the Isle of Dogs, and its attendant West India and Millwall Docks. The skyline is impressively punctuated by the grand buildings of the Royal Naval College, with the *Cutty Sark*, and Sir Francis Chichester's *Gipsy Moth* lying nearby.

About halfway along Limehouse Reach, on the W bank opposite the Isle of Dogs, is the recently developed project: The Marina at South Dock. Its lock opens +/- 2 hours HW and there is a shore-linked waiting pontoon to the north at Greenland Pier; midway between Greenwich and Tower Bridge. The many folk who are accustomed to and rejoice at the singular service offered at Hoo Marina (in the depths of the nearby Medway) will be pleased to know that this South Bank affair is that same Colin's hands.

Limehouse Reach is topped at its northerly end by Limehouse Lock and basin. This gives access to the Regents Canal, and thence the River Lee. As such, it falls under the jurisdiction of the BWB, and a licence is needed. The lock has recently been revamped to make it more appropriate for leisure craft.

Around the corner at the head of the straight of Upper Pool is Tower Bridge. From time to time, I fancy blowing the ship's whistle for it to open, but the £1000 or more fee that this would demand is beyond my means. If you want to be the cause of something opening hereabouts, it is better to arrive +/-2hrs either side of high water and call St Katharine's on Ch M to gain access to their locked entrance. An arrival outside of this time will leave you with a very uncomfortable stay on the 100ft St Katharine's Pier just down stream of the Yacht Haven, to which there is access at all states of the tide. The constant wash of passing vessels demands stout tackle to withstand the onslaught. There is no shore access from the pier and visitors are advised to contact the office prior to arrival. However, there is a telephone on the pier. Once inside, the mirror-calm waters in this Mecca for aspiring sea-going Thames motorboaters reflect the benefits of its decade and a half of remaking.

# Tower Bridge to Richmond

Once past Tower Bridge, London suddenly looms into a different focus as it begins to look its TV news/picture-postcard self, with easily recognisable views on both banks. As Wordsworth had it in his day, 'Ships, towers, domes, theatres, and temples lie'; and they still do. Now; while they may be 'Open to the sky', there is no way, as Prince Charles was recently quick to reinforce, that they are even 'Open unto the fields,' let alone being 'All bright and glittering in the smokeless air.'

Then comes a succession of bridges and places with names known all over the world: Tower Bridge, Chelsea, the Houses of Parliament, Harrods and on and on. Pick what you will, and if you have the time and the tide with you, in what order you like, for the stretch can afford delight after delight for the keen-eyed student of humans, humanity and our glorious heritage – complete with warts, wharfs and tarnishes. Happily, it is not impossible to find temporary moorings from which sightseeing and victualling can be undertaken. Discretion should be exercised when leaving the vessel. Fagin may no longer be alive and well, but his spirit, apostles and disciples are still at it.

Until I saw it from the water, I had always thought Chelsea to be a fat cat scene, where there was nothing but landlubbing reflections of the King's Road scene. Certainly, it has grown its own marina village in an appropriate image; but, in the more mundane world of boating business and interests, the venue has already achieved a level of fame as a much-needed fringe venue for the Earls Court Boat Show. Although local residents have first call on the 75 available berths, visitors are more than welcome to use the marina facility once having negotiated the 1hr+/-HW lock.

In contrast, Battersea and Wandsworth both cast gloom. Even the name of Hurlingham can do nothing to alleviate the riparian doom that hangs over the reaches. Incidentally, Wandsworth's bridge marks the end of the 'unrestricted' speed limit. From here on, up to Richmond, 8 knots is the maximum. *Valcon* and I find ourselves amused yet again.

Boat Race country is next, and with it the spotting of the locations that have over the TV years become well-known: Putney Bridge and University Stone; Hammersmith Bridge and nearby, the pier where you may, by grace and favour, land. Then Chiswick Ait, with not only eights in profusion but also sailing dinghies, inflatables, genuine slipper launches, all kinds of rowing boats and cruisers galore. Rowing and sailing clubs abound.

From here on, vessels with a draught approaching a metre should not attempt to navigate near low water, for the river shoals in many of the reaches. By now, the Thames has taken on its air of leisure and just as if to prove the point Mortlake Brewery and Chiswick Quay Marina (access HW+/-2hrs) appear on opposite banks. Then it is up to this particular journey's end. There are only two more diversions Brentford and Richmond.

At the former, you enter the world of the Grand Union Canal through Brentford Creek. The restricting dimensions on this BWB waterway are beam of 4m and a draught of just over a metre. Just upstream is Brentford Dock Marina where draught is no problem, but there is still an (albeit reasonable) beam restriction of 16ft at the waterline. The lock works HW+/-2½hrs marina can be called on Ch 14 or 16. Annual rates here are very good, and the many facilities include a full chandlery, a marine engineers' and a yacht club.

Old Chelsea.

Richmond Bridge

The famous first gateway to the non-tidal reaches, Richmond Lock and Footbridge are only a mile and a half up river. The Thames is maintained at half tide level at this point by overhead sluices. These are suspended from the bridge and are raised, allowing free passage, from HW+/2hrs.

It is said that water can rush through Richmond Bridge at such a rate of knots that often it will be standing as much as two feet higher on one side of the buttresses than on the other. Teddington is now just over two miles away and it is the first completely fresh water lock on the river. The section between is half tidal, being controlled by the weir gates and sluices. However, boats can get through whenever there is sufficient water to get up from Chelsea, by using the through navigation or the lock. When the sluices are down, all craft use the Richmond Lock. Dimensions: 76m x 8m and the limiting draught from Teddington to Windsor is 1·7m but with a very poor low water at Richmond you might be restricted to no more than a metre, though this is not common.

Up to this point, the river is under the jurisdiction of the Port of London Authority (PLA). The next port of call, Teddington, is under the National Rivers Authority (NRA). Here, a whole new set of rules applies. Craft are required to be registered and will be provided with a licence plate to prove it. From that moment on, they will be liable to inspection by official staff to insure they are toeing the line regarding engine, fuel, gas and loo installations. A new speed limit applies as well: 'a walking pace' being the limit, with a keen eye on wash as the recommendation.

As if in consolation, the historic and friendly yard of Tough's with its attendant chandlers lies immediately before Teddington Lock. Once through onto the 'inland' Thames, you now enter a land rich as if flowing with milk and honey, and pleasure takes over. From its source at Inglesham, in Gloucestershire, through its 44 locks, it is a 200 mile journey to the mouth at Shoeburyness. Not only is it a long haul from *Sea Reach No.1*, in miles of either measure to this sybaritic patch; it also takes a massive leap of the imagination to encompass the extremes of conditions that those watermarks signify.

# Estuary crossings

Above Richmond, the challenges and hazards that are likely to be encountered are of a socio-economic or domestic nature and hardly connected at all with pilotage or navigation. This tends to encourage one to forget the essence of the Estuary all those miles away on the salt side. I would not like to leave this section without a final note of caution. There are those intrepid cruising men who feel cheated if they have not sought out every gut, creek and swatchway; Ay to the very last ditch in the cruising itinerary. If there is no danger attached to this, I have no criticism to make; but when it involves foolhardy ventures I am no longer in favour. In this regard I would recommend readers of this volume to stick to the well tried channels when crossing the estuary and not feel they have been 'wet' if they have not followed an old compass course with dead reckoning their only guide across the banks and shoal waters of the Thames Estuary.

The channels shown at pp.169 are reliable and safe for novitiates as well as hardened sea dogs. Having used them personally many times, I have always found them to be first rate. However, I have not used the South Edinburgh Channel – let alone the Alexandra. Imray's *Pilot's Guide* says this about the latter: 'The channel is not recommended for use by day, and should never be attempted at night'. I am inclined to treat all other unlit, non-major channels in the same way. After all, if you are in the main channels and some mishap occurs, you are at least reasonably sure that someone will not be too far away – and I like to feel I have that reassurance in the maze of chances that go to make up the Thames Estuary.

The Thames is not the widest, the fastest nor the longest river in the world; nor is it the most beautiful, dramatic or treacherous but it has a variety that only few other waterways can challenge, and in that variety lies its claim to fame as the daddy of them all: Old Father Thames.

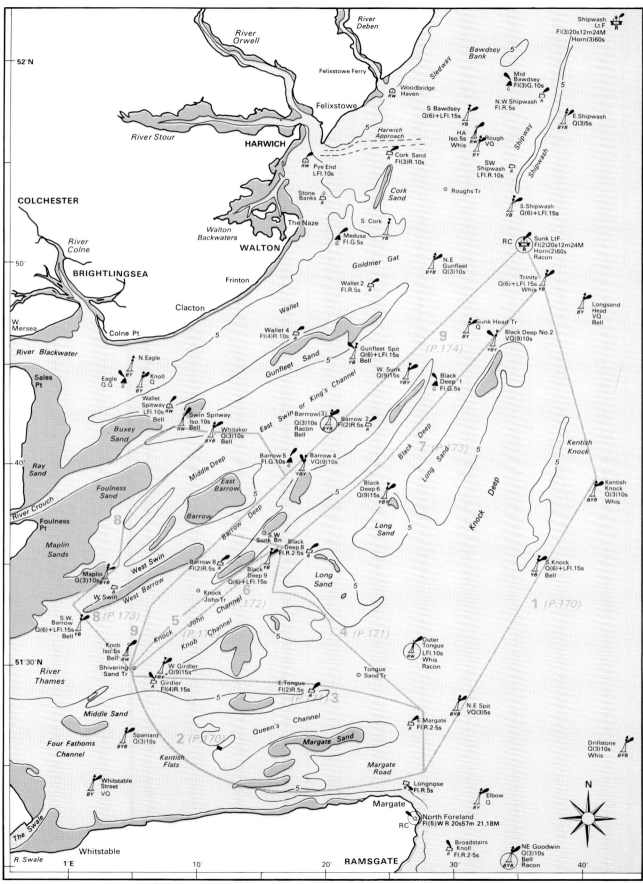

**ROUTES ACROSS THE THAMES ESTUARY**

## BUOYAGE

These diagrams apply to the routes shown on the chart on page 169.

### 1. N. Foreland to Sunk Lt Float Outside passage

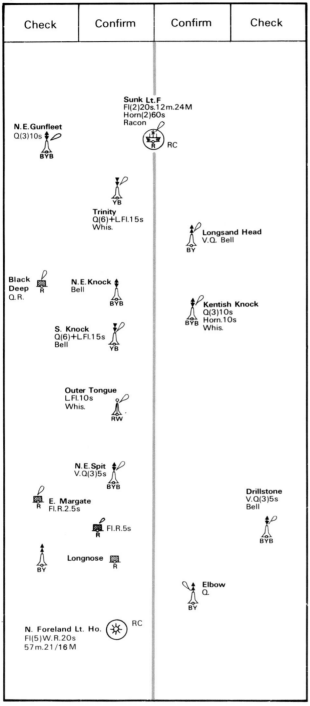

### 2. North Foreland to Shivering Sand Towers via Gore Channel and Kentish Flats

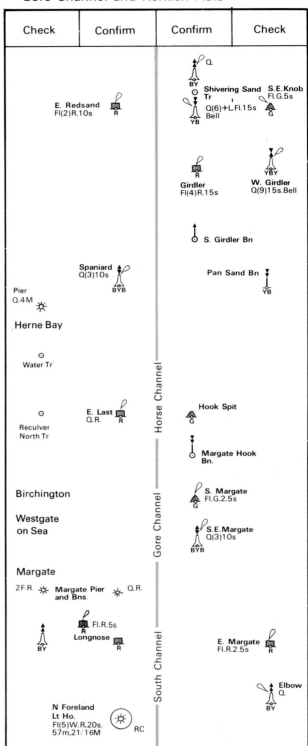

### 3. N. Foreland to Shivering Sand Tower via Princes Channel

| Check | Confirm | Confirm | Check |
|---|---|---|---|

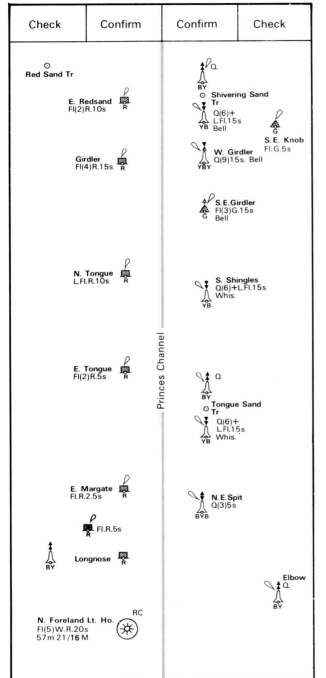

Princes Channel

- ○ Red Sand Tr
- E. Redsand — Fl(2)R.10s
- Girdler — Fl(4)R.15s
- N. Tongue — L.Fl.R.10s
- E. Tongue — Fl(2)R.5s
- E. Margate — Fl.R.2.5s
- Fl.R.5s
- Longnose — BY
- N. Foreland Lt. Ho. — Fl(5)W.R.20s — 57m 21/16 M — RC

- Q.
- ○ Shivering Sand Tr — Q(6)+L.Fl.15s Bell — YB
- S.E. Knob — Fl.G.5s
- W. Girdler — Q(9)15s. Bell — YBY
- S.E. Girdler — Fl(3)G.15s Bell
- S. Shingles — Q(6)+L.Fl.15s Whis. — YB
- Q — BY
- ○ Tongue Sand Tr — Q(6)+L.Fl.15s Whis. — YB
- N.E. Spit — Q(3)5s — BYB
- Elbow — Q. — BY

### 4. N. Foreland to Black Deep via N. Edinburgh Channel

| Check | Confirm | Confirm | Check |
|---|---|---|---|

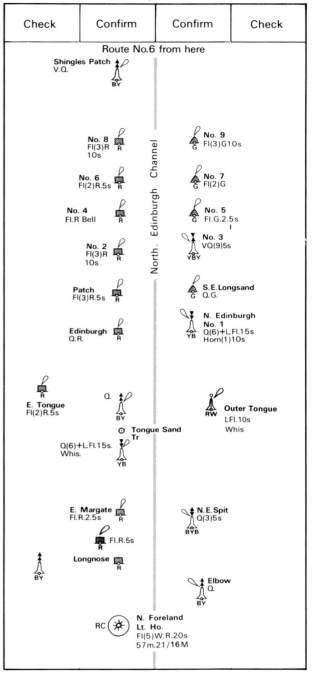

Route No.6 from here

North. Edinburgh Channel

- Shingles Patch — V.Q. — BY
- No. 8 — Fl(3)R 10s
- No. 6 — Fl(2)R.5s
- No. 4 — Fl.R Bell
- No. 2 — Fl(3)R 10s
- Patch — Fl(3)R.5s
- Edinburgh — Q.R.
- E. Tongue — Fl(2)R.5s
- Q(6)+L.Fl.15s. Whis.
- E. Margate — Fl.R.2.5s
- Fl.R.5s
- Longnose
- BY
- N. Foreland Lt. Ho. — Fl(5)W.R.20s — 57m.21/16 M — RC

- No. 9 — Fl(3)G10s
- No. 7 — Fl(2)G
- No. 5 — Fl.G.2.5s
- No. 3 — VQ(9)5s — YBY
- S.E. Longsand — Q.G.
- N. Edinburgh No. 1 — Q(6)+L.Fl.15s Horn(1)10s — YB
- Q. — BY
- ○ Tongue Sand Tr — YB
- Outer Tongue — L.Fl.10s Whis — RW
- N.E. Spit — Q(3)5s — BYB
- Elbow — Q. — BY

Shivering Sand Towers...with cardinal marker; always an encouraging sight for those who find the muddle of the Thames crossing at this stage something of a long and unrewarding haul

## 5. Shivering Sand Tower to Black Deep via Knock John Channel

| Check | Confirm | Confirm | Check |
|---|---|---|---|

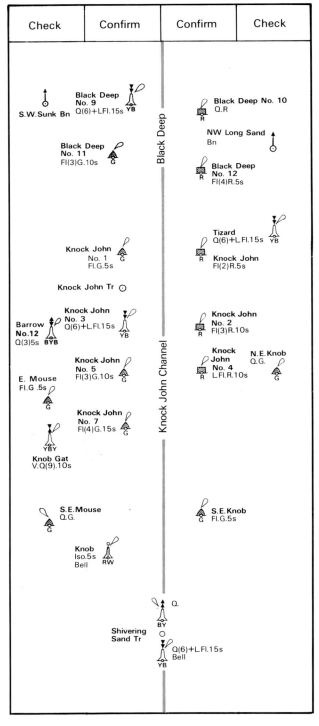

## 6. Shivering Sand Tower to Black Deep via Knob Channel

| Check | Confirm | Confirm | Check |
|---|---|---|---|

Continue with route No.7

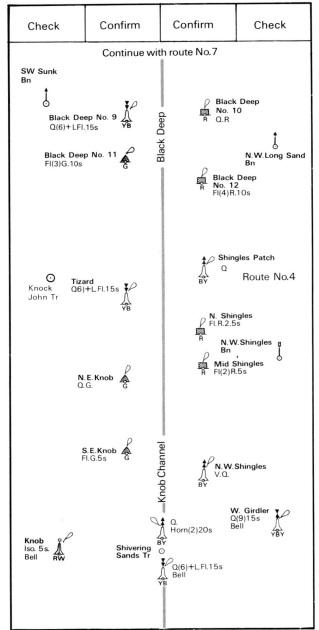

Tongue Sand Tower: the guns seem to have been 'at the ready' for years – and they still look pretty awesome and threatening if you first glimpse them arising out of an estuary fog

## 7. Black Deep to Sunk Lt. Float

| Check | Confirm | Confirm | Check |
|---|---|---|---|

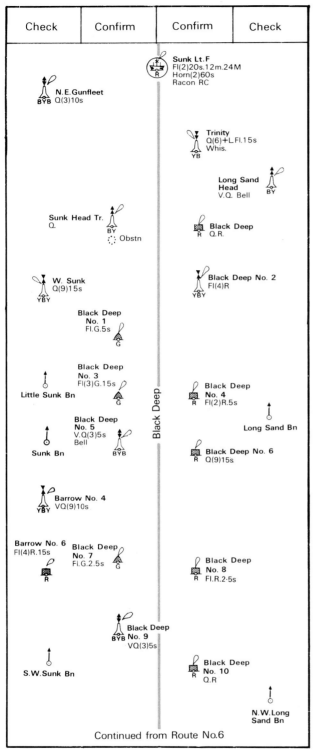

Sunk Lt. F
Fl(2)20s.12m.24M
Horn(2)60s
Racon RC

N.E. Gunfleet
BYB Q(3)10s

Trinity
Q(6)+LFl.15s
YB Whis.

Long Sand
Head
V.Q. Bell
BY

Sunk Head Tr.
Q.
BY
Obstn

Black Deep
R Q.R.

W. Sunk
Q(9)15s
YBY

Black Deep No. 2
Fl(4)R
YBY

Black Deep
No. 1
Fl.G.5s
G

Black Deep
No. 3
Fl(3)G.15s
Little Sunk Bn
G

Black Deep
No. 4
R Fl(2)R.5s

Black Deep
No. 5
V.Q(3)5s
Bell
Sunk Bn
BYB

Long Sand Bn

Black Deep No. 6
R Q(9)15s

Barrow No. 4
VQ(9)10s
YBY

Barrow No. 6
Fl(4)R.15s
R

Black Deep
No. 7
Fi.G.2.5s
G

Black Deep
No. 8
R Fl.R.2·5s

Black Deep
BYB No. 9
VQ(3)5s

S.W. Sunk Bn

Black Deep
No. 10
R Q.R

N.W. Long
Sand Bn

Black Deep

Continued from Route No.6

## 8. Shivering Sand Tower to Whitaker Buoy

| Check | Confirm | Confirm | Check |
|---|---|---|---|

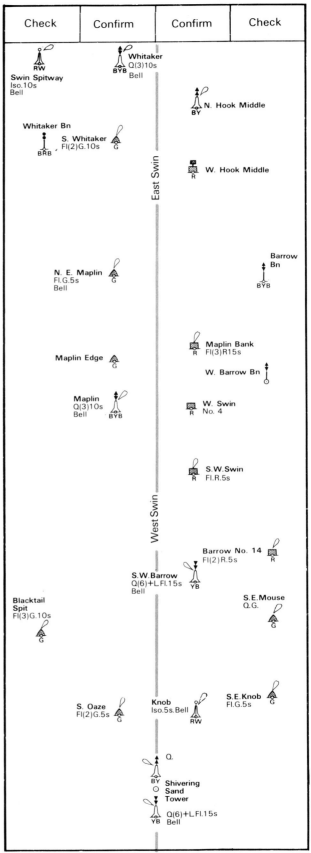

Swin Spitway
RW
Iso.10s
Bell

Whitaker
Q(3)10s
BYB Bell

N. Hook Middle
BY

Whitaker Bn
S. Whitaker
BRB Fl(2)G.10s
G

W. Hook Middle
R

East Swin

Barrow
Bn
BYB

N. E. Maplin
Fl.G.5s
Bell
G

Maplin Bank
R Fl(3)R15s

Maplin Edge
G

W. Barrow Bn

Maplin
Q(3)10s
Bell
BYB

W. Swin
R No. 4

S.W. Swin
R Fl.R.5s

West Swin

Barrow No. 14
Fl(2)R.5s
R

S.W. Barrow
Q(6)+LFl.15s
Bell
YB

S.E. Mouse
Q.G.
G

Blacktail
Spit
Fl(3)G.10s
G

S. Oaze
Fl(2)G.5s
G

Knob
Iso.5s.Bell
RW

S.E. Knob
Fl.G.5s
G

Q.
BY
Shivering
Sand
Tower
YB Q(6)+LFl.15s
Bell

An alternative is to use the Barrow Deep (Route No.9) and leave
it at Barrow No. 5 to pick up Heaps.

## 9. Shivering Sand Towers to Sunk Lt. Float
## via Barrow Deep

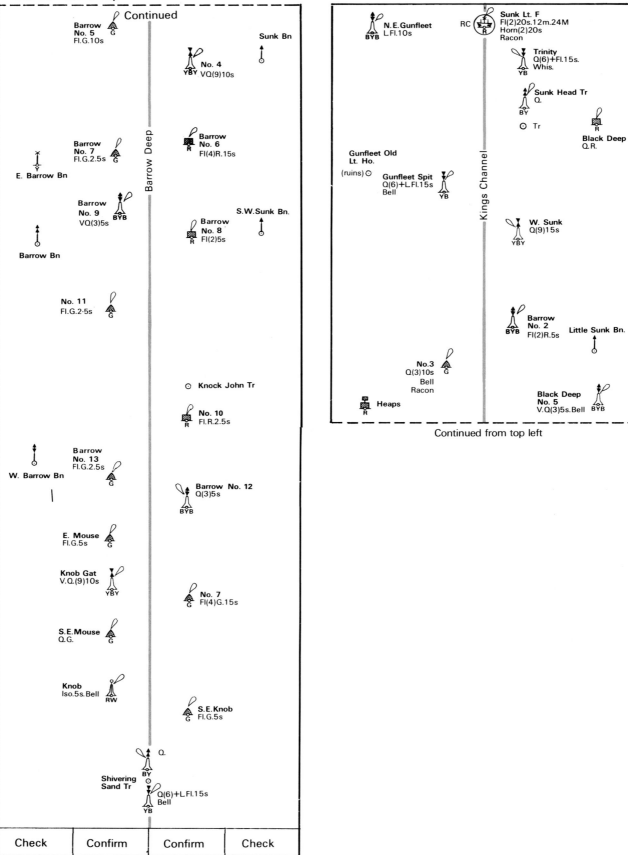

Continued

Barrow
No. 5
Fl.G.10s
G

Sunk Bn

No. 4
YBY  VQ(9)10s

Barrow Deep

Barrow
No. 7
Fl.G.2.5s
G

Barrow
No. 6
R  Fl(4)R.15s

E. Barrow Bn
Y

Barrow
No. 9
VQ(3)5s
BYB

S.W.Sunk Bn.

Barrow
No. 8
R  Fl(2)5s

Barrow Bn

No. 11
Fl.G.2·5s
G

Knock John Tr

No. 10
R  Fl.R.2.5s

Barrow
No. 13
Fl.G.2.5s
G

W. Barrow Bn

Barrow No. 12
Q(3)5s
BYB

E. Mouse
Fl.G.5s
G

Knob Gat
V.Q.(9)10s
YBY

No. 7
G  Fl(4)G.15s

S.E.Mouse
Q.G.
G

Knob
Iso.5s.Bell
RW

S.E.Knob
G  Fl.G.5s

Q.
BY

Shivering
Sand Tr
Q(6)+L.Fl.15s
YB  Bell

| Check | Confirm | Confirm | Check |
|---|---|---|---|

N.E.Gunfleet
L.Fl.10s
BYB

RC

Sunk Lt. F
Fl(2)20s.12m.24M
R  Horn(2)20s
Racon

Trinity
Q(6)+Fl.15s.
YB  Whis.

Sunk Head Tr
Q.
BY

Tr

Black Deep
R  Q.R.

Gunfleet Old
Lt. Ho.

(ruins)

Gunfleet Spit
Q(6)+L.Fl.15s
Bell
YB

Kings Channel

W. Sunk
Q(9)15s
YBY

Barrow
No. 2
BYB  Fl(2)R.5s

Little Sunk Bn.

No.3
Q(3)10s
Bell
Racon
G

Black Deep
No. 5
V.Q(3)5s.Bell  BYB

Heaps
R

Continued from top left

## LEIGH-ON-SEA

**Charts**
Imray C2, Y18
Admiralty 1185

**Tides**
Sheerness +0010, Dover +0120

## HOLEHAVEN

**Tides**
Sheerness +0010, Dover +0120

**Access**
Both Leigh and Holehaven are busy spots. They are equally inaccessible to boats drawing more than one metre except during the four hours each side of high water.

## THE MARINA AT SOUTH DOCK

South Dock Office, Rope Street, Plough Way, London SE16 1TX. ☎ 071 252 2244

**Tides**
As London Bridge, +0245 Dover

**Radio**
VHF Ch 37 and 80 – 24 hours

**Access**
Up to 3 hours either side of HW.
Maximum size of craft: 30m LOA – 6·0m Beam – 3·3m Draught

## ST KATHARINE YACHT HAVEN

**Tides**
As London Bridge, +0245 Dover

**Harbourmaster**
Ivory House, St Katharine-by-the-Tower, London EC1 9AT ☎ 071-488 2400.

**Radio**
VHF Ch 'M' (or, try Ch 14 to work 6). Lock hours only.

**Access**
Visitors from downstream are reminded that they must pass the Thames Flood Barrier. Please note the section above. Access is via a tidal lock 38m x 9·0m and draught of 5·0m: -2 to +1½ hours London Bridge.
*April–August* 0600–2030hrs
*Sept–March* 0800–1800hrs
*Nov–Feb* Tues.–Wed. Gates closed

## RIVER THAMES

**Charts**
Imray C2, C1
Admiralty 1185, 1186, 2151, 3337, 3319, 2484

**River Thames authorities**
Above Teddington the river is controlled by the National Rivers Authority. Below Teddington Lock the River Thames is under the jurisdiction of the Port of London Authority excepting Bow Creek and the River Lee (National Rivers) and the Regents and Grand Union Canals (British Waterways). The headquarters of the Port of London Authority is at London Dock House, 1 Thomas More Street, London E1 9AZ (☎ 071-476 6900).

The lower section of the river, below Crayfordness, is controlled by the Harbourmaster at Royal Terrace Pier, Gravesend (☎ Gravesend (0474) 357724). VHF Gravesend Radio Ch 12. Also from here, the Thames Navigational Service Centre controls the movement of traffic, with a subcentre at the Woolwich Thames Barrier Control. (☎ 071-855 5186 or 0315). VHF Woolwich Radio Ch 14.

The harbour offices of the upper section of the river are at Tower Pier Extension (☎ 071-481 0720) and Kew Pier 071-940 0634).

**Thames Barrier**
The Thames Barrier Navigation Centre controls navigation between Margaret Ness and Blackwell Point and is contacted by Radio (Woolwich Radio VHF 14, 22, 16). All vessels with VHF must make contact with the Controller on Ch 14 when passing Crayfordness going up-river or Tower Bridge going down to give ETA. permission to pass will be given once the vessel is at Blackwall or Margaret Ness. National Rivers Authority, Eastmoor Street, London SE7 8LX.

*EXTRACTS FROM THE PORT OF LONDON NOTICES TO MARINERS*
*Small vessels under 20m in length*
All small vessels and craft such as yachts, dinghies, power boats, sculls, rowing boats and canoes NOT fitted with VHF are advised that in general they should navigate inward through the northern most, and outward through the southern most span which is open to navigation.

*Vessels under sail*
Vessels proceeding under sail only, between the Woolwich Ferry Terminal and Island Jetty, must keep to the starboard side of the fairway and are not impede any other vessels. Wherever possible, vessels should take in their sails and use motor power to navigate through the Barrier.

All vessels are to comply with signals exhibited at the Barrier notice boards (Amber lights: proceed with caution. Red lights: Stop) and instructions received from the Barrier audio stations.

**Navigation lights and shapes**
Spans open to navigation in one direction will be closed to navigation in the opposite direction. Each end of the span exhibiting the appropriate signal.

The following navigation lights and signals will be displayed, both by day and by night.

*Spans open to navigation*
Green arrows will be exhibited from the ends of piers either side of the spans open to navigation. The arrows point inward towards the navigable span(s).

*Spans closed to navigation*
Red crosses will be exhibited from the ends of the piers either side of the closed span(s). Navigation between two red crosses prohibited.

*Spans permanently closed to navigation*
An inverted triangle, apex downward, consisting of three red discs or, by night three red lights situated in the centre of the span.

*Note* During the period of a Barrier closure for test, flood prevention or any other reason, the red crosses referred to above will operate in all navigable spans.

*Prohibited Anchoring*
Anchoring is prohibited 100 metres either side of the Barrier.

*Teddington Lock*
This the tidal limit of the river. The lock is manned 24 hours daily by the National Rivers Authority. ☎ 081-940 8723.

|  | LOA | Beam | Draught |
|---|---|---|---|
| New (Barge) Lock | 198m | 7·5m | 2·5m |
| Old (Launch) Lock | 54·0m | 7·3m | 2·8m |

*Signals* The signal lights indicate as follows:

| i. | An illuminated red cross | Barge and launch locks not available for upstream traffic |
|---|---|---|

## BUOYAGE
### The Thames: from Sea Reach No. 1 to Tilbury Cardinal Marker

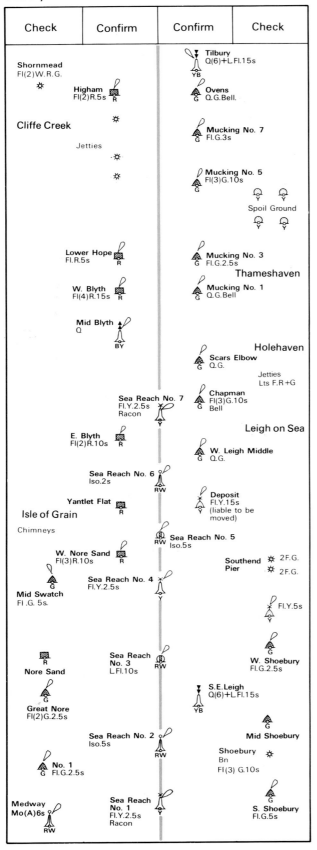

| Check | Confirm | Confirm | Check |
|---|---|---|---|

ii. A flashing illuminated white arrow pointing in respective lock

Barge lock available for upstream traffic. Launch lock the direction of the available for upstream traffic

**Richmond Lock**
This lock is half tidal, the necessary depths of water being controlled by lowering three separate vertical gates one in each navigation arch of Richmond Footbridge. These gates are generally raised for about 2 hours each side of HW. When the gates are lowered the lock must be used, the following signals being shown:
*By day* A red disc below the middle of each of the 3 centre arches.
*By night* A red light above the middle of each of the 3 centre arches. ☎ 081-940 0643. LOA 76·3m Beam 8m

**Grand Union Canal at Brentford**
This entrance is via Brentford Creek which leads to Thames Locks which open from 2 hours before HW until 2 hours after. Within 0600–2200 hours. For information and advice of ETA please ☎ 071-560 8942 (Ext 31) 0800–1800 Monday to Friday or ☎ 071-560 8924 outside these hours. LOA 21·9m. Beam 4·3m. Draught 1·1m. Headroom at MHWS: 2·1m. The Grand Union Canal is controlled by British Waterways and a licence is required for navigation. This is obtainable from British Waterways, Willow Grange, Church Road, Watford, Herts. WD1 3QA. ☎ Watford (0923) 26422.

**Useful contacts**
Port of London Authority ☎ (0375) 852325
HM upper section ☎ 071-481 0720
HM lower section (0474) 567684
National Rivers Authority, (Thames Region), King's Meadow House, King's Meadow Road, Reading RG1 8DQ ☎ (0734) 53500
Limehouse Ship Lock ☎ 071-790 9930
St Katharine's Yacht Haven ☎ 071-488 2400
Chelsea Harbour ☎ 071-351 4483
Chiswick Quay Marina ☎ 081-994 8743
Brentford Dock Marina ☎ 081-568 0287
Tough Shipyards ☎ 081-977 4494

Readers who are interested in comprehensive information regarding the River Thames are referred to: *London's Waterway Guide*, A guide to the River Thames, River Lee and canals in the London area, by Chris Cove-Smith, published by Imray.

# IX. THE MEDWAY

## Approaches

There are three ways of approaching the River Medway. One is from the outside seaside of the Northern Thames Estuary; another is from the southern border of the Estuary, perhaps on what is occasionally referred to, jokingly, as the 'Overland Route'; and the other involves creeping in from Old Man River himself, by the Yantlet back door from the Thames.

Actually, there is another way; and this fourth and last, from the River Swale, is the easiest, provided you just 'happen to be passing and thought I'd drop in.' Of course, this is all by way of a cheat, since to most yachtsmen's intents and purposes, the Rivers Swale and Medway can be treated as one river, making up in fact a single and assimilated cruising ground.

Coming down from London town, the route is along the south bank by Blyth Sands and Yantlet Flats up to Nore Sand and then, no doubt, through its Swatchway. In passing, it is worth mentioning that I generally find it difficult to pick out London Stone or the entrance to Yantlet Creek.

After Grain Spit and the Swatchway, if you are sensible you will then follow a course to take you, not across Sheerness Sand in any way, but right outside and then right round the wreck of the ammunition carrier, the *Richard Montgomery*; a long way round perhaps, but a safe and circumspect one. Then into the usual conglomerate of big ships in the anchorages awaiting the tide, bringing you up to Sheerness on the northwest tip of the Isle of Sheppey; marked and well known by the famous control and navigation nerve centre of Garrison Point.

Approaching from the northern side of the estuary, *Sea Reach No.1* stands sentinel between Maplin Sands and The Cant, and is a good signpost for the red and white safe water *Medway* pillar buoy.

From the southerly borders of the estuary, the approach is along the Kent Coast through the South and Gore Channels; and thence on past Whitstable and the Isle of Sheppey to the Medway red and white pillar safe water mark to the wreck of the *Montgomery*. While it is a relatively straightforward piece of pilotage, it can, nevertheless, frequently make quite severe demands upon all your seamanship skills. This is the famous overland route via the Kentish Flats. Past the old Wansum outlet near Reculvers, it can make the lower jaw of the tidal mouth of the Thames seem more to be identified with an experience off Cape Horn than anything connected with a shoresides leisure trip.

Whichever course you decide to chart, you will sooner or later come to view what has been perhaps not only the area's biggest attraction and conversation piece for many a year, but also its biggest hazard, peril and bugbear; and attitudes vary from the quietly reasoned through the wholly irrational to the vehemently superstitious.

### The *Montgomery* wreck and the entrance

That love/hate object lies just outside the River Medway itself and is the wreck of the *Richard Montgomery*, a Liberty ship from the United States, that went down in the 1939/45 war fully loaded with ammunition. She still carries her 'deadly' load, and there are those who believe that it is now just as much of a threat to the local area as it ever was. The topsides of her wreckage can be clearly seen; but in addition she is well marked with buoys ... and, of course, forms a prohibited zone. Whether she is 'safe' or not, she makes a telling and, surely, awesome sight even from a proper cruising distance.

So, the two main markers to the Medway are the safe water mark and a supposedly unstable wreck; and it is from there that you drop immediately into the extremely well buoyed and deep water channel straight into the Medway proper. Its actual gated entrance lies between the low fort on Garrison Point and the Martello tower and jetty ruins on the Isle of Grain. Garrison Point is unmistakable because of the tower with its radar station on top and the old Admiralty signal station behind. This is where the port operations and information service is situated. Sheerness

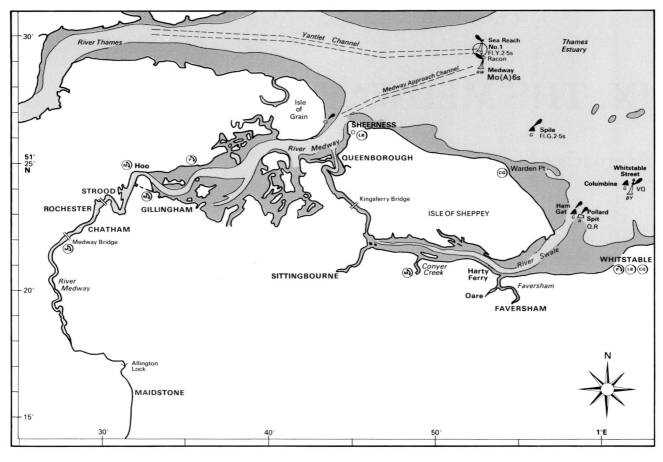

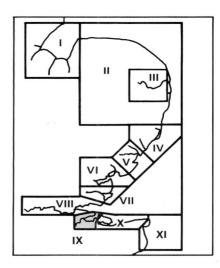

---

(LB)

Sheerness (and inshore lifeboat)
Whitstable (inshore lifeboat only)

(C)

N Foreland VHF 5, 26, 66
Thames VHF 2, 83

(P)

| Whitstable Harbour VHF | 9, 12 |
| Medway | VHF 9, 11, 22, |
| Medway Patrol | VHF 6, 11, 14, 22 |
| BP Kent | VHF 6, 19 |
| Kingsferry Bridge | VHF 10 |
| Pilots | VHF 9, 22, 14 (when on station) |

(M)

| Conyer Marine | VHF 16 and 'M' |
| Gillingham Marina | VHF 'M' |
| Hoo Marina | VHF 'M' |
| Medway Bridge Marina | VHF 16 and 'M' |

(CG) *see page 7*

## TIDAL CONSTANTS

Approximate times of HW
referred to HW Dover

Harty Ferry + 0120
Milton Creek +0130
Sheerness +0125
Queenborough +0130
Rochester Bridge +0150

The famous (or infamous?) wreck of the *Montgomery*.

(once a huge naval dockyard) is still busy but with cargo and ferry boats these days; it is also the headquarters of the Medway Ports Authority which runs the river from Garrison Point right up to Maidstone.

After the Medway approaches have been confirmed, the passage to Queenborough is straightforward: with the Grain power station firmly between your sights, to Garrison Point; then leaving the heavy architecture that is Sheerness well to port, pick up Queenborough Spit buoy off the Spit and Swale Ness; and, keeping to port, pass the dolphins at Queenborough Point and move into the fairway of the West Swale.

Whether you have approached from Garrison Point, passing Sheerness between the Isles of Sheppey and Grain, or from the Swale, through the straits and bends of Queenborough, you will have no difficulty in identifying the Medway, because of the way in which the quiet creeks, saltings and mud flats blend together not only with each other but also with the come-lately aliens; actually forming a strange composite, a truly unholy alliance, with the massive refineries and power stations. All in all, the pastoral and the petroleum; the aromatic and the mercenary; in brief, as it were, the refined and the unrefined, come together to form the kind of backcloth for the gathering big ships that would be appropriate only in some outlandish jig saw puzzle.

However, there is nothing for yachtsmen in the Medway in the vicinity of Sheerness. It is not until you are past the gate of the two green and red *N* and *S Kent* buoys and the Queenborough Spit cardinal marker, that you enter what can be properly be called hospitable home cruising grounds.

# Medway proper

These home waters come as you arrive at Saltpan Reach, and then you discover that various alternatives present themselves: tidal; non-tidal; anchor; drying mud berth; swinging mooring; marina; cruising club. Visitors may well think themselves spoilt for choice.

The creeks are many and various; the clubs are frequent and their members excellent talebearers, gossips, confidantes and first rate hosts towards bona fide visitors. In addition, there are four marinas before Rochester Bridge. So, those who are well disposed towards socialising are well catered for, in every way, for culinary standards are high in these parts.

Nearer to seaward and nearest to my inclinations are the creeks. Looking back over our shoulders for just one moment, there is the small Shepherds Creek on the West Swale side of Deadmans Island at Queenborough Spit, but I have not tried it personally, nor have I heard report of it. I would be most pleased to hear from any reader with personal knowledge.

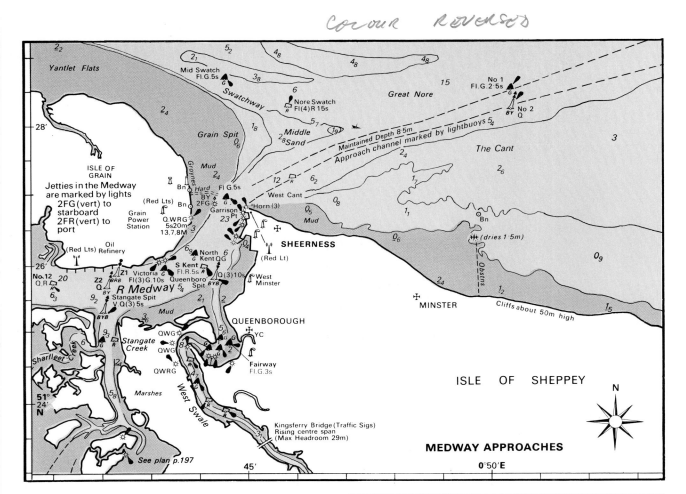

Colour Reversed

Yantlet Flats

Mid Swatch Fl.G.5s

Swatchway

Grain Spit

ISLE OF GRAIN

Jetties in the Medway are marked by lights
2FG (vert) to starboard
2FR (vert) to port

(Red Lts)

Grain Power Station

Oil Refinery

(Red Lts)

No.12 Q.R

R Medway

Stangate Spit V.Q(3) 5s

Sharfleet C.

Stangate Creek

Marshes

West Swale

See plan p.197

Nore Swatch Fl(4)R 15s

Middle Sand

Groynes

Mud

Bn Hard Fl G.5s

BY 2FG

(Red Lts) Bn

Q.WRG 5s20m 13,7,8M

Garrison Pt

North Kent QG

S Kent Fl.R.5s

Victoria Fl(3)G.10s

Z1

Z2

Queenboro Spit BYB

QUEENBOROUGH

QWG

QWG

QWRG

YC

Fairway Fl.G.3s

Horn (3)

West Cant

Mud

SHEERNESS

(Red Lt)

West Minster

Q(3)10s

Great Nore

Maintained Depth 8·5m
Approach channel marked by lightbuoys

No 1 Fl.G.2·5s

No 2 Q

The Cant

West Cant

Bn

(dries 1·5m)

Obstns

MINSTER

Cliffs about 50m high

ISLE OF SHEPPEY

N

**MEDWAY APPROACHES**

Kingsferry Bridge (Traffic Sigs)
Rising centre span
(Max Headroom 29m)

0°50′E

There are few places where you can find a berth at Queenborough

# BUOYAGE
River Medway: Sheerness harbour to
No. 32 buoy (Cockham Reach)

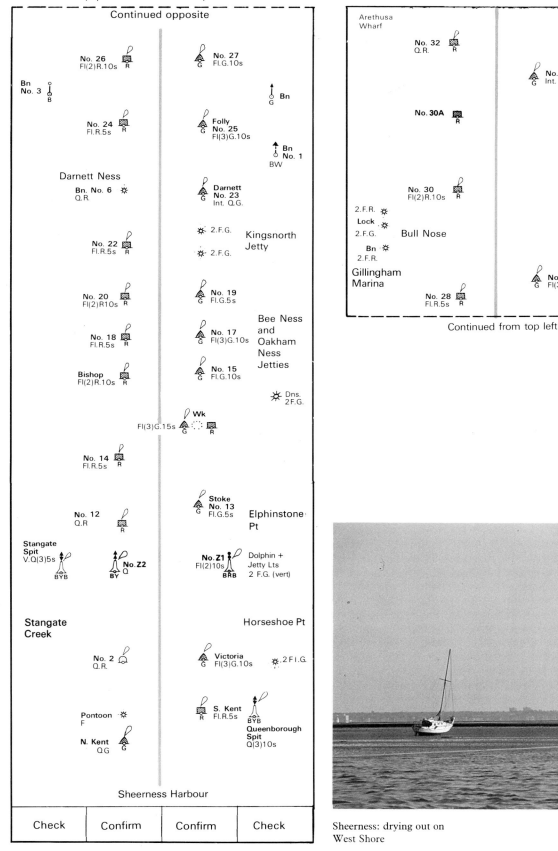

Continued opposite

No. 26
Fl(2)R.10s    R

Bn
No. 3       B

No. 24       R
Fl.R.5s

Darnett Ness
Bn. No. 6    ☼
Q.R.

No. 22       R
Fl.R.5s

No. 20       R
Fl(2)R10s

No. 18       R
Fl.R.5s

Bishop       R
Fl(2)R.10s

No. 14       R
Fl.R.5s

No. 12       R
Q.R.

Stangate
Spit        BYB
V.Q(3)5s

No. Z2    BY    Q

Stangate
Creek

No. 2    Q.R.

Pontoon   ☼
F

N. Kent   G
Q.G.

No. 27
Fl.G.10s    G

G   Bn

Folly     G
No. 25
Fl(3)G.10s

Bn
No. 1    BW

Darnett   G
No. 23
Int. Q.G.

☼ 2.F.G.    Kingsnorth
☼ 2.F.G.    Jetty

No. 19    G
Fl.G.5s

No. 17    G       Bee Ness
Fl(3)G.10s       and
Oakham
No. 15    G       Ness
Fl.G.10s          Jetties

☼ Dns.
2.F.G.

Wk
Fl(3)G.15s   G   R

Stoke     G
No. 13
Fl.G.5s    Elphinstone
Pt

No. Z1    Dolphin +
Fl(2)10s   BRB   Jetty Lts
2 F.G. (vert)

Horseshoe Pt

Victoria  G   ☼ 2 Fl.G.
Fl(3)G.10s

S. Kent   R
Fl.R.5s    BYB
Queenborough
Spit
Q(3)10s

Sheerness Harbour

| Check | Confirm | Confirm | Check |
|---|---|---|---|

Arethusa
Wharf

No. 32    R
Q.R.

No. 30A   R

No. 30    R
Fl(2)R.10s

2.F.R.   ☼
Lock     ☼
2.F.G.   ☼    Bull Nose

Bn   ☼
2.F.R.

Gillingham
Marina

No. 28    R
Fl.R.5s

No. 31    Hoo
Int. Q.G.   G    Marina

2.F.G.  ☼

☼

Hoo Ness

No. 29
G   Fl(3)G.10s

Hoo Island

Continued from top left

Sheerness: drying out on
West Shore

The Sheerness approach to the Medway.

## Stangate Creek and its familiars

Going upstream, leaving the junction with the Swale to port, you will find that the creeks are all well systematised with standard buoys and beacons. Stangate is the first creek both in situation and in stature. It is attractive in its own right, but it is also of particular interest because it gives on to five other creeks where there is much less movement. Although there is little commercial traffic to be encountered in Stangate these days, it is still neither feasible nor courteous to anchor in the fairway. Since it can be quite a busy spot, those more in search of solitude, and why else would one be in the creeks at all, usually take to one of the smaller creeks. Stangate affords access to their entrances at all states of the tide.

The first and by far the most blessed with deepish water is Sharfleet Creek, about half a mile on the starboard hand after the Stangate Spit cardinal marker. It bends its way around the landward side of Burntwick Island and finally leads, for those who have a nose for gutways, gullies and ditches, by the back door into Half Acre Creek. Sharfleet, with its near proliferation of good holes for anchor dropping, is a popular spot; but if you avoid the nastiness of weekend bank holidays, you will not be molested by intruders.

For my first essays into the creeks of the Medway I started by using Sharfleet exclusively, and enjoyed every sojourn. It is a detached discovery, with the fragile and delicate but still painfully plaintive cries of the marsh birds merging and mingling with the burdensome unceasing tumult and turmoil that emanates from the heavy machines of the surrounding power houses and refineries. The high-pitched sporadic bird cries pierce the low persistent hum of the infernal machines and together create a telling sound picture that in my experience is unique in the UK. Add to it the misty mystery of a late evening lit only by an autumn moon and you have the perfect recipe for cop out, drop out or lotus eating for life. However, it is only too easy to be lulled into a false sense of security hereabouts, being apparently so far away from raging tidal waters. So; beware: dragging anchors are not unknown in these creeks, and wise skippers will use ground tackle in which their confidence has already been proved. In particular, the 'holding' grounds cannot be wholly trusted near the second bend going into Sharfleet Creek from Stangate. The bottom is neither absolutely firm nor entirely unfoul, and there can be something of a tide rip, admittedly unsensational but enough to shift boats that are indifferently at anchor.

Just over a mile 'inland', that is to the south, comes the junction: the parting of the ways between Slaughterhouse Point and the near island of Chetney Hill. Here it is definitely a case of 'creeks to the right of them, creeks to the left of them', and, at sunny seasonal weekends, of the five hundred who are not to be thwarted as they onward ride.

More or less straight ahead, but in fact tending to the westward, is one channel that is out on a limb, for all the others turn to the east. It is the small channel known as the Shade. It leads to Funton Reach, which is about central in the drying patch, has those favourite features: numerous hulks to starboard and less numerous islands to port. However, the spot is so well protected, being in the shade of Raspberry Hill, that there is no danger of those other features, numerous white horses.

Funton finally over reaches itself to become no more than a shallow trickle as it takes on the optimistic title Funton Channel which is what it is when there are good tides. Here, it leaves the bewitchingly named Bedlam's Bottom to port and approaches the few small islands that are still separated from the mainland. These can all be approached on the tides and if you are well booted and oiled various landings are possible, but they will be attractive only to seekers after culture shock, wild life and social death. The last hope of staying afloat is situate on the bend where the Shade gives way to the Reach.

Taking the other main channel at Slaughterhouse point, we move easterly around the low lying point into what feels like a small inland lake. Counting from south to west, first comes Halstow Creek, which is approached along the narrow channel found to the east of the small island sitting between Millfordhope and Barksore Marshes. At the end of what is virtually a mile of mud flats that come and go and are mainly dry, there is civilisation at last in the form of the Lower Halstow Yacht Club and the LH Yachting Association. Comestibles and pub grub can also be got only short walks away in Lower Halstow itself.

On the other side of the tiny island, that is to the east of Millfordhope Marsh and the west of Halstow Creek, is the much less visited Twinney Creek that will finally lead you into the vagaries of Twinney Saltings. But here, and further to the northwest into the backwoods/hinterlands of Millfordhope and Ham Green Saltings, we begin to venture into water gypsy territory, where extra caution is required in parts that are only to be braved by those with of upright crafts, clean minds and pure hearts.

The last but not least of the Sharfleet Creeks genre is Millfordhope. It carries enough water for 1·5m craft to find a suitable 'Ole over a tide; however, there is a mini bar at he entrance that must be negotiated before this prize can be reached. It is if anything a spot that has the feeling of being even more remote than the others. Giving on, as it does, to Slayhills Marsh and Saltings it is easy for a visiting skipper of a fanciful mind to succumb to disquiet and unease in these quiet and secluded, but somehow oddly circumscribed and beset surroundings. For those who are seriously devoted or passionately dedicated to getting away from it once and for all, this is the place.

# Half Acre and more

Meanwhile, back in the Main Drag, we travel due west from Saltpan Reach across the shoals of Sharpness Shelf and into the deeps of Kethole Reach where we take a turn to the south and approach the second batch of Medway Creeks. Next geographically, as well as mainly next favoured, is Half Acre Creek. It is entered by leaving Bishop Spit, well marked by the red *Bishop No.16*, to starboard; not wanting to penetrate the no doubt immeasurably mysterious extent and excesses of Bishop Ooze.

After a good mile into Half Acre Creek we meet the red and white *Fairway* safe water mark where there are again tributarial choices: Otterham; Bartlett and Rainham; and South Yantlet. Moving once again in a clockwise direction we come across Otterham first, requiring a slight twitch to port as we pick up the buoyage past Wallop Stone. In fact, the buoyage gives the game away: good news of and for the continuing commercial traffic, but of no real attraction and little interest to yachtsmen. Visitors should take particular care that their presence near the fairway in no way impedes the progress of the surprisingly large vessels that still appear here, and quite speedily when, from time to time, they do. The area, which is well served with shoresides facilities once you can effect them, is best left to those local yachtsmen who know their own way around.

To a certain extent, the same must also be said to apply to Bartlett and Rainham Creeks. The former is no more than curate's eggishly accessible for about a mile in a generally westerly tendency after the *Fairway* buoy and its eponymous Spit; and here the visitor can seek and find various spots where they can keep out of trouble. The routes to Rainham and unbecomingly

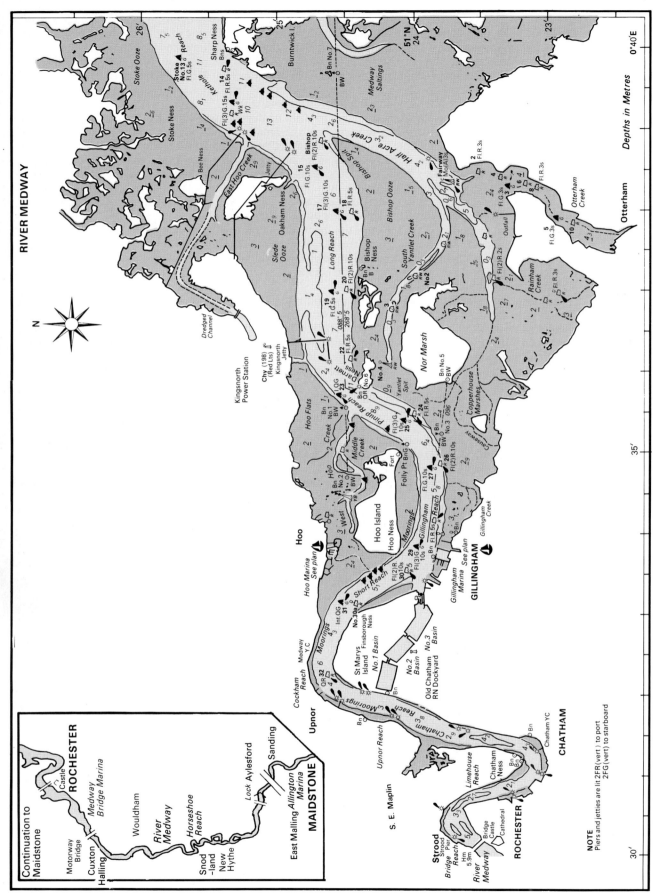

RIVER MEDWAY

*Depths in Metres*

0°40'E

51°N
24

26'

25

23

Stoke Ooze

Stoke Ness
Sharp Ness
Bee Ness

Keyhole Reach
**Stoke No.13**
Fl.G.5s
Bns

East Hoo Creek

Jetty

**14** Fl.5s
Wk
Fl(3)G.15s
**10**

Burntwick I.

Bn No.7
BW

Medway Saltings

Half Acre Creek

Bishop Spit

**Bishop**
Fl(2)R.10s

Oakham Ness

*Slede Ooze*

*Long Reach*
Fl.G.10s **15**
Fl(3)G.10s

**17**
**18**
Fl.R.5s

Bishop Ooze

**Fairway**
Mo(A)13s

Fl.R.3s

Fl.R.3s

Otterham Creek

Otterham

Dredged Channel

Kingsnorth Power Station

Chy (198)
(Red Lts)
Kingsnorth Jetty

**20**
**19** Fl.G.5s
Fl(2)R.10s

Bishop Ness

South Yantlet Creek

No.2

Fl(2)R.2s

*Rainham Creek*
Fl.R.3s

N

*Hoo Flats*

**Bn No.1**
BW

*Creek*

Darnet Ness
**22** Fl.R.5s
QG
QR
**No.4**
Bn
No.6

088°.5
268°.5

**23**

*Nor Marsh*
RW

Yantlet Spit

Bn No.5
BW

*Copperhouse Marshes*

Causeway

**24** Fl.R.5s
No.3
096

Hoo

*Hoo Flats*

**Bn No.2**
BW

*Middle Creek*

Fl(3)G.10s
**25**
Fort

Folly Pt Bn

**26**
Fl(2)R.10s

Hoo Island

Hoo Ness

*Moorings*

Fl.G.10s
**27**

Fl.R.5s
Bn
**29**

*Gillingham Reach*

*Gillingham Creek*

Gillingham Marina
*See plan*

**GILLINGHAM**

Hoo Marina
*See plan*

Fl(2)R
30
Fl(3)G
**5**

*Short Reach*

Int QG **31**
**No.3a** QG

Finsborough Ness

St Marys Island

*No.1 Basin*

*No.2 Basin*
*No.3 Basin*

Old Chatham
RN Dockyard

Medway YC

*Moorings*

Cockham Reach
QR **32**

**Upnor**

*Moorings*

*Upnor Reach*

S. E. Maplin

*Chatham Reach*

Chatham Ness

Chatham YC

*Limehouse Reach*

**CHATHAM**

Bn

**NOTE**
Piers and jetties are lit 2FR (vert) to port
2FG (vert) to starboard

35'

30'

Continuation to Maidstone

**ROCHESTER**
Castle

Motorway Bridge

Cuxton

Halling

Wouldham

*River Medway*

*Medway Bridge Marina*

*Horseshoe Reach*

Snod -land

New Hythe

Lock Aylesford

*Allington Marina*

East Malling

**MAIDSTONE**

Sanding

**Strood**
Strood Pier

*Bridge Reach*

Hm
5.9m

Bridge Castle
Cathedral

*River Medway*

**ROCHESTER**

named Bloors Wharf is not one to appeal to visiting yachtsmen, and while the area all round, but especially to the west, holds many leisure craft moorings, the thought of Horrid Hill has always symbolised for me the difficulties of relaxing in the neighbourhood.

However, all is not hopeless, for it is here that Mariners Farm Boatpark, is skippered by one Mister Robinson who runs a farm and a boatyard in a relaxed and friendly manner: side by side and hand in hand. All the berths are drying mud, either swinging or trots. It is an ideal spot for those who wish to work on their own boats in a friendly atmosphere. As the boss himself says, 'We're simple folk here. There aren't many bars around, and we haven't got a heli-pad.' Visitors are made informally welcome. The entrance is marked by an orange buoy marked 'Mariners Farm'. However, even the master himself will glowingly concede, 'The orange is a bit legendary. The seagulls seem to favour it'. They listen on Ch 'M', call sign *Mariners Farm*, at tide times, and also at other times by schizo-arrangement: the reclaimed saltings farmer taking the marsh mariner's VHF radio set into the fields.

We must not leave Bartlett without alluding to the presence of the elusive channel that just affords passage from the entrance to Rainham to the Medway. Passing Horrid Hill, it demands a careful negotiation of the Copperhouse Marshes causeway that crosses from Nor Marsh, where there are beacons, to the mainland. I have never succeeded in making a complete passage, chickening out about half way, and worrying whether I would make it back again before losing the water that way as well. However, I have seen it done, but it requires not only for the time and tides to be right but also for the skipper to have really sound and comprehensive local knowledge.

Then comes South Yantlet Creek. With its little explored Captains Creek, this is one of my favourite areas, and although it is extremely highly praised, it is in fact much less used than some of the other less attractive spots. It has an additional advantage in that without too much hassle or even local knowledge it can be approached from both east and west: the easterly main channel itself stemming from Bartlett Spit in Half Acre forming the usual entrance; and the westerly channel between the islands and emanating from Darnett Fort. This secondary channel dries more or less completely, nor is it possible not to take the tidal mud if you endeavour further west than the first red and white safe water markers. However, these buoys lead you all the way, and with a little help from reading the surface water and your friend the sounder it should not be too onerous for even the first time visitor to make the round trip.

In fact, it is possible to negotiate a way back to the main river from many of these creeks using a different return route. Special knowledge is needed for most but the local cruising populace must find it an absorbing relaxation for at least a couple of seasons.

I doubt that it is easy to find even remoter spots where, with a suitable vessel, you take the ground and let the rest of the world go not only by, but perhaps to rack and ruin. However, the strict whereabouts of these best spots is something that those who favour that kind of cruising like to delve into for themselves and then keep to themselves. Such information is beyond my learning and the scope of this guide. Those with a penchant for that approach will need to become an honorary local, and get well informed.

Any visiting stranger must be prepared not only to be beguiled by the Wills-o'-the-wisps and deluded by the Jacks-o'-the-saltings, but also to be surprised if not ambushed between the devils of the creeks and the deeps of the reaches: for the stranger, there is always the possibility of being run down by a commercial vessel if the fairway has not been observed accurately enough; of being doomed on a mud bank that seems to have no beginning and no end; of having to listen to the booming that is the night noise of industry and promises nothing at all to do with the sea; or of having to stare blankly at the chimneys and other vertical shafts of industry that pierce the skyline.

No matter where you anchor in this area, you will not be able to get much in the way of boating or domestic supplies without a dinghy; but that being, presumably, part and parcel of what is wanted from any excursion into these parts is not likely to be a drawback. If you haven't the time or the inclination to cruise the full blown estuary or the remoter locations of the Swale, these creeks will suffice to offer that kind of peace and quiet that is to be had further north on the East Coast in such places as the upper reaches of the Alde, and Walton's secret waters.

Indeed, it would be unkind and unfair to the Medway to report adversely on its commerce, and not to point out that the Walton Backwaters are almost overlooked by the massive works of Harwich and Felixstowe; or that the remote village of Orford suffers formidable works by disgrace and favour of the Ministry of Defence, together with the unavoidable legends of territorial rights and the obligatory notices bearing the abrupt dictum, 'KEEP OUT DANGER'.

Medway Fort and marker buoy.

Hoo Marina.

Unmistakable Medway power station plus smoke.

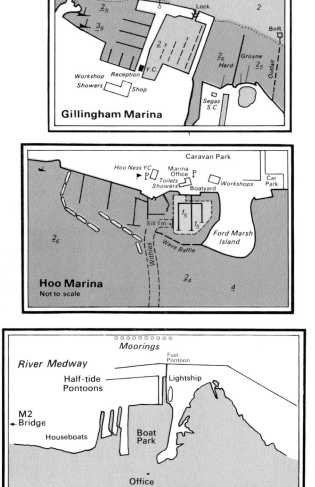

# Hoo Flats

The Half Acre collection represents almost the last outpost of the Medway anchoring creeks; but there is just one more: Hoo Island and its creeks and flats. Like the earlier examples, it can be reached from the east or the west. Working backwards, the approach from the west is probably the best known since it is also the well-withied channel to Hoo Marina, of which more later. After the clearly marked entrance in Short Reach, instead of taking the port fork to the marina, where there is a special withy with a 'V' topmark, you continue more or less straight ahead into the region behind Hoo Island to the north.

From the east, there are two main approaches and they both feature the fort at Darnett Ness. The main road keeps to Long Reach and leaves it before Pinup Reach to pick up Middle Creek just after green *Darnett No.23*; and this is almost opposite the fort. The secondary route is the creek crawler from Half Acre and brings you out just below the fort, all ready to make a strait crossing to the green *No.1* buoy and the *No.1* black and white beacon, a good example of those so beloved of the navigation authority. There is also a tide gauge.

You then move along a tortuous marked channel into a mudscape of gutways and mini-wrecks progressing ever landward towards a vista that seems to be made up exclusively of works, machines and industrial plant. If you cease from lifting your eyes unto the hills for a moment, you will find, at sea level, highlands of a different calibre; namely the Hoo Flats islands of such varying shapes and sizes that the Medway becomes once again a place of manageable proportions where the locale seems placed for nothing other than safe explorations and happy landings. There is little to blot the landscape if you keep your heads down, only one or two patches have been fouled with the excrescences of society's detritus; and it must be emphasised that the huge chimneys and some of the emissions can work near magical wonders on local sunsets.

# Hoo, Gillingham and Medway pier marinas

It is hereabouts that the first two of the major marinas are to be found. Gillingham Marina is not likely to be missed because its locked entrance is directly off the main river in Gillingham Reach and well marked not only by gas holders but also by its own commanding edifice: a control office and club HQ that can compete with any offering of the Bauhaus. This reception building is quite unmistakable.

Hoo Marina is different, in so far as it cannot be easily distinguished from the main river, so you are not likely to end up there by much in the way of a chance or accidental visit. You need to know it can be found only by those who know how to follow, not the yellow brick road, but the well withied path to the guardian sill.

So; Gillingham first: overnight and short-term berths are usually available for visitors. Arrangements are made through marina reception, which is in the main building. Initial contact is through VHF Ch 'M' to the lock keeper, or boatman who may be in attendance at high tide; and you are asked to specify whether you are calling the lock or the marina. There are pontoon berths with access 2 hours either side of high tide (HWS). You are asked to moor stern-on and 'Please use your own ropes bow, sterns and springs.' There are also deep-water moorings; provided to facilitate arrivals and departures. These consist of two trots where you moor fore and aft facing upriver. Access is made easier by a concrete footpath to the low water mark.

There could hardly be a greater contrast between Gillingham Marina and the creeks that are no distance at all downstream. Here are all the facilities a visitor could want for shopping, boating, eating, drinking or generally socialising at large. There is no hidden factor to be contended with; you know from the moment you arrive exactly who and what to expect and having discerned this, no visitor will go away disappointed.

And so to Hoo. Recent improvements and refurbishment have made Hoo Yacht Harbour an attractively new-looking facility. Friendly efficiency, disciplined by a measure of old-fashioned courtesy and laced with sparrow-bright wit is the hall mark of a marina once described as 'owned and operated by yachtsmen for yachtsmen.' However, there is nothing at all old-hat about their service, skills and business acumen. As well as their existing mud berths, there are now pontoon berths that stay afloat at all states of the tides. There is deep water access for 8 hours each tide. Visitors are welcomed and can make prior contact with the harbour master's office via VHF Ch 'M'.

There is another marina facility close by, and one that is often undeservedly overlooked by speedy travellers on their way up or downstream. It is managed by the Medway Pier Marine Ltd and is in operation at the end of Gillingham Pier. There are not many berths, just under 40 at the last count, but they are all deep water and have mains power, water and walk ashore access via floating pontoons. Visitors are made especially welcome and can often raise the marina on VHF

Ch 'M'. However, the master and his resident caretaker get around a lot, and their VHF boat sets are not always on and/or attended. That gives an idea of the relaxed attitude that is the essence of Dave Harris's operation. Access is about half tide. Ashore it is their proud avowal that they uniquely enjoy the talents of a boilermaker, sheet metal worker, fitter and turner, all in one person. If you want anything ferrous or indeed metallically otherwise, this has to be something of an importance and advantage.

The remaining choices are swinging moorings or alongside berths from one of the cruising clubs or marinas below Rochester Bridge. There is plenty of choice with facilities varying from the basically decent to the basically luxurious. Perhaps the best approach is to decide, roughly, on the bit of the Medway that you want to settle on first, and then enquire of the clubs and marinas nearby. Most of them are contactable by phone during office hours, and many in the evenings as well.

# More Medway to Rochester

If it is not one of the creeks, marinas or clubs that you are seeking, your next stopping place (perhaps perforce by let or hindrance) will turn out to be the bridge at Rochester where the clearance at HWS is between 5m and 6m. Thus, yachts with masts must lower them before proceeding further.

Up to this point, the river will have offered no serious problem, being impeccably buoyed right up to *No.32* by Upnor Reach. All the way, the channel is clear and plain and all the vistas from Queenborough Spit onwards offer plenty of contrasts: predominately of course, the architecture of commerce with its attendant fingers of long horizontally searching jetties and tall symbolically reaching chimneys; the looming, glooming grey of Her Majesty's naval colour scheme; the desolate flats of Bishop Ooze and Bedlam's Bottom and the surrounding hosts of diminutive isolated islands; the derelict, circular fort at Folly Point on Hoo Island; and the splendid surprise of the grandeur of Cockham's wooded hills and the stone splendours of Upnor Castle.

From Gillingham onwards, through the pretty Cockham Reach and the unpretty Upnor and Chatham Reaches, the river shows by its many buoys, moorings, berths and cruising clubs that it is an extremely popular cruising base. In addition, there is history all round with old military and naval fortifications, training, fitting and supply bases. Ashore, there is a plethora of services, marine, domestic and social; as well as plentiful voyages of discovery for those with an interest in our past glories and preserved culture; with the shame of Chatham Dockyard a living and partly living indictment of the philosophy, morals and politics of our '80s lords and masters or should that read lady and mistress?

The virtual bridgehead of unencumbered Medway navigation.

As we move towards the grand bend of Chatham Ness and on towards the greater glories of Limehouse Reach and Gashouse Point before the head of navigation for masted craft at Rochester Bridge, the architecture begins to present a more appealing facade as riparian interests become not only more varied but also of more national commercial significance and consequently more affluent. Typical in this latter respect but atypical in its cannon assisted design is the recently erected edifice of Lloyds close by the monolithic home of Homecare, have a nice day, Texas style, and, in contrast to both, the near nonentity that is Sun Pier, where it is possible to moor for a few hours on the tide. This is a popular port of call, for there is easy access to the myriad attractions and services to be found shoreside in Chatham and the surrounding area. It is also useful for handing masts, but please see below.

So many and varied are the shoresides attractions that large scale Ordnance Survey maps, holiday guides and history books are all excellent companions on the stretch between Queenborough and Rochester since there is not likely to be a major problem on the navigational side and most of the interest will be found to be shoresides.

Once into Limehouse Reach, the waterway begins to take on something of the nature of its London/Liverpool counterparts as maritime commerce leaves its imprint on all the wharves, the jetties, the old waterside warehouses and the massive moorings.

While the area is no longer seething with foreign trade or Barbary pirates it is still a busy place and skippers must always be on the look out for big ships movements. Between Gashouse Point and Rochester Bridge, with Strood to port and Rochester's Acorn Wharf to starboard, barges and coasters throng the quays and waters with the red crescent (that I last encountered on the French canals) being much in evidence.

Below Rochester Bridge there will have been masts aplenty, but above it they are in short supply and motor cruisers take over in a massive majority. This state of affairs is dictated by the disciplines of Rochester Bridge relative to the state of the tide and the height of the water.

When it comes to the question of raising or lowering masts, the two most popular spots for visiting skippers who can manage without cranes, are the Sun Pier at Chatham and Strood Public Pier. Personally I have always used the Sun Pier finding it helpful to settle for an hour or so at LW on the soft mud and know that there will be a completely stable period when any tricky adjustments can be made in the masting or demasting process; it is also close to a mass of facilities that must be described as comprehensive.

However, it is here that masted vessels should pause for thought: is it really worth it? There are the various problems of logistics regarding the deployment of crew forces and the employment of forced labour in the handing masts and booms.

Even when they are down, not all the obstacles will have been overcome: those that follow relate to length, beam and draught. Sizes that may have been no more than reasonable in coastal waters, or perhaps over-modest indeed for the North Sea's short, sharp shocks; sizes that have in fact been quite appropriate for the Medway up to this point, can suddenly become an embarrassment once the vessel is past the charms of Maidstone. So critical and limiting are some of the overall restrictions that some may not even fancy trying to get up to Allington, let alone navigating beyond it.

Sun Pier is the best known stopping off place in this area. However, by diligent searching, looking and asking around, it is possible to find other spots and even 'better oles' for a short stay. Caution should be the keynote; there is a lot of fairly heavy, 'bright and breezy at best' traffic, and many of the locals are indeed jealous of their rights and their territory.

There is 6m available for air draught under Rochester Bridge at MHWS. At low springs, there tends to be little water and it not a good idea for a stranger to be navigating the arches until at least an hour after low water. There is little point in doing so anyway, since unhappily not much further upstream the bottom has foul patches and irregular shoal banks and shallows with which the mariner has regularly to contend; and which he will encounter if too early on the tide. The arch to use is the northerly one; that is, to starboard, going upstream. It carries 1·5m at MLWS.

# Last tidal to Allington

Imray's transit map, *Rochester to Allington Lock* which is part of their *Map of the Upper Reaches of the River Medway*, describes the river bed as follows: 'Lower reaches soft mud in banks. Upper reaches rocky and very foul. Dries out almost completely at Snodland at spring tides. If stranded, moor only where indicated (on map) or anchor so that you settle on the bottom of the bed'; and for the bridge: 'Rochester road and rail bridge: a clearance of 5·96m at the centre of the middle arch at MHWS. At low water (chart datum) the clearance is 11·9m but with a depth of only 0·9m. Passage at Rochester Bridge shall not be attempted by vessels drawing more than 0·6m at MLWS. A safe rule when navigating through the bridge is only to do so 3 hrs either side of HW'.

Once above the bridge, the famous Rochester Castle dominates the scene and the Medway becomes a different creature, afloat or ashore. Social cruising looms into view with a pleasant and charming vengeance; and the first establishment to receive you into its everlastingly hospitable arms is the Rochester Cruising Club. Visitors are made welcome especially at their clubhouse at 10, The Esplanade, Rochester. Their moorings are in the river nearby. While Strood Yacht Club, just across the way, offers an equally warm invitations and maintains marked mooring buoys for visitors.

Next comes the unmistakable motorway bridge and the Medway Bridge Marina. The two main eye-catching features here are the massive but slender span of the M2 motorway bridge, and the unmistakable lines of the oldest surviving light vessel, the old *Inner Dowsing*, now in good retirement service as the Lightship Club with its club, bar, restaurant and the attendant navigation school, the Medway Bridge Motor Cruising School.

Medway Bridge Marina has half-tide and deep water pontoons, mud berths and swinging moorings. Their obviously marked berths for visitors' boats are to be found at the downstream end of the deep water pontoons which accept craft up to 12m. The marina publishes a most useful and comprehensive guide to the area under the guise of a Medway tide table and marina brochure.

After a successful if spellbound negotiation (if that is the word) of the M2 motorway bridge, Cuxton Marina is almost the first thing you will notice. You can generally count on there being a few moorings available for visitors; with some on the outside where craft up to 1·5m will generally stay afloat. The pontoons have electricity and water. Some emergency domestic supplies are held by the office staff who will do all they can to make sure you are not deprived because of the relative isolation of the marina. In any case, the railway station is very close and comprehensive shopping facilities are to be found in easily accessible Maidstone and Rochester.

Only a little further upstream is Elmhaven Marina. It is a quiet, secluded spot with pleasant views of the much improved scenery. Most of the berths, which have mains power and water, are usually occupied by permanent holders. However, visitors are made more than welcome and will usually be found a space either alongside one of the pontoons or outside an already moored vessel.

Elmhaven is the last mooring post on the Medway, with the next port of call not appearing until you have reached the haven of the non-tidal waters that are the main reason for the long haul up to Allington Lock. Sadly, the Medway from here up to Allington is nothing but a melancholy and depressing experience. There are many shoal patches and the sides of the river are consistently foul and dangerous. It is wise to leave your passage as long as possible before high water to prevent the problems associated with a fast flood up the stern over an uneven bottom. A word with the Allington lock keeper, giving him your draught and point of departure, will pay dividends and relieve you, and crew, of a lot of anxiety. The bottom is not the only particular hazard you are likely to encounter, and a careful watch must be kept for floating islands of debris that include large and heavy logs, trunks of trees and sodden, wooden sleepers, as well as the usual collection of jerry cans, oil drums and plastic grot in all colours, shapes and sizes – but all equally lethal to props and stern drives.

At this stage on its inland progress, the river looks in general a pathetic, uncared for creature; leaving an overall impression of decaying boats, uninspiring landscapes and more mere factories. In particular, the paper mills, with their acres of bulk storage apparently awaiting recycling, are responsible for some severe eyesores.

# Allington lock and on to Maidstone and Farleigh

On the whole, pleasing things are few and far between until after Allington Lock, with, however, honourable exceptions to offer some compensation. For example, there are some interesting, attractive and really well-cared for craft, often moored in one of the few extremely pleasing scenic vistas. Moreover, there is the outstanding Carmelite friary and at Aylesford one of the most attractive stone bridges I have ever seen.

The times of high water at Allington Lock are something of a mystery. The last lock keeper I consulted said that it is 30 minutes on Rochester; the official Imray figure is given as 60 minutes on Rochester; in the Shell *Book of Inland Waterways*, Hugh McKnight says it is 40 minutes on Rochester; and my experience is that it has been as much as two hours on Rochester. So; when planning a cruise up to the lock, the best thing is to talk to the duty lock keeper and take his advice (and when has it not been a good idea to take lock keepers' advice?).

The only problem in working out when to leave (say) Rochester Bridge, comes if you are likely to have difficulty with air draught at Aylesford Bridge where the briggage is 2·9m at high water springs and 3·9m at high water neaps. Most skippers tend to set off too soon and risk finding bottom, rather than get caught below the bridge and have to wait for the tide to turn and then

The Medway's famous Allington Lock.

punch it. The bottom of the river is not so 'unfoul' that encountering it can be said to be without worry. The logistics can only be worked out with reference to each boat's specific dimensions and speed.

The lock is manned at all times but normally opens from three hours before to two hours after high water. The limits are the lock are: 50m x 6m x 2·0m draught.

Once you have passed through Allington Lock, you will find the River Medway changes dramatically to become an altogether safer, calmer and much more picturesque proposition. There are various ports of call immediately after the lock dependant upon your needs: Allington Marina; Allington Castle; the Malta Inn; and Aylesford village with nearby priory only minutes down the road.

If you can negotiate the lock, you can berth in Allington Marina. Visitors are made extremely welcome in what are very much away-from-it-all arboreal quarters. At most times is it a place 'full of noises, sounds and sweet airs, that give delight and hurt not.' There is hardly a more appealing location on the river.

The reach on to Maidstone is made up of two and a half miles of absolute delight. There are many interesting and well kept boats, including some fine specimens of beautifully converted Thames sailing barges. The delightful terrain consists for much of its time of gorgeous trees that hang in profusion well into the centre of the river and so form a protective canopy for cruising. That is, if you are in a mood to tolerate such hazards to navigation and interpret them in idyllic mode.

Maidstone itself offers well designed quayside moorings that look good and are within easy striking distance of all the shops you are likely to need. I have berthed at the quayside many times, but as yet have never been charged for the privilege. The city fathers are to be congratulated for their expertise, their thoughtful planning and its successful execution; for it extends to providing spotless and efficient public toilets, a treat and rarity indeed. Maidstone is a splendid place to visit: it has charm; is in touch with the many facets of its history, heritage and culture; but is not without all those up to date features that give contemporary life its zapp, such as fast food bars and speedy supermarkets. The brewery has a foot in all camps and is a visitor's must.

Upstream from Maidstone, the river continues in its well treed and leafed apparel as befits the most prestigious waterway of the Garden of England. However, there is a serpent in this mariner's Garden of Eden, for the river begins to lose depth and the banks encroach. The bottom, other than dead centre, tends to be foul with the sides especially so, because of their poor state of repair;

none of which is helped by the increasing presence of fishermen behaving in their typically gloomy non-helpful manner.

It is only a short leg (two miles or so) to Farleigh where there is a lock and a bridge: but what a lock; what a bridge; and what a combination. There is a telling shortage of both depth and height, as water is down to 2m at best and the Farleigh Bridge height is limited to no better than 2·4m when the beam of your air draught is 3m. *Valcon* was quite unable to pass through, and the downstream side of this lock is head of navigation for this guide.

# End piece

There can be no doubt that the River Medway is a major waterway. Indeed, from the wreck of the *Montgomery*, it must be considered a trip and a half, with the last leg from Rochester Bridge, which bars the way of masted vessels, being one that should be undertaken during daylight hours and even then, not when skipper or crew are feeling frail or fraught after a long day's arduous cruising or even more arduous family-holiday-making or socialising.

Since the waterways for cruising vessels are so expansive; since there is an abundance of navigational aids as well as all kinds of shipping movements; and since the tidal waters are known for their power and speed (for example, the rise and fall at Strood is between 4·5m and 5·8m) there are always opportunities galore for any skipper to practise pilotage and seamanship skills. Since, in addition, there are anchorages, marinas and clubs with their surrounding towns and attendant services to suit all tastes, it is difficult to fault the river for a quick weekend visit, a month's leisurely cruise or a permanent sailing base.

The following extract from Ms. Driscoll's letter has special relevance to the Medway: 'Now you mention about riding lights, and it is good advice. I don't think you should anchor anywhere without displaying a riding light. I have lost count of the yachts that I have nearly hit because they neglected this precaution. In the summer months especially one had to exercise extra caution because one knew that there would be an unlit yacht anchored in the worst possible place. Yet the Department of Trade's *Seaway Guide*, when first published, said not a word about lights when anchored, which I thought was a remarkable omission and told them so.

Now when you talk about Queenborough it's not a bad thing to mention that once the wind goes round NW you've got to get out, as there's no shelter with the wind this way. Shepherds Creek I know. Not much water, and plenty of old wooden barges, run in here to get rid of them. I've been in here a couple of times in our 14ft. dinghy to get photos of these remains. Plenty of water in Stangate Creek, but beware barge remains. There's one which is well in the centre of the creek, opposite some hulks on the side, but if you avoid this then it's a nice quiet anchorage.

If you want to get to Otterham Quay (via Half Acre Creek) the best way I found to pick up the entrance was to shape in from *Medway* channel buoy *No.14*. Then you see the remains of an old steel tug stuck on its side, and close to this is a small lit buoy marking the creek entrance. On the other side of the Medway in Slede Creek you will find two lots of remains of German U-boats (1914–18 type). Two together with only the bottoms still there, and another with quite a bit of the sub remaining. Not a nice thing to find on a dark night.....

Now the flagstones on the piers of Rochester Bridge are a very useful tide gauge. If five of them were showing we would get under way (in a loaded barge) if bound for New Hythe. Similarly, when the water just reached the barge blocks at Crescent Shipping's yard you then get under way if bound for Maidstone. Not that I can vouch for that one as I've only once been in a craft capable of getting under Aylesford Bridge, and while I was in her we never got a freight to Maidstone.

Once through the bridge and just below New Hythe you can see a much over-grown waterway opening up to port. This is known as 'Burham Old River' and is, or so I was told, the original course of the Medway, made into an 'ox bow' when the river was straightened at this point when Reed's created New Hythe. This is a place I'd like to have explored, but never had the opportunity. I can remember when I was mate of the *Olive May* (at 100ft overall one of the biggest barges to be found) we lay at New Hythe awaiting discharge, and so did two other craft, whose mates asked my skipper to lend our boat so that they could explore this lost river. He lent them the boat then they got stuck there and had to wait for the next tide before they could get back. So I think an inflatable boat is probably the best bet. In a way I would like to have joined in this trip, but there was work for me to do on board, so I missed it, but in view of what happened, and my skipper's wrath, it was just as well I never went!

There was another point about the Medway that I should have made. This is particularly noticeable above Rochester Bridge and is the 'land water' effect, where fresh water draining into the river, especially after heavy rain, forms a top layer of water so that it might be flood tide, but to all intents and purposes it is ebb. Off Sheerness Pier (now the late pier, I think) there is a tidal eddy so that it is always ebb here, whatever it might be doing elsewhere, but I suppose a yacht would not need to be here.'

The Medway is a river rich in contrasts.

## RIVER MEDWAY

**Chart**
Imray Y18
Admiralty 1834, 1835

**Tides**
+0130 -0200 on HW Dover.

**Authorities**
*Medway Ports Authority* VHF 9, 11, 22, 74, 16 (24hrs) ☎
*Medway Patrol* VHF 6, 11, 14, 22 16 (24 hrs) Medway Ports Authority ☎ Sheerness (0795) 580003

**Access**
The main channels of the River Medway are accessible at all times, but the moorings and marinas are restricted to between 2 and 3 hours on each side of high water.

**Marinas – from seaward**
*Mariners Farm Boatpark*, Lower Rainham Road, Gillingham ☎ Medway (0634) 33179. South Bank
*Gillingham Marina*, 173 Pier Road, Gillingham, Kent, ME7 1UB ☎ Medway (0634) 280022. South Bank
*Medway Pier Marina Ltd* Gillingham Pier, Medway ☎ (0634) 511113, after hours (842427). South Bank
*Hoo Marina*, Vicarage Lane, Hoo, Rochester, Kent ME3 9LE ☎ Medway (0634) 250311. North Bank
*Medway Bridge Marina*, Manor Lane, Rochester ME1 3HS ☎ Medway (0634) 43576
*Cuxton Marina*, Station Road, Cuxton, Rochester, Kent, ME2 1AB ☎ Medway (0634) 721941
*Elmhaven Marina*, Rochester Road, Halling. ☎ Medway (0634) 240489
*Allington Marina*, Allington, Maidstone, Kent. ☎ Maidstone (0622) 52864

**Allington Lock**
☎ Maidstone (0622) 52864

Contrasting perspectives and perceptions of life on the Medway.

# X. THE ISLE OF SHEPPEY TO NORTH FORELAND

## By way of introduction

The River Swale can be approached from east or west. From the west, you will have left the confluence with its much mightier sister river, the Medway, at the Queenborough Spit buoy. This westward 'urban-overland' approach is definitely the simpler of the two but by the same urban token it is also much the busier.

A cruise from the Kent coast to Maidstone via the River Swale offers a variety of experiences: there is an interesting if brief coastal passage (perhaps also going round the outside of the Isle of Sheppey to start with); a busy commercial waterway; two highly contrasting rivers; a multitude of quiet creeks; and a miniature excursion into the soft underbelly of the riparian aspects of 'The Garden of England'. What is more you can get away from it all yet have all that you want readily to hand; for nowhere along the cruise will you be really far away from some small village (like Conyer), a busily thriving town (like Maidstone) or one of the dozen or so marinas or moorings that lie between Harty Ferry (just inside the Swale) and Allington Lock (just below Maidstone).

You will also encounter a splendid cross-section of a vast variety of craft: from the huge commercial tankers and container vessels that bear down in an amazing juggernaut fashion, to the fleets and flocks of sailing dinghies that skirt and flirt with incredible agility right under their bows or stern as the mood/whim/need takes them; from rotting hulks to splendidly maintained Thames barges some of them still performing miracles of handling under sail; and from enormously expensive modern motor cruisers to tiny, neatly converted fishing boats of a grand old age but always with a known history.

The area is also a great one to sail but only if you have plenty of time, since the vagaries of the British climate will make it extremely difficult to negotiate the narrow (and often tortuous) channels that make up a substantial part of the cruising grounds. Seldom is the wind of the right strength to get anywhere at all under such conditions; and even when it is, it is probably coming from the worst possible direction and, in any case, will probably die round the next bend because of some vast windbreak in the form of a power station. No; although it is quite a delightful area for the use of sail, unless your time is ample (preferably even unlimited) a reliable motor will serve you best in these parts...although the sailing buffs of the Swale will take hot issue with me here.

If you are approaching the east end of the Swale, you will probably be coming from the North Foreland or the Shivering Sand Towers and the Spaniard. In any case, the marker you will want to pick up first is probably the *Whitstable Street*. Unless you are lucky and have a day of exceptional visibility you will find it difficult to identify either the *Whitstable Street* black and yellow north cardinal light buoy or the green buoys of the *Columbine* or the *Columbine Spit* since they tend to get lost in the confusion of images that make up the low lying coast behind them. Since both Pollard and Columbine Spits are inhospitable places, and since the two or three miles in this approach to the Swale can be as boisterous as any waters in the neighbourhood, it is worthwhile taking things slowly until *Ham Gat* and *Pollard Spit* buoys have been confirmed. With these two in sight, the Swale entrance offers no serious problem or hazard; the challenges come when you try to find your way into Conyer Creek for the first time or try to get up to Faversham on the top of a big spring tide when there is little to indicate the presence or absence of channel or saltings. But first, let us deal with the navigation round Sheppey to Queenborough on the outside.

## From the east

From the east, you are more than likely to have left behind the North Foreland or those strangely named monuments in the Thames mid-stream, the Shivering Sand Towers. While this is an almost traffic free passage, there are complications awaiting the visitor. First, it is essential to

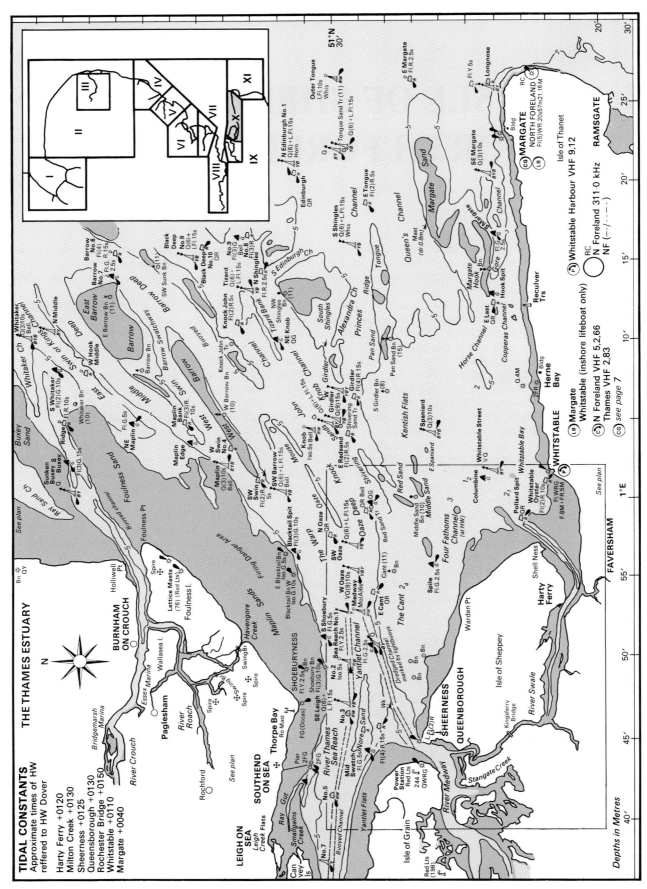

THE THAMES ESTUARY

TIDAL CONSTANTS
Approximate times of HW
reffered to HW Dover

Harty Ferry +0120
Milton Creek +0130
Sheerness +0125
Queensborough +0130
Rochester Bridge +0150
Whitstable +0110
Margate +0040

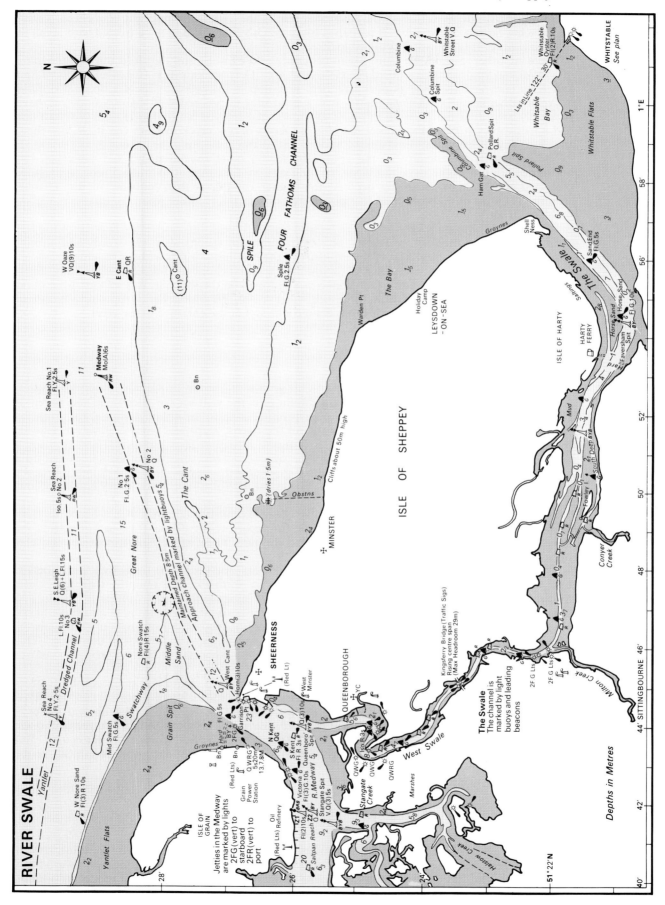

RIVER SWALE

ISLE OF SHEPPEY

FOUR FATHOMS CHANNEL

SPILE

SHEERNESS

QUEENBOROUGH

MINSTER

LEYSDOWN-ON-SEA

WHITSTABLE
See plan

Whitstable Bay

Whitstable Flats

The Swale

ISLE OF HARTY

HARTY FERRY

Milton Creek

SITTINGBOURNE

Depths in Metres

The Swale
The channel is marked by light buoys and leading beacons

Jetties in the Medway are marked by lights
2FG(vert) to starboard
2FR(vert) to port

Kingsferry Bridge (Traffic Sigs)
Rising centre span
(Max Headroom 29m)

51°22'N

make a positive identification of the buoy that marks the extremely long spit of rock hard sand that reaches far out into the sea. It is shaped like a witch's finger and is to be treated with about as much intimacy. It is known as Whitstable Street.

There are other intriguingly named markers closer to the Swale, and they lead through the maze of wrecks and sandbanks that guard the close entrance. They are known as *Columbine, Pollard Spit* and *Ham Gat*; and the wise skipper has them non stop in his eyeballs. Indeed, from *Whitstable Street* or either of the *Columbine* buoys, it is a good idea to proceed with caution until you have positively identified the *Ham* and *Pollard* green and red buoyed 'gate' that is no more than one and a half cables at best. Take note; not only is there a drying creek in Ham Gat itself, but there are also many variations on the theme of underwater nastiness awaiting the unwary.

The waters in the vicinity of the approach can be quite exceptionally, and unexpectedly, boisterous. It can come as a nasty jolt to strangers to find that, two miles inside apparently protected waters, they are being exposed to rougher conditions than 'outside' in the Thames estuary. They are of the same kind that plague mariners in the Humber when the infamous Barton bulldogs strike.

The first sign of human habitation is to be seen on Shell Ness, the most easterly point of the Isle of Sheppey, where there is a collection of robust homes for the stalwart, the sturdy and strong: those who can face the bleakness of the exposure to the Northeast winds without flinching.

A nominal 225° can be maintained until you have a visual check on *Sand End* light buoy. Shell Ness stands out clearly and while this stretch can be tough on the way out, it is seldom difficult on the way in. Soon after Sand End come the wreck buoy, off Horse Sand opposite Faversham Creek, and the north cardinal marker that denotes the spit at the entrance to the creek.

# Harty Ferry

Just round the corner from these low lying dwellings is the well known anchorage and haven of Harty Ferry. In true English style the nomenclature lingers on although there has been no working ferry for years, and it still features on all the charts, maps and guides. However, legend, tradition and atmosphere die hard and all is hale and hearty at Hardy Harty. There is many a Southeasterly cruising skipper who considers his summer as of naught if he has not picked up a buoy, or better, anchored off, and rowed ashore (for outboards, even the classic doughty Seagull, are frowned upon hereabouts) to the special bit on the Isle of Sheppey for water and spirituous liquors.

On the other ('mainland') side, there is a well marked gut-cum-slipway that is much used by local fishermen and others in the know as a point of departure for fishing trips or just getting the dinghy to the swinging moorings, of which there are quite a few just offshore most permanently booked and usually occupied to boot.

The moorings to the west of the hard belong to Brents Boatyard. The majority are numbered, but the methodology behind the numerololgy is so complex and obscure that few locals understand it fully and strangers are left at a loss. In general, the usual courtesies obtain, and unoccupied buoys may be taken by visitors on a pro tem basis. It is something of a mistake to ask for advice or permission from one of the occupied boats: if they are strangers you learn nothing; and if locals, the answer usually comes: 'They are all private,; and you're not to use them.' This is not the case; but for further information on use of these moorings at Harty Ferry, you contact Brents Boatyard, Faversham (0795) 537809.

This is generally a quiet spot, for in spite of its well-protected charm and the accessibility of its liquid provision, it is seldom unpleasantly crowded. What is more, joy of joys, you can stay afloat at all stages of the tide. There are few places on the Swale where you can do this and yet have access to reasonable facilities. Perhaps the visitors' moorings at Queenborough and the anchorage through South Deep on the south side of Fowley Island are the best known and most used. But here you have an excellent waiting station for anyone wanting to get out to the North Sea or the English Channel.

# Faversham Creek

Faversham Creek is entered by leaving the north cardinal marker off Faversham Spit and known locally as Creek Mouth buoy, the proper distance from its proper side. This has not always been the case, but it has been moved and now marks a channel that is central. There was never a lot of room for manoeuvre and there isn't now, but at least visitors can feel free and legal when entering.

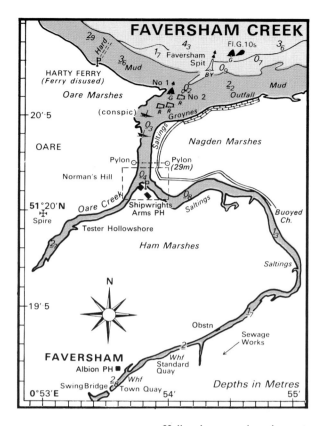

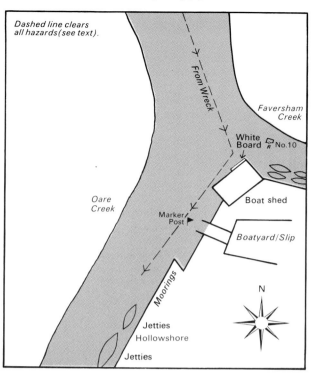

Hollowshore moorings; low water at the junction of Faversham and Oare Creek

After the immediate entrance, the next main markers are the wreck buoy (to starboard about 1½ cables inside the creek) and the white board on the boatyard shed; this latter gives a good leading line down the main channel, which is shared by Oare and Faversham Creeks.

This board will lead to the junction (see chartlet) where there is a spit (on the starboard, west bank) opposite the boatyard that reaches far out into the stream. If you are proposing to go into Oare Creek to try for a mooring on one of the jetties belonging to Barry Tester (whose yard is called Hollowshore) it is best to keep fairly close to the post marking the end of the boatyard slipway. This will clear all obstacles. There are few moorings at Hollowshore anyway, and most of them are usually taken up by their regular occupants, so it is best to contact Barry Tester before arriving.

The small community of Hollowshore is a close one. Here, you will discover (and dis-cover is the right word, for nothing here is conspicuous) Barry Tester's boatyard; the clubhouse of the sailing fraternity; and that favourite of Swale enthusiasts, the Shipwright's Arms. Once a notorious spot for smugglers, there still lingers about the area an air of 'brandy for the parson and baccy for the clerk' and some say there is always the chance of a late, late drink nearby.

It is a remote spot, without mains power or water, and is most easily reached by boat, since the road is neither A nor B, and is probably beyond the reach of the alphabet. The company and the beers (one of them a special local brew going by the name of Fremlins) make a visit not only worthwhile but mandatory for any Swale crusader.

At one time the landlord of the inn was an Auxiliary Coastguard at Sea and ran a VHF station for the convenience of local cruising folk (no doubt to encourage the placing of early orders). There was also a comprehensively-equipped weather station. As is the way with sailing landlords, he has upped anchor, but VHF and even better communications facilities will soon be available.

Somehow, the legend still hangs on that it is safe to moor to the steps by the Shipwright's Arms. For a good long time now, there has been a motley collection of underwater items, rendering it quite a tricky spot. For really shoal craft at the top of the tide there will be no anxiety, but for visitors it must surely be best to anchor just off and use an inflatable.

Hollowshore and the Shipwright's make probably one of the finest stopping-off stages on the whole of the southeast coast. I'm not one for going overboard about pubs, but this one is really special. Otherwise the facilities are basic: there is no mains water, so you can only rely on emergency provisioning for that; nor is there mains electricity nor a full fuelling service (although once again Hollowshore will see you alright in a genuine emergency); indeed, there is not even a full-blown postal delivery. However there is a phone which cruising folk may use just inside the entrance to the clubhouse.

I can think of no better mooring place than Barry Tester's Hollowshore moorings at the junction of Faversham and Oare creeks; indeed, it must rank as one of my favourites on the southeast coast. Hollowshore's master has got it just right: 'We're trying all the time to get and keep the place just as it was 100 years ago, as much as possible. If people like it here just as it is, we tend to get on all right with them. But we are not a marina and can't spend our time rushing around with lots of rope and hundreds of gallons of water. Nor can we keep touching our forelocks all the time to people who will keep calling you My Man and are never likely to bring their expensive cruisers here again.'

The Hollowshore jetty is an excellent place in every way; it is comfortable, protected, close to the facilities and decent on the ride for an early getaway. The last time I left there, for example, the tide started to make at 1020 (HW Dover +1220) and I was afloat at 1120. By 1130 there was enough water over the mud 'bar' of the berth to enable me to get into the channel and leave the Swale without problem.

So; you can certainly get in and out of the Faversham channel at better than half tide, although the course is not a wide one. However, it is well marked and the local boating fraternity and fishermen are always helpful and friendly to strangers whether they get themselves stranded or not.

There is now a good channel to the small and attractive town of Faversham. Different from the Oare branch line, it is marked on both port and starboard well up towards the town: after the junction, the red buoys go from 10 to 16, and the green from 3 to 11. Alertness and a reliable crew are still highly desirable if you are not to find 'ground' which, in this area, is, of course, soft mud, glorious mud. So, while there is no serious hazard in navigating this creek, it is not a place to get neaped and certainly not along its lower reaches. I have always found it a creek of special appeal, and a joy of a haven for any East Coast and saltings man: remote and quiet so that there is little likelihood of being badgered by unwelcome socialites-cum-isers, but not too far if you desperately need to contact civilisation. The improved buoyage has made life much easier for boating visitors, and that is to be particularly welcomed, for it is a veritable jewel of a place.

Once the town has been reached, the channel to the town quay is on the port hand. On that side is the wall against which you can lie if you are to stay just below the bridge. If you do, make sure you have plenty of stout rope and hoisting gear (for vessel, self, goods and chattels) for once you are down you are out for the count and nothing takes longer than a neap tide to float you up here. The mud is too soft to allow any decent crossing, unless you happen to have arctic-type snow shoes or those legendary (and now priceless) Thames smuggling boots.

On the opposite side are the small landing stages that are the Faversham town council moorings (☎ Faversham (0795) 533234). If you draw more than 1·5m it will be difficult to negotiate since the stagings are off a mud shelf that is well above the rest of the channel. Such manoeuvres should, therefore, be kept for rising spring tides that are still making.

Close by is the Albion Tavern, on the bankside in fact, where you can not only get food and drink, but arrange for basic provision too and if you are in luck you may find the milkman ready to leave you a couple of pintas at the end of the catwalk. The Anchor Inn, on the opposite bank, just above Iron Wharf, is an ancient cott-like pub where you can also get good food. In a slightly different league not far away are the good old real ale premises of Shepherd Neame. They are still an independent, family brewery and more than happyby appointment to show visitors around the place and the brewing action (☎ Faversham (0795) 532206).

There are other candidates for a comfortable berth. Mud berths and other facilities can be had at Brents Boatyard ☎ (0795) 537809 (on the west bank just below the Albion); at the Quay Lane Wharf ☎ (0795) 531660/537805 (on the east bank just below the bridge); and at Iron Wharf Boatyard ☎ (0795) 536296/537122 (on the east bank below the Anchor) where they tend to specialise in providing facilities for DIY enthusiasts.

If you draw a drop over 1·5m it is worth checking with the boatyard of your choice for their advice and guidance. In any case, berths are not so little sought after that chance arrivals can be automatically accommodated.

Sadly, the city fathers seem to have made little or no progress near the head of the navigation in getting the riparian owners together to improve the looks of the place or to provide decent welcoming facilities for visiting yachtsmen. Indeed, most things to do with the river have been let go into some state of disrepair over the years. No evidence lingers of what was a thriving and attractive quayside. There would be no threat to conservation or the peace and quiet of the backwater if the council promoted a small marina scheme. Everyone would benefit from a project with discreet development rather than commercial exploitation. It is to be hoped that they will soon feel so uncomfortable about the squalid aura both above and below the bridge (unpleasant enough to spoil any visiting yachtsmen's perception of what is otherwise a beautiful town) that they will be moved to renew their endeavours. Apart from its restricted access and visitors' facilities, and it must be said they are slowly but only slowly improving, I can find nothing but good to report about Faversham.

Faversham Creek possesses an arm, armlet or rivulet: Oare Creek, leading to a small boatyard and mooring facility. If you draw more than a metre you will experience more than some trouble and strife to reach the head of navigation. The channel to Oare is a tortuous affair, but if you know it well, you can get a boat of 2·10m up on the big springs; but not only is it tortuous, it is also a narrow job, with its sides deeply scarred by those who tried in error or in vain. I remember the words of one local expert very well: 'I've been using the creek for more than twenty years and I must go out at least four times a week in the season, but I still get caught by it every year. It's a monkey!' Oare Creek is no more than a mile at best length, but it comprises more twists and turns than many a much longer river.

The creek to the Oare is just over a mile from the entrance at its 'full' length; Faversham itself is about 2½ miles. Oare Creek is twisty and tortuous in miniature; Faversham Creek is just the same but on a larger scale: where the Oare has twists and turns, Faversham has bends and corners. They are both equally difficult to follow: Oare because it is so narrow; and Faversham because, although wider in the main channel, it is enclosed between saltings that extend over an extremely wide area (even by East Coast standards) and consequently tend to mislead.

From the marker at Faversham Spit, a course of 303° will bring in line a first rate lead on a large chimney immediately next to a clutch of smaller ones. This can be a help since this stretch is known to have strong tidal sets. In fact, on one occasion, I found, steaming at six knots, I was being set off a good 15°.

After the *No.1* buoy comes an east cardinal marker on the extreme end of the mud bank of Fowley Island nearly opposite Spit End. If you are going into Conyer Creek this is where you take the port fork into South Deep; but if you are on your way up the Swale, this mark is left to port and a course set that will pick up the *Nos 2,4,6* and *8* red can buoys that mark the channel to the old Elmley ferry. These buoys should be left close to port for the channel is extremely narrow (and at is shallowest) during this stretch. After *No.8* buoy come the notice boards and the red and green buoys that denote the now discontinued ferry and the extremely noticeable hulk by the south bank. Nearby, just past the hard and on the south side, there is a reasonable anchorage off the Lilies where the end of the saltings is marked by a red beacon. The Lilies must be well rounded if you are to make a trouble-free entrance into Milton Creek.

The moorings to the west of the hard belong to Brents Boatyard. The majority are numbered, but the methodology behind the numerology is so complex and obscure that few locals understand it fully and stranger are left at a loss. In general, the usual courtesies obtain, and unoccupied buoys may be taken by visitors on a pro tem basis. It is something of a mistake to ask for advice or permission from one of the occupied boats: if they are strangers you learn nothing; and if locals, the answer usually comes: 'They are all private, and you're not to use them.' This is not the case; but for further information on use of these moorings at Harty Ferry, you contact Brents Boatyard, Faversham ☎ (0795) 537809.

## BUOYAGE
### Whitstable Street lightbuoy to Queenborough via The Swale

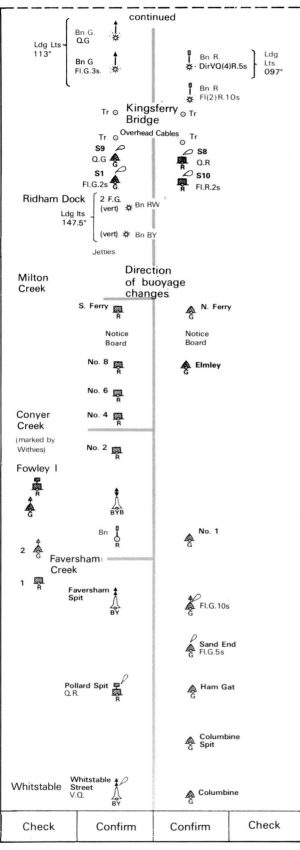

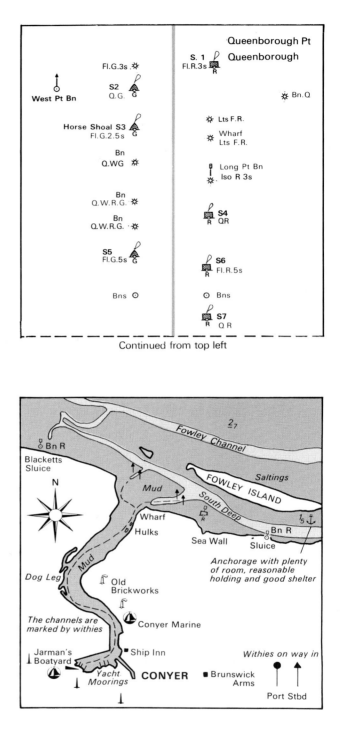

Continued from top left

Conyer Creek: the head of the creek is a popular spot and it is not always easy to find a berth – even on the outside of the creek itself.

Conyer Creek: a moody, muddy study at low water. Conyer almost always seems to be at low water and getting in and out needs to be carefully timed

# Conyer Creek

Meanwhile, back on the Creeks Trail comes Conyer. It has an even more restricted and difficult entry as well as a more convoluted channel than Faversham; but it is not quite in the miniature league of Oare. There are two entrances to Conyer Creek: the east and the west and both have markers that are getting better year by year. If there ever was a case of 'never the twain shall met' this is it....although of course they do, well inside the creek. The 'deep water' entrance, the one that seems to be the main entry on the Admiralty chart, and known locally as The Butterfly, is the westerly one. Once you know it well, you can gain something between two and three hours on the standard easterly entrance. It is extremely narrow and has some very sharp turns.

Whichever way in you use, you will need to find the withies: a much simpler task now that Conyer has improved them so that they can be recognised. They have also has produced a sketch map complete with cartoon by Mike Peyton. Some are topped with white circles to be left to port and white triangles to be left to starboard.

In fact, the creek is even better marked now than ever before, and while it is still necessary to exercise caution there is no danger these days of mistaking the odd piece of flotsam or a rogue willow for a properly stuck marker, nor, praise be, for the actual, if modest, official buoyage. Nevertheless, it is still a good idea to hitch a ride with a local at half tide to see for yourself the convolutions of Conyer's ins and outs.

On the top of a good tide can you cut across from *No.6* or *No.4* buoy in the main Swale channel to get to the west side; so generally the approach is from the east. In this case you take the port-hand fork at the east cardinal marker at the end of Fowley Island leaving it close to starboard on the way in. After which, the better water tends towards the south shore. At low water there is never very much of it around, so care and regular soundings are called for. It is not until about half-tide that a craft drawing more than 1·5m will be able to reach the withies that mark the easterly entrance or pass them in the river to get to the Butterfly.

If you can approach the withies at the easterly entrance without bottoming, there is every chance that you should be able to make the channel into Conyer without problems. This is, of course, by no means foolproof, but the chances against getting caught out are as slender as the withies that take you in. The first withies should be left close to starboard. 'Close' too is a comparative term. On a couple of occasions, I have stuck *Valcon*'s bows in the mud by being too close to a couple of withies and also by being too far from some others. On average, around about the metre mark is the least that should be left and about two to two and a half the most. Often, you will be forced into the right position because of approaching traffic and natural caution on all counts will see you right.

There is a nasty shoaling patch in the middle of the channel about half a mile into the creek; in fact it is a sort of dog leg and if you are really familiar with the channel you will be able to avoid it. Otherwise just watch out with extra care about a cable or so down from the major turn to port where there is an old sluice/drainage entrapment.

As in Faversham, an eye should be kept on the sounder and also on the remaining posts and withies that have suffered damage over the years and are still leaning over in decrepitude. For these, as well as the other fairly obvious reasons, Conyer Creek is not a place to try to enter at night until you know it intimately.

For a first time visit I would suggest you contact Conyer Marine, the expanding boatbuilders at Conyer Quay, if you really want to know the eccentricities of the Butterfly without getting caught yourself. You can do this by phone or on VHF (16 or M) and father Ernie, the presiding genius of the marina pontoons, or indeed son Ted or other Brother, for it is a family affair in very truth, will be pleased to sort you out mainly for the pleasure of doing so. But also perhaps for the (token?) payment that can usually be offered in pints at the local during your stay at the marina berths. They will also pilot you through the usual (easterly) entrance channel if you wish, but there you stand a goodly chance of finding your own way in while keeping out of trouble; or a fair one of getting out again if the best does not entirely come about.

Because of Conyer Creek's intricacies combined with tidal restrictions, many skippers have given up even trying to get in. They just anchor outside in the Swale at a little spot between Fowley Island and the mainland known as South Deep. In very truth it is only a touch southerly and hardly deep at all, but all things are comparative. From this anchorage, it is only a short row and a brief walk to Conyer itself; and that is much more appealing than the long wait for a neap tide. Conyer itself is, I think, a dream of a place. The village is an old-fashioned hideaway that is well worth seeking out. It may not be easy to enter, but its charms are plentiful once you are there and it is well worth all the effort.

There are comprehensive boating facilities, firstly at Conyer Marine at Conyer Quay, where recently they were fully occupied (in every sense of the word) with the completion of a massive project, the 30m leisure live-aboard barge for use on the Continental waterways. There is usually work proceeding on non run-of-the-mill craft here; but they can generally find time to spare for boat, ship-and-shop talk — even laced with dashes of gossip and crack. If they haven't got what you want, or can't do what you ask (as they most often can) they always know a man who has or can.

Secondly, upstream at Conyer Wharf, where the name of Jarman's was once supremely well known if not actually supreme, there is now Swale Marina, run by Mr and Mrs Parry. On the site there is Swale Rigging and Chandlery and the Wilkinson lady sailmakers. Regarding the latter, the more intriguing and challenging your rig or request, the more favourably you will be received; the size of the order is not the prime factor or concern. Tip! They do not go a bundle on dodgers. They also work closely with the boatbuilders on both the new and converted craft that are fabricated there. They are still known as Wilkinson Sails, after their initiator, but Sindy Staley is now at their helm. Relocated in their new, refurbished loft, they are going from strength to strength.

Alan Staley (Wooden Boats and Service, also husband of Sindy Sails) is available at Faversham and, more recently at Conyer Wharf, where he indulges his passionate devotion to classic craft but will work on almost any practical project you care to offer him.

When visiting the creek, I tend to stay back at Conyer Marine and not get involved with the possible stick-in-the-mud games that can occur if, as unsure stranger, you venture right up to what is euphemistically known as the 'head of navigation'.

There are two pubs: the nearer of the two, the Ship, has real ales galore, a restaurant with an exotic menu, a heady wine list and prices to correspond. Up the road, at the Brunswick Arms, the menu is more blunt; the fare much more candid; and the prices are neither threatening nor extortionate. Basic provisions can be found only with difficulty, although frozen goods are to hand at Swale Marina Chandlery and the Ship Inn; but a trip into one of the nearby (but not walking nearby) towns is necessary for anything other than basics.

Early in the season, there is another traditional rite: the annual Conyer Mud Sports an event that has to be seen to be believed ... especially when Page 3 *Sun* Girls invade. But early or late, seasonal or not, you will find that the locals will always welcome you.

Conyer is something of a double bind: it can be difficult to reach because of the awkwardness of the Creek; and it can be even more difficult to quit because of the delights of the place itself. With regard to the exceptional case of Conyer, Stevenson was wrong; it is not really better to travel than to arrive.

Conyer represents the ultimate in the journey from the easterly entrance; for the rest it is more appropriate to start again from the other beginning: the approach from the west and then via the Medway.

## BUOYAGE
### Whitstable to Queenborough via Four Fathoms Channel

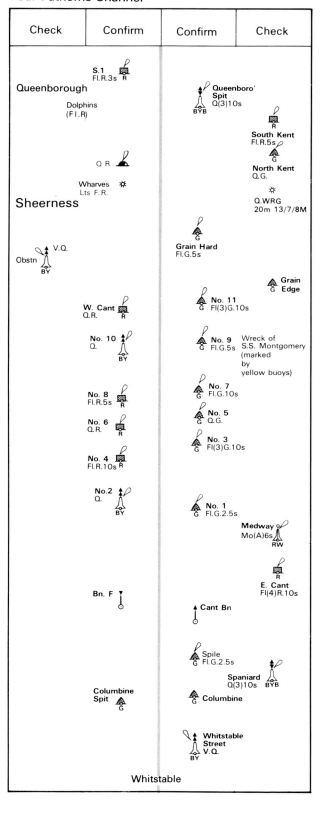

| Check | Confirm | Confirm | Check |
|---|---|---|---|

## BUOYAGE
### Ramsgate to East Swale

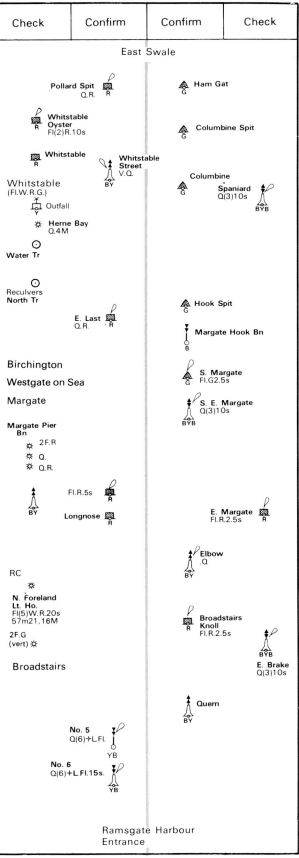

| Check | Confirm | Confirm | Check |
|---|---|---|---|

# The Four Fathoms Channel:
# Whitstable to Queenborough

Let us first turn to the Admiralty *Pilot*: 'The name Four Fathoms Channel is no longer apt as there is now barely 7·3m (that is, 24 feet or 4 fathoms) of water at HW spring tides. Caution: There are numerous pieces of wreckage, some of which dry, on The Cant'.

And now to Imray's 1960 *Pilot's Guide to the Thames Estuary*: 'Overland Route. This passage should only be used by light draught craft under fine conditions, as it is exposed to the full force of northerly and easterly winds, and yachtsmen should on no account run the risk of being caught in it in bad weather. Avoid if possible bringing up anywhere along the route. The shoals are intricate and very difficult to clear'.

Even 'under fine conditions' and with the aid of two sound working sounders, I have still always found this passage to cause prickly erections on the hairs of my neck. It is difficult to explain, since nothing has ever actually gone wrong; but there never seems to be quite the right amount of water under the keel and *Valcon* has a habit of misbehaving whenever the bottom is near sniffing distance.

For craft up to 1·8m there is little or no danger provided the channel is used at or near HW, and the sailing directions themselves are not difficult: from Whitstable Street, set a course for midway between the *Spile* light buoy and the Middle Sand beacon. From there make for the beacon 'F' and then on to the rest of the beacons or a buoy of your choice in the Medway approaches off the Cheyney Spit.

Coming from the northern side of the estuary, you leave the Shivering Sands towers behind and make for the safe water marked by the *Middle Sand* beacon and then carefully round the *Spile*. The alternative being to go down to the Spaniard, follow a westerly course straight to the Spile, and then continue as before. All of which seems a lot of trouble when there are other, safer and more reliable courses to follow; but some kind of special attraction still attaches to this channel as I know from the number of skippers who have mentioned it to me. True, round the Isle of Sheppey can make a pleasant day's cruise if you have plenty of power and the weather is settled fair; but for anyone but the experimentalist who feels cheated unless he has tried all the variations, the disadvantages and risks must outweigh the rewards which certainly do not come in the form of beautiful coastal scenery. No; the main reason for using the FFC must be found when going from Whitstable or further east to Queenborough, the first port of call on the West Swale.

## From the west

The Swale is entered from the Medway, leaving the Queenborough Spit cardinal marker just to starboard and The Lappel, a vast area of drying mud flats, well to port. Shortly after, for the first time in the area, the banks of the river approach one another so that there is a feeling of an inland waterway as opposed to a seaway. Then it is past Deadman's Island and Shepherd's Creek to starboard until the red buoy marking the Queenborough Hard and the Creek appear on the port hand after no more than a mile.

The title 'Queenborough Harbour' must surely be something of a euphemism for the conglomerate that starts at a line running from Swale Ness to the ruins of the pier off the point. There is a concrete lighter on the west side of the channel, green lit (Fl.G.3s), and this can furnish an alongside berth provided you get there soon enough, for it is a popular location. It carries a legend: 'Mooring at the discretion of the Harbour Controller. Medway Ports Authority: Berthing alongside this lighter is prohibited until consent has been obtained from Harbour Master.'

There are large black buoys that will take about half a dozen craft and a number of smaller ones, usually with two white ones near the creek reserved for visitors. The buoys are all to the west and the concrete lighter barge to the east. Skippers thinking of making use of the facilities for a short stay should contact the harbour master. With regard to the two conjectural white visitors' mooring buoys: I have never been in the fortunate position of having appropriated or even identified one. Otherwise, there are many private yacht moorings and usually a vacant one can be found on the east side. There are also other lighters that may seem to be of use and appeal. You should stalwartly resist succumbing to any temptation without thoroughly checking it out from those with real local knowledge: otherwise the process might well be tricky and something of a snare and a delusion.

The Creek, is a small drying creek just by the hard, well buoyed in standard red and green, that runs right into the centre of the town. It is used by commercial and fishing vessels, so unless you have real business there, it should be avoided. There are three boatyards there and it is usually busy. While their trade is mainly vested in the 'big stuff', it is just possible, with much persuasion, to get non-essential work done on small leisure craft. However, if your boat is in desperate need, you will find that you can reach the ministering angels at the quaysides on the top of the tide, and they will be very quick to get and keep you right. While they generally have to deal with ships and craft much larger than those used by visitors, they are not beyond approach.

There is the public wharf where fishing boats lurk, but you may be lucky and find a vacant space for lying alongside to scrub, paint or just check underwater things over. Access is completely restricted to the top of the tide, and since the locals refer to it as a shoal-draught job, it is worthwhile taking advice if you draw much more than a metre. There is also hardstanding nearby.

Queenborough is dominated by the Grain power station, and there is really no escape from its dominating edifice. But the town has plenty of facilities, all no more than a dinghy row. Probably the best and quaintest shop is the chandlery known as the Bosun's Stores: it is an Aladdin's cave, staffed and patronised by a range of sea-son characters. They do all that they can to keep not open house but also open hours and every conceivable item of chandlery. Their establishment is a source of character, charisma and comedy; as well as the not-at-all-comic HM Coastguard connection and service. You can count on them for advice and help. Together with the agreeable Queenborough Yacht Club, one of the most hospitable in the area, they just could be the reason that makes it so very popular.

In Loden Hope, just after West Point with its beacon, there is the green buoyed Horse Shoal almost opposite the jetty. I was once advised by a local non-expert that it is perfectly safe and problem free to pass it either side. I tried it the once and failed to find sufficient water; and that once was enough. If a man deceive me once, shame on him; if a man deceive me twice, shame on me.

The Swale then makes an incipient Ox Bow as Loden Hope turns from dead southerly dramatically up to the northwest before circling violently round to end up facing towards the southeast, which course it holds for the three miles to Milton Creek, after which it settles in an east–west parameter.

Long Point, well named and well marked with its beacon, and Loden Hope offer fascinating views of the really big ships back in the Medway as they apparently land-glide over Dead Man's Island.

# Kingsferry Bridge

After Loden's Bend Long Reach, Horse Reach and Ferry Reach bring you to something quite different: the pillars that are the buttresses of Kingsferry Bridge. It is a wondrous construction to contemplate, especially when it is in the process of opening.

By tradition, myth and legend, you can arrange passage in a number of ways: getting into touch with the bridgemaster by telephone landline well in advance to arrange a time; calling him on VHF Ch 10; signalling with the ship's whistle: 1 long and 4 short blasts; addressing the bridgemaster by means of a loud hailer; hoisting a bucket or other suitable object in the rigging; signalling by flag; or signalling in the classic manner by the use of arm signals.

The famous Kingsferry bridge is almost as well known up as it is down.

I was intrigued by all these ideas, some more than others I must confess, and so tried out a few. Much as I would have liked to be able to recount immediate success having hoisted a 'suitable object' in the rigging, I have to report complete failure of all methods except VHF. This has worked without fail every time and, as a result of checking in advance on Ch 10, I have never had to wait more than a few minutes.

I felt it worthwhile discussing the case with the Kingsferry Bridge staff. One of the team put it this way: 'A bucket's all very well, but it really means 'I want to take on water'; and many of the smaller craft have got all kinds of things in their rigging – including the day's washing. When it comes to flags, well yachts have all got all kinds of flags in all kinds of places; you just can't rely on them. Many is the time I have opened the bridge for a yacht displaying a flag, only to hear some upper class voice with 'I say, my man; that's not for us, is it? I mean, we don't want the jolly old bridge, you know.' We all do our best, but you just can't win. The best method is VHF Ch 10 on the VHF. That's why we have it, and I can't see any reason not to use it. I mean, all little ships should have a licensed set shouldn't they?'

So close to Horse Reach I accept that as coming from the horse's mouth. I have found the bridge very regular. It is likely to lift on the hour, or the half hour, or at the behest of a big ship; so it seems sensible to arrange your itinerary accordingly and enjoy the wait, if any, for there is usually a fair amount happening, shoresides or waterways. But the staff are as friendly and efficient as you could ask for in bridgemasters; and, after all, they must have something in common with lock keepers, and bearing in mind the treatment they so frequently get offered from leisure craft, they have every reason to be a law unto themselves.

Kingsferry Bridge is a road and rail bridge with a rising centre span. It is unusual in that the span rises vertically, but all of a piece horizontally. It is an excellent candidate for photography. The clearance when the bridge is down is 3·3m and 29·0m when it is up. When the bridge is raised, you should add 25 metres to the figure on the tide gauge. The gauge is mounted on the bridge itself and is easy to read. All inner sides of the four pillars are lit and the traffic signals are as follows:

| No light | Bridge down |
|---|---|
| Q.R/Q.G | Bridge lifting |
| F.G | Bridge up |
| Q.R | Bridge descending |
| Q.Or | Bridge out of action |

This is a busy stretch, and I once found myself negotiating four separate tugs; three sloops a'sailing; two water skiers; and a coaster with three tugs; but happily there was not a partridge nor a pear tree in sight. Wits are certainly needed at the ready.

Shortly after the bridge, on the starboard hand, are many moorings belonging to the Kingsferry Boat Club. While the membership is friendly, the likelihood of finding a vacant place is remote. It must also be said that the major entity in the area is the accumulation of buildings on the south bank, and the main item of interest for visiting mariners is the possibility of heavy sea-going traffic emerging from the unappealing constructions that go to make up Ridham Dock. It is a place devoted exclusively to commercial craft and completely unavailable to yachtsmen.

The aptly named Clay Reach is an oppressive stretch with demolition, desolation, wreckage, remains and debris creating the deadly landscapes that on both sides of the water.

Elmley Reach is of some importance for three reasons. First, it is where the direction of buoyage changes: it comes inward from east and west to meet at the Kemsley paper mill and it is on this side of the river that the best water is to be found, until Clay Reach, where the channel becomes central again. From here right up to Queenborough the middle course in the river is clear to be seen since the banks are now much closer; and there is always much more water in this western half than in the eastern.

Second, it is one of the places where tidal separation occurs. The other two are Kingsferry Bridge and Fowley Island. However, there is still little reliable information about exactly what happens, and, as the Admiralty *Pilot* says: 'Tidal streams in the Swale are subject to considerable variations, and all data must be considered approximate.' However, in general, the stream will separate as follows:

| Kingsferry | HW Dover +0330 |
|---|---|
| Milton Creek (The Lilies) | HW Dover +0430 |
| Fowley Island (Conyer Creek) | HW Dover +0530 |

It is important to know that both in-going and out-going streams can exceed 4 knots, mainly between Elmley Reach and Kingsferry.

Third, it is the home of the Lilies, the small islands that mark the entrance to Milton Creek. While Conyer and Faversham are the two best known creeks in the Swale, there are others. Many of them are quite small; for example, the miniature rivulet in the saltings near the entrance by Shell Ness and the other miniatures by the Lily Banks near Harty Ferry. Then there are the slightly larger but no longer whirling Windmill and Bell's Creeks by Dutchmans Island, Flanders Mere and Spitend Point, as well as the three heroics at Cockleshell, Wellmarsh and Sharfleet, which latter is not to be confused with the Medway Sharfleet – this is Swale style, and a different kettle altogether. In addition, there is the much larger commercial creek, called proudly just the Creek, already mentioned at Queenborough itself; and finally, there is this one by the Lilies: Milton Creek.

Many of the smaller creeks are suitable only for wading (birds or humans) or days in the dinghy, unless of course you have a purpose crafted shoal boat, in which case you can have a whale, or a porpoise, of a time. That leaves Milton.

## Milton Creek

Both the poet's name and the cleansing brand are well known, but nothing could be further removed from the healthily antiseptic or the powerfully poetic than this last of the Swale creeks. Sadly, it is difficult to find anything good to say about this creek. However, it can be said that it leads to Sittingbourne; its waters are oddly coloured, implying pollution; and its air is heavy with odours that confirm the implication. The creek is neither clear either to look at nor plain to navigate, since it is difficult to identify features above or below the waterline. At the head of the creek, the water seems to thicken and the air to hang heavy with evil rankness and stench. There are few facilities of any kind and nothing to recommend to a visiting yachtsman except the Dolphin Sailing Barge Museum. That is undoubtedly worth a visit but I would suggest that it should be made by road and not by water.

Sittingbourne itself is a place to be avoided except as a matter of urgency. True it has plenty of shops but it is also possessed of all the ugly attributes of the worst of the United Kingdom's noisome urbanisation. Should you be overcome by some perverse and wayward obduracy that leads you inexorably to the entrance of Milton Creek, make sure you give the Lilies a wide berth and take the water towards the wharfs on the west bank. I have tried the trip a few times, but on each occasion have not only found it to be an area of dereliction but also to have its bottom liberally bespattered with hazardous submerged objects and to be fairly short of navigable channels even at high water. A careful study of the chart will show the main features to be wrecks, chimneys, brickworks, hulks, wharfs and a sewage works.

## Swale End

From the Lilies eastward towards Conyer Creek the channel is entered between the gate of the *North* and *South Ferry* green and red buoys. They are situate just to the west of the hard that was part and parcel of the one time Elmley Ferry. Now there is naught but the residual and the skeletal; and that description might well be given to the narrow strip of navigable water that runs a pretty middle course through the vast wides of the flats that make up the Heart of the Swale. It is not realistically possible to hope to float through with a one and a half metre boat at anything better than half tide; although I did once succeed in making a muddy progress all the way to Fowley on a median neap. It is easy to feel slight disorientation in the middle of this featureless stretch.

Although the Swale is not a long river, nevertheless, in its few miles it packs more to intrigue, absorb and fascinate than do many others. The river is a place of charm and eccentricity where you can find plenty of good socialising company whenever you want it; or you can just keep to your own self solus without any difficulty; apart from fish, birds and bees, that is, for wild life has a charmed life in these parts. For me, its appeal is quite compelling.

Ms. Driscoll has had experience of the Swale: 'That old smack whose remains can be seen by the entrance to Oare Creek was an ex-Brixham trawler, the Toreador, which was bound away about 1947 and got stuck there. Her mast stood until quite recently, when it was removed and re-used when a smack was re-rigged. At Faversham you are liable to run out of water in the stretch of the creek where Pollock's Shipyard used to be. The smell to be found in Sittingbourne (Milton) Creek is something to do with the waste from the paper mills. It used to be a lot worse, an it would make paint go a most peculiar lead-like colour and the brass used to be covered with a strange milky sheen, preparatory to tarnishing badly. I used to cover all exposed brass with a light film of oil if bound for Sittingbourne. What it did to the human 'Innards' I hate to think ... '

# Whitstable

So; out in the big wide world again, the main hazard upon leaving the Swale bound for Whitstable are the sand banks that lurk between Pollard Spit and the long finger of hard, hard sand known as Whitstable Street. It is tempting to make straight for the red can *Whitstable Oyster*, but having been guided across those flats and nearly flats by two local divers, I am apprised of the detritus, the bits and pieces that have accumulated on the bottom. I no longer cut off any of that corner but go right outside.

Others may be more hardy than I; but from the east I think there is no doubt at all: it is essential to make a positive identification of its cardinal marker before trying to make an approach to Whitstable itself, or the mooring buoy facilities of the yacht club.

Visiting yachtsmen are neither barred nor aggressively discouraged from using this small commercial port that has a growing traffic with the rest of Europe. This commercial expansion explains any lack of warmth in the reception accorded to visiting yachtsmen. Otherwise, it would be an ideal staging post for many cruising craft from north, east and west. But as things stand, it can on no account be looked on as a possible port-of-call when on a leisure trip.

The harbour itself is of an unusual and pretty design, but in the main is packed with cargo ships up to 1000 tons carrying stone, slag, grain, timber, steel and so on as well as all the local craft employed in fishing, oyster and shell, for which the name Whitstable is well known.

The entrance is not easy to see even on the clearest of days. There is little doubt as to where it is, and it is simplicity itself to set the right course from either Whitstable Street or Columbine Spit; but to pick out any really helpful sign is a feat of considerable difficulty at day or night. By daytime, the best mark is the green girdered construction by the asphalt lift; and by night, try to line up the harbour entrance red lights with the top light of an unmistakable streak of yellow street lights. Following this until about a half mile off will enable you to pick up the leading lights.

Care is needed at night not to line up one of the leading lights with one of the entrance lights. In fact there is a plethora of red lights including one on the nearby pub. I still recall the story of the skipper who, while having been in and out of the port with his coaster on numerous occasions, had, at one Christmas time, had to send out a VHF call from the wrong side of the Street shingle: 'Help; I'm lost! What the hell have you done with the entrance?' He had in fact, picked up one of the red lights on the Christmas tree in the window of one of Whitstable's larger houses.

The tide can run strongly past the entrance and a decent amount of power is needed in order to negotiate it satisfactorily. The Whitstable Street shingle bank dries for nearly two miles out and

Whitstable Street is impressive seen from shoresides above.

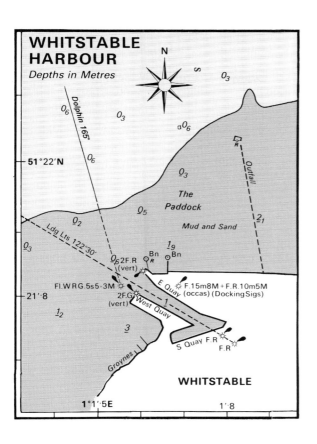

## WHITSTABLE HARBOUR

*Depths in Metres*

Although you will never be refused Whitstable if in need the harbour is no place for pleasure craft.

for up to 2·0m in places. Each season there are fatalities or nasty accidents among holidaymakers: they walk out too far and then get caught by one or other of the various pools and eddies that can be treacherous on a rising spring tide.

However, notwithstanding all the pressures just mentioned, during the summer season, the berthing officer is, if prevailing conditions are reasonable (and that covers a multitude of factors, sinful or pure) prepared to try to house one or two visiting yachts next to the fishing vessels. 'If we get any more than one or two, we just haven't anywhere to put them. If you haven't got space, you haven't got it, and that's that; and you can't get it neither, and that's that as well.' You will need sturdy fenders, and a plank will not go amiss.

In addition, and not at all as a compromise, the yacht club will do everything possible to sort you out with a suitable mooring offshore. It is sensible to call the mooring master in advance of any proposed call. The club offers the usual facilities, and has also a few places for an overnight kip in their bunk room. They also keep a list of names and addresses of suitable lodgings if a more sybaritic situation is preferred.

Gathered round the harbour are all the usual occupations and facilities that you would expect in a busyish small port. Chandlery and rigging requirements can be satisfied near the harbour by Messrs Rigden and Joiner respectively. Not able to match the punning euphony of their names, but offering splendid service nevertheless, is Heron Marine, where Dave Challis is the electronics marine wizard; and for wooden boat enthusiasts, Alan Staley, who is not only a boatbuilder, bender and refurbisher, but also a enthusiastic devotee himself and now at Conyer Wharf.

While Whitstable Harbour is not the easiest to find at the best of times, nor one to be running for at the worst of times; and while it should be looked upon really as only a refuge in time of distress, the town itself is a highly desirable spot for the visitor and by no means a last resort. It is a joy not the be missed. It has been well visited in the past, just like Ramsgate and the hinterland of Pegwell Bay; but cruising folk are now more popular in the town than were the foreigners who foraged, scrounged and scavenged in the days before Domesday.

# And so to Margate

Between Whitstable and Margate there is little to catch the eye on the shore line; the main features being Herne Bay and its pier, the modern 'contemporary' style water tower, and the very old Reculvers Towers. This seaside resort is no longer what it was, and its piers are in ruins although they still show up well on radar.

Navigation along the section is straightforward: steaming eastward, the first pair of buoys, green *Hook Spit* and red *East Last*, are close together marking the 'gate' that leads from Horse Channel into Gore Channel. There is also the inshore alternative of the Copperas Channel between them and the Reculver Sand. The drying sands known in the main as Margate Hook and Last are much in evidence just over a mile off-shore and are clearly marked by their buoys and beacon.

Margate's small harbour dries to about 2·0m, gently if sometimes unevenly, shelving from the head of Stone Pier to the town shore. Vessels of nearly 4m can get to this pier at HW spring tides.

Reculvers is always impressive, even in an East coast mist.

However, the 1960 edition of Imray's *Pilot's Guide to the Thames Estuary* says this: 'Craft can only enter the harbour towards high water, and if intending to stay must be prepared to take the mud. There is little shelter, and yachtsmen are not recommended to enter without special reason.' My own visits to the place gave me no cause for disagreement.

Margate had two piers: Stone that forms the harbour; and Promenade, known as Iron Jetty. This was damaged by storms in the winter of 1979, and the leftovers look just about as inviting from seaward as they do from the shore. They are an emblem of Margate's spiky weaknesses, sharp practices and shrill commercialism: a resort lacking in revelation and inspiration.

It is important to stand well clear of the Longnose. On occasions it looks as if there is a tempting 'close inshore passage' round the headland, but attention to the chart will show that to be erroneous as the rocks of Longnose Spit reach the cardinal marker. Nevertheless, not a year goes by without some skipper (usually of a motor cruiser from the Thames or Medway) clipping the corner to his lasting regret.

Once round North Foreland, and past its experimental VHF lighthouses, we move into the symbolically deep waters of the English Channel.

Margate is still awaiting its marina development .

Margate offers various sites and sights.

**QUEENBOROUGH**

**Charts**
Imray Y18
Admiralty 1834

**Tides**
0000 Sheerness, +0130 Dover

**EAST SWALE AND HARTY FERRY**

**Charts**
Imray Y14
Admiralty 2571

**Tides**
Whitstable: −0015 Sheerness and about +0110 on HW Dover

**FAVERSHAM CREEK**

**Chart**
Imray Y14

**Tides**
0000 Sheerness, +0130 Dover

**Marinas and boatyards**
*Barry Tester (Hollowshore Boatyard)* ☎ Sittingbourne (0795) 532317
*Shipwrights' Arms* ☎ Sittingbourne (0795) 533163
*Brents Boatyard* ☎ Faversham (0795) 537809
*Iron Wharf Boatyard* ☎ Faversham (0795) 536296/537122
*Quay Lane Wharf* ☎ Faversham (0795) 531660/537805

## CONYER CREEK

**Chart**

Imray Y14

**Tides**

0000 Sheerness, +0130 Dover

**Radio**

Conyer Marine: VHF Ch 'M', 16

**Marinas and boatyards**

*Conyer Marine* ☎ Sittingbourne (0795) 521285

*Wilkinson Sail*, (Marina moorings – Ernie ☎ Sittingbourne 0795 521285) Conyer Quay ☎ Sittingbourne (0795) 521503

*Heron Marine* (Electronics & Radio) ☎ (02273) 61255

*Alan Staley* (Wooden Boats Service) ☎ Sittingbourne (0795) 522590/536088

*Swale Marina*, ☎ Teynham (0795) 521562


## WHITSTABLE HARBOUR

**Charts**

Imray Y14

Admiralty 2571

**Tides**

−0015 Sheerness, +0110 Dover

**Harbourmaster**

☎ Whitstable (0227) 274086

**Radio**

VHF Ch 9, 12, 16 (Weekdays 0800–1700 or +/−0330hrs HW)

**Access**

+/−0100 hrs HW (Dries max. −1m)

**Approach**

The approach is from the N with the dolphin light Fl (green sector) bearing 165°M and when about 50m from the dolphin go SE until the harbour leading lights are in line at 122°.

**Signals**

A fixed red light shown below the harbour white light at night means entry of vessels is prohibited. A fixed white light only means Port open for entry. In the event of VHF radio breakdown only: On day tides between the hours of sunrise to sunset (from 3 hours before to 1 hours after high water), a docking light signal may be in operation exhibited from the light tower. Fixed white: Port closed; Fl.3s white: Port open and clear for entry.

**Moorings**

Yacht moorings NW of harbour: contact Whitstable Yacht Club. Clubhouse:- ☎ Whitstable (0227) 272343. Office:- ☎ Whitstable (0227) 272942. The yacht club is also contactable on VHF Ch 'M': call sign Whitstable Yacht Club. (For their own very good reasons, their radio is restricted, in the main, to club licensing hours.)

**Reminder**

Whitstable is a busy, commercial port and yachts are expected to use it only when seeking refuge, or in other emergencies.

# XI. NORTH FORELAND TO RAMSGATE

## Foreland to Ramsgate

The four miles of coastline from the North Foreland to Ramsgate consist mainly of sheer, chalk cliffs that rise from 60 to 120 feet, sometimes in stark perpendicularity. This in itself is enough to tell us quite clearly that we have come round the bend from the flats of the east coast and are now into something quite different. And so we are, for the scenery continues to improve as the cliffs are relieved from time to time by verdant slopes like those near Broadstairs and Dumpton Gap.

Close-to inspection shows that there is little that has not been built on. If time and weather permit, you will be able to muse on the site that is, by quite misguided local tradition, the setting of John Buchan's *Thirty Nine Steps* and also to be suitably awed, if not indeed completely subdued, by the genuine original of Charles Dicken's *Bleak House*.

The area between the Foreland and Ramsgate is not renowned for its visibility and the *Broadstairs Knoll* buoy never seems to stand out very much. So; you are unlikely to spot it, the *Gull* or the *Elbow*.

It can at times seem a bit tedious if not quite unnecessary to take the deep-water, dredged channel all the way in and out of Ramsgate but I do it mainly for two reasons. First, I like to remain on the safe side, checking all the local navigational aids whenever possible. For example, the Ramsgate *Fairway* buoy in its day seemed to spend more time on the harbour wall than on station. I like to check the performance of my radar before finally setting off; and also to take every opportunity to check my own performance in reading it accurately.

Second, because the waters close by the harbour wall and 'Ramsgate Sands' are seldom quiet enough to tempt me their way. Once out of the buoyed stretch, there is a trouble free passage about a mile offshore, which is about where the yellow channel buoys are, to and from the North Foreland.

Thanks to the prevailing weather, not often is the North Foreland to be seen as clearly as this

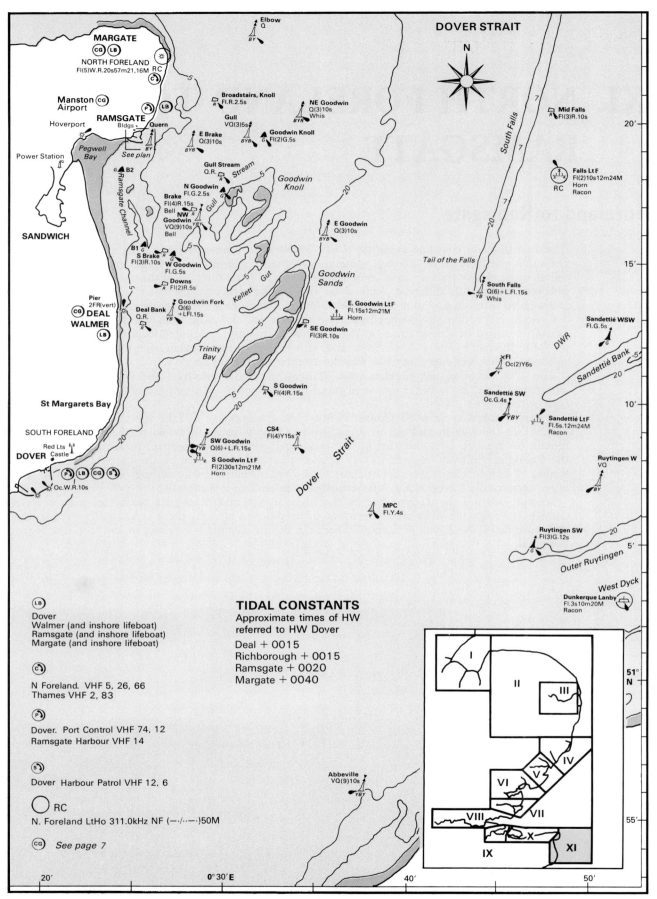

**DOVER STRAIT**

Elbow
Q
BY

NORTH FORELAND
Fl(5)W.R.20s57m21,16M

Broadstairs, Knoll
Fl.R.2.5s
R

NE Goodwin
Q(3)10s
Whis
BYB

Gull
VQ(3)5s

Goodwin Knoll
Fl(2)G.5s
BYB

E Brake
Q(3)10s
BYB

Mid Falls
Fl(3)R.10s
R

Gull Stream
Q.R.
R

Goodwin
Knoll

Falls Lt F
Fl(2)10s12m24M
Horn
Racon
RC

N Goodwin
Fl.G.2.5s
G

Brake
Fl(4)R.15s
Bell
R

NW
Goodwin
VQ(9)10s
Bell

E Goodwin
Q(3)10s
BYB

B1
S Brake
Fl(3)R.10s
R

W Goodwin
Fl.G.5s
G

Goodwin
Sands

Downs
Fl(2)R.5s
R

South Falls
Q(6)+L.Fl.15s
Whis
YB

Sandettié WSW
Fl.G.5s
G

Goodwin Fork
Q(6)
+L.Fl.15s
YB

Deal Bank
Q.R.
R

E. Goodwin Lt F
Fl.15s12m21M
Horn

SE Goodwin
Fl(3)R.10s

Fl
Oc(2)Y6s
Y

DWR

Sandettié Bank

Trinity Bay

S Goodwin
Fl(4)R.15s
R

Sandettié SW
Oc.G.4s
YBY

Sandettié Lt F
Fl.5s.12m24M
Racon

SW Goodwin
Q(6)+L.Fl.15s
YB

CS4
Fl(4)Y15s

S Goodwin Lt F
Fl(2)30s12m21M
Horn

Ruytingen W
VQ
BY

Dover
Strait

MPC
Fl.Y.4s
Y

Ruytingen SW
Fl(3)G.12s
G

Outer Ruytingen

West Dyck

Dunkerque Lanby
Fl.3s10m20M
Racon

**TIDAL CONSTANTS**
Approximate times of HW
referred to HW Dover

Deal + 0015
Richborough + 0015
Ramsgate + 0020
Margate + 0040

(LB)
Dover
Walmer (and inshore lifeboat)
Ramsgate (and inshore lifeboat)
Margate (and inshore lifeboat)

(C)
N Foreland. VHF 5, 26, 66
Thames VHF 2, 83

(P)
Dover. Port Control VHF 74, 12
Ramsgate Harbour VHF 14

(S)
Dover Harbour Patrol VHF 12, 6

◯ RC
N. Foreland LtHo 311.0kHz NF (—·/··—·)50M

(CG)  *See page 7*

Abbeville
VQ(9)10s
YBY

# BUOYAGE

## S. Foreland to N. Foreland: Outside Goodwins

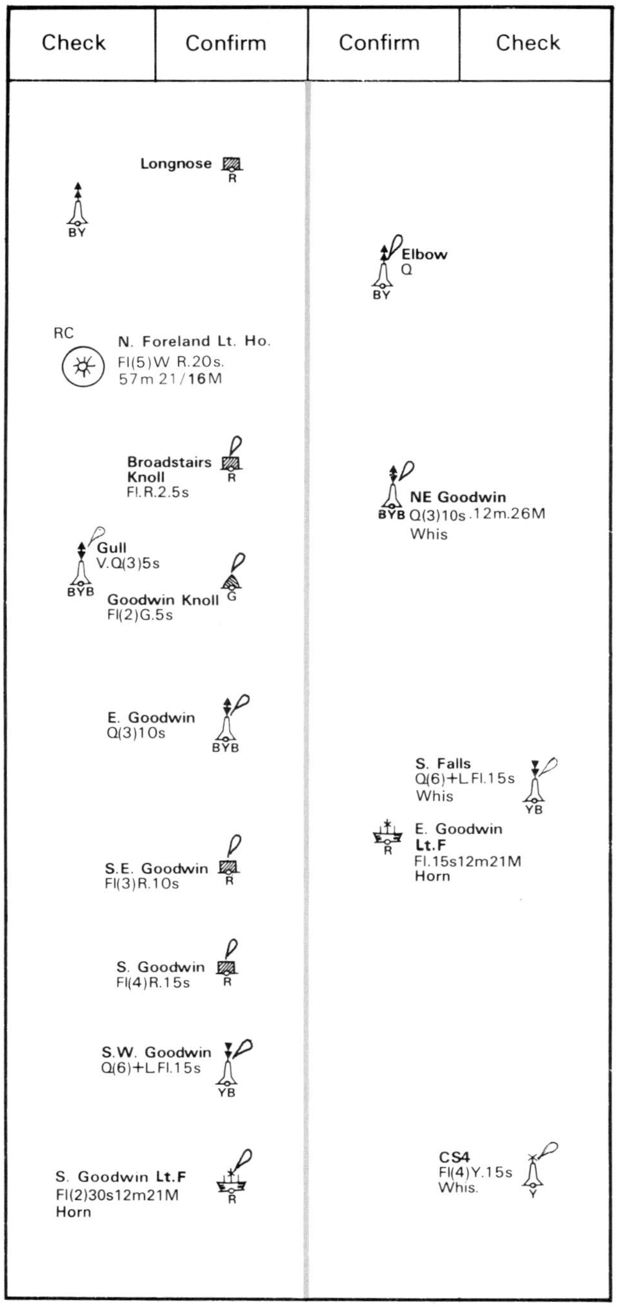

| Check | Confirm | Confirm | Check |
|---|---|---|---|

Longnose
R
BY

Elbow
Q
BY

RC
N. Foreland Lt. Ho.
Fl(5)W R.20s.
57m 21/16M

Broadstairs
Knoll
Fl.R.2.5s
R

NE Goodwin
BYB Q(3)10s .12m.26M
Whis

Gull
V.Q(3)5s
BYB
Goodwin Knoll G
Fl(2)G.5s

E. Goodwin
Q(3)10s
BYB

S. Falls
Q(6)+LFl.15s
Whis
YB

E. Goodwin
Lt.F
Fl.15s12m21M
Horn

S.E. Goodwin
Fl(3)R.10s
R

S. Goodwin
Fl(4)R.15s
R

S.W. Goodwin
Q(6)+LFl.15s
YB

S. Goodwin Lt.F
Fl(2)30s12m21M
Horn

CS4
Fl(4)Y.15s
Whis.

## S. Foreland to N. Foreland: Inside Goodwins

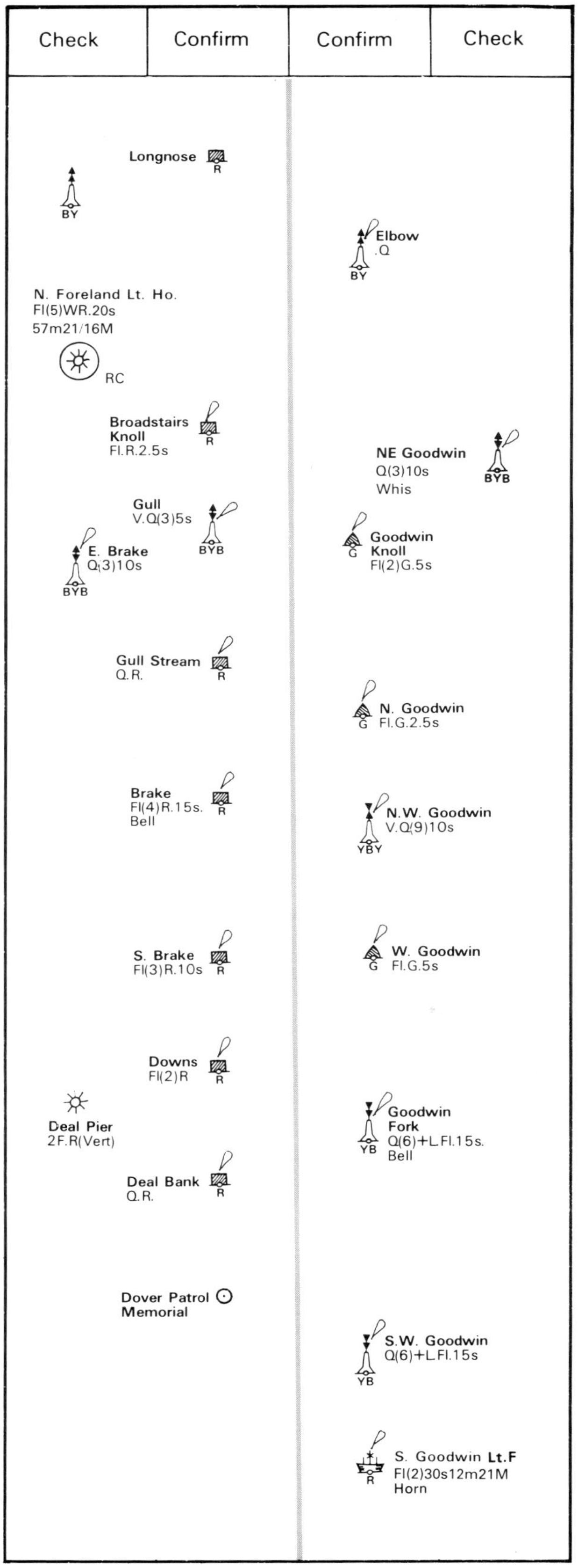

| Check | Confirm | Confirm | Check |
|---|---|---|---|

Longnose
R
BY

Elbow
.Q
BY

N. Foreland Lt. Ho.
Fl(5)WR.20s
57m21/16M
RC

Broadstairs
Knoll
Fl.R.2.5s
R

NE Goodwin
Q(3)10s
Whis
BYB

Gull
V.Q(3)5s
BYB
E. Brake
Q(3)10s
BYB

Goodwin
Knoll
G
Fl(2)G.5s

Gull Stream
Q.R.
R

N. Goodwin
G Fl.G.2.5s

Brake
Fl(4)R.15s.
Bell
R

N.W. Goodwin
V.Q(9)10s
YBY

S. Brake
Fl(3)R.10s
R

W. Goodwin
G Fl.G.5s

Downs
Fl(2)R
R

Goodwin
Fork
Q(6)+LFl.15s.
YB Bell

Deal Pier
2.F.R(Vert)

Deal Bank
Q.R.
R

Dover Patrol ☉
Memorial

S.W. Goodwin
Q(6)+LFl.15s
YB

S. Goodwin Lt.F
Fl(2)30s12m21M
Horn
R

Seldom is an approach to Ramsgate Harbour smooth. My own experiences of it are of one of the most hyperactive areas on the East and Southeast coasts. The waters are often settled enough for peaceful entry and exit, but visitors should be prepared for a disturbed time one way or another. The general shallowness of that coastal stretch and the plenitude of shoal banks are two important causes. Another is the exposed limb on which the harbour is perched. In addition, it is completely artificial and formed of stone piers, thus possessing none of the natural protection afforded to ports and havens of a less manufactured origin. Its immovable mass of stone stands against the irresistible force of the North Sea and the Atlantic as they conjoin in the narrowness of the Dover Strait, creating a fervent breaking swell. All these can combine to make the area one of troubled waters.

However, in less than a mile or so from the entrance everything usually calms down. At that distance, the backlash from the walls and the wakes left by the pilots die away to no more than unpleasant memory. However, it is worth noting that the waters surrounding the North Foreland itself and the stretch to Ramsgate are more often than not lumpy. When the wind is against the tide, most folk who want to go east decide to stay another day in Ramsgate Marina – and to hell with the expense.

# Ramsgate Harbour

## Approach

The harbour authorities give the following advice to yachtsmen.

*Approach from the East*
Enter the 6·5m dredged channel at the Dike buoy.

*Approach from the south*
The approach is through the 'Ramsgate Channel' which is entered after Deal, the Goodwin Fork and The Downs. Sandbanks are all left to starboard. A minimum depth of 3·4m may be carried in the fairway as far as Ramsgate Road, between Brake and the flats extending from the coast fronting Sandwich. Cross Ledge, with a minimum depth of 0·9m lies on the eastern side of the fairway, about 1½ miles south-southwestward of the entrance to the harbour. A drying patch lies near the centre of Cross Ledge. Craft should pass 1 cable westward of B1 and B2 green conical buoys that mark the westward edge of Brake and the western edge of Cross Ledge.

## Entrance

The harbour is accessible to craft of 1·8m at most states of the tide; with only exceptional conditions making an approach difficult at dead low water at springs. The tide goes slack about two hours before high water. It is always worth being prepared for a possible strong sheer as you approach the breakwater entrance.

Over the years, Ramsgate has undergone some veritable sea changes

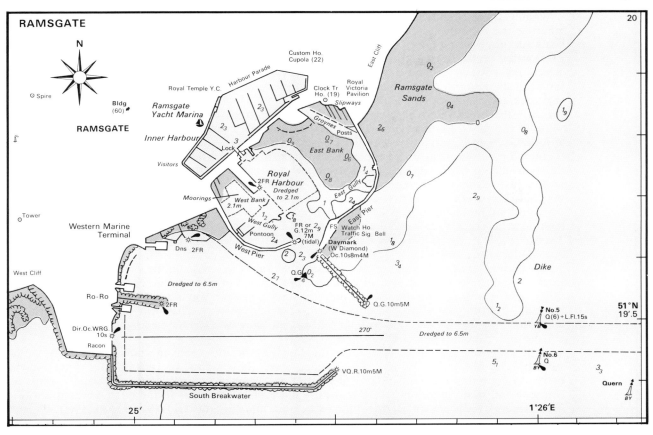

Valcon in the outer harbour of Ramsgate, once her home port.

Whatever the conditions, it is important to check with port control on VHF Ch 14 before entering the recently improved shipping channel. This will lead to the new protective harbour walls via the *Dike* and *Quern* beacon buoys (S and N cardinals, both lit) and to the north and south breakwater heads beacons, green/white and red/white, both lit. There are also leading lights (Occulting 10s and 5s) and daymarks (black and orange triangles) for the centre of the channel, but with dredging to 6·5m, it is not likely that pleasure craft will seriously need to navigate with that accuracy.

Inside the breakwaters a green conical buoy with green conical topmark (Fl.G) indicates the route to the actual harbour entrance. It has always been a good idea to round up before the final approach. Nothing in the recent works has changed this idea, and the establishment of the harbour buoy reinforces it. There are 63m between the pierheads, and while the severity of the local turbulence has been mitigated by the new projects, nevertheless, it is still a wise precaution to veer just to the east of centre. This avoids most of the backwash and any silting or sanding that may have occurred; all of which is being scrutinized by the harbour authorities.

Careful attention must be paid to the harbour signals. The new system is in keeping with the continentals, but I must confess to a sneaking affinity for the old rig. I reckon it a sad day when Ramsgate lost its black flags and balls; a bit like the apes leaving Gibraltar. But the new coloured ones do look very smart.

The harbour staff on watch are always more than ready to advise on the state of water conditions in the entrance, as well, of course, as on the movements of any commercial shipping. If there is likely to be a wait of more than a few minutes, they will keep you advised; and, unlike many port controls, it is not necessary to remind them of your presence. They will not keep you hanging about for a quarter of an hour without letting you know what is happening. Shoresides staff are equally alert to collect your fee.

Some visitors seem not to have done their homework and steam in and out with little or no reference to the traffic signals. Or if they have, they follow the example of some of the contravening locals who, in the grip of frustration, anger or anxiety ignore the signals, common courtesy and basic safety by trying to steal a place. The entrances to the outer harbour and the marina can be locations for scenes of unpleasantness and stupidity. But the Ramsgate watch has an eagle eye and an elephant memory.

## Ramsgate shoresides

Ramsgate has all the facilities any visiting yachtsman could want. Most usual supplies and services can be found along Military Road, and even the most esoteric request can usually be met as the result of a phone call. After all, the marina is the closest to the continental coast and no more than an hour or so from London. Sadly, its marina charges compare very unfavourably with those of its cross channel neighbour, Calais; and for no additional services.

There is a characterful chandler for your delectation: The Bosun's Locker (0843) 597158, run by a man of ancient mariner-like brightness of the eyeballs, and the character of a true gent. He is one Mike Haines, and he describes himself disarmingly on his business card as 'partner'. He will serve you service, advise you advice, and deliver you goods and chattels without fear or favour but with much fervour, for that is his inimitable way. The place is not always jumping, but it is usually good for five minute's crack. In Mike's absence, the younger, but equally friendly and even more obliging, partner will attend you and your needs; no matter how esoteric they may be. It is a delightfully jumbled place where chaos is not unknown to reign, but where benevolent service to the always-right clientele always comes first.

Also worth conning in the same vicinity are Jacob's Ladder by the car entry to the ferry areas, which also gives access to High Road above; and the 1881 Ramsgate Home for Smack Boys and the current Sailors' Home.

Any first-time visitor should consider two factors. First approaching from seaward at night, it is important to try for calm, unsettled weather, not only because the surrounding shallows can be unruly, but also because the town lights proliferate with so many confusing characteristics, that it is quite often difficult to disassociate them from navigational lights.

Second, shoresides, there are still midday cowboys as well as midnight operators around, perhaps in greater profusion here than in other ports. Their only purpose in life is to take you for a quick ride in pursuit of the fast buck. Caution, but above all, reliable, personal recommendation are called for.

Ramsgate is proud of its royal patronage: The Royal Temple Yacht Club enjoys an enviable position overlooking the harbour, and from it can be seen the obelisk erected to George IV 'as a grateful record of His Majesty's gracious condescension is selecting this port for his embarkation to His Kingdom of Hanover'. Today, that sycophantic tribute is surrounded by tokens of the town's changed style and status: Club Tiberius (casino); Stardust and Pleasurama (penny lanes);

and Cinderellas and Snobs (licensed houses). All is not lost however, for tradition and heritage are represented by Bert's Whelk Stall, the R.N.L.I., the Shipwright's Arms and the superb red-brick customs house....as well as the harbour itself.

Ramsgate's first harbour was built in 1750, but suffered greatly from silting – a factor which is still not completely overcome today; but the harbour and its marina flourish, providing a base for the residual fishing fleet and an excellent centre for cruising the East and South coasts, the Thames, the Swale and the Medway....as well as 'going foreign' for all the duty-free.

Hengist and Horsa landed in nearby Pegwell Bay in 448 AD. They found the countryside fertile and the inhabitants unable to resist their advances; and so it has been ever since; Bishop Wilfrid in 664, the Danes around 1000, Canute in 1014, and the Black Prince in 1356. 1500 years after the first invader, came the *Hugin*, a replica ship, rowed across the North Sea by 53 land-lubbing Danes; and she sits there still, presiding over the hovercraft and quite immune to their deafening roar and threatening aspect as they come and go like maritime behemoths aroused in anger from the shipwreck-littered crypts of the Goodwin Sands.

If you stand on the top of Ramsgate's west-side cliff, the quayside, the harbour and the marina will appear below as if featured on a picture postcard of a miniature Côte d'Azur haven with the whole panorama giving promise of Mediterranean bliss. At least, it will, if you are protected from the prevailing winds that dispose (or should it be indispose?) many of the locals to proclaim Ramsgate to be one of the windiest spots in Britain.

When I first went there, I thought that comment was of the usual kind of exaggeration to be expected from disenchanted natives. Very similar to the view of the old sea-dog who described Ramsgate as 'the arse-hole of England'. Since then, I have been into so many ports, harbours and havens that have been similarly decried that I can now happily dismiss such views. In addition, for many years I lived just off Hartland Point on Devon's north coast and found it almost impossible to believe that anywhere else could be as wind-beleaguered and certainly not more so. However, a few winters in the grip of the Ramsgate-to-North Foreland variety soon disabused me of any doubts; and even in the height of the summer season, there is always a good chance that a NE force 6+ will take you by surprise and then hang around for a week or more. But for anyone with a head for heights and a liking for strong air (or for the equally strong real ale that abounds in this particular part of Ramsgate) the prospect will provide entertainment for days on end; and even the visiting yachtsmen should not leave the harbour without giving the view at least the once over if only for the navigationally useful perspective of the bay and the run down to Deal. With good visibility, you can in fact see very much further from that vantage point, picking out many of the navigational aids especially the red and white of the light-vessels. Laid out as if on a table for our inspection, in daylight their aspects and attitudes to one another are unmistakable. However, at night, there is a distinct possibility that a skipper can be considerably put out by the navigation lights and the gaggles of fishing boats in the area that have been known to exhibit some unusual displays. On one occasion only a radar enabled me to 'place' the lights correctly.

# Pegwell Bay and the Stour to Sandwich

It is by no means a long haul from Ramsgate to Pegwell Bay (be it as the falcon flies or as the *Valcon* sails); but in terms of ethos, character, aura and genius loci the distance must be measured in light years. Ramsgate is municipal not elegant; noisy but not entirely noisome; raucous without a mellow hint; and essentially vulgar. Pegwell Bay is indistinctly remote and virtually unpeopled; almost without intrusive sound or smell; and most of the time given over to wild and natural rustic ways. Ways that demand humans shall respect them or retire from the scene; quite different from the capital of Thanet which invites invasion and abuse from any person with coin of the realm (any coin, any realm) to spare.

When the tide is out, Pegwell Bay seems to stretch to France; and that might be said to be its downfall or achievement according to your point of view. At one time, there used to be juggernauts of the sea regularly coming and going from the Bay to France. I know they looked like real hovercraft, but I am persuaded that they were space leviathans, professionally disguised.

And that would be no more than in keeping with a history of raid, rapine and onslaught. For example, Hengist and Horsa landed there in 448 AD. They found a fertile countryside inhabited by folk so unresistant to their advances that they were able to spread their talent(s) like wildfire. They were only the first: then there was Bishop Wilfrid in 664; the Danes around 1000; Canute in 1014; and the Black Prince in 1356. There is now only one relic of all that: the *Hugin*, sitting sentinel over the Bay, utterly immune. She was rowed across the North Sea some 1500 years after the first landing by some 53 routinely land-lubbing Danes.

The landmarks that dominate the countryside for miles around are the chimney and twin cooling towers of the power station on the nearby A256/8 from Ramsgate to Deal; a road always

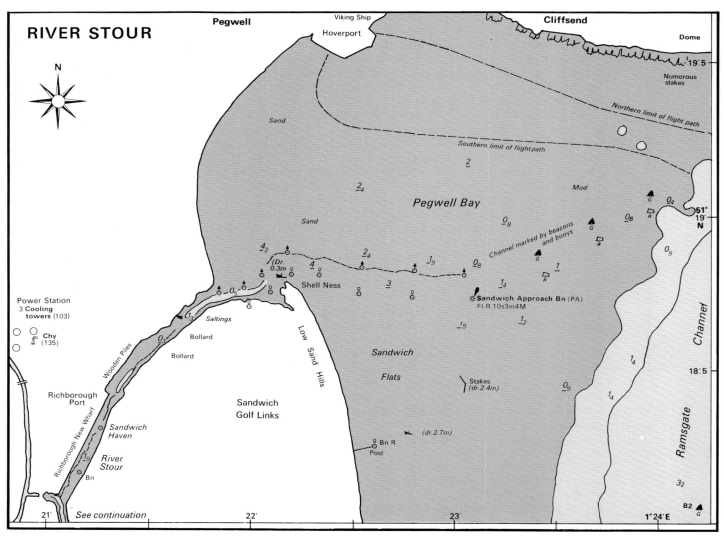

## RIVER STOUR

heavy with fumes, dust and dirt. Keen eyes are an advantage in Pegwell Bay, where the orange buoys that mark the hovercraft flight-path and the standard red and green buoys that mark the approach to the river are seldom easy to spot and are never what can be called conspicuous.

On leaving Ramsgate, once clear of the ferry terminal and its associated pillars and buoyage, it is almost straightforward enough to steer on to the cooling towers for a satisfactory course to the Stour. The bay gently slopes and there is no serious navigational hazard. When coming from Deal, the best plan is to set a straight course for Ramsgate Harbour from the *B2* buoy. About halfway there it should be possible to pick out the buoys and the beacons marking the approach to the river. If they have not become apparent at the halfway stage, then make slowly for the very obvious chimney and three cooling towers at Richborough power station.

Some skippers have been tempted to cut Shell Ness and have spent a boring time regretting it. The buoys and the beacons are simplicity themselves once you are on top of them. (The tendency of near-cormorants and other shag-shaped birds to perch on the top of some of the port hand beacons can make them appear to be starboard markers. Don't be deceived.) I have found the best water to be on the starboard side going in; and since this is well away from the Shell Ness bank it is the course I prefer. Once inside the river, the channel is more or less central; and the old decaying dolphin that used to be right in the middle of the channel has now finally gone.

The Admiralty *Pilot* suggests that the channel by Shell Ness is quarter of a cable wide and is marked by five beacons on each side. There is no reason to disagree with the width of the channel (except that, as usual, it seems even less when you are trying to sail in and avoid a school of dinghies) but I have on a number of occasions counted eight beacons. In any case, they are enough and the first port hand is a very large one, and is lit (Fl.R.10s). Just less than a mile up the river is the wharf of Richborough Port and this is used from time to time by coasters. Part of it is reasonably new and is in good order, but the seaward end is in a very poor state and should be avoided. Further upstream, the banks tend to be littered with all kinds of obstacles and there is little to make the cruising man pause until the Cinque Port of Sandwich is reached. There are

The unmistakeable landmark of the Richborough Power Station, as it looms over the Stour.

## BUOYAGE
### S. Foreland to Pegwell Bay

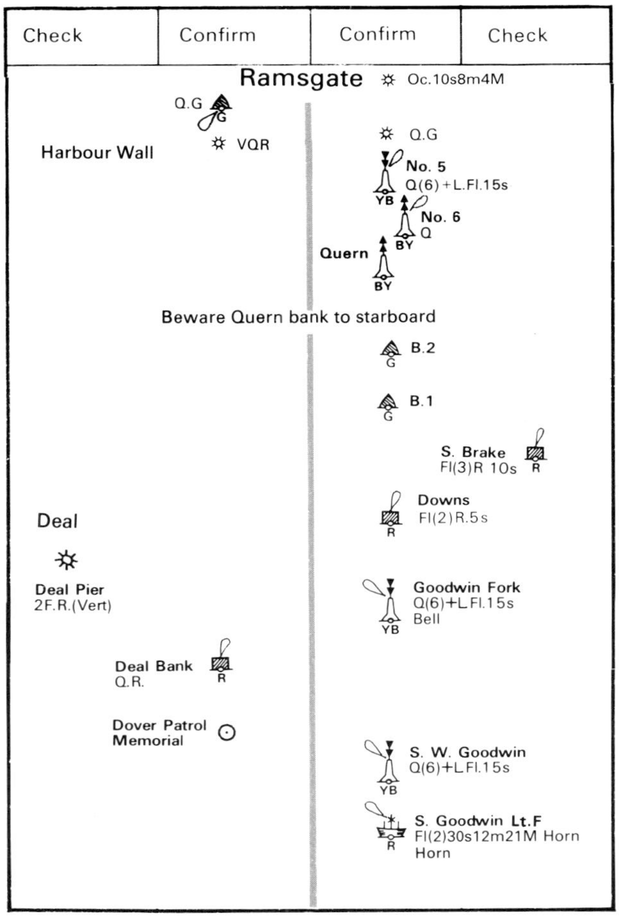

| Check | Confirm | Confirm | Check |
|---|---|---|---|
| | | **Ramsgate** ☼ Oc.10s8m4M | |
| | Q.G 🔺G<br>☼ VQR | ☼ Q.G | |
| Harbour Wall | | 🔻 **No. 5**<br>Q(6)+L.Fl.15s<br>YB | |
| | | 🔺 **No. 6**<br>BY Q | |
| | **Quern**<br>BY | | |
| | Beware Quern bank to starboard | | |
| | | 🔺G **B.2** | |
| | | 🔺G **B.1** | |
| | | **S. Brake** ▨R<br>Fl(3)R 10s | |
| **Deal** | | ▨R **Downs**<br>Fl(2)R.5s | |
| ☼ | | | |
| **Deal Pier**<br>2F.R.(Vert) | | 🔻 **Goodwin Fork**<br>Q(6)+L.Fl.15s<br>YB Bell | |
| | **Deal Bank**<br>Q.R. ▨R | | |
| | **Dover Patrol**<br>**Memorial** ⊙ | | |
| | | 🔻 **S. W. Goodwin**<br>Q(6)+L.Fl.15s<br>YB | |
| | | **S. Goodwin Lt.F**<br>R Fl(2)30s12m21M Horn<br>Horn | |

### River Stour approaches

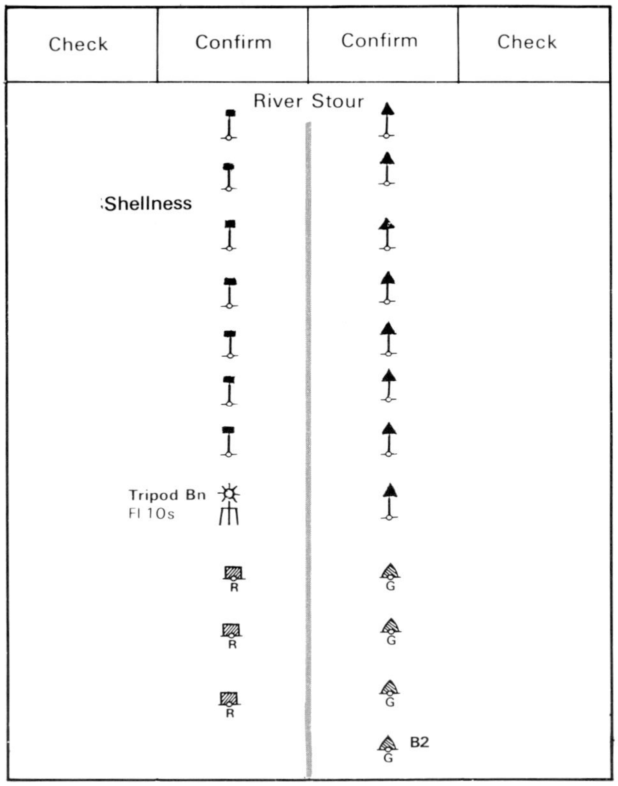

| Check | Confirm | Confirm | Check |
|---|---|---|---|
| | | **River Stour** ▲ | |
| | �🀆 | ▲ | |
| **Shellness** | ⍿ | ▲ | |
| | ⍿ | ▲ | |
| | ⍿ | ▲ | |
| | ⍿ | ▲ | |
| | ⍿ | ▲ | |
| | ⍿ | ▲ | |
| **Tripod Bn** ☼<br>Fl 10s | 🕆 | ▲ | |
| | ▨R | 🔺G | |
| | ▨R | 🔺G | |
| | ▨R | 🔺G | |
| | | 🔺G **B2** | |

Sandwich is not the easiest of top of the tide trips but the berths are pleasant enough although drying in the main.

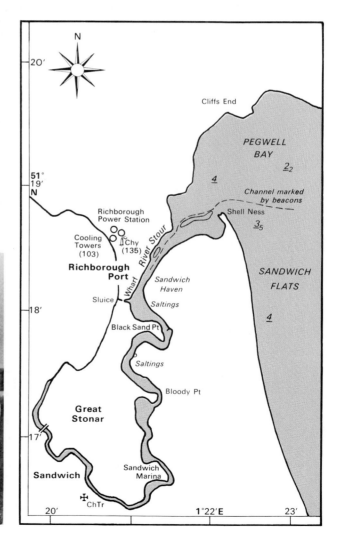

pontoons and there are also the vestigial traces of boatyards and boating clubs along the river banks, but they are all best given a wide berth unless you have a specific reason to venture in and have made advance arrangements to do so. Pfizers (marked by its chimney just over half a mile up from Richborough) shows its soft underbelly to be as hard as its frontal carapace. Often in the past have I heard the cries of apparently pent up animals.

## Sandwich

The Stour was once busy with commercial traffic. It is now little used except by leisure traffic. It is not one of England's prettiest rivers, suffering from a disarray of development and banks that are in many places falling not only into disrepair but also disrepute.

However, it does improve scenically as it closes with Sandwich. It is always tortuous and sometimes annoying, as when a pushing spring tide exacerbates the traffic situation at a crowded bend. There is no official pilot for yachtsmen, and visitors should watch out for a pseudo Trinity House official offering his services.

Sandwich is probably best known as a Cinque Port and a small holiday resort. It is a thoroughly pleasing old town, still retaining its olde-worlde charm, and providing as many domestic facilities as one might expect of such a dreamy spot. There are some facilities for yachtsmen, but not enough to justify a trip since Ramsgate is so much better equipped. It is Sandwich's peace and quiet that make the potentially tedious trip up the Stour's 6 miles to the quayside and opening bridge really worthwhile. The first day's mooring is sadly no longer free, but the quayside is a small experience not to be missed.

It is best to arrive at Sandwich just before high water (the river is not properly accessible to boats of more than 1·2m until well clear of half tide) for there is not a lot of room to turn and the stream by the quayside can be quite vicious at springs and the bank opposite the quay carries not a lot of water....and more than its fair share of weed, branches and other obstructions.

Manoeuvring against a too strong tide is not to be recommended here at a time when the quayside can be extremely busy. Generally speaking, you will have to take the mud, but is it possible to find a substantial boat by the quayside and to gain permission to lay alongside; on which case, if you are anything at all under 2·0m you should just stay afloat. There is now a public slipway at the town quay for the use of which no charge is made. The slipway is limited to vessels not exceeding 6·0m and 4 tons in weight. The slipway is only operable 2 hours either side of high water owing to its length. The old toll-bridge over the river has an opening section (no charge) and a 16th century gatehouse. There was a drawbridge here until the end of the century. The 15 miles of waterway above Sandwich is very pretty and Fordwich itself (the virtual head of navigation) is an idyllic spot; the river being tidal until this point where it is impeded by a mill dam. There is a maximum of 6·0m under the four bridges to Fordwich; and a 0·9m to the village (mainly determined by weeds and all the other predictable obstructions of a hardly used navigation).

# Pegwell to South Foreland

The sea route from Pegwell Bay to the South Foreland may give no hint of the infelicitous hazards to be found ashore on the highway, but nevertheless, it does have those of its own: plastic bags of all shapes and sizes; floating oddities lost from fishing vessels or their anchors on the sea-bed; and the many natural shoal patches in which the area abounds.

By way of the Ramsgate Channel, there is a general shortage of water, and one specific sandbank, the Brake. It may not be as mighty or as well written up as its neighbouring big brothers, the notorious Goodwins, but it is a trap for the unwary and has caught out many a disdainful yachtsman in its time.

The low coastline, with its shingle and sand beaches, is much relieved by golf-links and caravan parks; churches, castles and windmills; a gas-holder, a water tower, a radar station and a cupola. Deal pier stands out at a point where, ashore, there is a castle built by Henry VIII around 1540; a maritime and local history museum; and the famous Timeball Tower, home of the 1820 semaphore and later converted to a time ball.

The beaches of Deal are used by local fishermen to launch their small fishing boats, most of which look more like Yorkshire cobles than the locally designed and built Men o' Kent that they are.

The Downs and Small Downs are very popular with local fishermen (especially when they are chasing the flat fish from the North Foreland that make a habit of rushing to their doom off Deal Bank) and there is usually more of interest afloat on the water than there is on the shore. As I have already hinted, it is important to pick up *B1* and *B2* buoys and to keep a constant eye on the echo sounder when moving into Pegwell Bay, as there tends to be less water than is charted. In the vicinity of Cross Ledge, there is also likely to be a collection of fishermen's rubbish floating just below the surface. The stretch between *B2* and Ramsgate seems to attract detached pots, markers, lines and quite heavy gauge plastic sheets in the kind of profusion that spells disaster to props and rudders if not spotted well in time.

In fine, settled weather, there is little to choose between going east or west of The Brake. Close by the Gull Stream usually affords a reasonably comfortable deep water passage. Otherwise, in any kind of blow (especially with east in it) it is wisest to take The Downs, Small Downs and Ramsgate Channel out of Pegwell Bay.

It is important not to flirt with the steeply edging shoals of the banks in this area. They have a habit of moving in advance of the buoyage and are best given a substantial margin. Even the small Brake and Cross Ledge sands and patches are not to be trifled with since they, too, change their contours pretty rapidly from time to time. Indeed, during one two month period when the first of the Sally Viking ferries was going through its paces and there was still much dredging in evidence by Ramsgate's approaches, I estimated that the shelf between the *B1* and *B2* buoys in the Ramsgate Channel had shifted about 2–3 metres to the west. Discussions with local skippers and fishermen showed that they were of the same opinion yet the buoyage, of course, stayed the same. Whether dealing with estuaries, rivers or bars, of just closing the coastal waters of the East Coast, the theme of shifting sands/expanding saltings/moving mudbanks is one that has continually occurred in this guide. In addition, Trinity House and the port authorities are constantly at work. Indeed, the whole area ought properly to be covered by one of the Admiralty's cautions, 'Owing to the frequent changes in the buoyage/channel, the channel/buoyage are likely to be changed without notice.'

There is no denying the perils that are associated with The Goodwins. The Admiralty *Pilot* describes these Sands as 'shifting, and subject to movement by the prevailing tidal streams to such an extent as at times to alter their form considerably.' As if that is not sufficient, it goes on, 'Goodwin Sands and the area around the sands, are littered with wrecks.'

On the other hand, I have, more than once in Ramsgate's hostelries, been accosted by that certain kind of homme sportif who is not satisfied until he has exhausted the worlds of its challenges and its listeners and been bombarded by tales of derring-do cricket and football matches played on the Goodwins....with everyone 'in' and 'out' as well as done and dusted between tides, with much fun'n'games and wining and dining all round. I do believe that such games were once played. I have little choice in fact having been faced with photographs. But I am not convinced that the tale spinners of Ramsgate were ever among those present.

From the ruins of Sandown Castle past Deal Pier to the South Foreland, standing a mile off, will provide a problem free course; with the more or less featureless, low level continuum of the coastline slowly growing into the white cliffs of Dover. Once off off the South Foreland with its two lighthouses; the conspicuous windmill; and the Dover Patrol Memorial in view, you are well away from the dangers of the Goodwins. However, you are well into the waters of Dover Strait and the English Channel, with all their attendant traffic hazards: including the increasingly popular cross-channel ferries.

But to end on another note: it will not be long before we are all sailing over a much more encumbered track: the long awaited and even longer delayed Channel Tunnel.

### RAMSGATE HARBOUR
**Charts**
Imray C1, C8
Admiralty 1827, 1828
**Tides**
+0020 Dover
**Harbourmaster**
*Radio* VHF Ch 14 ☎ Ramsgate (0843) 592277

# Appendix

## CONVERSION TABLES

### metres–feet

| m | ft/m | ft |
|---|---|---|
| 0·3 | 1 | 3·3 |
| 0·6 | 2 | 6·6 |
| 0·9 | 3 | 9·8 |
| 1·2 | 4 | 13·1 |
| 1·5 | 5 | 16·4 |
| 1·8 | 6 | 19·7 |
| 2·1 | 7 | 23·0 |
| 2·4 | 8 | 26·2 |
| 2·7 | 9 | 29·5 |
| 3·0 | 10 | 32·8 |
| 6·1 | 20 | 65·6 |
| 9·1 | 30 | 98·4 |
| 12·2 | 40 | 131·2 |
| 15·2 | 50 | 164·0 |
| 30·5 | 100 | 328·1 |

### centimetres–inches

| cm | in/cm | in |
|---|---|---|
| 2·5 | 1 | 0·4 |
| 5·1 | 2 | 0·8 |
| 7·6 | 3 | 1·2 |
| 10·2 | 4 | 1·6 |
| 12·7 | 5 | 2·0 |
| 15·2 | 6 | 2·4 |
| 17·8 | 7 | 2·8 |
| 20·3 | 8 | 3·1 |
| 22·9 | 9 | 3·5 |
| 25·4 | 10 | 3·9 |
| 50·8 | 20 | 7·9 |
| 76·2 | 30 | 11·8 |
| 101·6 | 40 | 15·7 |
| 127·0 | 50 | 19·7 |
| 254·0 | 100 | 39·4 |

### metres–fathoms–feet

| m | fathoms | ft |
|---|---|---|
| 0·9 | 0·5 | 3 |
| 1·8 | 1 | 6 |
| 3·7 | 2 | 12 |
| 5·5 | 3 | 18 |
| 7·3 | 4 | 24 |
| 9·1 | 5 | 30 |
| 11·0 | 6 | 36 |
| 12·8 | 7 | 42 |
| 14·6 | 8 | 48 |
| 16·5 | 9 | 54 |
| 18·3 | 10 | 60 |
| 36·6 | 20 | 120 |
| 54·9 | 30 | 180 |
| 73·2 | 40 | 240 |
| 91·4 | 50 | 300 |

### kilometres–statute miles

| km | M/km | M |
|---|---|---|
| 1·6 | 1 | 0·6 |
| 3·2 | 2 | 1·2 |
| 4·8 | 3 | 1·9 |
| 6·4 | 4 | 2·5 |
| 8·0 | 5 | 3·1 |
| 9·7 | 6 | 3·7 |
| 11·3 | 7 | 4·3 |
| 12·9 | 8 | 5·0 |
| 14·5 | 9 | 5·6 |
| 16·1 | 10 | 6·2 |
| 32·2 | 20 | 12·4 |
| 48·3 | 30 | 18·6 |
| 64·4 | 40 | 24·9 |
| 80·5 | 50 | 31·1 |
| 120·7 | 75 | 46·6 |
| 160·9 | 100 | 62·1 |
| 402·3 | 250 | 155·3 |
| 804·7 | 500 | 310·7 |
| 1609·3 | 1000 | 621·4 |

### kilograms–pounds

| kg | lb/kg | lb |
|---|---|---|
| 0·5 | 1 | 2·2 |
| 0·9 | 2 | 4·4 |
| 1·4 | 3 | 6·6 |
| 1·8 | 4 | 8·8 |
| 2·3 | 5 | 11·0 |
| 2·7 | 6 | 13·2 |
| 3·2 | 7 | 15·4 |
| 3·6 | 8 | 17·6 |
| 4·1 | 9 | 19·8 |
| 4·5 | 10 | 22·0 |
| 9·1 | 20 | 44·1 |
| 13·6 | 30 | 66·1 |
| 18·1 | 40 | 88·2 |
| 22·7 | 50 | 110·2 |
| 34·0 | 75 | 165·3 |
| 45·4 | 100 | 220·5 |
| 113·4 | 250 | 551·2 |
| 226·8 | 500 | 1102·3 |
| 453·6 | 1000 | 2204·6 |

### litres–gallons

| l | gal/l | gal |
|---|---|---|
| 4·5 | 1 | 0·2 |
| 9·1 | 2 | 0·4 |
| 13·6 | 3 | 0·7 |
| 18·2 | 4 | 0·9 |
| 22·7 | 5 | 1·1 |
| 27·3 | 6 | 1·3 |
| 31·8 | 7 | 1·5 |
| 36·4 | 8 | 1·8 |
| 40·9 | 9 | 2·0 |
| 45·5 | 10 | 2·2 |
| 90·9 | 20 | 4·4 |
| 136·4 | 30 | 6·6 |
| 181·8 | 40 | 8·8 |
| 227·3 | 50 | 11·0 |
| 341·0 | 75 | 16·5 |
| 454·6 | 100 | 22·0 |
| 1136·5 | 250 | 55·0 |
| 2273·0 | 500 | 110·0 |
| 4546·1 | 1000 | 220·0 |

# Index